D0835546

Patrick Bisho̶p̶ ̶w̶a̶s̶ ̶b̶o̶r̶n̶
1979 and cov̶e̶r̶e̶d̶ ̶I̶r̶e̶l̶
going to the F̶a̶l̶k̶l̶a̶n̶d̶
which he wrote with John wit̶h̶ ̶t̶h̶e̶ ̶t̶a̶s̶k̶ ̶f̶o̶r̶c̶e̶ ̶i̶n̶
the Falklands. He has been on the staff of ITN, and the *Sunday Times* and is now a correspondent for the *Sunday Telegraph*.

Eamonn Mallie was born in 1951 and educated at Trinity College, Dublin. He has worked for the last ten years as a political journalist in Ireland. He is a regular contributor to nationally networked programmes on Independent Radio and LBC and is political correspondent with Downtown Radio in Belfast.

THE
PROVISIONAL IRA

Patrick Bishop
and Eamonn Mallie

CORGI BOOKS

To Ernest and Kathleen Bishop
and
Michael and Eileen Mallie

THE PROVISIONAL IRA

A CORGI BOOK 0 552 13337 X

Originally published in Great Britain by Hamish Hamilton Ltd.

PRINTING HISTORY

Heinemann edition published 1987
Heinemann edition reprinted 1987
Corgi edition published 1988
Corgi edition published 1988
Corgi edition reprinted 1989 (twice)
Corgi edition reprinted 1992 (twice)
Corgi edition reprinted 1993
Corgi edition reprinted 1994

Every effort has been made to trace copyright holders of material in this book;
unfortunately, in some cases, this has proved impossible. The Authors and Publishers
would be glad to hear from any copyright holders they have been unable to approach and
to print due acknowledgements at the earliest opportunity.
The maps on pp. Vii, Viii, ix, x are from pp.284, 285, 286 of *Pig in the Middle* by Desmond
Hamill, and are reproduced by permission of Meuthuen, London.

Copyright © Patrick Bishop and Eamonn Mallie 1987

Corgi Books are published by Transworld Publishers Ltd.,
61-63 Uxbridge Road, Ealing, London W5 5SA,
in Australia by Transworld Publishers (Australia) Pty. Ltd.,
15-25 Helles Avenue, Moorebank NSW 2170, and in
New Zealand by Transworld Publishers (N.Z.) Ltd.,
3 William Pickering Drive, Albany, Auckland.
Printed and bound in Great Britain by
BPC Paperbacks Ltd
A member of
The British Printing Company Ltd

CONTENTS

ACKNOWLEDGEMENTS

During the writing of this book we received generous help and encouragement from a large number of people who, because of the nature of the subject matter, we are unable to thank by name. We owe a great debt of gratitude to the officers of the Royal Ulster Constabulary, the British Army, the Northern Ireland prison service and numerous anonymous republicans from all parts of the movement for their reminiscences, expertise and opinion.

We would also like to thank Mr Humphrey Atkins, Dr Paul Bew, Mr Andrew Boyd, Mr W.D. Flackes, Mr David Gilliland, Mr Desmond Hamill, Mr Fred Heatley, Ms Mary Holland, Mr John Hume, Mr Patsy McArdle, Dr Maurice Manning, Mr Michael Noonan, Professor Cornelius O'Leary, Mr James Prior, Mr Merlyn Rees, Brigadier Michael Rose, and Mr Harry West for their advice.

Our gratitude is also owed to Dr Philip Beresford for his generous permission to allow us to use material from his masterly thesis and to Mr David McKittrick, *doyen* of Northern Ireland correspondents, for giving us access to his researches on the Loyalist paramilitaries.

Our thanks too, to Mr Walter McCauley, chief librarian of the *Belfast Telegraph* and to the kind and efficient staff of the Belfast Linehall Library.

We are also grateful to our editors over the period when the book was being researched and written, Andrew Neil of the *Sunday Times* and Peregrine Worsthorne of the *Sunday Telegraph*, and David Sloan and Ivan Tinman of Downtown Radio, for their understanding attitude

We also wish to express our thanks to Amanda Conquy of Heinemann for her shrewd and perceptive suggestions and to Naomi Klein for her meticulous copy-editing.

We are also indebted to our friends and family for their support and encouragement. To Louise Baring, Simon Freeman, Kim Fletcher, Felicity Hawkins and Alexandra Hay, and to Detta, Ciara, Laura Kate and Michael Mallie, honour and affection.

A NOTE ON SOURCES

Writing the history of secretive organisations is inevitably circumscribed by a dearth of written evidence. The IRA commits little to paper and the few scant records it does keep are underground, buried away in arms dumps. Much of the book therefore is based on numerous personal interviews with the main participants in the events described, republicans, civilians, politicians and members of the security forces. Wherever possible, this has been augmented by archival research. The research was shared between the two authors. The majority of the republican interviews were conducted by Eamonn Mallie. The manuscript was written by Patrick Bishop.

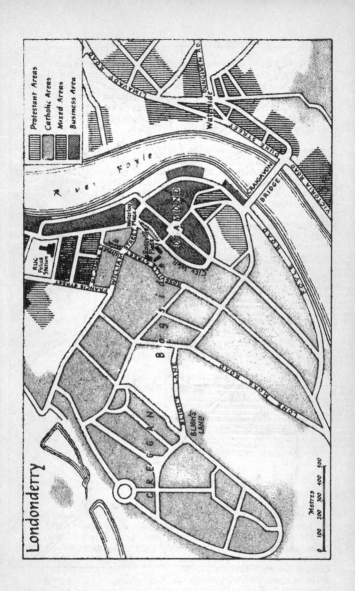

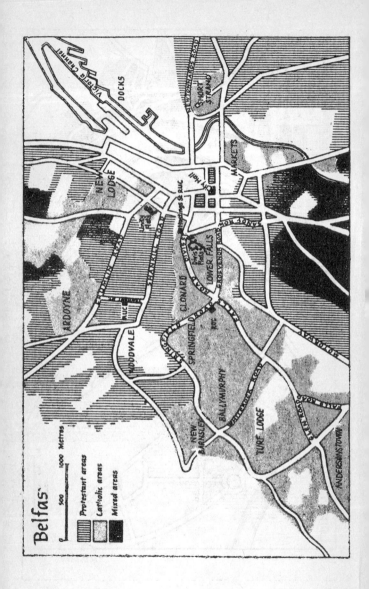

Belfast

Ireland

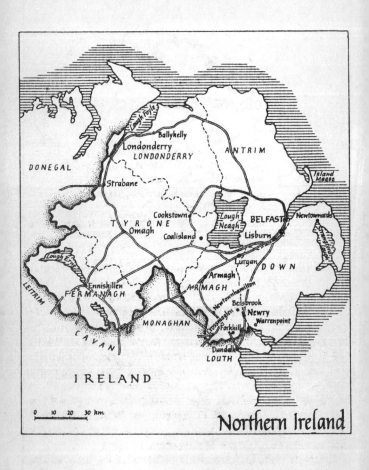

Northern Ireland

CHAPTER ONE

Prologue: Fanatic Hearts

> Out of Ireland have we come
> Great hatred, little room
> Maimed us at the start
> I carry from my mother's womb
> A fanatic heart.
>
> W. B. Yeats, 28 August 1931

Travelling south on the motorway out of Belfast two sights catch the eye. The first straggles over the slopes of West Belfast at the point where the city peters out and the hills begin. If it is not raining or the mist has not come down from Divis Mountain you can just make out the green, white and orange flags that mark the graves of the Republican plot. This is Milltown cemetery. Ten miles down the road you slowly become aware of a high, flat wall, broken here and there by towers, running through the middle of unworked fields off to the right of the road. At night it is bathed in orange sodium light, accentuating its air of remoteness. What could it be? A military airfield? A scientific research centre? Slowly it dawns on you: it is the Maze prison.

Recruits to the IRA are taught in their training lectures that their involvement in the republican movement will probably lead them to Milltown or to Long Kesh, as the IRA persist in calling the Maze. This is only a slight exaggeration. Between 1969 and November 1986 281 IRA men and women have been killed and, the IRA claim, between eight and ten thousand imprisoned — high odds in an organisation which the IRA also claim has seen between eight and ten thousand pass through it. Nine hundred and ten people are currently held in jails in Northern Ireland and Britain for IRA-related offences. Most of those who have been to jail will have been locked up during what for most people is the most carefree and optimistic period of their lives — their late teens and twenties — when they might otherwise have been going to university or college or starting a trade, a career or a marriage.

Outside the prison walls, life is barely more rewarding. There is no money in belonging to the IRA. It is a working-class organisation and its members lead working-class lives. Home for most of the Belfast volunteers is a council estate or a terraced house in the remaining streets that have not been redeveloped. If they are in work they are expected to finance themselves. For the unemployed there is a weekly handout of £20 (drawing the dole is theoretically discouraged because of the state surveillance it entails), but only when the war chest is full.

There is little kudos to be gained in becoming a member. From time to time — during a hunger strike, or a spate of killings by loyalist murderers — it is not a bad thing to be known as an IRA man. There is not much enjoyment to be had either. The fact of membership leeches normality out of life. There is always the fear of arrest or betrayal. Once you are in, friendships with those outside the ranks become awkward, circumscribed by the need for secrecy. In the bleak, barn-like social clubs of West Belfast, the IRA men drink with each other, while their wives and girlfriends form a separate, exclusive huddle. This rock-pool atmosphere is addictive. Many of those who have left the movement or been forced out miss its conspiratorial closeness; they find the open water cold and daunting. It is a problem they share with the soldiers and policemen they shoot at.

Unlike the soldiers and policemen they have few of the compensations of a regimented life. The IRA gives no medals. Nor does it offer much extra status or reward to those who rise through the hierarchy. The top and the bottom are separated by only a narrow band of privilege. There is not much praise or recognition. Republicanism is a hypercritical tradition: 'You are not as good as your last job, you are as good as your next one' the operators tell each other. The cult of personality has never caught on. Flamboyance is regarded with suspicion. The 'Green Book', the IRA manual, preaches the merits of modesty, abstemiousness and discretion. Drinking is officially frowned on (but, accepting that enforced teetotalism is unrealistic, the leadership in Belfast request that members stay out of bars before seven in the evening) and those with irregular domestic arrangements are asked not to flaunt them. Unlike most contemporary guerrilla organisations and unlike the old IRA of the War of Independence, the modern IRA has produced few heroes. Bobby Sands, who came closest to being one, did so not by bravery in the field against the British forces but by starving himself to death in prison. Indeed, given the secret nature of the organisation, it is necessary to die before you can become a hero.

Even when tucked away inside the hermetic world of the movement, it is hard to feel really safe. Conspirators rely on each other, a fact of which they are only too aware, and mutual reliance encourages mutual suspicion. One of the most important developments in recent years in the Belfast IRA has been the establishment of a security department charged with vetting members, and each 'battalion' in the North now has a security officer on the staff. The price of treachery is high: interrogation in a slum back room, a haphazard 'trial', then a hood, a piece of wasteland and a bullet through the back of the head. Mere suspicion can be enough to doom you, or at best thrust you out of the organisation.

This is wartime justice and these are wartime privations, yet there is not even the compensation of an end in sight. The leaders insist with heart-sinking regularity that they cannot expect victory, this year, next year or even by the end of the century.

Why then should anybody want to join the IRA? One answer is that it is in the blood. About eighty per cent of the current

13

membership have fathers, uncles or brothers in the movement. Republicanism is a hereditary tradition and certain families exert a dominating influence on its history. Gerry Adams, the Sinn Fein president and the pre-eminent figure among the small group that directs the Republican movement, has three brothers who are, or have been, in the organisation including one who until recently was head of the Belfast organisation. As time has gone on, and the number of those who have experienced the death, wounding or imprisonment of a member of the family has multiplied, the potential recruiting base of the IRA has expanded correspondingly.

Tradition and family expectations on their own, though, are not enough to overcome the drawbacks. Three great and frequently cited attractions are: the fact that the republican movement offers a simple and easily understood political and military objective (the removal of the border), an easily identifiable enemy (the British and their Northern Irish allies who keep the border there) and the immediate means of revenge.

Recruits to the IRA often cite 'the feeling that I was striking back' as a crucial motive for joining. The IRA has obviously been able to do that. By March 1988 it had killed 253 policemen, 391 soldiers and 172 members of the Ulster Defence Regiment. In all 2,640 people have died in the troubles since 1969. It has proved itself able to reach out to hit the powerful and the high, assassinating judges, diplomats and politicians, striking even Earl Mountbatten and missing Margaret Thatcher by a hair's breadth. It has proved that it can change things, albeit not necessarily to its liking. Its activities have warped the politics of Ireland for a generation.

In joining the IRA, recruits are entering an organisation that regards itself as an elite and exclusive band. This offers to the working class youth of the Catholic ghettoes an opportunity to gain esteem and a chance to exercise initiative that they are unlikely to find elsewhere in the dismal economic climate of Northern Ireland in recent years. The IRA's members sincerely believe themselves to be soldiers, and now that the republican movement is concentrating its energies on political activities

14

the same military sense of purpose and *esprit de corps* is to be seen among Sinn Fein workers.

This outlook precludes guilt. It is as unrewarding to expect remorse from a 'volunteer' over the killing of a policeman or a politician as it is to expect regret from a soldier who shoots a sniper or a minister who allows a hunger striker to die.

A Belfast psychiatrist who examined many IRA men convicted of murder found them resilient, relaxed and 'a reasonably stable group of people', (Dr H. A. Lyons quoted in the *Independent*, 29 November 1986.) 'They have clear ideals and goals, they have leadership, they get strong support from other members of the group and that helps to keep them well. It helps to keep any guilt from coming to the surface.'

Until recently the exclusivity of the republican movement was reinforced by the doctrine that it had inherited the legal government of Ireland, forfeited by all Irish governments since the second Dail (parliament) of 1919 by their acceptance of the treaty that divided the island.

The importance of that belief now appears to be waning. At the 1986 Sinn Fein ard fheis (annual conference) the movement finally voted to abandon its ban on sitting in Leinster House (the Republic of Ireland's parliament); IRA violence has subsided and most of the movement's effort is being put into political activity. Politicians and policemen occasionally claim to detect in this process signs of the same 'benign corruption' which has brought previous generations of violent republicans down from the hills and on to the path of peaceful politics. The history of the present IRA shows that this is a forlorn hope. The most important lesson the current leadership has learnt over the past seventeen years is that without the IRA standing behind it the republican movement would be insignificant. Even if the leadership were to abandon violence, another violent republican organisation would spring up in its place. As long as Ireland is divided, violent republicanism will be an ineradicable tradition.

15

CHAPTER TWO

The Roots of Republicanism

On the morning of 2 June 1866 a group of 800 armed men joined battle with a hastily assembled force of young militiamen on Lime Ridge, also known as Ridgeway, just inside the Canadian border. They carried before them a green flag adorned with the gold harp of Ireland and the letters 'IRA'. In the ensuing skirmish, the Canadians, mostly students who had volunteered at short notice to defend their country against these bizarre invaders, lost twelve dead and forty wounded. Their assailants, mostly emigré Irishmen of the Fenian Brotherhood, retreated back over the border into the United States after sustaining eight losses and twenty wounded. This inglorious encounter was the first time that a force calling itself the Irish Republican Army had ever taken the field. The action was the American branch of the Fenians' contribution to the abortive uprising that was planned to sweep the British from Ireland. It was a characteristically optimistic effort. Before the battle the expedition's commander, Colonel John Roberts, had predicted that before the summer was out, 'the green flag will by flying independently to freedom's breeze and we will have a base of operations from which we can not only emancipate Ireland but annihilate England'.[1]

In fact, the soldiers of Roberts' force never fought again, though the name of the IRA continued to be heard in America from time to time. In July 1868 *The Buffalo Express*, a newspaper covering the affairs of a small town in New York State, reported that the funeral had taken place of 'Sergeant

John Lynch, of Grace's Ohio Unit of Fenians', who had been wounded in the groin at Ridgeway. According to the paper's anonymous reporter, between 300 and 400 'Finini' of Buffalo's 'Seventh IRA Regiment' had marched behind the coffin to the chapel where they were disappointed to hear the priest, Father Gleason, announce that 'he would refuse to pray over the coffin if there were going to be green uniforms in the chapel . . . accordingly they were removed before the burial in the churchyard.' Lynch was laid to rest near a headstone bearing the name of Edward K. Lonergan, described as a 'Lieutenant of the Seventh Regiment IRA who fell gallantly fighting Ireland's enemies on the famous field of Ridgeway'.[2]

With the decline of the Fenians, the name of the IRA disappeared. It re-emerged in Dublin almost exactly fifty years later when, with British shells falling around them, the rebel forces occupying the General Post Office building issued proclamations in the name of the 'Irish Republican Army'. After the uprising had been crushed the letters 'IRA' began to appear appended to the names of the imprisoned insurgents in their correspondence home. It was not until three years later, when the guerrilla war against the British forces was well advanced, that the name Irish Republican Army was used to unite the disparate groups that made up the rebel forces.

These different groups were not linked by any firm political creed or institutional bond but by a shared aim and a common belief in the method of achieving it. Put simply, this was that Ireland's ills derived from the British presence, that the British would have to be removed before Ireland could be a nation and that force was the best means of bringing this about.

These men and women saw themselves as part of a tradition that stretched back to the sixteenth century when the first nobles rose against English rule in Ireland. Some parts of rebel history seemed to be more relevant than others. In particular, those who supported the use of physical force saw themselves as descendants of the United Irishmen who rebelled in 1798.

Among the leaders of the United Irishmen was Theobald Wolfe Tone, an intellectually restless Protestant lawyer and the man who has had more influence on Irish republican thinking than any other. He was born in Dublin in 1763, the son of a respectable farmer turned coachbuilder. He was a spirited young man who wanted to be a soldier but was persuaded to complete his education. After studying logic at Trinity College in the city, he married and travelled to London to read law. He showed an early interest in imaginative political scheming when he proposed that the English Crown should establish a colony in the recently discovered South Sea islands, in order to 'put a bridle on Spain in time of peace and annoy her grievously in time of war'.

By the time he returned to Ireland his ideas seem to have undergone a profound change, for he was soon annoying the Protestant establishment with his pamphlet arguing that Ireland was an independent nation and should not be obliged to support England in the event of a war with Spain. His radicalism had yet to set hard, however, for he was later to revive his colonial plan, this time receiving a message of approval from the British foreign secretary.

Like many Irishmen he was deeply affected by the French Revolution of 1789, which, he wrote, 'changed in an instant the politics of Ireland'. Tone was naturally on the side of the French democrats and he turned to the question of Roman Catholic rights. Irish independence, he believed, depended on a rapprochement between Catholics and Protestant dissenters. He made contact with middle-class dissenters in Ulster where the combination of prosperity and Presbyterianism, with its anti-hierarchical tradition, had created a climate of radicalism. In 1791 he was invited to Belfast to meet them and the Society of United Irishmen was founded there.

The society's original ambitions were lawful enough: the union of Irishmen of all religions and the establishment of an annual parliament elected by universal male suffrage. With the outbreak of war between England and France in 1793, the radicals attracted the attention of the French. An agent was dispatched to Ireland to make contact with Tone. The prospect of French assistance helped to turn him from a radical into a revolutionary. As the republican truism had it, England's difficulty was Ireland's opportunity.

The revelation of the links between the radicals and the French resulted in the suppression of the United Irishmen by the English government, which ultimately transformed it from a debating club into a revolutionary conspiracy dedicated to establishing a republican and separate Ireland. The discontent felt by the radical middle class was more than matched by the grievances of the Catholic peasantry. In 1796 the United Irishmen began to plan an uprising using the forces of the 'defenders', as the secret societies formed by aggrieved rural Catholics called themselves. The rising was to be complemented by a French military invasion which Tone had organised during a trip to France. The first French expedition ended in disaster when gales prevented the fleet from putting ashore. By the time the second arrived in August 1798, the rebellion was over — crushed with great brutality by the English.

Tone was captured and sentenced to death, but was refused a soldier's execution by firing squad. He cheated the gallows by inexpertly cutting his throat and suffered a lingering end. He was but one of many organisers of the United Irishmen's revolt and but one contributor to their philosophy. His fame, while other leaders remain obscure — even in Ireland — has something to do with the attractiveness of his personality, his warm-hearted and optimistic character, a distillation of the qualities that are sentimentally attributed to Irish people generally. But it also reflects the succinctness with which he summarised Ireland's problem and its solution. His beliefs are best conveyed in the words that were to become one of the most heavily-thumbed texts of republicanism in later years:

> To subvert the tyranny of our execrable government, to break the connection with England, the never failing source of all our political evils, and to assert the independence of my country — these were my objects. To unite the whole people of Ireland, to abolish the memory of all past

19

dissensions, and to substitute the common name of Irishmen in place of the denomination of Protestant, Catholic and Dissenter – these were my means.

Despite their failure, the United Irishmen succeeded in establishing a strain of 'physical force' republicanism that has persisted ever since.

The United Irishmen's activities set the basic theme of Irish events for the next 124 years – the struggle for a form of independence from Britain. This struggle was to acquire a familiar rhythm – long, slow passages of peaceful agitation punctuated by eruptions of violence. The former was carried out by Irish constitutional nationalists such as Daniel O'Connell; the latter by the inheritors of the violent tradition of the United Irishmen. The constitutional camp was prepared to compromise; the physical force camp was all-or-nothing. It was a difference of outlook that was ultimately to provoke the Irish Civil War of 1922-3.

After the failure of the United Irishmen Irish energies shifted back towards peaceful agitation for Emancipation – the granting of political rights to Catholics. But the pace of events was too slow for young nationalists. In 1848 physical force republicanism reasserted itself in the Young Ireland movement, a group of mainly middle-class Protestants who drew their inspiration from the 1798 uprising. Their rebellion had even less success. One brief skirmish in Tipperary marked the end of their challenge. They fled, many of them to America, taking their revolutionary aspirations with them.

America had a large Irish population which had been swollen by the flood of emigrants who left Ireland in the late 1840s to escape the famine that descended with the successive failure of the potato crop. One million Irish had died of hunger, a catastrophe that was laid at Britain's door. The rebels saw in America a reservoir of sentiment, men and material they could draw on to help overthrow the British. In 1858 they founded there a secret society called the Fenian Brotherhood, whose name was derived from the *fian*, the band of warriors who

20

attended the legendary Irish king, Finn MacCool. At the same time one of the participants in the Young Ireland fiasco, James Stephens, returned to Ireland after exile in France. On St Patrick's Day 1858 he founded a new revolutionary organisation, which came to be known as the Irish Republican Brotherhood (IRB). Both movements were dedicated to the swift, violent removal of British rule. The Fenians were energetic and impatient. Their motto was 'revolution sooner or never'. They took violence to the home of their enemies, planting bombs in London and killing a policeman in Manchester. But their schemes tended to end badly, often farcically.

Despite their supposed secrecy they were riddled with spies and informers. Before the planned date for the great rising in 1867, the British had already moved in to arrest the ringleaders. The rebellion went ahead anyway, without the help promised from America, and ended up another chapter in a chronicle of glorious failures.

Still, the rebels had continued the tradition and added to it. From the outset, the Fenians' clear aim was to make Ireland an 'independent democratic republic'.[3] Unlike their predecessors, the Fenian rebels were from the lower-middling reaches of Irish society — clerks, schoolteachers, people who had less to lose than their social superiors, who if nationalist at all were naturally inclined towards the constitutionalist approach. It was this approach that dominated Irish political life as it entered the twentieth century. The Irish National Party (INP), which was made up of MPs sitting for Irish constituencies in the Westminster parliament, extracted a commitment to Home Rule from the Liberals as the price of keeping them in power. Although the measure fell far short of republican aspirations it was passionately opposed with threats of violence by the Protestants of Ulster.

By the start of the First World War in 1914 it seemed that the constitutionalists' strategy would succeed where the physical force tradition had failed. On 18 September the Government of Ireland Act was passed, which set up an Irish parliament with jurisdiction over its own domestic affairs.

21

But the Irish would have to wait for the war to finish before the act was implemented. The King's assent to the act was met with delight and relief by most of the population, who had feared that Ulster's intransigence would finally succeed in wrecking it. But it did not impress republicans and extreme nationalists, categories which by 1914 covered a diverse, but small collection of people.

One strand of the republican rope was the Gaelic revival and its adherents. By 1900 Ireland was undergoing a small but important cultural renaissance. After years of neglect and suppression, Irish customs, art forms and language were being dusted off and admired by a small band of intellectuals. Irish folk stories enjoyed a vogue among the sophisticated. At the Abbey Theatre in Dublin (founded by the poet W. B. Yeats and his friend, Lady Gregory) people could for the first time watch plays set in and concerned with their own country.

The political manifestation of this development was Sinn Fein. It was founded in 1905 by Arthur Griffith, a printer who had spent some time in South Africa before returning home. Sinn Fein means 'Ourselves Alone'. Griffith's programme, spelt out in his newspaper the *United Irishman*, was that Ireland should sever all political and economic links with Britain and stand or fall on its own resources. Griffith was not a deep-dyed republican. Initially he advocated passive resistance to British rule and he believed that Ireland and England should have a duel monarchy such as in Austro-Hungary. Nevertheless he and his newspaper became a mustering point for republicanism.

The cultural revival nudged back into wakefulness the IRB, and many republicans had joint membership of Sinn Fein and the IRB. They were a disparate crew. Sinn Fein included Constance Markiewicz, née Gore-Booth, who was of an ancient Sligo Anglo-Irish family and who pronounced her birthplace 'Ahland', and Denis McCullough from the Falls Road in Belfast. Their aspirations and ideas were as mixed as their backgrounds. But as time went on some of them became united in their impatience. Griffith believed in giving Home Rule a chance but influence began to pass to the IRB with its strong insurrectionary tradition (exemplified by veteran Fenian dynamiter Tom Clarke, who had returned from America in 1907).

There was a third element in the republican hotchpotch: the Irish labour movement. Through the efforts of Jim Larkin, a fearless and energetic Liverpudlian, and James Connolly, the son of an Edinburgh carter, the socialist ideal of the trade union movement was married to republicanism. In 1913 they organised a transport strike in Dublin, which resulted in an employers' lock-out, rioting and, for Connolly, jail. After his release he organised the Irish Citizen Army – the third unofficial army in Ireland – whose original purpose was to protect the workers.

Meanwhile, the Protestants in the North had formed them-selves into the Ulster Volunteers pledged to fighting any attempt to impose Home Rule on them. In November 1913 the nationalists in the South had countered with the Irish Volun-teers, a nationwide force waiting in the wings to press the passage of Home Rule should Britain let them down. When war came, republicans found themselves confronted with a dilemma. They had, or they thought they had, Home Rule, which was at least a start towards full independence. On the other hand, they also found themselves in a potentially revolutionary situation. As Wolfe Tone had pointed out, England's difficulty was Ireland's opportunity.

In August 1914 a small group on the extremist edge of the IRB met in secret in Dublin and pledged to mount a rebellion aimed at gaining Ireland's total independence at some time during the war. The idea must have seemed grandiose, even to the conspirators. Most nationalist Irishmen were con-tent with Home Rule and supported the patient, reasonable approach which John Redmond, the leader of the constitutional INP, was employing. When Redmond appealed to Irishmen to enlist in the British Army as a gesture of Irish goodwill, 27,000 members of the Volunteers marched off to war.

There were some dissidents, however. Redmond's recruiting drive produced a split in the Volunteers' ranks and some 13,000 left to form a breakaway movement known as the Sinn

23

Fein Volunteers. The new force was not intended as a revolutionary one. Its leader, Eoin MacNeill, simply felt that committing the Irish Volunteers to the British war effort would reduce the pressure on Britain to implement Home Rule, and it was necessary to maintain a force to ensure that it carried out its stated intentions. But unbeknown to most of its members and even to MacNeill himself, the leadership of the Volunteers had been infiltrated by the revolutionary wing of the IRB who saw it as the means by which an uprising could be carried out. In the summer of 1915 the conspirators set up a military council of three men, Partick Pearse, a militaristic schoolmaster, Joseph Plunkett, a literary jounalist and poet, and Eamonn Ceannt (Kent), who worked for Dublin Corporation as a clerk, to plan the event. Pearse and Ceannt held high positions in the Sinn Fein Volunteers, one as director of operations, the other as head of communications. As time went on, the conspiracy widened. In the autumn, Tom Clarke, the dynamiter, and Sean MacDermott, who had been imprisoned for agitating against British Army recruitment, were admitted to the planning council. The following January Connolly added the small weight of the Citizen Army to the scales.

America was brought in on the plan. Clann na Gael, the IRB organisation in the United States, approached the Germans as potential allies and Sir Roger Casement, an Antrim man knighted for his services as a British consular official, travelled to Germany to negotiate for arms. In return he was to help raise a renegade brigade from Irish prisoners-of-war who would be used to fight their former comrades. The action, planned in the main by Plunkett, was timed for Easter 1916. Once the German guns were there, Volunteer units infiltrated by the IRB would rise. Eoin MacNeill would have no choice but to follow.

The conspirators expected the rising to fail. Pearse seemed positively to wish it to. He believed in the rejuvenating power of blood. Writing in December 1915, when the scale of the horror of the Western Front was becoming clear, he observed that 'the old heart of the earth needed to be warmed with the

24

red wine of the battlefields'. For him the rising was a sacrificial act which would ultimately inspire the Irish people to overthrow British rule once and for all.

Had it not been for its consequences, the Easter Rising might now be looked upon as just another bloody fiasco. The German vessel carrying the vital arms was intercepted by a British ship and Casement taken prisoner. When MacNeill finally learned of the plot he cancelled the Easter Monday Volunteer manoeuvres in Dublin's Phoenix Park where the conspirators had intended to launch the uprising.

It went ahead none the less. At about noon on Easter Monday, a group of Volunteers and Citizen Army men marching down O'Connell Street in the heart of Dublin suddenly wheeled right and entered the General Post Office building, an imposing neo-classical edifice. With the odd pistol shot, they cleared it of customers and staff. Shortly afterwards Pearse appeared and read a proclamation from the 'provisional government' of the new republic of Ireland to the baffled crowd that had gathered. Meanwhile, all round the city units of Volunteers and the Citizen Army had taken up positions. A detachment of the Citizen Army succeeded in entering Dublin Castle, the bastion of British power in Ireland, which had been emptied of most of its garrison. Inexplicably, the rebel force withdrew, perhaps not believing their luck.

Within five days the uprising had been crushed. There were only 1,300 Volunteers and 200 troops of the Citizen Army and they had taken up fixed positions which the British systematically surrounded and reduced with artillery fire. Pearse and his men were bombarded out of the Post Office, where they had done little but sit and endure. In asking to treat with the enemy Pearse styled himself the 'Commandant General of the Irish Republican Army', a term he first used in a communiqué issued from the Post Office on the second day of the rising.

Pearse had had his blood sacrifice but the uprising had failed to move the Irish population in the way that its organisers had hoped. People were curious and surprised by the violence but had little idea what it meant. If anything there was hostility towards the rebels. They had started the fighting but inevitably it was the civilians who had suffered most; 220 were killed by shot and shell against sixty-four rebels and 134 Crown forces. As the rebels were led away under guard they were jeered at by Dublin slum women along the route.

But within a matter of three months this opposition had given way to admiration. The reason for the transformation lay in the British response to the affair. On 3 May, four days after the rebellion had ended, the firing squads got busy, working their way through the leadership. Pearse, Clarke and Thomas MacDonagh (another poet, who had signed the proclamation of the republic) were the first to go, shot at dawn in Kilmainham jail. Plunkett, the main planner, went the following day. Connolly was shot eight days later, head held upright grasping the arms of the chair he was forced to sit in because his ankle had been broken by a bullet in the fighting. Altogether there were sixteen executions, including Casement, who was hanged at Pentonville in London in August. Most of the victims went to their deaths confident that history would find in their favour. 'We shall be remembered by posterity and blessed by unborn generations,' Pearse wrote to his mother.

In themselves the executions were not enough to swing the population towards the rebel camp. The increase in sympathy for the Sinn Feiners, as they were beginning to be termed, was only possible because of a corresponding decline in popular confidence in Redmond and the constitutional Nationalist Party.

Soon after the rising it became clear that the British government was preparing to renege on the terms of the Home Rule Act. The presence of the unionist supporters of the Ulster Protestants in the wartime cabinet had greatly strengthened their hand. While Ireland was still absorbing the shock of the executions, moderate nationalists learned that the best deal they were likely to get from the British now was Home Rule over twenty-six of the thirty-two counties of Ireland. Six of the nine counties of Ulster — Antrim, Armagh, Londonderry, Down, Fermanagh and Tyrone — were to be permanently excluded.

Partition was very unpopular, even to some unionists who felt that the dismemberment of the island would be disastrous.[4] That Redmond was prepared to countenance it contributed greatly to the downfall of himself and his party.

The rebels hardly seemed in any condition to push themselves forward as an alternative. The men who led the uprising did not constitute a political entity speaking with one tongue. They represented a bundle of ideologies: the Fenian conspiratorial dedication to physical force of Clarke; the revolutionary socialism of Connolly; the mystical nationalism of Pearse. The political aspirations of those who followed them were even more cloudy.

The nearest thing to a serviceable roof under which they could all shelter was Sinn Fein, which had taken no direct part in the events of Easter 1916. At this stage, Sinn Fein was set on ideas rather than a political party. It was for independence, against partition and in favour of Irish participation at the great conference that would decide the future of Europe at the end of the war. How these ends were to be achieved was far from clear.

In 1917 Sinn Fein candidates stood in by-elections in Ireland with highly encouraging results. At the Sinn Fein ard fheis at the end of the year one of the victors, Eamonn de Valera, a mathematics lecturer who had commanded a battalion of volunteers in the uprising, replaced Griffith as President of Sinn Fein. De Valera, like Griffith, preached that the end-of-war conference was where Ireland's independence could best be achieved. His tone was more belligerent than that of the moderate Sinn Feiners and he repeatedly upheld the right of the Irish to take up arms in certain circumstances, such as any attempt by Britain to impose conscription on Ireland. By April 1918 this prospect had moved closer to a reality, when Parliament passed a measure enabling conscription to be extended across the Irish Sea. Conscription was an extreme measure, the result of the need to restock the trenches with fresh troops after the slaughter that followed the German March offensive. It was also an act of extraordinary political insensitivity. Why should young Irish men be pressed into service to die in the cause of a principle — the right of small nations to their independence — which was being consistently denied to them? In the end the need to conscript in Ireland receded. But Sinn Fein had benefited, as it almost invariably did, from the government's crassness. Then the government arrested seventy-three leading Sinn Feiners, including de Valera, on the pretext that they had been involved in a plot with the Germans.

The depth of Sinn Fein's new popularity was put to the test in the general election of December 1918. The results underlined the political bankruptcy of the old nationalist Home Rule party, now without Redmond who had died earlier in the year. They won only six seats. Their new leader, John Dillon, was defeated by de Valera, who fought his campaign from a cell in Lincoln jail. The Nationalists conceded defeat almost from the outset and in twenty-six constituencies they did not bother to field a candidate.

From the start all Sinn Fein candidates pledged that if elected they would abstain from taking their seats at Westminster. After the election they took this policy further by setting up their own parliament, Dail Eireann, in the Mansion House in Dublin. At the opening session on 21 January 1919 they established a provisional government and a constitution and issued a declaration of independence which linked Dail Eireann with the republic 'proclaimed in Dublin on Easter Monday, 1916, by the Irish Republican Army on behalf of the Irish people.'

As Sinn Fein's political strength had been growing, so had that of its sister organisation, the Volunteers. During 1918 the Volunteers became increasingly bold, drilling openly, raiding houses and demanding arms, and generally defying authority. Indeed, in August 1918 the Volunteers' official newspaper *An tOghlach* (The Volunteer) had declared that 'the Irish Volunteers are the Army of the Irish Republic'.[5] They had hard and clever leaders, notably Michael Collins, a former bank clerk who had returned from London in time to take part in the Easter Rising. As with Sinn Fein there was a certain confusion about the aims and policies of the Volunteers. Many

28

members saw themselves in the traditional role as a bulwark against British bad faith in the matter of Home Rule. Others were already dedicated to another uprising to finish the work begun by the 'men of 1916'.

About the time the Dail met, two constables in the Royal Irish Constabulary (RIC) the 9,000-strong national police force, who were escorting a waggon loaded with gelignite to a quarry in Tipperary, were shot dead by Volunteers; they stripped them of their weapons and made off with the explosives. The Volunteers were led by Dan Breen and Sean Treacy and they were acting without orders either from the Volunteers' headquarters staff in Dublin or from the Dail. The cold-hearted manner of the killings aroused widespread disgust and was condemned by the Church, though not by the new government. Indeed, *An tOghlach* gave limited approval to the action.[6] By the end of the year there had been dozens of similar incidents and eighteen RIC men were dead. There was nothing in the highly unspecific manifesto Sinn Fein put before the Irish people which said that killing policemen and soldiers was part of their plans, but if there had been it would certainly have been rejected by the electorate.

At the start of 1919 Sinn Fein was still seeking political solutions to the Irish problem. Indeed, de Valera, after being sprung from Lincoln jail by the audacious Collins, left Ireland for the United States to mobilise American support for Ireland's claims. But he believed that violence would have to be used again if peaceful agitation failed. Other prominent members of the Dail, such as Collins and Cathal Brugha, who were both ministers of Dail Eireann and leaders of the IRA, believed that violence was the only means to Sinn Fein's ends. Less than a fortnight after the Dail met for the first time, Brugha, who was chief-of-staff, sanctioned a directive issued to the IRA which authorised them to 'slay' members of the armed forces to overcome their resistance. Most of the policemen who were shot during 1919 died at the instruction of Collins, who was a politician by day, soberly addressing the Dail on financial matters, while plotting death by night. The silence of Dail Eireann as RIC men were shot from behind hedgerows and ditches showed that even the moderate members of Sinn Fein were not prepared to dissent.

Public disquiet over the IRA tactics was diminished by the behaviour of the Crown forces. Terror was met with counter-terror. In March 1920 the ranks of the RIC, depleted by resignations, were stiffened by recruits from Britain, called Black and Tans because of the mixture of uniforms they wore. They were heavy-handed and vindictive and their name a by-word for British brutality. There were other Crown forces: regular soldiers and later, Auxiliaries, but to the IRA the Black and Tans symbolised all they were fighting. In republican circles the conflict is still known as the Tan War.

The Troubles threw up a steady stream of martyrs. Terence McSwiney, the Mayor of Cork whose predecessor had been murdered by the RIC, died on hunger-strike in Brixton prison in London. A young medical student, Kevin Barry, was hanged in Dublin for his part in an IRA raid, inspiring a mawkish but powerful ballad. This conflict was markedly different from any previous Irish rebellion. The insurgents were infinitely better disciplined and organised than their political ancestors. They now avoided suicidal head-on confrontations with their better-armed opponents. Instead, under the tutelage of Collins and local commanders like Dan Breen in Tipperary and Tom Barry in Cork, they learnt how to keep a much larger enemy force in a wearying state of perpetual insecurity by frequent ambush and assassination. Despite later myth-making this was not a heroic war. There was considerable popular acquiescence among the population to the IRA; but when it was not forth-coming there was intimidation. In the first three months of 1921, for example, seventy-three people adorned with placards denouncing them as spies were found trussed and shot.

In a unique turnabout, it was the British who were now riddled with informers. Collins had a superb network reaching deep inside Dublin Castle. In November 1920 his men surprised fourteen British undercover agents in their beds in Dublin and shot them dead. The same day the Black and Tans replied by firing into the crowd at a football game at Croke Park, killing twelve and wounding sixty.

The violence eventually wrung some political concessions from the British. At the end of 1920 the Prime Minister, Lloyd George, produced the Government of Ireland bill which finally conceded Home Rule to Ireland. The great problem was that the island would still be divided. There was to be one Home Rule parliament in Dublin, and another in Belfast to govern Ulster. This was entirely unacceptable to Sinn Fein. In May 1921 they fought the election for the Southern assembly on the principle of opposition to Home Rule and partition and the demand for independence in an all-Ireland state. They won 124 of the 128 seats. The deputies swore their allegiance to the provisional government of Ireland and took their seats as the Second Dail Eireann. A few days later the Dublin Brigade of the IRA entered the Custom House, one of the main centres of the British administration in Ireland, and burnt it down.

By June Britain had about 65,000 soldiers and policemen in Ireland. Yet there was no sign that military might was about to pacify the island. On 25 June Lloyd George suggested a peace conference to de Valera, who was now back from America. On 11 July both sides began a truce. For the first time since the reign of Elizabeth I it was the British government who had been forced to come to the Irish to negotiate.

But the fighting that had brought about this state of affairs had not been of the making of the Irish people or even its self-proclaimed government. The population and the Dail had been hustled into the conflict by the IRA. Despite the pious claim of de Valera that 'the Republican Army is the constitutional military arm of the Government of the Republic,'[7] the IRA's main loyalty was to itself. The government had little claim over its actions. Even Michael Collins, who had personal command of the bulk of the organisation, was sometimes incapable of controlling some of the rural divisions which operated more like the old rural secret societies of the eighteenth and nineteenth centuries than a disciplined guerrilla army.

The negotiations between Collins and Griffith and the British government went on all through the remainder of 1921. On 6 December, under the threat of a renewal of the war and with great misgivings, the Irish delegates signed 'the articles of

...ement for a treaty between Great Britain and Northern Ireland.' The treaty established a new political entity, the Irish Free State, which would have dominion status. Members of its parliament would still be required to take an oath of allegiance to the British Crown. The British Navy would maintain bases in Ireland, the so-called 'treaty ports'.

The Free State had a greater degree of independence from Britain than the Home Rule state. Ireland could make its own foreign policy. The price of this, however, was partition. Northern Ireland, where the Protestants had greeted news of the treaty by attacking the Catholic ghettoes, would have the right to opt out of the new state. If it chose to do so, then a boundary commission would establish the frontiers of the new mini-state. The Northern Ireland parliament in Belfast established by the elections in May that year immediately announced it would exercise their right to secede.

Collins and Griffith returned to Dublin to a divided Dail. The fighting and the subsequent negotiations had not gained much. Ireland was now divided and the new Free State was still not completely independent of Britain. Collins interpreted events optimistically. Partition, he believed, could not last. Only four of the counties of Northern Ireland had Protestant majorities. A new state of Northern Ireland based on Antrim, Armagh, Down and Derry could not survive for long. What the treaty had provided, he declared, was 'not the ultimate freedom that all nations aspire and develop to, but the freedom to achieve it.' When the treaty was put to the Dail on 7 January 1922 it was accepted by sixty-four votes to fifty-seven. De Valera, who had stayed out of the negotiations, rejected the decision and resigned as President of the Dail. He was replaced by Collins.

This division was probably not an accurate reflection of Irish opinion as a whole. In the country at large the treaty was not unpopular. Many people felt, like Griffith, that it was a considerable achievement. For the first time in 700 years British troops would be removed from the soil of three of Ireland's four provinces. Many others, though dissatisfied, accepted Collins' stepping-stone theory.

The most immediate issue in the fortunes of the treaty was the attitude of the IRA, which in 1922 was the most powerful institution in the as yet unformed Irish state. The organisation's 100,000 members had been fighting for a republic and they felt the treaty's shortcomings more sharply than did the non-combatants. At the top, the General Headquarters staff split on much the same lines as the Dail cabinet had, with half accepting Collins' assurances that they were halfway home. In the ranks there was suspicion and anger, which increased as the new pro-treaty government began recruiting its own army and police force. In March the IRA held a convention to discuss its relationship with the new state. Motions calling for a military dictatorship were only narrowly defeated.

As always, the violent republican tradition did not feel itself to be bound by the wishes of the majority of Irish men and women. Most IRA men accepted that the country backed the treaty. But in the eyes of the extreme republicans, the country was wrong. If it had been left to the population, the argument ran, there would have been no 1916 rising. If it had been up to the conventional politicians of the First Dail, there would have been no Anglo-Irish war and therefore no treaty. Why stop now when with one more push they could achieve the sacred goal of an independent, thirty-two county republic?

Throughout the spring and early summer there were continual attempts to heal the breach. The government and the 'irregulars', as the dissident IRA men were called, co-operated in an attempt to relieve the pressure on the Catholic population in the North after sectarian rioting broke out once again in May. Collins hoped that the general election of 14 June would also relieve the political pressures. The republicans, under the leadership of de Valera, gained only twenty-six of 128 seats.

Four days later the IRA held an extraordinary general army convention in which Tom Barry, the veteran Cork commander, denounced the new government and proposed that the IRA should immediately resume the war against Britain.

This situation could not be allowed to continue. The Irish government, under the leadership of William Cosgrave, a veteran of the uprising whose death sentence had been commuted, was coming to the conclusion that if the new state was to survive, the IRA would have to be crushed. In June the IRA provided the government with an excuse when it kidnapped a member of the Dail in retaliation for the arrest of one of their officers. The government replied by bombarding the IRA headquarters in the Four Courts on the banks of the Liffey in Dublin.

In the Civil War that followed the IRA had none of the advantages that had brought them such success against the British. The rural population was now largely indifferent to it. The Free State government showed itself capable of acting with greater ruthlessness than the British. They locked up republicans by the thousand — at the end of the war there were more than 12,000 in Irish jails. The firing squads executed seventy-seven IRA men. Retaliation was swift and brutal. When the IRA assassinated two Dail deputies, four senior IRA prisoners, Rory O'Connor, Liam Mellows, Joseph McKelvey and Richard Barrett, were taken out and shot.

The IRA had some successes. In August 1922, for example, they managed to ambush and kill Michael Collins, the chief of the Free State forces, thereby fulfilling his own prophecy that by signing the treaty he was 'signing my own death warrant.' But the superiority of the Government troops, the harshness of their tactics and the indifference of most of the population made an IRA victory impossible. On 24 May 1923 a ceasefire was declared. The remnants of the irregulars dumped their arms and dispersed.

The IRA had now been defeated politically and militarily, but in the eyes of the extremists that did not reduce the legitimacy of its cause. As the decade progressed, however, the number of members prepared to accept its almost theological approach to politics decreased. In November 1925 the IRA removed its support from the Sinn Fein deputies who were still operating a theoretical 'republican government' after withdrawing from the Dail, and invested power in its own Army Council. The Army Council was to consist of seven officers, elected from within a 12-man executive who in turn were elected by IRA delegates from units all over the country. The Army Council chose a commanding officer or chief-of-staff, who was expected to consult with his Army Council comrades on important matters. The planning and implementation of decisions taken by the Army Council was carried out by the General Headquarters staff, which usually contained most of the Army Council. This system is still basically the same today.

The IRA's faith in Sinn Fein had been weakened by the fact that a section led by de Valera had been edging away from abstentionism and toward entering the Dail, declaring, in an argument that was to be repeated at regular intervals during the years to come, that abstentionism was merely a tactic, not a principle. After failing to persuade the party, de Valera withdrew and founded a new organisation, Fianna Fail (Soldiers of Destiny), who contested the June 1927 elections as non-violent republicans committed to a united Ireland by peaceful means. The new party did well, a tribute in part to de Valera's popularity, and won forty-four seats against forty-seven by William T. Cosgrave's Cumann na nGaedhal party. Sinn Fein won three.

The main obstacle to the victorious Fianna Fail deputies taking their seats in the Dail was the existence of the oath of allegiance to the British Crown, stipulated by the treaty. De Valera overcame this difficulty by denying that it had any moral validity and treating it as merely a distasteful formality. Despite de Valera's continued ambivalence towards the constitution, the arrival of Fianna Fail in the Dail set the seal on the validity of the Free State. It also provided a constitutional safety valve for anti-treaty, anti-partition sentiment in the country.

With Fianna Fail's success, the IRA's standing sank further. By the end of the decade it had been reduced to a dedicated rump of conspirators, bound together by a sense of betrayal, in the service of an invisible republic. With each successive desertion it acquired a more exaggerated sense of its own legitimacy and grew further away from the realities of Irish political life. Even in this reduced role its effectiveness was sapped by a series of repressive acts passed by the Cosgrave government including the Public Safety Act of 1931 which declared the IRA illegal, extended police powers of arrest and detention and set up military tribunals to deal with political crimes.

The IRA had no coherent idea of what direction it should follow. To a great extent it was still a coalition of the disparate political forces that had brought about the Easter Rising — intense traditionalism, Fenianism and revolutionary socialism. The latter expressed itself in the shape of Saor Eire (Free Ireland), founded by Peadar O'Donnell, a socialist who tried to push the movement to champion the grievances of workers and small farmers.

By the 1930s most of those with a developed political sense had already left the IRA. Those who remained were hostile and mistrustful of politics. They believed — and history provided much evidence to support them — that violent action was the most effective way of edging Ireland towards the ultimate goal of becoming a fully-fledged, thirty-two-county republic.

The question was, what action should they take? The leader of the militarists was Sean Russell, a fervent, pious figure who had inherited the physical force instincts of the Fenians. In 1939, the year he took over the IRA organisation, he revived an old Fenian tactic by sending bombing teams to the mainland of England. They set off 127 bombs, including one in Coventry that killed five civilians. De Valera, by now prime minister and anxious about the trouble the IRA could make in the war that was looming, took hard, unsentimental action. The Offences Against the State Act introduced internment without trial, a measure the government made liberal use of to lock up 400 republicans during the war years.

One of de Valera's fears was of a pact between the IRA and the Nazis, which could jeopardise Ireland's precious neutrality. The intense fastidiousness that the IRA displayed in its choice of allies in Ireland did not extend abroad. In a tragi-comic repeat of the Casement episode, Russell sought help from Nazi Germany. It came to nothing.

By the end of the war the IRA was almost as insubstantial

36

as the republic it sought. The General Headquarters staff in Dublin had first been split by accusations of treachery, then virtually wiped out by arrests and imprisonment so that at the end of the war there was only one member at large, Harry White, who kept one jump ahead of the police moving around the country playing the banjo in the Magnet Showband. There were still those who were prepared to keep the tradition alive. As the jails began to empty at the end of the war, the nucleus of a new organisation began to take shape. By 1947 the new GHQ staff estimated there were 200 activists. In 1948 they elected a new chief-of-staff, Tony Magan. Magan was conservative, puritanical and a martinet. Under his control the IRA acquired a concrete purpose — to launch a guerrilla war against the British troops occupying Northern Ireland. After the confusion and feuding of the 1940s this new clarity was attractive. The IRA began to draw a new generation of idealistic young men who had no experience of the Tan War or the Civil War.

At long last the IRA was beginning to focus its attention on Northern Ireland. In 1925 the Northern state had hardened into the frontiers set by the 1920 Government of Ireland Act. The boundary commission, which Collins had fondly hoped would return part of the Six Counties to the Free State, had actually tried to add part of Donegal to the North. The British relented in negotiation, but Ulster would be viable after all. Viable, that is, for the Protestants. The institutions of Northern Ireland had been rapidly turned to the Protestants' overwhelming advantage. Within the Six Counties Protestants outnumbered Catholics by two to one. As politics were conducted along sectarian lines, the Unionists had a perpetual majority at Stormont, the seat of the Northern Ireland parliament. It was, as its first prime minister, Sir James Craig (later Lord Craigavon), boasted, 'a Protestant parliament and a Protestant state'.[8] It had its own police force, the Royal Ulster Constabulary (RUC), backed up by the 25,000-strong Ulster Special Constabulary, (the 'B' Specials), whose main function was to stifle republican activities, which they carried out with great success. Although there was a strong IRA presence in Belfast and Londonderry (or Derry as it is always called by nationalists) it was constantly depleted by arrests and was generally incapable of anything other than occasional, token activity.

The arrival of Fianna Fail in the Dail revived the Northern Ireland question. In 1937 de Valera had introduced a new constitution which laid claim to the whole thirty-two counties of Ireland as the 'national territory'. In the late 1940s attention had been drawn to the issue once again when a former IRA man, Sean MacBride, had left to form a constitutional republican party, Clann na Phoblachta, which won nine seats in the Dail. Later, in the early 1950s, the Southern government had funded nationalist candidates in elections in the North. None of this had had the slightest effect on the Northern Protestants' determination to maintain the union with Britain, or on the British government's willingness to go on preserving it.

The IRA border campaign was conceived in the same spirit as the 1916 uprising and the war against the Crown forces. On paper the enterprise seemed ludicrous, given the huge imbalance in forces, but Magan and his men still believed that isolated acts of revolutionary violence had the potential to alter utterly an apparently immutable situation, just as the rebellion of 1916 had done.

Before the fighting could begin the IRA needed guns and, as usual, it had no money. In 1951 the Army Council began authorising arms raids. The first took place on a British Air Force and Navy barracks in the North and was a complete, and rather surprising, success. The next was in Britain. Cathal Goulding, one of a new generation of IRA men, was sent to Britain to team up with a British-born recruit, John Stephenson (later better known as Sean MacStiofain), and Manus Canning from the Derry unit, to raid the armoury of Felsted, a public school in Dunmow, Essex. The operation was not a success. After making off with eight bren guns, a dozen sten guns, an anti-tank gun, a mortar and 109 rifles, their heavily-laden van was stopped by a police patrol. All three were subsequently sentenced to eight years in prison.

In June 1954 an IRA team mounted a daring and well-executed raid on a British Army barracks in Armagh, which brought them 250 rifles, 37 sub-machine-guns, nine bren guns and forty training rifles. The next raid on an Army barracks at Omagh ended in a firefight and the capture of eight of the unit, but the mere fact that the IRA was active again was enough to maintain morale and attract recruits.

* Republican spirits were further raised by the success of Sinn Fein in elections to the Westminster parliament in the North in 1956: they polled 152,310 votes and won two seats. In 1949 Sinn Fein and the IRA had entered the mutually supporting embrace they are still locked in. Most IRA men retained their fundamental suspicion of politics, but Sinn Fein was different. Like them, it had kept the faith, doggedly sticking to its refusal to accept the authority of the Dail. Besides, discussions that had gone on among internees in prisons all over Ireland during the war years had led some to accept the need for political outlet. At an Army Convention, called to discuss significant policy changes, IRA men had been authorised to infiltrate and take control of the movement. Sinn Fein submitted willingly, electing a member of the Army Council, Patrick McLogan, as their new president. *

In the autumn of 1956 IRA training officers arrived in the North to begin recruiting and training local men. The initial thrust, however, was to be provided by 'flying columns' from the South who would move over the border and begin operations in their allotted area. According to an IRA document seized in the South, the task of each force was

> to cut all communications, telephone, road and rail . . . our mission is to maintain and strengthen our resistance centres throughout the occupied areas and also to break down the enemy's administration in the occupied area until he is forced to withdraw his forces. Our method of doing this is use of guerrilla warfare within the occupied area and propaganda directed at inhabitants. In time, as we build up

39

our forces, we hope to be in a position to liberate large areas and tie these in with other liberated areas – that is areas where the enemy's writ no longer runs.

The campaign was an old-fashioned and, by the standards of what was to come, chivalrous affair. It aimed at destroying property rather than people and all units were under instruction to avoid civilian bloodshed. For this reason, and because there were doubts about the reliability of the Belfast IRA, which GHQ in Dublin believed to contain a traitor, there would be no action in the city.

The hostilities opened up on 11 December, a night when rain, sleet and snow lashed the length of the border. Altogether 150 men went into action, with mixed fortunes. In County Derry a five-man unit bombed a BBC transmitter, further south at Magherafelt the quarter sessions courthouse was set on fire and destroyed; at Newry a team burned down a hut used by the 'B' Specials, the part-time police force set up in 1920 to counter the IRA; and in Enniskillen a half-built barracks intended for the British Army Territorials was blown up. The main action of the evening was directed at Armagh Barracks, scene of the successful arms raid, but it fizzled out in a characteristic mixture of bad planning and bad luck. The lorry that was due to carry the unit to the raid failed to turn up on time, not an unusual occurrence in IRA operations. When it finally appeared the men were appalled to see that it was missing an exhaust pipe and billowing smoke.[9] The raiders, led by Sean Garland, a young ginger-haired Dubliner who had enlisted in the British Army at Armagh in order to gain intelligence for the arms raid, were spotted immediately, and had to content themselves with a few lame bursts of automatic gunfire before roaring off towards the border.

This failure did not prevent the IRA from issuing a gradiloquent statement the following morning:

Spearheaded by Ireland's freedom fighters, our people have carried the fight to the enemy . . . Out of this national liberation struggle a new Ireland will emerge, upright and

40

free. In that new Ireland we shall build a country fit for all our people to live in. That then is our aim: an independent, united democratic Irish Republic. For this we shall fight until the invader is driven from our soil and victory is ours.[10]

The phraseology of the statement betrayed the vagueness of the IRA leadership's thinking. How was a campaign of sabotage and assassination going to hasten the dawn of the republic? What sort of republic would it be? The IRA had no clear answers to these questions themselves. The energy that had gone into preparing and planning the campaign had precluded any consideration of where it was going to lead. It was action for action's sake. Two days later the attacks resumed with more success. Garland's column moved west to Fermanagh and attacked the RUC barracks in Lisnaskea, blowing in the front of the building with a 50-pound gelignite mine and riddling the buldings with bullets. There were further attacks at Derrylin and Roslea Barracks which were beaten off by the RUC.

GHQ suspended the campaign for Christmas, but on New Year's Eve the columns were back in action. Noel Kavanagh decided to lead the South Fermanagh column back to Derrylin. Once again the RUC constables put up a spirited fight. The attack opened with a long burst of machine-gun fire that killed one of the officers, Constable John Scally. His companion, Constable Ferguson, a veteran of the previous attack, managed to scramble upstairs and return fire with his sub-machine-gun, before a mine demolished the front door and brought down the staircase. Ferguson struggled free from under a pile of plaster and resumed shooting, by which time the IRA column had withdrawn.

The following night, a short distance to the north at Brookeborough, Garland, who had now been joined by Daithi O'Connaill, an intense, bony schoolteacher from County Cork, as his second-in-command, decided to mount a similar attack, which was to become the most famous action of the campaign.

Shortly after dusk the unit arrived in the high street of

Brookeborough in a stolen tipper lorry. As all the previous attacks had taken place in the small hours of the morning, Garland believed the early timing would give them the advantage of surprise. The lorry parked by the corner of the barracks and two men ran forward to place a mine against the wall. Meanwhile, Sean South, a 27-year-old clerk from Garryowen, County Limerick, who had served as an officer in the Irish Army reserve, opened up on the building with a bren gun mounted on the back of the truck. The mine failed to explode. Another mine was planted, which also declined to go off, even when sprayed with fire by O'Connaill. One of the raiders threw a hand grenade at the window but it bounced off the iron casement, rolled back under the truck and exploded. By now the bren gun had run through its woefully inadequate three magazines of ammunition and the inhabitants of the barracks had recovered from their initial surprise and were returning fire with devastating effect. Garland decided it was time to pull out. As they fell back to the lorry he was hit in the leg. South was badly wounded and fell over his gun. Another member of the party, 19-year-old Feargal O'Hanlon, had been hit in the leg, and an artery was pumping blood. The lorry, now riddled with bullets and with the back see-sawing, lurched off towards the border.

Five miles out of Brookeborough they abandoned the lorry and took to the fields. It was obvious that South was dying and that O'Hanlon had not long to go. With reluctance, they were left in a cow byre, where they were discovered by the RUC a short time later. The rest staggered on through the night, evading 400 RUC men, 'B' Specials and British soldiers who were hunting them and eventually crossed the border.

● The episode made excellent propaganda. South and O'Hanlon were model young men. South was a member of the Legion of Mary, a lay organisation dedicated to good works, and a devotee of the Irish language. O'Hanlon played football for Monaghan. South (Sabhat in Gaelic) became the subject of a ballad elevating him to the republican pantheon which ended with the words, 'He has gone to join the gallant band of

Plunkett, Pearse and Tone, A martyr for old Ireland, Sean Sabhat of Garryowen.'

Until now the campaign had been relatively untroubled by the attentions of the Irish police and army, but after the raid the climate rapidly changed. The Special Branch began rounding up known republicans under the Offences Against the State Act including the current chief-of-staff, Sean Cronin, and by the end of January most members of the GHQ were in jail. The Fine Gael government under John Costello had been prodded into action by two considerations: the IRA's activities were threatening to propel the republic into a diplomatic confrontation with Britain, and it seemed that the IRA could mount a serious challenge to the state itself. Fifty thousand people had attended Sean South's funeral in Limerick. The proof that this sentiment could be translated into political terms appeared to come when Fine Gael's coalition partner, Clann na Phoblachta, forced a vote of no confidence in Costello over his treatment of the IRA. In the ensuing general election, Sinn Fein stood in support of the IRA campaign, won four seats and received 65,640 first preference votes. This represented only five per cent of the electorate, yet after years starved of encouragement the IRA was inclined to believe that the original justification for the campaign was being realised and that the action in the North had indeed sparked off a process of 'republicanisation' among the Irish nation. The election, however, had placed a new and more formidable opponent in power. De Valera had proved in the past that he was capable of unflinching toughness against republicans. In July 1957, after an RUC constable was killed in an IRA ambush in Armagh, he ordered wholesale internments, just as he had during the war years. Most of the Sinn Fein executive, the Army Council and the GHQ staff were picked up. But even with the old leadership locked up and a new one on the run the campaign continued. In 1957 there were 341 incidents. Many failed to rise much above the level of vandalism. Roads and customs posts were blown up and occasionally bridges were destroyed to 'reunite' temporarily patches of Northern Irish counties with the hinterland.

The IRA seemed particularly prone to bad luck. In November 1958 an active service unit (ASU) was preparing a gelignite mine in a cottage a hundred yards from the border at Edentubber, County Louth, when it went off, demolishing the building and killing all four members and the owner of the cottage. An IRA team in Carrickmore, County Tyrone who dug a hideout under the floor of a farmyard piggery nearly suffocated after they forgot to put in any ventilation.

Once they had lost the element of surprise of the initial raids, the IRA units lacked the weapons to mount a serious threat to the RUC. They had only rifles, grenades and Thompson machine-guns which made little impression on the armour-plating of the RUC vehicles and every attempt to obtain anti-tank weaponry, including a raid on a British army camp in Dorset, failed.

Their opponents, the RUC and the 'B' Specials, had a comprehensive knowledge of the social geography of their areas, which enabled them to identify republican sympathisers and shut down the supply of possible safe houses. Many IRA teams were forced to operate out of dank and freezing foxholes cut into inhospitable hillsides. On top of this, they had to contend with anti-republican legislation in the North that was just as formidable as the Republic's. The Stormont government had waited only ten days after the border campaign opened before reintroducing internment. From 21 December 1956 hundreds of republicans, even those who had long since aged beyond the point where they could use a Thompson gun even if they had wanted to, were locked away. To compound the IRA's difficulties, after the first swoops in the South, the direction of the campaign was complicated by internal quarrelling which arose when the imprisoned leadership began finding fault with the way operations were being conducted outside.

This combination of arrests, lack of funds and equipment and poor organisation began to erode the high morale of the early part of the campaign, especially as it became clear that the political effects of the violence were far less dramatic than the IRA had expected. After a short time even the most

44

optimistic among them had reached the conclusion that military victory was not possible. But there was still a general expectation that the campaign would provoke a crisis — of what sort no one was sure. Occasionally an assassination would move the campaign back into the headlines, but after the initial flurry of anxiety, both Northern and Southern governments and the government of Britain were for the most part able to treat it as a relatively minor consideration.

The ability and the will to carry out operations began to run down. In 1959 there were only seventy-seven incidents. The following year there were twenty-six. By January 1962, when the Army Council met to consider calling it off, the campaign was already effectively over. In all there had been about 500 incidents ranging from road craterings to full-scale assaults. Eight IRA men and four republican supporters had been killed. Six RUC men had died and thirty-two members of the British security forces were wounded.

The campaign had been a classic manifestation of the physical force tradition. All the energies of the participants had gone into military preparations, and almost no thought had been devoted to the political consequences of their actions or how these might be turned to bringing their goal of a republic nearer. The insurgents had promised in their declaration of war 'a new Ireland, upright and free,' without offering the people of Ireland to whom they were constantly appealing, the slightest idea of what this new state would be like.

The Army Council statement announcing that 'all arms and other material have been dumped and all full-time active service Volunteers have been withdrawn', issued on the evening of 26 February, concluded with a belligerent declaration:

The Irish resistance movement renews its pledge of eternal hostility to the British Forces of Occupation in Ireland. It calls on the Irish people for increased support and looks forward with confidence — in co-operation for the final and victorious phase of the struggle for the full freedom of Ireland.

* * *

At the time this seemed to many inside the republican movement to be mere empty defiance, the last gasp of a tradition whose day had finally drawn to a close. The events of the new decade were to show that this view was mistaken and that the doctrine of physical force would not be eradicated by simple defeat. In the 1960s it would become clear that adherence to this doctrine was still a cardinal principle to a substantial number of republicans, and one that would eventually play a large part in splitting the movement in half.

CHAPTER THREE

Becalmed

Early on the morning of 25 April 1961, the last batch of republican prisoners to be interned by the Northern Ireland authorities during the IRA's border campaign filed through the massive oak and steel door of the Crumlin Road prison in Belfast and out into an unwelcoming and indifferent world. There was no one waiting in the thin spring sunshine to welcome them. As always they had only learnt of their release at the last moment. The Belfast contingent set off down the narrow streets running off the Crumlin Road to their ghetto homes. The rest headed for the station, armed with the one-way rail warrant provided by the authorities to ease their passage into the outside world.

Many of the internees who were released from Northern Ireland prisons in January 1960 as the IRA campaign fizzled into insignificance found that the elation of being free did not survive their homecoming. Jimmy Drumm, a Belfast republican, returned to find that 'some of the people in the street we lived in didn't even know we were in prison'.[1] Sean Keenan, another IRA veteran, went back to the area of Derry where he had grown up to find he was an outsider.[2] To Drumm it seemed that republicans had become 'a forgotten race of people'. Of the 256 republican prisoners interned in the North eighty-nine had registered their disillusionment with the campaign and their unwillingness to continue to sacrifice their private lives and employment prospects to the movement by 'signing out', pledging themselves to renounce violence

47

in return for their freedom. When the gates clanged behind those who stayed the course, many decided that enough was enough. Instead of 'reporting back to their units', as the IRA rules instructed, they put their energies into building their family lives and their careers. John Kelly, for example, who had been arrested on 'active service' and sentenced to six years in the Crum, drew the dole for nine months before finding work on a building-site and was happily married and installed in a good job as a planning engineer with ICI when he returned to the movement in 1969.

Those who remained tried to explain and analyse the catastrophic events of the preceding six years. Even by the standards of an organisation as steeped in failure as the IRA had been, the border campaign was a disaster. By the close the IRA had shown a complete inability to mobilise popular support or to influence political events. More than 400 of its men had been locked up without provoking much more than token noises of protest. As the remnants gathered to take stock it seemed to many of them that the campaign had merely succeeded in furnishing them with the final proof of the hopelessness of their cause. Their frustration shone through the communiqué issued on 25 February 1962, which finally declared that the episode was dead; after announcing the termination of the 'campaign of resistance to British Occupation' the statement went on to blame the attitude of the Irish public 'whose minds have been deliberately distracted from the supreme issue facing the Irish people -- the unity and freedom of Ireland'.

Among the veterans of the campaign who remained in the movement, in pub back rooms and dingy republican drinking clubs, a debate began as to the lessons to be drawn from failure. Most of the men who took part had been dismayed by the almost complete indifference that the Catholic popula-tion in the border areas had shown towards them. The point had been made forcibly in the Republic of Ireland's elections in October 1961 when Sinn Fein polled only three per cent of the first preference votes, a considerable decline from the five per cent they had won in 1957. The first lesson, it was generally agreed, was that the IRA needed to develop a coherent political philosophy that had some relevance to the lives of contemporary Irish men and women, to replace the appeals to an ill-defined republic that constituted the IRA's current manifesto. The second, as seen by Jim Sullivan, a participant in the campaign who went on to become one of the Official IRA's leaders in Belfast, was that 'the brute military stance would never achieve anything in Ireland. It was as simple as that. The campaign had bloody well proved it for us'.[3]

Everyone, even the proponents of physical force republicanism who were to lead the breakaway by the Provisionals at the end of the decade, accepted that for the moment at least, any thoughts of a further campaign would have to be shelved. It seemed to Jimmy Drumm, emerging from prison, that there was 'no future. I had been in prison in the forties and after I got out it had been ten years before anything got moving. We all agreed that this time it was going to be even worse. It was going to be twenty years before anything got off the ground again.'[1] Most agreed with the necessity to develop an attractive political philosophy. Two of the leading dissenters who went on to found the Provisionals, Ruairi O'Bradaigh, the last IRA chief-of-staff during the border campaign, and Daithi O'Connaill, one of the most energetic commanders, both enthusiastically supported the injection of some socialism into the moribund philosophy of the movement. But the argument that was to develop through the decade and ultimately to split the movement did not concern the desirability of developing a new political formula. It concerned the nature of the recipe and the proportions of the ingredients it contained.

The republican movement's reassessment of itself had begun long before the campaign ended. As usual, the experience of imprisonment during the years of the campaign had forced the IRA to rethink its position. In the Crumlin Road jail, a secret newspaper, *Saoirse* (Freedom), which circulated among the prisoners, carried an article by Eamon Timoney, the leader of the Derry IRA, entitled 'Quo Vadis Hibernia?' It urged republicans to involve themselves in local government and co-operatives and advocated increased discussion of the social and economic issues. A similar view was emerging among the prisoners south of the border in The Curragh. This dismal collection of huts near the famous racetrack in County Kildare was reserved for republican internees and convicts in times of emergency. Tomas MacGiolla, interned in the camp from 1957 to 1959, came to view the campaign as an incongruity. 'We were ignoring mass unemployment and the fact that 50,000 people were being forced to emigrate from the Twenty-six Counties [the Irish Republic] every year. All this was to wait until the battle was over.'[4] Like most of the other prisoners who bothered to take part in the debate, he came to the conclusion that 'our attitude had to change to "bread today" rather than "roses tomorrow" '.

In September 1962, six months after the campaign had been officially abandoned, the Army Council met in Dublin to consider the future. The most significant outcome of the gathering was the resignation as chief-of-staff of Ruairi O'Bradaigh, who was exhausted after two years attempting to command a military campaign while on the run from the authorities. He was replaced by 40-year-old Cathal Goulding, who had impeccable qualifications for the job. Two previous generations of his Dublin working-class family had produced republican revolutionaries. He had left school at 14 to be a house-painter, joined the IRA and was interned during the war. The lack of manpower in 1945 meant that he was soon on the staff and he later ran training camps in the Wicklow Mountains before going to Britian in 1953 to join up with John Stephenson (Sean MacStiofain). The fact that Goulding had been absent in Wormwood Scrubs prison in London during most of the border campaign spared him from being blamed for its unhappy outcome. He returned to Ireland in 1959.

At first sight Goulding's personality and background made him an unlikely force for radical change in the IRA. He was relentlessly cheery, an old friend of the Dublin playwright Brendan Behan and fond of company and a drink. After much reading and reflection in the Scrubs, however, he came to the conclusion that 'what we needed to do was to sit down and have a good look at the whole revolutionary movement in Ireland, from 1798 to the present day. I and others felt that the movement as a whole had never given a thought to winning a war. They only thought of starting one.'[5]

On his own it was doubtful that Goulding would have been able to make much headway in altering the philosophy of the IRA, dispirited and hungry for new hope though it was at the end of the campaign. But on returning to Ireland he had become friendly with Tomas MacGiolla and, more significantly, with Roy Johnston.

Johnston, a young computer scientist, had come back to Dublin from England where he had been an active member of the Connolly Society, a small discussion group that subjected contemporary Ireland to a marxist analysis. He was an awkward, scholarly man who travelled round Dublin on a bicycle. He found Goulding a romantic and attractive figure as he held forth in the Dublin pubs, often surrounded by pretty girls and Trinity College students. Goulding in turn was impressed by Johnston's refreshingly scientific approach to republicanism. It seemed modern and took account of the facts of contemporary Irish life while providing a long-term strategy for achieving republican aims. He seemed to offer hope for a new start. Within a year of his meeting with Goulding, MacGiolla and Sean Garland, Johnston and another Trinity lecturer, Tony Coughlan, had become indispensable members of any Republican gathering. Johnston's swift progress and the ease with which his ideas gained ground are a testimony to the intellectual feebleness of the IRA when he came on the scene. In 1962 no one in the organisation could say with any great certainty what the movement stood for beyond the removal of the border and the eradication of all remaining traces of British rule. There were many, though, as the new leadership of the IRA was to discover, who knew what the movement stood against.

Johnston's approach seemed modern but much of his philosophy was based on the writings and example of Wolfe Tone. 1963 was the 200th anniversary of Tone's birth. The

51

republican leadership, at the suggestion of Johnston, marked the occasion by founding a Wolfe Tone Society as a forum where the re-evaluation of beliefs and strategy that the failure of the border campaign had shown to be necessary could take place. Other societies were founded in Cork and Belfast. At meetings there would be a lecture or a paper followed by a discussion. Among the most frequent speakers were two veterans of the left who had struggled to steer the IRA away from a course of predominant militarism in the 1930s, George Gilmore and Peadar O'Donnell, the founder of the short-lived experiment in socialist republicanism, Saor Eire. During the course of the discussions in the cavernous, mildewed rooms of the Sinn Fein headquarters in Dublin, a programme of action emerged. The credit for the introduction of the strategy lies largely with Johnston, but the ideas themselves were hardly new – conventional marxism mixed in with a large helping of traditional republican wisdom enlivened by borrowings from the tactics of the Campaign for Nuclear Disarmament in Britain and the civil rights movement in America. Later it became known as 'the stages theory', though it was never called so at the time.

The plan was based on a marxist analysis of Ireland's future, but it was self-deluding: it took little account of the historical realities of the North. It envisaged workers in the Six Counties conducting a civil rights campaign that would establish equality for the Catholic minority. In the process, the sectarian barriers between the two communities would be broken down, enabling the proletariat to recognise their communal class interest. At that point a Sinn Fein political agitation in the South would transform the working classes' ingrained conservatism into a progressive non-sectarian attitude. Parallel to this process, the dynamics of capitalism would be forging a strong bourgeoisie all over the island, which would eventually become equally oppressive to workers of all creeds. At some point the workers would band together to overthrow capitalism; whether it was by violent or peaceful means would be a matter for their own choice.

If there was one element of Tone's teaching that the Goulding leadership had taken to heart it was his insistence that Catholics and Protestants would have to achieve a complete reconciliation before a properly independent and equitable state could be founded. With characteristic optimism, Tone did not bother himself too much about how this unlikely combination was to take place, assuming that the logic of the proposition was almost sufficient in itself to bring it about.

The IRA leaders came to regard non-sectarianism as a crucial principle, an attitude that ended up paralysing them when the sectarian violence in the North broke out in the autumn of 1968. The realities of Northern Ireland, where Protestant supremacy was built into the system of government and backed up with the threat of force, were not allowed to spoil the symmetry of Johnston's theories.

In any case, the problem of the North did not occupy much of the discussion in the early days of the republican revision. The painful memory of the border campaign and the complexity of the border question meant that the IRA with its Southern-based, Southern-oriented leadership was content to leave it lie. Instead they concentrated on organising agitation over housing, jobs, agricultural injustices and fishing rights. In 1963 they began making contact with Irish trade union leaders and later with the leftward fringes of the Irish Labour Party. Despite the adherence to the military rankings and structures, the prospect of a campaign grew so remote in the minds of the leadership as to be almost unthinkable. For once in the Irish history the experience of defeat bred contempt for violent methods. By 1964 training had more or less ceased everywhere in Ireland though some may have periodically brought out the weapons hidden at the close of the campaign to strip and clean them and give them a new coat of grease.

The antipathy to violence was not universally felt. After taking over as chief-of-staff, Goulding had been lobbied by members calling for a military overhaul: better weapons, better training and new tactics. Goulding squashed the proposal, pointing out that 'this had been done before and it always ended up as it had done in 1962'.[5] The IRA at the top was thinking and behaving like a small, conventional, left-wing political

53

party. The extent to which this process had progressed became apparent to the rank and file after an extraordinary meeting of the Army Convention, the supreme policy-making body of the IRA made up of delegates from every unit in the island, in 1964. The gathering was presented with a document containing nine points. Among them were the recommendations that the IRA should combine with other left-wing organisations in a 'National Liberation Front' to throw themselves into a programme of social and political agitation and that the IRA should discard the abstention ban dating back to 1917 which prevented Sinn Fein members taking their seats in Dail Eireann (the Irish parliament), the Northern Ireland parliament at Stormont or the British parliament at Westminster. The proposals had caused disquiet when they were circulated to the units around the country before the convention and the debate was long and angry. The most contentious issue was the proposal to discard abstentionism. Abstentionism, as Sean MacStiofain — who later emerged as one of the leaders of the opposition to Goulding's revision — was to point out, was 'the policy on which the entire republican position rested'.[6]

The IRA's doctrine at the time was that the last legitimate government of Ireland had been the national parliament, overwhelmingly composed of Sinn Fein representatives, which entered the Dail after elections of May 1921, the famous Second Dail. Once it had approved the treaty signed with Britain in December 1921 ceding six of the nine counties of Ulster to British rule, its legitimacy ceased. Naturally, all subsequent parliaments had been illegal, hence Sinn Fein's refusal to sit in them. Legal authority, the IRA believed, was vested in the Army Council. Republican history bred a certain contempt for democracy. At the back of the abstentionists' minds was the belief, not unfounded in fact, that almost every step along the road to Irish freedom had been the result of the actions of dedicated and self-sacrificing conspirators rather than any initiative by the masses. It was the IRA or their ancestors who had brought the Free State into existence (transformed at the stroke of a pen into the Republic of Ireland

54

in 1939). The right of government, therefore, lay with them rather than with politicians elected by a duped electorate.

This view was sincerely and fervently held by many honest republicans. But there was no denying it had many advantages. It released the IRA from the need to obtain any popular backing for its actions and even lent them a quasi-official status. To reverse the policy of abstentionism was not only to recognise, however much you might protest to the contrary, the legitimacy of Leinster House. It was also the beginning of an acceptance of the sovereignty of the ballot-box.

For most of the supporters of abstentionism the issue was simple. Abstentionism was a principle as immutable and inscrutable as religious belief. When it was put to the vote, the leadership's proposal was comprehensively voted down. This did not stop Tomas MacGiolla pledging at the Sinn Fein ard fheis the following year that the movement would win a majority in the Dail before the end of the decade. The abstentionists' brand of republicanism was beginning to appear incompatible with Goulding, MacGiolla and Johnston's view of the future of the movement.

In the months following the Army Convention the Dublin leadership grew steadily more remote from the rank and file in most of the rest of the country. Ireland is a small country, roughly 300 miles long and 200 miles across at the widest point, yet Headquarters had always had difficulty in keeping in touch with the regions. Under Goulding communications became even more tenuous. He, MacGiolla and Johnston seemed to prefer Dublin and the company of fellow left-wing intellectuals, especially those from the Communist Party of Ireland, to that of the rural membership. The vehicle for much of the new thinking was the *United Irishman*, the descendant of the paper that Arthur Griffith had founded at the turn of the century. It had been edited since 1962 by a former inmate of Crumlin Road jail, Denis Foley, who swept away the celtic typefaces and eulogistic memoirs of old IRA heroes, in favour of sharp analytical articles which must have mystified some of the older subscribers. Despite the leadership's belief that the movement's strength was growing, outside Dublin the IRA was in pitiful shape. By the mid-sixties the organisation had sunk into total inactivity in large parts of the country. Where it operated there was fractiousness. In Belfast in 1963 a serious row blew up over whether the Tricolour, the flag of the Irish Republic, should be carried at a march to commemorate the 120th anniversary of Daniel O'Connells 'monster rallies' to repeal the Act of Union with Britain (an arcane event, even given the backward-looking habits of the IRA).

The IRA commander in Belfast, Billy McKee, had been told by the police that if the green, white and orange colours were paraded, the marchers risked prosecution under the flags and emblems legislation, which forbids displays that could provoke a breach of the peace. McKee decided to heed the warning, to the anger of some of the marchers, one of whom, Bobby McKnight, announced he was ready to risk jail to show the flag. McKee insisted and carried the day but the incident did not end there. After the parade Dublin HQ received petitions from the Belfast group demanding the removal of McKee. Goulding was forced to come North to sort out the squabble and left confirming McKee's command. Within a year, however, McKee had lost the confidence of so many of the active IRA members in the city that he resigned, taking some of his supporters with him, including such veterans as Jimmy Steele, who had been jailed in the thirties and forties for numerous republican escapades in the North and who had been part of a celebrated escape from the Crum. These men were to form the core of the Belfast Provisionals when the division eventually came.[3]

McKee was succeeded as Belfast commander by Billy McMillen, who with his second-in-command, Jim Sullivan, was sympathetic to the direction being taken in Dublin. Some republicans in the North felt that Goulding, MacGiolla and Johnston were too concerned about bruising the feelings of the old timers and wanted to force the pace down the road to constitutional politics. Sean Caughey, a Sinn Fein vice-president from Belfast, resigned from the movement in June 1965 because it would not officially recognise the Stormont and Dublin Governments.

Most of the dissatisfaction, though, came from the traditionalists in the ranks. The new philosophy succeeded in alienating socialists like Ruairi O'Bradaigh who had initially welcomed the intellectual overhaul of the movement as a 'long overdue opening of windows and letting in of fresh air' but came to regard it as the first step down the path trodden by de Valera and Sean MacBride (the jurist, diplomat and IRA leader who embraced constitutionalism in the forties but remained an energetic apologist for republicanism): 'The formation of another constitutional party from within the republican movement.'[7]

O'Bradaigh felt that the new apostates should pursue their fortunes outside the movement rather than stay inside and attempt to subvert its cardinal principles. Concern about constitutionalism was reinforced by alarm over the agnostic and atheistic tendencies of the leadership. Despite the frequent official denunciations of their activities by the Catholic hierarchy, IRA men were traditionally devout. During the border campaign they would often hear Mass before an operation and make their confession to a sympathetic priest afterwards. This was a practice dating from the early days of the organisation, as Tom Barry, the commander of the IRA 'flying column' in West Cork during the war against the British, described in his memoirs:

At 3 am the men were told for the first time they were moving in to attack the Auxiliaries between Macroom and Dunmanway. Father O'Connell, parish priest, Ballineen, had riiden out to hear the men's Confessions, and was waiting by the side of a ditch, some distance from the road. Silently, one by one, their rifles slung, the IRA went to him, and then returned to the ranks. Soon the priest came on the road. In a low voice he spoke: 'Are the boys going to attack the Sassanach, Tom?' 'Yes father, we hope so.' He asked no further question, but said in a loud voice, 'Good luck boys, I know you will win. God keep ye all. Now I will give you my Blessing.' He rode away into the darkness of the night.[8]

Johnston quickly made it clear that Catholicism was no longer the official religion of the IRA. Adherence to the Church could only reinforce the Protestants' belief that republicanism was a sectarian force and delay the union of Catholic and Protestant workers in the joint fight against capitalism. This attitude soon provoked trouble. Johnston wrote an article in the *United Irishman* condemning the tradition of reciting the rosary at republican commemorations as a 'sectarian practice'. Sean MacStiofain, Goulding's companion in the Felsted escapade and a devout man, responded by stopping the distribution of the paper in South Kerry where he was republican organiser. For this he was summoned to Dublin by the Army Council and suspended from the movement for six months. Earlier, in 1964, he had raised the issue of Johnston's marxism, a matter of much concern to the devout members of the rank and file who had been taught by their Catholic teachers to regard communists as the Antichrist. At an Army Council meeting in 1964 MacStiofain helpfully pointed out that under IRA regulations, communists could not be members of the republican movement, and proposed that Johnston be removed. Goulding replied that if Johnston went, he would go with him. The matter was dropped.[9]

MacStiofain's concern about the leadership was shared by another Army Council member, Daithi O'Connaill, the Cork schoolmaster who was second-in-command for the ill-fated Brookeborough raid and who had subsequently been badly wounded in an ambush in Ardboe, County Derry. Both were in favour of broadening the base of republican activities, but it seemed to MacStiofain that the Goulding group was 'becoming obsessed with the idea of parliamentary politics and wished to confine the movement almost entirely to social and economic agitation'.[9] The movement's energies were now being poured into demonstrations against poor housing conditions and 'fish-ins' to protest against fishing restrictions of the Republic's waterways.

MacGiolla was frequently badgered by young men 'wanting to know when the campaign was going to start. I had to say to them, ''This *is* the campaign.'' '[4] This was not what the younger elements had joined the IRA for. Pressure for an operation reached the point in the summer of 1965 when the leadership reluctantly authorised an attack on a British torpedo boat, *Brave Borderer*, as she lay in Waterford Harbour on an official visit. The action could be justified by the pledge to 'eternal hostility to the British Forces of occupation in Ireland' delivered in the statement announcing the end of the border campaign. The three men — led by a local romantic, Richard Behal — who fired on the boat were later arrested and imprisoned, but less than six months later were freed from Limerick prison by a raiding party of sympathisers. Behal then embarked on a wave of inconsequential violence, blowing up an automatic telephone exchange in Kilmacow, south Kilkenny, and firing shots down the main street. The republican publicity bureau issued a denial of responsibility for his actions stating that 'the republican movement is directed solely against British rule in Ireland and the movement is prepared only to engage in actions against British Forces in Ireland.'

There was a further embarrassment in March 1966, again involving Behal, when Nelson's Pillar, a remnant of British rule that dominated O'Connell Street, Dublin's main thoroughfare, was blown up. The incident was treated tolerantly in the British Press as a piece of Irish buffoonery rather than an act of terrorism. The publicity bureau responded with another prim denial: 'The republican movement has not concerned itself in the slightest way with the destruction of monuments of foreign origin, nor has the movement aided implicitly or explicity such demolitions.' In case there was any doubt about the priority that the use of violence had assumed in the republican movement, Goulding spelt it out in June 1967 in a speech at Bodenstown, a small Kildare village where Wolfe Tone was buried. Republicans gather there every year to reaffirm their faith and to hear speeches about the movement's future. On this occasion Goulding told them that 'the revolution is a matter of organisation and demonstration' and explicitly rejected the 'physical force tradition of Dan Breen'. Breen, it will be remembered, had been the first IRA man to shoot a policeman during the Anglo-Irish war.

This attitude posed certain logical problems for the leadership. The IRA was still organised as an army with a military command structure and it retained its military instincts. Tim Pat Coogan remembers attending a reinternment service in July 1967 for Joseph O'Sullivan and Reginald Dunne, two IRA men executed for the assassination in London in June 1922 of the chief of the Imperial General Staff, Sir Henry Wilson:

> A guard of honour of the contemporary IRA marched openly on either side of the two coffins through the streets of Dublin. The guards were set-face, stern young men, moving to military commands and dressed in a strange 'uniform' of ordinary peaked cap and gloves. Police kept the crowds back as men who had been under sentence of death by the state which those police were guarding honoured their dead, some praying openly.[10]

If Goulding wanted to hold on to authority, such as it was, bestowed upon him by his leadership of the IRA then the option of force would have to be retained. In 1968 the Army Council sanctioned two operations which could be justified by their purportedly revolutionary nature. In May an IRA team burned buses belonging to the American-owned EI company of Shannon, during a dispute over union recognition. On the Connemara coast a boat owned by an American-backed company which was held to be threatening the livelihoods of local fishermen was blown up. Headline-catching as these activities were, there was no evidence to suggest that they were going to be any more successful than the old tradition of romantic violence had been in reviving the fortunes of republicanism.

CHAPTER FOUR

Civil Rights

In 1966 celebrations were held all over Ireland to commemorate the fiftieth anniversary of the Easter Rising. In the South the memory of the event no longer carried any political dangers. It was marked by marches, long newspaper articles, innumerable documentaries on Radio Telefis Eireann, (RTE, the Irish broadcasting corporation) and nostalgic speeches by politicians of all parties, regardless of where they had stood in the Civil War. A coin was struck bearing the head of Patrick Pearse, the author of the notion that blood sacrifice was needed to liberate Ireland.

In the North the tradition still had the power to alarm the authorities. The eighty officers of the RUC's Special Branch were placed on alert for any commemorative action by the IRA. None came. On the whole, the celebrations passed off in an atmosphere of tolerance. Raymond Shearer, a doctor in the Falls Road, which runs the length of Catholic West Belfast, remembers policemen holding ladders for Catholics as they hung out bunting on the lampposts. On Easter Sunday 10,000 people marched to Casement Park for a rally. To most of the younger people in the parade, and to the onlookers, it appeared a celebration of an important chapter of the past that was now closed. Among them was Danny Morrison, now education officer for Sinn Fein. 'As far as we were concerned there was absolutely no chance of the IRA appearing again. They were something in history books.'[1] The Belfast republicans had hoped that the event might lead to a recruiting

61

boom. They were disappointed. One of the few to join was Gerry Adams (now the Sinn Fein president) whose long family tradition of IRA membership would probably have led him into the movement anyway.

The relatively relaxed attitude Stormont showed towards the celebrations was another sign of a slight easing of the mistrust that the government had felt towards the Catholic minority of Northern Ireland since the foundation of the state in 1922. The previous year, the Prime Minister, Captain Terence O'Neill, an Old Etonian and former Guards officer who was descended from an old Anglo-Irish family, had taken the daring step of receiving the Irish Premier, Sean Lemass, at Stormont, in a gesture of reconciliation with the Republic. It was the first time that the heads of the two governments had met since the island was divided. O'Neill's brand of unionism consistently underestimated the depth of working-class and lower middle-class Protestant feeling against any alteration in relations between the North and the South, or any improvement in the status of Northern Catholics. The extent of the fears that 'liberal' unionism was capable of arousing, at least among some semi-criminal loyalists, was illustrated a few weeks after the Easter anniversary celebrations when a petrol bomb was thrown from a speeding car at a Catholic-owned pub in the Shankill Road, the backbone of Protestant West Belfast. It missed its target and crashed through the window of a 77-year-old Protestant widow, who later died of the burns she received in the fire. Responsibility for the attack was claimed by the Ulster Volunteer Force (UVF), a revival of the name used by the citizen army inspired by Edward Carson in 1912 to band together against the Liberal government's plans to introduce Home Rule for the whole of Ireland.

Their statement warned that 'from this day on we declare war on the IRA and its splinter groups. Known IRA men will be executed mercilessly and without hesitation.' This was the first appearance of Protestant 'murder gangs' in Belfast since the 1930s. Even during the border campaign, when sectarian antagonism might have been expected to run high, Catholics had not been harmed. A few days after the fire bombing a

UVF gang went looking in the Catholic streets that form the frontier between the Catholic and Protestant quarters of West Belfast for Leo Martin, a well-known local republican. Instead, they came across 28-year-old Patrick Scullion, who was making his way home singing republican songs after an evening in the pub. The UVF men shot him with revolvers and he later died of his wounds. On 26 June a UVF band fired on four young Catholics as they left a pub in Malvern Street off the Shankill Road, killing 18-year-old Peter Ward. Three men, including Augustus ('Gusty') Spence, were later imprisoned for the murders.

These crimes could not dispel the general feeling among Northern Irish Catholics in 1966 that life was beginning to change for the better. In the late 1950s a reasonably-sized Catholic middle class had started to form, the result, to a large extent, of the British 1948 Education Act which established a grants system and opened up higher education to working-class Catholic men and women. There was a sour old joke that the only way a Catholic could get into Queen's University in Belfast was by leaving his body for medical research. In the 1953-4 academic year there were 442 students in the faculty of applied science and technology, of whom fifty-one (11.5 per cent) were Catholic. By 1967-8 there were 1,056, 202 of them Catholic (19.63 per cent). The numbers were still far from equitable but they were an indication that the door to managerial jobs with the Protestant industrial firms was at least theoretically ajar. By the mid-sixties numbers in the arts and law faculties were sometimes even, a reflection of the teaching priorities of Catholic schools and of the tendency of Catholic graduates to seek careers as teachers, lawyers or doctors.[2] Catholic entrants to these professions were often the offspring of bookmakers and publicans. Presbyterian scruples over following these trades meant that they were almost entirely Catholic-dominated. Those who prospered were able to fund their children through the grantless extra years of study necessary to qualify.

There were also signs that blatant economic discrimination against Catholics was softening. On coming to power in 1963

O'Neill had commissioned a report which recommended that Northern Ireland should accept that its traditional industries, such as shipbuilding and textiles, were in terminal decline and concentrate on attracting outside companies to replace them. Lured by massive grants, international manufacturers like Michelin, DuPont, Enkalon and ICI moved to the Province. The newcomers did not discriminate when they hired and Catholics found themselves being treated as equals.

The changing townscapes of Derry and Belfast added to the general impression that things were improving. At the start of the 1960s West Belfast, Catholic and Protestant, still appeared a monstrous marxist model of the dynamic of capitalism, with the brutal simplicity of the wage-workers' relationship with capital enshrined in bricks and mortar. The narrow streets were dominated by the high red walls of the old linen mills, built along the streams that run off Divis Mountain to take advantage of the continuous water supply needed for textile manufacturing. Huddled in their flanks were row upon row of brick terraces with smoke gusting from the chimneys. They had been put up during the nineteenth century to house workers who gave up the drudgery and uncertainty of rural labour for the relatively secure existence offered by the mills and factories. They came in droves. In 1806 Belfast was as Wolfe Tone had known it, a busy but compact port of 22,000 people. By 1896 it was a monument to industrial imperialism with a population of 340,000.

The standard of living in Ulster was always poor compared with Great Britain and West Belfast was generally poor compared with Ulster. People did — and do — eat badly, and disease struck frequently and hard. In 1897 there was an outbreak of typhoid which infected 27,000 people. Respiratory illnesses were frequent, the result of inhaling fibres from the flax. Most workers died before they were 45 and children were usually underdeveloped and sickly. The millworkers' houses had a living-room and kitchen on the ground floor, two bedrooms upstairs and a lavatory in the backyard. Today, many of the ones that remain are scrupulously maintained, the doorsteps reddened and buffed and the tiny front rooms stuffed with furniture. Others are dirty and smell of unwashed bodies and stale frying fat – the smell of Northern European poverty. Some have been abandoned and the windows sealed with breeze blocks. Some are simply derelict. Peering into the wrecked interiors you see a shoe or an empty picture frame.

During the 1960s the Stormont government began to knock down the terraces and decant the inhabitants to new estates to the west and the south of the old mill areas. The programme was partly in response to a British government report in 1962 which criticised the sluggish rate of house-building in the Province, then running at 6,000 a year, and demanded that it be increased to at least 10,000. This figure, according to the report, was the minimum if Northern Ireland was to even maintain the status quo. In 1961 Northern Ireland, and particularly Derry and Belfast, had more than its fair share of slums. In the Province as a whole, one in five of the houses had no piped water supply and twenty-two per cent were without a flush lavatory.

The religious composition of the old quarters of Belfast was transferred to the new estates, the Catholics to Andersonstown at the south end of the Falls Road and Ballymurphy to the West, and the Protestants of the Shankill Road moving west up the hill to Woodvale. There were a few attempts at mixing the communities, notably at the Unity Flats at the foot of the Shankill Road. The most striking development was the Divis Flats, six multi-storey apartment blocks sited on the city centre side of West Belfast. Before long it was to become the most notorious.

Both Catholics and the Protestants of West Belfast were ambivalent towards the changes. A local committee was set up to complain about the construction of the Divis Flats, by people who were reluctant to give up the snug squalor of the terraces for an apartment without a backyard or a proper front door. The nostalgia for the slums is reflected in Gerry Adams' memoir of growing up in West Belfast, in which he reproduces a lament for the Falls by a priest at

St Peter's pro-cathedral, which dominates the area:

> The body of the parish lies stretched below the tower
> Its main arteries are weakened and dying by the hour
> There are clots of bricks and mortar in the little veins of
>   the streets
> And the talk is all of 'flitting' with everyone one meets[3]

The exodus continued throughout the following decade. In 1973 there were 25,000 people on the parish register of St Peter's. In 1985 there were 7,800.

Protestants and Catholics of West Belfast lived in the same grim houses, ate the same diet and earned the same wages. But they kept their ritual distance. There were points at which the communities brushed: Catholic women often did their shopping in the cheaper supermarkets in the Shankill Road. Traditionally, the dance halls advertised 'Catholic dances' or 'Protestant dances' but by the mid-sixties Maxim's club was offering 'mixed' entertainments. The police lived unremarked among both communities. Dr Shearer remembers Andersonstown police station in those days as resembling 'a small country house'.

> There was a small triangular plot at the front of it which was kept as a lawn. At the side of it was a small greenhouse and a couple of rows of peas and beans. The constables would have taken their shirts off and dug over it in the summer season. Although it was a private path through the station from the Falls Road to the Glen Road it was continuously open.[4]

The RUC was around ten per cent Catholic (a figure that has remained surprisingly steady) and they lived among their charges. They went to the local dances and sent their children to the neighbourhood schools. Their immersion in local life was to cause bitterness later. In the street where a local Catholic businessman lived, in Finaghy, south-west Belfast,

66

there would have been four or five policemen, and more in the estates opposite, not all of them Catholic. The Catholics sent their children to Irish dancing, to camogie [Gaelic hockey] and to football and they were accepted . . . When the troubles came in 1969 a lot of us realised they had done a good job infiltrating. They had made themselves the best friends of the people on the road. It was the police who could fix a parking fine or stop a row getting to court. It was the same policemen, though, who identified the people who were picked up . . . Things like that were manipulated by the IRA who would say: 'Look, the police you trusted are the people who are now fingering people for internment.' And the disillusionment came overnight and the police left overnight. They just up and went.[4]

It was remarkable that they had remained there unmolested for so long.

The problem with Terence O'Neill's liberalism was that it raised Catholic expectations but dodged real reforms. After a few years of O'Neill's government it was clear that his commitments to change would be confined to rhetorical appeals for reconciliation and well-publicised encounters with mother superiors. O'Neill admitted as much. After his resignation he wrote: 'As the party would never stand for change I was really reduced to trying to improve relations between North and South, and in the North itself between two sections of the community.' A climate of dissatisfaction was created. The result was the civil rights movement.

In 1964, encouraged by the success of the American civil rights movement, a Dungannon doctor, Conn McCluskey, and his wife Patricia founded the Campaign for Social Justice. Its members were middle-class, Catholic and politically cautious, and it aimed to publicise grievances and injustices by researching employment, housing and electoral malpractices, notably the blatant gerrymandering of boundaries in the Catholic areas. There was no lack of material to illustrate the State's institutionalised unfairness towards the minority. In the

1960s, as from the first day of its inception, the machinery of the Stormont government was still geared to hindering the Catholics and promoting the Protestants. Posts and appointments in the gift of the State, from the high court bench to the humblest labouring job in a municipal park, were allocated with ruthless partiality. In 1961, of the senior officials in the professional and technical grades of the Northern Ireland civil service, 209 were Protestant and thirteen Catholic.[5] Of Northern Ireland's eighty-four legal officers, seventy-six were Protestant. There were six Protestant high court judges and one Catholic; four Protestant county court judges and one Catholic; eight Crown solicitors and no Catholics; twenty-six clerks of petty sessions and no Catholics. It was the same story on the public boards: of the 332 appointees in 1969, 283 were Protestant. On the eight-man Housing Trust there was one Catholic. On the twenty-four strong General Health Services Board there were two. Among the twenty-one trustees of the Ulster Folk Museum, the minority tradition was represented by a single Catholic.

In the private sector, local Protestant firms overwhelmingly hired Protestant workers. In 1961 Robert Babington, a barrister who later became a Unionist Stormont MP, suggested that in response to the decline in the shipbuilding and textile industries 'registers of unemployed loyalists should be kept by the Unionist Party and employers invited to pick employees from them. The Unionist Party should make it quite clear that the loyalists have first choice of jobs.'[6] (This view, however, was repudiated by the Northern Ireland government the following day.)

On the face of it, Ulster under O'Neill was making an effort to drag itself into line with society on the mainland. During his leadership, two great symbols of the decade appeared, redolent of change: new motorways and a new university. But instead of connecting Belfast with the Province's second, and predominantly Catholic, city of Derry, as logic and fairness suggested, the roads were driven north to Protestant Ballymena, and south to Protestant Portadown. Derry was due to have been the site of Northern Ireland's second university but under pressure from Unionist politicians it was switched to the inconsequential, but Protestant, town of Coleraine. Derry Unionists supported this move because they feared that the siting of the university in their own city would swell the Catholic majority to the point where it would swamp the carefully gerrymandered political boundaries that gave Protestants a majority on the council, even though they were a minority of the population.

The Campaign for Social Justice was energetic in publicising these grievances and forging links with the Labour Government in London but it was reluctant to take an active political role in Northern Ireland. The impetus for a full-scale civil rights campaign came instead from the Wolfe Tone Society (founded after the bicentenary celebrations of Tone's birth) and from left-wing Northern trade unionists, together with a sprinkling of Ulster liberal professionals and *bien pensants*.

The branches of the Wolfe Tone Society were tiny. Belfast and Dublin were the largest, and Belfast never had more than a dozen members. Their aim was to foster republicanism by educating the Irish public, Catholic and Protestant, in the cultural and political heritage exemplified by Tone. However, there were considerable differences of view about how this was best done. The Belfast branch, which contained a local headmaster, Alec Foster, and a Queen's University professor, Michael Dolley, was pragmatic and inclined to be careful. They were watchful, lest it be dominated by the IRA or Sinn Fein and, according to one member, Fred Heatley, keen to keep it 'an autonomous adjunct of the republican movement'. In Dublin the society was more or less an IRA debating club with Roy Johnston, Tomas MacGiolla and Cathal Goulding the leading lights. For them, at first sight, the stirring of Catholic resentments in the North was not merely a chance to redress injustices but an unmissable opportunity to promote the IRA's political fortunes. On Friday 13 August 1966 at the suggestion of the Dublin branch, a weekend meeting of all the Wolfe Tone Societies was held at Rathlure House in Maghera, County Derry, the spacious home of Kevin Agnew, a solicitor and republican. It was to be a social as well as a political occasion and many of the members brought their wives. The proceedings opened at 10.00 pm after a good dinner, when Eoghan Harris, a writer from Cork, read a forty-minute-long dissertation on the future of republican socialism in the North. It advocated, among other tactics, the infiltration of Northern trade unions as a precondition of creating a revolutionary consciousness that would bind together the Catholic and Protestant working class of Ulster.

The paper drew loud applause from Cathal Goulding and most of the six Southerners present. This was unsurprising in the case of Roy Johnston, who was the author of the document. To him the ideas were of a few years' vintage but to the Belfast members they were new, and alarming. Only one of the eleven Northerners gave the strategy any backing. Billy McMillen (later the leader of the Official IRA in Belfast) remarked pointedly that whereas trade unionism and republicanism were a potentially successful mix in the South, they represented a more improbably political cocktail in the Six Counties. Professor Dolley of Queen's found the dissertation 'embarrassing'. Ciaran Mac and Aili, a Dublin lawyer, president of the Irish Pacifist Association and a member of the International Federation of Jurists, said he detected in it many of the ideas of the IRA's 'communist' period in the thirties. The meeting broke up at midnight with a promise that the discussion would continue the next day. Instead, at the prompting of Mac an Aili, the conversation on the afternoon of 14 August turned to the prospect of launching a full-blooded civil liberties caompaign. Once again the Southerners seemed to be out of touch with the realities of the North, advocating a 'boycott of Stormont'. Kevin Murphy, a workman at a small experiment in co-operative farming in Swatragh, County Derry, pointed out that this bold venture in socialist economics would never have got off the ground without a grant administered through the Northern Ireland goverment.

Mac an Aili suggested that the campaign should adopt as its immediate aims the lowering of the voting age to eighteen and the abolition of the arrangement which allowed only

70

householders and tenants the vote in local elections, a restriction that favoured the Protestants. The meeting voted to start a civil rights crusade. It was left open whether the campaign should be based in Belfast or Dublin and whether it should band together with other groups. The National Democratic Party, formed the previous year to try to reform the old Nationalist Party, which was looking increasingly traditionalist and priest-ridden, had also been talking about a civil rights campaign. In the end, the idea of an alliance with it was rejected on the grounds that it was 'too Catholic'.[7] The last act of the gathering was to decide that in future they would operate as a civil rights group and that the banner of the Wolfe Tone Society would be dropped.

Despite their coolness towards a coalition with the National Democrats Mac an Aili, Heatley and the moderate theoretical republicans at the meeting were anxious to draw as many progressive elements to the campaign as possible. In October Heatley organised a meeting in the Queen's Hall of the War Memorial Building in Belfast. He invited a non-republican Protestant academic, John D. Stewart, to chair it. By the time the Northern Ireland Civil Rights Association (NICRA) steering committee was elected in February 1967, the republicans were, on paper at least, outnumbered by representatives of other ideologies. Of the fourteen members, only four had straightforward republican affiliations and the rest were a motley collection that included trade unionists, communists and even the former chairman of Queen's University Young Unionists.

In Dublin, Goulding, Johnston and MacGiolla were simultaneously irritated and gratified by the development. On the one hand, they had been edged to the margins of a movement whose birth they had attended, shoved there by fellow republicans. On the other, NICRA, with its alliance of Catholics and predominantly Protestant trade unionists, appeared to have the potential to bring about the cross-sectarian fusion of the Northern Ireland working class that Johnston's theories defined as the first stage in the revolutionary transformation of the whole island. The potential of the movement

71

filled them with excitement. In the early sixties it had seemed to MacGiolla that it would be decades before the republican movement would be able to make any significant political progress in Ireland. Yet here, within a few years of the movement's darkest hours, was a vehicle that could transform Irish society. It was vital to get on board.

Throughout the life of the civil rights movement Unionist politicians claimed that it was a front for the resurgence of the IRA. Many still believe that. Despite the involvement of many IRA members and republicans, including many of the people who went on to found the Provisional IRA, the charge is untrue. When the IRA did attempt to turn the movement to their advantage the manoeuvre was easily spotted and defeated. In the summer of 1968, before the first civil rights march in Dungannon, Roy Johnston, by now director of information on the Army Council, tried to have an IRA message of support read from the platform. Fred Heatley, according to his own account, 'tore it up in front of his eyes'.[8] Even for the theoretical republicans of the Wolfe Tone Society like Heatley, the success of the civil rights campaign, with its potential of short-term gains for Northern Catholics, was infinitely more important than the distant ambitions of the IRA, and a hawk-eyed watch was kept for attempts at subversion. On the other hand, the civil rights organisers were quite happy to use IRA muscle when it suited them. IRA men acted as stewards at every civil rights march of any size during the late sixties and early seventies. All along, the IRA contingent was swamped by groups who were either ignorant, indifferent or hostile to them: trade unionists who had no time for republicanism; students inspired by the Paris *événements* who regarded the trench-coat and revolver image that still clung to the IRA — despite Dublin's best efforts — as hopelessly unfashionable; and ordinary men and women who gave the movement no thought at all.

The IRA leadership was keenly aware of this and behaved with caution, even timidity. There were only four republicans on the NICRA steering committee, but if they banded together with their three communist allies in the association they could command a majority. The Special Branch of the RUC calculated that at the first annual meeting of NICRA in February 1968 thirty of the eighty people attending were 'actively engaged in IRA activities',[9] yet only two more republicans were elected to the executive committee. Rather then launching into a programme of full-scale agitation, NICRA started off hesitantly. According to Heatley, 'the most annoying aspect of the early period was the lack of real interest shown by our first council members — at times we couldn't muster up the required six members for a quorum at the monthly meetings'. Activity was on the whole confined to issuing condemnations of police harassment of tinkers and republicans. Later the republicans' restraint was to be acknowledged by the moderates. Attacking the extremist tendencies of the student People's Democracy element in NICRA in 1969, Dr McCluskey was moved to 'point out how correctly republicans have adhered to the spirit of our movement, never at any time trying to promote their own political views'.[10]

In Dublin, the IRA leadership's euphoria at its good fortune produced a corresponding reluctance to rock the boat, at least for the time being. According to MacGiolla a decision was taken early on that the IRA element would restrict their energies to pushing for the basic demands of the association — electoral reform, an end to discrimination in jobs and housing and the abolition of repressive anti-subversion legislation — and no more: 'It wasn't to be a republican committee, it wasn't to be a socialist committee, it was to be a civil rights committee.'[11]

This attitude was not as innocent as it seemed. The IRA had a compelling tactical reason for sticking to the civil rights issue. If they were to extend their Southern 'anti-imperialist' housing, fishing rights and land ownership campaigns northwards it would be a great help to operate openly. In the Republic they were able to organise through their political wing, Sinn Fein. In the North, however, there was no such cover organisation. The Government had banned Sinn Fein in 1964 along with its newspaper, the *United Irishman*. The movement had briefly circumvented the ban by setting up Republican Clubs instead, but they were outlawed in 1967. The inaugural act of the Civil Rights Association was to denounce the ban and call for the repeal of the Special Powers Act, the legislation under which it had been imposed. A second great advantage of the Civil Rights Association was that it provided a perfect framework in the North for the sort of left-wing link-up that the IRA had been trying to forge in the Republic. The three-man sub-committee (which included Billy McMillen, a leading Belfast IRA man) charged with drawing up the NICRA constitution proposed that the fundamental rule of the association was to 'place no bar on membership because of particular political affiliations'. The result was that from the outset NICRA was well populated with the communists and trade unionists that Goulding, Johnston and MacGiolla were so eager to befriend.

These considerations were to play a large part in the leadership's responses to the great drama that was about to begin in the North. The leaders were all of a theoretical cast of mind and the civil rights campaign seemed to confirm that their political analysis of the future was basically correct. Johnston envisaged civil rights educating Catholic and Protestant workers towards a new revolutionary consciousness. As events started to go awry, the leadership appeared to be hypnotised by the symmetry of their strategy and incapable of making the deviations that changing pragmatic considerations demanded. By the summer of 1968 it was apparent that the Civil Rights Association was losing its importance. The initiative was passing to the civil rights movement, of which NICRA was only a part. The new element was the Catholic Nationalist Party, politically more conservative than NICRA but tactically more radical. At their party conference in June they discussed the adoption of a civil disobedience policy, suggested by Austin Currie, a young MP in the Northern Ireland parliament. Shortly afterwards Currie, aided by members of the local Brantry Republican Club, drew the attention of a huge media audience to housing injustices by occupying a council house in Caledon, County Tyrone, which had been allocated to a 19-year-old single girl — a Protestant.

By the time the first civil rights march took place on 24

August 1968, NICRA played no part in the organisation and simply acted as the sponsoring body for the event. The planning was done by Austin Currie. About 2,000 people turned up for the short walk from Coalisland to Dungannon, including the bulk of the IRA's Northern units; the IRA provided the seventy stewards, who responsibly steered the marchers away from a confrontation with a gang of counter-demonstrators who had gathered to jeer. As an exercise in attracting publicity the march was a success. A group of republicans and left-wingers who had been conducting a vigorous campaign against housing abuses in Derry decided to invite the Civil Rights Association to stage its next march there. NICRA agreed to sponsor the march, which was set for 5 October. As the association had no representation in the city it was decided to place the organisation in the hands of members of Derry's James Connolly Republican Club (named after the revolutionary socialist leader executed after the 1916 uprising) and the local Labour Party. In fact, the planning committee never functioned and the preparations fell into the hands of two prominent local activists, Eamonn McCann, a trotskyist member of the Labour Party, and Eamonn Melaugh, an independent radical. Both had already demonstrated a taste for the confrontational street politics of the time, organising marches, occupations and sit-ins and disrupting the proceedings of the city corporation throughout the summer. McCann made little secret of the aim of all this. It was to 'provoke the police into over reaction and thus spark off mass reaction against the authorities'.[12] As the day of the march approached the atmosphere grew ominous. To the delight of McCann, the Government responded to a series of goading press statements by banning the demonstration, thereby increasing the chances of encouraging 'thousands of outraged citizens who would not otherwise have marched to come and demonstrate their disgust'. According to Billy McMillen, the RUC Special Branch received a tip that the IRA intended to use the march to provoke riots and when 4 October dawned they were deployed in strength and anticipating trouble.

* * *

Despite hopes of a massive show of strength, only 400 turned up, including a busload of republicans from Belfast and a contingent from the far left Young Socialist Alliance. They gathered on the Protestant bank of the River Foyle, the Waterside, and set off across the bridge towards the city centre. The police were waiting for them, stretched in a phalanx across the span. After some pushing and shoving the Young Socialists began hurling their placards at the RUC lines and the police responded by charging the demonstrators, batons flailing. A second police cordon moved up behind the marchers, sandwiching them on the bridge as two water cannon opened up. The panic-stricken marchers fled across the bridge and into the city centre. Some made for the Catholic Bogside quarter on the west bank, pursued by the police. Others took shelter in shops and hotels. According to Eamonn McCann, 'in the evening the lounge of the City Hotel looked like a casualty clearing station, all bandaged heads and arms in slings . . . Later there was sporadic fighting at the edges of the Bogside which lasted until early morning. Police cars were stoned, shop windows smashed and a flimsy, token barricade erected in Rossville Street. A few petrol bombs were thrown . . .'[13]

The Derry organisers had set out to provoke the police but they had underestimated what McCann called the 'animal brutality' of the RUC. None the less, the event had the desired effect. At the next civil rights march in Derry on 15 November nearly 15,000 turned out. At Armagh on 30 November there were between 5,000 and 8,000. Branches of the Civil Rights Association sprang up in Newry, Strabane, Dungannon and Omagh. The transformation of the campaign into a mass movement had resulted in a dilution of republican influence as conventional Catholic politicians began to dominate the new committees. In Newry, for example, the eighteen-strong citizens action committee formed on 9 November contained only one declared republican. Still republicans continued to watch events with excited anticipation. As Seamus Rodgers of Donegal Sinn Fein told a discussion on civil rights held in Strabane in December, 'the civil rights movement had done more in a few weeks to damage the unionist structure than decades of IRA activity'.[14]

For the first time in their long, obdurate history, unionists were now prepared to introduce serious reforms. On 22 November Prime Minister O'Neill announced that the Londonderry Corporation, the living symbol of politcal contortionism in the Province, was to be abolished and replaced by a nominated commission. An ombudsman was appointed to arbitrate grievances. Henceforth housing would be allocated on an equitable points system. The Government would consider suspending parts of the Special Powers Act. The Derry march had been televised and the images of respectable, middle-aged Catholic politicians having their heads broken by RUC truncheons had dragged the Northern Ireland question to the top of the political agenda for the first time in nearly fifty years. The Labour Government warned O'Neill that Stormont's continued existence depended on reform. On 9 December O'Neill made a television appeal to the civil rights activists: 'Your voice has been heard, and clearly heard. Your duty now is to take the heat out of the situation.'

When O'Neill's hard-line home affairs minister William Craig denounced the speech the following day he was sacked. The Unionist Party at Stormont backed the move by twenty-eight to one with four abstentions. Newspaper polls and bumper stickers, trade union leaders and prominent academics all announced support for O'Neill's approach. McCann observed that 'a casual visitor to Northern Ireland might have wondered who it was, apart from William Craig and Ian Paisley, who had ever been against reform'. But Craig and Paisley represented the views of a far greater proportion of the Protestant population than the media — or the republicans — were prepared to concede. As usual the Dublin leadership put a rosy complexion on the new turn of events. Civil rights had opened a split in the unionist monolith and that was all to the good. The position of the movement, as stated in an official publication of 1969, was that 'by winning civil rights and thereby weakening the Unionist Party, the nationally minded people would be

77

in a much better position to push forward to ending partition and winning independence'.[15] At the same time it was hoped that the impending crisis in the Unionist Party would bring the Protestant working class to its senses. One spectacularly optimistic article in the *United Irishman* exhorted republicans to retrieve the initiative in the civil rights movement and 'seek to prove by the quality of public service and leadership they gave therein that they were the best champions of the needs of the ordinary people. In this way, Republicans would win the friendship and respect of members of the Protestant and Unionist community who were not utterly blinded by bigotry and hatred'.[16]

The extent of the ill-feeling towards the civil rights movement was to be fully demonstrated during the course of a march organised by the Queen's University-based People's Democracy on New Year's Day 1969. The trek, from Belfast to Derry, was in violation of a feeling held by most of the civil rights movement (including the Dublin leadership of the IRA who later denounced it as 'an exercise in ultra-leftism') that O'Neill should be allowed a breathing space to fight off the opponents of change inside his own party. From the outset the straggling column was harassed and hindered by the Paisleyites, led by a former British Army major, Ronald Bunting. On the second day, at Randalstown, the path was barred by loyalists carrying cudgels and sticks. The police made no attempt to shift them and rerouted the march instead. The marchers had intended to stay that night at Maghera but, on police advice that another Protestant mob lay waiting for them there, they stopped for the night at a hall at Brackaghreilly near the small village of Gulladuff. The loyalists consoled themselves by rampaging through Maghera attacking Catholic shops and homes. The following day the police again informed them that Maghera was unsafe. The marchers trudged over the Sperrin Mountains to the Catholic town of Dungiven, where they were warmly received. On leaving, the police warned them that there were hostile crowds waiting in two villages ahead, Feeny and Claudy. 'The marchers had had enough,' wrote Michael Farrell, one of the organisers. 'They broke through the police

78

cordon and went straight through the villages. There was no hostile crowd. There was one at the diversion suggested by the RUC.'[17]

The march stopped that night at Claudy. The following day at Burntollet Bridge, a few miles outside the village, a loyalist mob who had been lying in ambush showered the marchers with bricks, stones and bottles from the banks on either side of the road, then swooped down on them with iron bars and cudgels. No attempt was made to arrest the ambush party. Later it transpired that nearly 100 of them were off-duty members of the part-time 'B' Specials, the anti-republican auxiliary force of the RUC. When the 200-300 marchers struggled into Derry later that day groups of Protestants stoned them from street corners. That night the Derry police, many of them drunk, entered the Bogside and beat anyone they encountered, breaking doors and windows and shouting sectarian slogans.

By the organisers' own admission, the march had been designed to provoke. Michael Farrell's calculation had been that 'either the government would face up to the extreme right of its own unionist party and protect the march . . . or it would be exposed as impotent in the face of sectarian thuggery, and Westminster would be forced to intervene, reopening the whole Irish question for the first time in 50 years'.[18] O'Neill responded to the attacks by condemning the marchers' irresponsibility and offering only the mildest rebuke to their assailants. His speech ended with the words: 'We have heard sufficient for now about civil rights, let us hear a little about civil responsibility.' It was the wrong note to strike. The systematic violence that had been done to the People's Democracy and the cynical role of the police hardened the attitudes of many of the large section of ordinary civil rights supporters who had been opposed to the march going ahead.

From now on almost every demonstration ended in violence, some of it engineered by the student revolutionaries of the People's Democracy. On 11 January civil rights supporters arrived in the border town of Newry to be told by the police that they would not be allowed to march through the town centre. According to one of the marchers:

> While the organisers were telling the marchers to wait and show restraint, [one of the People's Democracy officials] was speaking to the crowd, telling them that people were well capable of making their own decisions — why leave it to the leaders? For example, they could take a decision to attack some of the 'British fortresses' in the town, like the Post Office. 'All those in favour?' All the young fellows put up their hands. Carried unanimously! 'That's what I mean by power,' he said. And the next thing you saw was a hundred youths storming the Post Office and smashing every pane of glass.[19]

It was not just the young who were in a combustible mood. 'I saw a middle-aged man, Dr Haughey, beating a police tender with his umbrella and shouting, "Fifty years of Unionist misrule!" ' said Margot Collins, a Newry civil rights activist. 'I shared a house with that man. I had no idea that there was such discontent beneath the surface.'[20]

The People's Democracy march and its aftermath formed a political watershed. Enough Catholics lost confidence in the State to make the prospect of peaceful reform impossible. As the Province began to descend into violence the cautious revolutionary strategy sketched out by the IRA theorists began to look increasingly inappropriate. By the start of 1969 the dynamic of the civil rights movement was slipping out of the control of conventional Nationalist politicians and into the hands of the young working-class Catholic demonstrators, the radicals of Derry and the People's Democracy. None had any allegiance to the IRA, and little interest in its political programme. What they did have a use for was the very military tradition that the new leadership of Goulding and MacGiolla had tried so hard to shed. In the early hours of 2 January, on the second day of the People's Democracy march, a Catholic politician whose daughter was among the marchers telephoned the republican solicitor Kevin Agnew at his home in Maghera. The marchers were due to stop there the following night and the politician asked what provision could be made for their safety. Later that day Agnew toured the South Derry countryside calling at the homes of old IRA men. A cache of revolvers hidden since the end of the border campaign was exhumed, stripped and cleaned; shotguns were commandeered. That night the IRA men kept a discreet armed watch over the marchers. When the attack came in Burntollet the next day, the middle-aged escorts could do little to prevent it. But their presence had a symbolic importance. The IRA was once again acting in the role which it had traditionally played in the sectarian history of the North — that of defenders of Catholics against Protestant violence.

CHAPTER FIVE

The Return of the Troubles

Far from improving its fortunes, the IRA's involvement in the civil rights campaign had the effect of aggravating the tensions inside the movement and hastening it along the path towards confrontation. In unionist demonology the IRA was a seamless organisation – devious, single-minded and tireless in its work of overthrowing the State and dragging the Protestants into the superstitious theocracy of the South. This was a necessary invention if the North's massive anti-republican security apparatus was to be justified.

In fact, Brendan Behan's joke – that whenever the IRA met, the first item on the agenda was the split – was much closer to the truth. The IRA was a hybrid, an unlikely cross-fertilisation of revolutionary socialism and romantic nationalism, and these traditions had rubbed along uncomfortably ever since. It had a diverse membership. In 1969 it contained both atheist revolutionaries and God-fearing conservatives. Unlike later on, IRA men came from a variety of backgrounds. Tomas MacGiolla was an accountant with the Electricity Board. Sean MacStiofain was a storeman before he became a full-time republican official. There were small farmers and factory hands, shopkeepers and schoolteachers. As 1969 opened, the movement's old antagonisms were sharpened by the realisation among even the most blinkered members that Northern Ireland was approaching a historic crossroads.

The leadership came under attack from left, right and centre. In late 1968 as Tomas MacGiolla was waiting at Manchester airport for a flight back to Dublin after attending a ceremony to mark the centenary of the execution of three Fenian 'martyrs' for the killing of a policeman, he was approached by Joe Cahill, an old Belfast IRA man. Cahill told him 'very forcibly what my thoughts were – that the IRA was being run down, and that civil rights were taking over and that in the end the movement would be content with civil rights'.[1] Cahill was like many Belfast men who had dropped out of the IRA at the close of the border campaign and who now confined their republicanism to sentimental get-togethers under the auspices of organisations like the National Graves Association, which tended the resting places of dead IRA heroes, and the Republican Welfare Association, which helped the dependents of those who had suffered for the cause.

They were exemplified by Jimmy Steele, a daring if ineffectual operator in the 1940s who had taken part in two celebrated jail-breaks. He had voiced the traditionalist discontent at a republican gathering at Mullingar in the summer of 1968. Despite frantic attempts by Cathal Goulding to keep him off the platform, Steele had launched into a vivid denunciation of the movement's politically accented approach, claiming that the leadership was more or less accepting the existence of the six-county state. Steele's opinion was shared outside Belfast, especially by the older IRA members in the remote parts of the country – Tipperary, the West, Leitrim and the border counties – who found Johnston's theorising either mystifying or a treasonable departure from republican doctrine.

The traditionalists had friends inside the Army Council, notably Ruairi O'Bradaigh, Sean MacStiofain (who was appointed director of intelligence in 1966) and Daithi O'Connaill. O'Bradaigh was 37, small and bespectacled, with prominent teeth. A devout Catholic, he wore the badge of the Pioneers, the church abstinence society, in his lapel. His quiet and courteous manner overlaid a strong will and an unshakable belief in the correctness of his own views as to what constituted republicanism. O'Connaill was tall and lean, with a restless, driven manner. He looked hard, with a thin, scimitar-shaped mouth and smoked incessantly. Despite his military appearance, he was generally thought to be O'Bradaigh's intellectual superior.

Goulding's most formidable enemy among the traditionalists, though, was MacStiofain. Their personalities and backgrounds could not have been more opposite. Goulding was light-hearted and gregarious; he made friends easily. In 1969 he was often to be found in the fashionable bars around St Stephen's Green drinking with writers, musicians and painters, and became a recognised feature of Dublin bohemia. His revolutionary style at that time was closer to Berkeley campus and the Rive Gauche than the bogs and backstreets where the IRA tradition was rooted. He appeared reflective, well read and impressed by intellectuals — too much so according to the traditionalists. It was a testimony to his personal popularity that critics of his leadership invariably portrayed him as a good but easily influenced man fallen among marxist highbrows.

Goulding benefited from impeccable republican antecedents, important in a movement where a good bloodline is appreciated. His grandfather had been a member of the Invincibles, the clandestine revolutionary group who hacked to death Lord Frederick Cavendish, the British chief secretary for Ireland, in Phoenix Park in 1882. His father fought the Black and Tans and in the civil war — on the right side.

MacStiofain was born John Stephenson in Leytonstone, north-east London in 1928 and never managed to eradicate his slight cockney accent. His mother was strict and by his own account, 'old fashioned in her outlook and ideas'.[2] She was from Belfast and proud of it. His father, a solicitor's clerk with a fondness for drink, whom he appears to have disliked, also had Irish connections but was indifferent to them. His mother died when he was 10, by which time the formative experience of his life had taken place.

When I was very young, not more than seven, my mother said to me, 'I'm Irish, therefore you're Irish. You're half Irish anyway. Don't forget it.' I never did. This is the incident to which I attribute the fact that in spite of having been born and brought up in England I never considered myself anything but Irish.[3]

Successive experiences in his early life turned him against the British. Evacuated to an aristocratic household in Bedfordshire during the Second World War, he had his 'first clear insight into the English class system. When we asked if we could hear the news on the radio, they made us stand outside the window to listen to it.'

After leaving school at 16 and starting work in the building trade he was 'staggered by the vehement prejudices of labourers, bricklayers, plumbers' against the Irish. He spent his spare hours mixing with Irish exiles in the dance-halls of north London and reading Irish history. In 1945 he was conscripted into the Royal Air Force and served as a storeman. A tour of duty in Jamaica exposed him to the 'racism and poverty' of the British colonial system. He also discovered rum and 'for a while got very fond of it. But I didn't want to develop into a hard drinker, so I went easy on it the rest of the time I was in Jamaica and when I returned to England I cut out drinking altogether.'

Back in London he began learning Irish, married an Irish girl and immersed himself in expatriate Irish political groups, where he swiftly became disillusioned with the 'desperate hypocrisy and make-believe of the Free State politicians'. One hot August night, restless and frustrated, he crept up to Pentonville jail and painted the words 'Roger Casement Died for Ireland' on the walls in memory of the patriot who still lay buried behind them. He had yet to visit Erin.

At last he met some republicans who introduced him to the movement's English membership organisation, the United Irishmen. MacStiofain joined expecting it to be a front for the IRA. He was disappointed. Its leaders had no wish to start trouble in London. Together with some like-minded young men he sent word to the IRA in Dublin. After a visit from a Headquarters representative they eventually received confirmation — on official IRA notepaper — that they could

85

consider themselves a unit, with MacStiofain as the officer commanding. MacStiofain's English IRA activities began and ended with the Felsted School raid. He and Goulding got five years each, and served part of their sentence together in Wormwood Scrubs. Like many IRA men before and after him, jail brought about a political conversion. It turned Goulding away from raw militarism and toward conventional left-wing agitation. But the experience seems to have confirmed MacStiofain's belief in the value and inevitability of force, without advancing his frequently professed but ill-defined socialism. He was particularly impressed in prison by the Greek-Cypriot EOKA guerrillas who were locked up with him and attempts were later made by the IRA to forge links with them.

The respect that Goulding and MacStiofain had for each other in prison did not survive long after their release. MacStiofain's noisy defence of the old republican traditions against the assaults of 'communist' infiltrators like Johnston inspired Goulding's observation that he was 'continually trying to prove that he is as much an Irishman as anyone else', and that he was a 'petty-minded conspirator'.[4] Matters were not helped by MacStiofain's dour and angular personality. 'Not the sort of fellow I'd look for after a political meeting to have a drink with,' was Goulding's view.

The traditionalists at the top of the organisation could do little to protect the dissidents when the leadership reacted with customary sharpness to challenges to the official line. After the Mullingar incident, Steele was expelled from the movement. The traditionalists' grievances against the leadership focused on abstentionism and on Goulding and his supporters' growing hesitancy and ambivalence towards the use of violence. A year after the proposal to end the abstentionist policy had been comprehensively voted down at the army convention, it surfaced again at the 1965 Sinn Fein ard fheis and was again soundly defeated. Under the party's rules, no policy could be overturned without the approval of two-thirds of the delegates. The leadership was not deterred.

In June 1968, at the annual Bodenstown Wolfe Tone

memorial celebration the national organiser of Sinn Fein, Sean Garland, another border campaign veteran, warned the crowd:

> Let no mealy-mouthed sentimentalist tell us that we must preserve the movement as traditionally constituted if this proves impractical and hand on these impracticalities to the next generation . . . By saddling the next generation with useless tools and tactics we are not helping them, but destroying their chances of success by binding them to a line of thought and action that was a failure with one generation and must just as surely be a failure with the rest.

The scene seemed set for another blood-letting debate at the ard fheis that autumn but a confrontation was averted when Garland proposed a compromise motion calling for a commission to examine electoral policy. The calm could not last long. The 'politicals', in the IRA, as MacStiofain disdainfully called them, and those republicans who had been most active in the civil rights movement in the North and the housing and fishing agitation in the South had arrived at the conclusion that agitation in a vacuum was pointless; that abstentionism was a tactic not a principle; and that if the movement was going to progress, abstentionism would have to be removed.

The matter came to a head in N. Ireland. In January 1969 six prominent republicans in Tyrone resigned from the movement citing their 'disillusionment with the leadership', which stemmed, they said 'from [its] inability to face up to the present situation in the six counties and from the complete disregard for the advice of the Northern leadership when decisions concerning that area are being taken. We believe that the abstentionist policy bears no relevance to conditions in 1969.'[5] These were precisely the feelings of Goulding and his friends, but without the backing of the Sinn Fein ard fheis, the supreme policy-making body, they could not alter course without risking a split.

When, early in 1969, George Forrest, the Unionist MP representing Mid-Ulster at Westminster, died, the issue could be avoided no longer. The constituency had an anti-Unionist majority, a fact proved in 1955 when an IRA prisoner, Tom Mitchell, had won the seat. In the highly charged atmosphere of the time — with the civil rights campaign in full swing and the Province in political ferment — abstentionism seemed to most Catholics in Northern Ireland to be a self-defeating principle.

> In the past, [observed Bernadette Devlin, at the time a young crusader with the People's Democracy and a native of Mid-Ulster] voters hadn't minded if you went to Westminster or not, so long as you kept the Unionists out. But by now the civil rights movement was having its effect and people saw this by-election as an opportunity to project Northern Ireland into British politics and keep it there, even after the election was over.[6]

However, republicans and Nationalists found it impossible to agree on a candidate. At first Tom Mitchell had been approached to represent Sinn Fein but had refused to stand on an abstentionist ticket, so Kevin Agnew, the Maghera solicitor, had been chosen instead. In response, the Nationalists decided to field their own candidate, Austin Currie, the hero of the Caledon sit-in. To avert the prospect of the prize slipping away as a result of a split Catholic vote, the well-meaning McCluskeys, founders of the Campaign for Social Justice, were drafted in to smooth a compromise by presiding over a panel entrusted with the task of deciding which candidate should stand.

At meetings to choose the contender, republican and Nationalist supporters howled each other down. The leadership was in a panic of indecision. They had never wanted to fight the election in the first place, fearing the loss of face that a defeat would bring, and were also acutely aware of the opprobrium they would attract from the Catholic community if they persisted in fielding their own candidate, an abstentionist to boot. Eventually, they decided to back off. Official backing was withdrawn from Agnew and MacGiolla, and Mitchell persuaded local republicans that they should back an independent compromise choice, Bernadette Devlin, who was duly elected.

This half-hearted intervention aroused the resentment of republican traditionalists in the North, both in the rural areas and in Belfast, who felt that Goulding and his cronies had engineered the election of Devlin as a device to circumvent abstentionism. The Belfast IRA had proved resistant to the new strain of republicanism, opposing the ending of abstentionism at the 1966 ard fheis, and according to their leader, Billy McMillen, were 'still very reluctant to discard the physical force role . . . and to adopt the unfamiliar role of political activists'.[7]

The North, as Dublin HQ was about to discover, was different. Considering that it was the first city in the territory that republicanism was sworn to liberate, the Belfast IRA had played remarkably little part in the activities of the movement. During the thirties and forties IRA units (which included a company of Protestants from the Shankhill Road) had mounted a number of arms raids and killed five policemen. The resulting police operation practically destroyed the movement in the North. Belfast had been excluded from the border campaign. According to the veterans of the period who stayed in the 'official' camp after the movement divided, this was a deliberate policy to avert the prospect of a sectarian bloodbath. By the account of Joe Cahill, there was thought to be a traitor in the organisation: several operations in 1953 designed to show republican displeasure at the coronation of Queen Elizabeth, including an attempt to blow up a radio mast on top of Divis Mountain, were mysteriously intercepted by the police. Any plans to involve Belfast became academic when the IRA organiser there, Paddy Doyle, was arrested.

Where the IRA had proved itself to be active and effective in Belfast was as a minor bulwark against sectarian violence in a city where Protestants outnumbered Catholics by two to one. In the early 1920s they mounted patrols in the Catholic areas to guard them against the 'murder gang', a collection of ex-servicemen, police and 'B' Specials responsible for a number of random killings; in 1935 they formed vigilante groups during sectarian rioting that resulted in eleven deaths and 574 injuries. The Belfast IRA tended to be enclosed and backward-looking. Historically it had been poorly represented on the Army Council and successive leaderships in Dublin had been negligent about maintaining contact. The membership, in turn, tended to feel all the usual resentment of the front-line soldier towards the cosily billeted headquarters staff. Life for a Belfast IRA man had always been fraught with more danger than for his Southern counterpart. The attitude of the State was implacably and tirelessly hostile and the RUC, armed with draconian anti-republican legislation, waged a continuous war against the movement. The contrast with the South was considerable: there was still a large reservoir of sentimental guilt towards the IRA. During its quiescent periods its members were treated with surprising indulgence. Even during the border campaign, the authorities were sometimes reluctant to apply the full weight of the law. Early in the hostilities, an Army and police patrol ran into an IRA unit sheltering in a farmhouse on the Republic's side of the border. All were released without being charged, even though they had a land-mine and a number of incriminating documents with them.

In 1969 there were fewer than sixty men in Belfast who would regard themselves as members of the IRA. At least half of these were lapsed: drop-outs after the border campaign for whom republicanism was now mainly a social event, with the steady round of commemorations of the births and deaths of long-gone heroes on the IRA calendar providing the opportunity for drink and reminiscence. The low state of the movement's fortunes was illustrated by the fact that the Belfast contingent at the 1966 Wolfe Tone commemoration at Bodenstown was able to travel there by minibus. Billy McMillen and his pro-Dublin deputy, Jim Sullivan, attempted to involve the remaining members in protests in West Belfast in 1966 against the building of the Divis Flats. One of the few who showed any enthusiasm was the 16-year-old Gerry Adams.

By 1969 all military activity had ceased. No drilling or arms training had taken place for years, and little attempt was made by the traditionalists to get into a more military posture as the year progressed and the likelihood of widespread violence increased. One reason for this inactivity was that Belfast was curiously distanced from the drama of the year. Civil rights had had little effect on the city. There had been no marches and only a few, unspectacular, demonstrations by the People's Democracy and its supporters. It was not until April 1969 that a Civil Rights Association branch was organised in the city.

The centre of events was Derry. The city lies along the banks of the River Foyle at the point where it widens into a broad and beautiful sea loch. Viewed from the east bank its seventeenth-century stone ramparts and the mountains beyond give it the appearance of an illustration in a book of fairy-tales. The effect is heightened by the weather. Even in summer, rain, wind and cloud scud around its steeples and walls. There are frequent rainbows. This uplifting sight is only slightly marred by the city cemetery which dominates the west bank. Even from the opposite side of the river you can make out the celtic crosses standing among the headstones, and the green, white and orange tricolours flying over the graves of IRA men and women. Behind the cemetery, smoke rises in ranks from the chimneys of the Creggan Estate, a modern development of brick boxes separated by large open stretches of grass which, whatever the planners' intentions, have a depressing effect on the spirits. The atmosphere could not be more different from the muggy intimacy of the terraces they were built to replace. Some terraces still remain, below the Creggan in the Bogside, the marshy part of town underneath the city walls which was historically the main Catholic quarter. It was in these narrow streets that the pitched battles between the Catholics, the Protestants, the police and the Army were later fought.

By the early months of 1969 a mood of latent anarchy had set in in the Catholic areas of Derry. Unemployed youths had taken to stoning casually any police car that came their way. Within a few weeks of the February general election, there were regular small-scale riots on the streets where the Bogside touches the city centre.

91

On Saturday 19 April about 200 civil rights supporters organised a protest sit-in in the centre of the city. They were attacked by a group of Paisleyites, reinforced by the police who baton-charged the demonstrators and drove them into the Bogside, where they regrouped and fought back with stones. Water-cannon were brought out, but they had little effect on the Catholic youths who began erecting barricades and hurling petrol-bombs. As the police advanced behind armoured vehicles to clear the streets, they were pelted with stones from the high flats in Rossville Street, a tactic that would be used repeatedly in the coming months. At one stage a police sergeant had to fire his revolver in the air to frighten off a group of rioters who were advancing on his men. It was the bloodiest day Derry had so far seen. The Altnagelvin hospital treated 165 people for injuries, eighty-six policemen and seventy-nine civilians. Among the day's casualties was Samuel Devenney, a 42-year-old Catholic from the Bogside who, while his wife and children stood by, was kicked and batoned by a group of policemen who broke into his house. He died of his injuries three months later, the first martyr of the troubles.

For the first time, the riots produced an echo in Belfast. The following day, at the end of a civil rights rally, a crowd gathered outside the RUC station in Hastings Street in West Belfast and smashed the windows with stones in retaliation for the events in Derry. Late in the evening nine post offices and two buses in a depot in the Falls Road were set on fire. Although Goulding was quick to deny these events were the work of the IRA they had in fact been carried out by a small group of members from West Belfast who were hoping to divert the attention of the RUC away from Derry.

Since 5 October, when the Derry march had ended in riot, the IRA leadership had been under increasing pressure to mount some sort of defence for civil rights supporters. At the December 1968 ard fheis, the mild-tempered Sinn Fein director of publicity, Sean O'Bradaigh (Ruairi's brother), declared that 'we would be prepared to help them and meet violence with violence. The three main political parties have ruled out violence, but we have not.'[8] Immediately after the

Burntollet Bridge ambush Goulding had been urged by MacStiofain to sanction retaliatory attacks on policemen but was turned down. As the year progressed the demands for action grew more urgent. Goulding gave a mildly belligerent interview in February warning that 'the IRA has never gone out of existence and we don't intend that it ever should', but it did little to stop the criticisms.

In May 1969 the question was debated at a rancorous meeting in Dublin. There were twenty people present, including all the Dublin leadership and representatives from the North. During the discussion Ruairi O'Bradaigh suggested setting up vigilante groups to keep 'pro-British elements out of the Catholic areas', arguing that it was the 'height of irresponsibility and madness to have the pressure continue from the civil rights movement knowing where it was going to lead and being unable then to meet the logical consequences'.[9] O'Bradaigh claims that Goulding's reply was that 'it was up to the official forces of the British Army and the RUC to defend the people'. When asked by O'Bradaigh how much weaponry and material the Belfast units could lay their hands on Billy McMillen replied there was 'enough for one operation' — that is a pistol, a machine-gun and some ammunition.

O'Bradaigh's concern for the safety of civil rights supporters was shared by their leaders. In June the chairman of NICRA, Frank Gogarty, visited Goulding in Dublin to ask if he could rely on the protection of the IRA if the violence continued to worsen.[4] He left dissatisfied. In his autobiography MacStiofain painted a lurid picture of the behaviour of the leadership as the crisis approached. According to his account, they regarded the events in the North as an unwelcome disruption to their plans and spent more time worrying about the final shape of their definitive political programme 'Ireland Today', which was published in March. 'From the chairman of the army council and from the adjutant general [he wrote] the same answer came repeatedly: 'The time is not yet ripe for military action.' They sat there poring endlessly over their volumes of documents as though the North was a million miles away.'[10]

There is no doubt that the Goulding group felt a strong aversion to MacStiofain's attitudes and an extreme reluctance to do anything that smacked of a reversion to the militaristic policies of the past. According to MacGiolla, 'What we were trying to do was to avoid getting involved in any campaign. That's why MacStiofain was such an embarrassment. The objective was to avoid military confrontation and to avoid any appearance of sectarianism.'[11] The IRA's political strategy depended on a rapprochement between Catholic and Protestant workers. Any action of the kind MacStiofain was proposing would wreck the fantasy for ever. Instead, the leadership had been urging members to involve themselves in the citizens' defence committees that were set up in Derry, Belfast and Newry as the year progressed.

What the leadership had in mind was not to infiltrate and subvert the committees, as the Special Branch officers of RUC had immediately assumed, but to shift the burden of defence away from the IRA and on to the shoulders of the Catholic population itself. 'The objective was,' said MacGiolla, 'to try and help the people defend the areas rather than have the IRA come out and start a new campaign. We never wanted the role of the defenders of the Catholics. No one could, who had come through the re-analysis of the 1960s.'[12] However, the Army Council did promise the release for defence purposes of some Thompson machine-guns hidden in farmyard dumps, but by the time of the critical riots of 12-15 August they still had not arrived.*

Early in 1969 IRA units and individuals had stopped expecting any encouragement from Dublin and prepared to fight. Immediately after the police assault on the Bogside, Derry republicans had set up vigilante street committees. The first was the St Columb's Wells Street Committee under the chairmanship of Sean Keenan, the city's leading republican;

* The fact was that there was very little to give. 'We were broke in every way,' said Goulding. 'We just hadn't got the stuff, and we feared that the limited amount that we did have would just produce the reaction that the attackers wanted — and they had more guns than us.'[13]

94

they put up barricades and mounted patrols for a few days until they were persuaded to stop by the Derry Citizens' Action Committee. The DCAC was the official voice of the Catholics in the city at the start of the year and was composed of 'moderate' Nationalist politicians and prominent citizens. But as the Bogside youths grew more aggressive and the likelihood of a sectarian pogrom increased, its influence diminished correspondingly. Control passed instead to the defence committees. Concern about civil rights, the *raison d'être* of the DCAC, was beginning to look irrelevant to many Bogsiders. Defence was a more pressing issue.

The defence committees were revived once again after the April rioting, with two in the Bogside, another next door in Brandywell and one on the other side of the river in the Waterside. According to Eamonn McCann, 'the [Citizens' Action Committee] died in Derry after the riots of 19 April. It was difficult after that to organize a demonstration that did not end in riot, and the CAC was not about to assume such responsibility . . . The rage and frustration which lay just beneath the surface of life in the Bogside could no longer be contained within the thin shell of the CAC's timid respectability. The 'hooligans' had taken over and the stage was set for a decisive clash between them and the forces of the state.'[14]

The obvious flashpoint was the marching season of July and August when the Orangemen, the Blackmen and other Protestant triumphalist societies parade around the Province in an orgy of celebration of the victories that saved Ulster from Roman Catholicism. In June a new form of violence appeared in the city. Individuals were stopped in the street and asked their religion. If they gave the wrong answer they were beaten. 12 July is the day Orangemen honour the victory of the Protestant William of Orange over the Catholic James II at the Battle of the Boyne in 1690. The previous evening, the traditional bonfires were lit in the city. As they died down, crowds of Protestants and Catholics gathered and exchanged missiles, but were eventually broken up and ushered back to their homes by civil rights activists led by McCann on one side and the police on the other. The 'Twelfth' was not celebrated as fervently in Derry as it was in the rest of the Province. The Orangemen went off to the nearby town of Limavady for their celebration and most of the city shops stayed open.

Youths gathered to throw stones at the procession when it returned at about six o'clock but they were easily dispersed. It seemed the day might pass relatively peacefully. At eight o'clock, however, the youths reappeared inside the city walls and, ignoring the pleas of some stewards from the DCAC, began stoning the police. An appeal by Bernadette Devlin to move back only seemed to make the crowd, by now reinforced with older men, more restless and they began looting shops. The RUC moved in with their truncheons whirling, driving the Catholics back through Butcher's Gate, one of the entrances in the walls. The pattern of the ensuing fighting was to become familiar in the years ahead. A duel with bricks, bottles and catapults developed and at one stage a propane gas cylinder was ignited and rolled across Butcher's Gate to make a fiery barricade. Late in the evening a group of youths set off to attack the Victoria Police Barracks (brushing aside a cordon of Catholic men led by Father Mulvey, a priest from St Eugene's Cathedral, who tried to prevent them) where they smashed windows. Eventually the police turned up in Land-Rover vehicles to clear the area. The mob replied with petrol-bombs and they threw up barricades in the surrounding streets. The riot finally petered out at five o'clock in the morning.

Next day, Sunday, the youths of the Bogside did not rise till late. In mid-afternoon they grouped in Waterloo Place, outside the Victoria police station and stoned shop windows. Most of them were aged between 14 and 17 and it was clear that they were spoiling for a fight. County Inspector Corbett of the Derry police observed that:

The [crowd's] hostility was first not to the police and the DCAC stewards: it had been equally hostile to Brother O'Sullivan [Principal of the local Christian Brothers' school and the headmaster of many of the crowd]. By the later stage they had thrown stones at some of the tourist traffic going along the street and it was a case that the crowd was absolutely determined, come what may, that it was going to force police action against it.[15]

The police moved in to disperse them, hosing them with water-cannon and driving their Land-Rovers into their ranks. The ensuing riot continued all evening. Rossville Hall, a local community centre, went up in flames. At one point the police asked to be allowed to fire CS gas (tear gas) but the request was turned down by the Northern Ireland Minister of Home Affairs, Robert Porter, who was one of the strongest advocates of reform in the Unionist ranks. A small group of policemen who found themselves trapped in a side street with a mob advancing on them fired a volley over their heads, wounding an onlooker.

The approach of 12 August made the prospect of a further outbreak of violence seem inevitable. This is the proudest day in the calendar of Derry Protestantism, the anniversary of the siege of the city in 1689 when the Apprentice Boys baulked the attempts of the English governor to surrender to the army of James II and successfully held out. The event was celebrated with the same fierce pride as if it had happened yesterday.

The DCAC called a meeting on 17 July in a desperate effort to work out a peace-keeping plan, but was unable to agree on what action to take if the Bogside was attacked. Despite the fact that it had been Catholic youths who had started the last disturbances, the fear of a Protestant reprisal by police or loyalist mobs had, if anything, increased. The inhabitants of the Bogside were now less interested in the hand-wringing dilemmas of the moderates on the DCAC than in securing a proper defence. A few days after their meeting, a group of Derry republicans, members of the James Connolly Republican Club and headed as usual by Sean Keenan, formed the Derry Citizens Defence Committee (DCDC).

Keenan was the leading representative of what remained of the IRA tradition in the city. According to Eamonn McCann there were perhaps ten people in Derry who regarded themselves as members when the troubles broke out. Their initiative in assuming the defenders' role caused some annoyance among other groups on the left, and the original eight members were later increased to forty to widen the representative base. The committee began immediate preparations for trouble. A 'Peace Corps' was set up to enrol stewards for order-keeping duties, but it does not seem to have operated very efficiently; the director, a man of no previous experience, never received a list of those who were under his control. First aid posts and evacuation points were set up and a communications system using walkie-talkies 'liberated' from a film crew. But most of the energy went into preparing the Bogside's defences. Barricade-building materials were collected and experiments conducted in how long it would take to put them up. Petrol bombs and stones were stockpiled, but the use of firearms was ruled out.

'Sticks, stones and the good old petrol bomb,' as Sean Keenan declared at a meeting on 4 August, were justifiable means of defence. A dairy delivering milk in the centre of the city collected suspiciously few empty bottles on the morning of 10 August. The next day there were none at all. As the day of the Apprentice Boys' parade approached a series of mass meetings in the Creggan and the Bogside organised by the Defence Association deepened the apocalyptic atmosphere. In Celtic Park on 10 August a long-serving republican, Neil Gillespie, declared: 'If attacked and only then, let us in God's name fight as peace-loving men know how to fight and in a way which will give pause to those who in future may toy with the idea of again attacking us.' 'If this is indeed our hour of trial at hand,' said Eddie McAteer, the local Nationalist MP, in another speech that day, 'if we are to be beaten into the ground in this city as a helpless minority then I pray to God that our watching brethren [in the South] will not stand aside any longer.'

At one o'clock on the afternoon of Tuesday 12 August 15,000 Apprentice Boys moved off to parade around the city, drums pounding and pipes playing. As they arrived in Waterloo Place two middle-aged women broke away and capered about singing *The Sash*, a Protestant anthem which ends with the words: 'It's a terror to them Papish boys, The sash my father wore!' The Papish boys were behind crush barriers just off Waterloo Place. At 2.30 someone threw a handful of nails at the police, swiftly followed by stones and bricks. One reporter saw an apparently respectable middle-aged man produce a catapult and fire marbles into the Apprentice Boys' ranks.

The riot that followed lasted two days and nights and was not brought under control until the Army arrived in Derry at 5.00 pm on 14 August. For two and a half hours the police stood their ground in Waterloo Place, while the Bogsiders showered them with missiles. In the late afternoon a baton charge was ordered which drove the Catholics back into the Bogside. There the rioters were able to fall back on prepared defences. At 3.30, two hours before the police advance, Sean Keenan had given the order to raise the barricades. As the police advanced into the narrow streets of the Bogside in armoured vehicles and on foot, they were brought to a standstill by a sustained barrage of bricks, rocks and petrol bombs from surrounding roofs. Water-cannon deployed to douse the crowd had to be used to quench the fires that sprang up in houses and shops. Detective Inspector Slevin and the contingent of police drafted in from County Down he was commanding found themselves in William Street locked in 'a fight for survival' with the mob. Of fifty-nine officers, forty-three were treated later for injuries. A hundred yards away in Sackville Street the scene resembled a battle from the ancient world, with the Bogsiders throwing steel reinforced rods into the police lines. Sergeant Pendleton of the RUC was ordered to take his armoured Humber — fitted with a barrier-breaking grid — to clear the obstacles to the entrance of the Bogside. All the tiny streets on the east flank of the quarter seemed to be barricaded. He drove through hostile crowds, destroying barriers in Little James Street, the Little Diamond, Frederic Street and Union Street before returning with the hull of his Humber ablaze from petrol bombs to William Street, now comparatively quiet.

The police decided that their best chance of containing the

riot lay in breaching the huge barricade that stretched across Rossville Street, the main thoroughfare in the Bogside. The Bogsiders had been working on it all afternoon and by 6.00 pm it was nearly complete, a solid structure built from scaffold poles, trestles and concrete slabs. Pendleton's Humber was brought up again. It took six attempts before the barrier was broken. The police poured through and into the Bogside, closely followed by a crowd of 200 Protestants, who stoned the fleeing Catholics and then began smashing the windows of their homes. The arrival of the Protestants, mostly teenage boys, dispelled any remaining qualms of the Bogside moderates, who saw the move as a deliberate attack on them by a coalition of police and Protestants acting together. Although it lasted only twenty minutes according to Father Mulvey, the incursion 'brushed aside any hope of moderation or any hope of restoring calm . . . there was . . . an apparent unanimity in opposition to the police force. Over the next few days the determination was so unanimous that I would only regard it as a community in revolt rather than just a street disturbance or a riot.'

When the police withdrew, the Bogsiders followed them out again. They built a barricade at the junction of Little James Street and William Street, on the corner of Waterloo Place, and began a steady bombardment of the now demoralised and exhausted police. On the other side of the police line an angry Protestant mob gathered. Some of the policemen were being set on fire by petrol bombs. It was obvious that they could not keep the two sides apart for much longer. Earlier in the day Porter had finally authorised the use of 'tear smoke', as CS gas was quaintly termed, if it became necessary. Deputy Inspector General Shillington of the RUC, who had heard news of the authorisation on his car radio as he drove from Belfast, took one look at the dazed constables lolling with fatigue in the doorways of the narrow streets and gave the order to fire gas. As the choking cloud rolled towards them the rioters withdrew, which allowed the fire brigade to get in and begin dealing with the fires raging in William Street and Little James Street. In the morning a pall of gas still lay on the Bogside. A stalemate held for most of the day. The Bogsiders used the time to build up stocks of paving-stones and petrol bombs. There was sporadic stoning during the afternoon and evening. At 9.00 pm everything stopped so that people could listen to a broadcast by the Prime Minister of the Republic, Jack Lynch, who promised that the South 'would not stand idly by' if the situation worsened. The Irish Government had asked Britain to request the assistance of a United Nations peace-keeping force as Stormont was no longer in control. According to McCann, 'this put new heart into the fight. News that "the Free State [Republic] soldiers are coming" spread rapidly. The radio station operating from Eamonn Melaugh's house in Creggan was pumping out republican music and exhortations to "keep the murderers out. Don't weaken now." '

The battles between the Catholics, the police and the Paisleyite mobs in tartan tam-o'-shanters continued into the small hours. The following day it was clear to senior police officers that their men were too tired and too few to restore order. They decided to deploy the 'B' Specials. The sight of them advancing on the Bogside bearing pickaxe handles and batons created near panic. ' "Have we guns?" people shouted to one another, hoping that someone would know, inching forward more slowly now as the police retreated, suddenly fearful of what was about to happen. We were about halfway down William Street when the word came that British soldiers were marching across the bridge.' The arrival of the First Battalion of the Prince of Wales Regiment in company strength marked the end of the riot. To the disgust of the republicans, the Bogsiders welcomed them. Local republicans had to a large extent been responsible for organising the defences of the Bogside but they by no means controlled the population and gained little kudos for their efforts. The introduction of the Army and the political upheavals that followed the rioting moved conventional politicians to the fore once again and Derry republicans were unable to reap much political advantage from the situation. None the less, the army of increasingly nihilistic

and daring youths who had led the fighting represented
a fertile field of potential recruits, among them Martin
McGuinness who was to go on to become a leader of the
Provisional IRA. It would be at least another year, however, before the Provisionals had a proper organisation in
the city.

CHAPTER SIX

August 1969

Soon after the rioting had started in Derry, Sean Keenan, Eamonn McCann and others contacted Frank Gogarty of NICRA and appealed to him to organise demonstrations around the Province to divert police resources away from the city. Significantly, Keenan did not think of approaching the IRA leadership in Dublin or the members in Belfast. There had been virtually no contact between Derry and Dublin since the start of the year, though Sean MacStiofain had visited Keenan from time to time on his regular weekend visits to the North. Gogarty's call for diversionary meetings was published in the morning papers of 13 August and that evening there were demonstrations in Dungannon and Armagh. NICRA decided against a rally in Belfast for fear of inflaming sectarian tensions, which had been worsening in the preceding months. Both ·ommunities were in the grip of a mounting paranoia about the other's intentions. Catholics were convinced that they were about to become the victims of a Protestant pogrom; Protestants that they were on the eve of a republican insurrection. Two illustrations from July give an indication of the mood:

> It had been the insistent habit of a Mrs Gilmour, an elderly Protestant living in the predominantly Catholic Chatham Street to display a Union Jack about this time of year. This had caused irritation in the past and extra police attention had had to be given. In 1969 tension was greater. On

9 July the flag was torn down and some damage was done to Mrs Gilmour's house . . . on 11 July a crowd gathered outside the house in Hooker Street of Mrs Gilmour's daughter and chanted threats such as 'burn Minnie Baillie out' and 'get Minnie Baillie out'.

Another incident concerned an Orange parade:

As the first procession passed the Edenderry Inn [on 11 July] a Tricolour was held up to a window. Some members of the Orange Lodge attempted to break ranks but were kept in line by stewards . . . Police then came over to the Inn where they spoke to the manager, who had meantime been locked out by the customers and was standing on the Crumlin Road. While the second procession was passing the Tricolour was again displayed. Afterwards the police went over to the bar and broke down the door with batons. After a struggle they arrested a Mr Deeds and a Mr Corrigan who, it was said, had been recognised holding the Tricolour up to the window.[1]

In May a defence committee had been set up following brawling between the police and crowds leaving the pubs at closing time in Ardoyne, a Catholic area just off the largely Protestant Crumlin Road and the scene of the two incidents quoted above. As in Derry, the committee was initiated by republicans. But when two of its founders, Joseph Graham and Anthony Cosgrove, spoke against the continuation of the Northern Ireland constitution at an open air meeting they were 'soon told by a crowd to get out and stay out.'[2] In July the committee was revived by Frank McGlade, a long-standing republican who urged local people to band together against attacks by 'strangers'. For a time there were nightly vigilante patrols, and families who lived in mixed streets lodged with relations, leaving the religious boundaries of the terraces clearly defined.

In the early days of August there were repeated clashes in Belfast between the police and Protestant crowds as Orange celebrations came to a close in the evening. The Scarman inquiry into the riots later reported that on the evening of 2 August, after a procession of Junior Orangemen had passed by the Unity Flats, 'a large part of the crowd in Peters Hill dispersed'.

> However, this still left about 1,000 people in Peters Hill who showed no readiness to leave. Among this crowd were a number of rowdy, aggressive youths, some of whom had been drinking. Indeed a senior police officer described the crowd . . . as consisting of 'hooligans, agitators and criminals'.[3]

On the same evening, 'a report reached Tennent Street Police Station that a crowd was moving up the Crumlin Road from the Unity Flats area. A small group of police went to the area of Disraeli Street/Hooker Street. After dark they heard a crowd approaching. It was chanting "we are the people" and "let's wreck the fucking pope heads". It had no identifiable leaders but two people in front carried the Union Jack.'[4]

Despite the worries of the NICRA executive on 13 August about provoking more sectarian trouble, a group of young civil rights activists went ahead with a rally. A crowd of about 500 met outside the Divis Flats and marched to the Springfield Road RUC station where they handed in a petition protesting about events in Derry. Disorder soon broke out all over West Belfast. The crowd began throwing petrol bombs and missiles at the police station. A police Humber which drew up at the mouth of Leeson Street nearby was suddenly rocked by an explosion from a Second World War American-made grenade, and then came under rifle fire. The attackers have never been identified.

The episode was to have important consequences, for it reinforced febrile RUC intelligence reports that the IRA were planning an uprising in Belfast, and led to a fatal police decision to mount high-velocity heavy-calibre Browning machine-guns on their Shorland armoured cars to counter the threat. A little later a mob set fire to the showrooms of Isaac Agnew, a Protestant car dealer who had recently moved his business to the Falls Road from a Protestant part of the city. A fire officer's car, which the mob took for a police vehicle, was fire-bombed and crashed out of control. The crowd then returned to Springfield Road and unknown gunmen fired shots at the station. When the police fired back, injuring two young men, the crowd dispersed but returned a short time afterwards with crates of petrol bombs; they withdrew only when sub-machine-gun bursts were sprayed over their heads. Watching these dramas were groups of Protestants who formed in the frontier streets where the communites met: Cupar Street, North Howard Street and Third Street. They began stock-piling missiles and petrol bombs. Sometime before midnight the first barricades went up.

Around seven o'clock the following evening, a crowd of young Catholic men began gathering around bonfires in Divis Street and the Lower Falls Road, singing republican songs and throwing the occasional stone at passing cars. By nine, they had started moving up Divis Street towards the Protestant streets at the foot of the Shankill Road. Divis Street, with its continuation the Falls Road, is one of the two main religious frontiers in West Belfast. South of the line is mainly Catholic, though there were Catholics living in the southern end of Percy Street and Dover Street and they occupied the whole of Beverley Street and Ardmoulin Avenue. To the west of the line, Catholics also inhabited the Clonard area, a block of streets jutting north of Falls Road into the flank of the Shankill. As the crowd moved along Divis Street petrol bombs began to fly. One set fire to the Arkle Bar, a Catholic pub named after a legendary Irish racehorse, a favourite with the two-shilling punters who gambled away their dole money in the numerous bookies' shops of the district. If the Catholics were looking for a fight, the Protestants were willing to give them one, and crowds began to build up at the street corners, shouting abuse at the 'Fenians'. By 10.40 the Catholics had arrived outside the Hastings Street police station, which faced Divis Street. Some of them made their way up on to the vantage point of the roof of the newly constructed

Whitehall maisonettes; they showered police vehicles lying in the side streets below with bricks, petrol bombs, concrete blocks and scaffolding tubes. One of those on the roof, a Mr McGarrigan, later told the Scarman tribunal that the action had been taken because 'women and children in the flats were terrified that the RUC would do to them what they had done in Derry'.

By now, the Protestant crowds, who had watched the action from the foot of Dover Street and Percy Street, were fighting with a thin screen of 'B' Specials to get at the Catholics in Divis Street. The Catholic crowd, like foot-soldiers in a Homeric skirmish, formed up behind sheets of corrugated iron fencing and drove the Protestants back up Dover Street, only to be halted and pushed back themselves. Petrol bombs and dustbin lids flew between the sides. The Sarsfield bingo hall and several houses were aflame. Police reinforcements arrived in armoured vehicles and broke through the Catholics' by now battered mobile barricade and the 'B' Specials swarmed into the breach followed by the Protestant crowd. The street was full of writhing, punching bodies, dramatically illuminated by the light from the burning buildings.

There were similar scenes the length of Divis Street and its offshoots. In Cupar Street, a mixed street where Catholics occupied the southern end, a police patrol arriving at 11.30 found 400 Catholics and Protestants facing each other and duelling with bricks and petrol bombs in front of blazing buildings. Head Constable Rooney decided to baton charge the Catholics, judging them to be the greater danger to his men. While leading one of these charges he heard what he thought were three revolver shots coming from the Catholic crowd in front of him. Another officer, Constable Elliot, saw a man emerge from the crowd, drop on one knee and fire towards him. Their shots were the first to be fired by members of the IRA in the present conflict.

Earlier on the evening of 14 August the adjutant or second-in-command of the Belfast IRA had set off from his home off

107

the Falls Road for a drink in the Bush Bar, only to find that it was shut due to the 'riots up the road'.

> I was getting different wild tales of mobs moving in to burn people out of homes. As far as I was concerned they were stories. I could not see that sort of thing happening. I finally reached Conway Street [next to Cupar Street] and met a few of our people coming up towards the Falls. I stopped them and I said, 'Where are you going?' They said, 'We're going up there, we've been told they're burning houses.' I told them to hold on until we found out for definite it was happening. Eventually we moved up and it was obvious that there were 'B' Specials and mobs trying to burn people out in the Conway Street area. It was then that instructions had to be given.[5]

He dispatched runners to round up all available members and weapons. The first trawl produced only thirteen men, though as the word spread other members surfaced. There was a desperate shortage of guns. Since the Belfast commander, McMillen, had reported to the Army Council earlier in the summer that there was little more than a machine-gun and a pistol in Belfast IRA's armoury, further weapons had been unearthed, but the total was still woefully inadequate to the circumstances. According to the adjutant, on the night of the rioting there were only two Thompsons, a sten gun, one Lee-Enfield rifle and nine hand-guns. Other accounts by Belfast IRA men present put the figures even lower. (Phil McCullough, a Belfast republican, for example, claims there was only one Thompson, one rifle and four hand-guns.)

According to the adjutant, who assumed command while waiting for McMillen's arrival, half a dozen men were dispatched to Cupar Street, Conway Street and Percy Street. If any attempt was made to burn houses they were to disperse those responsible, if necessary by force but 'under no circumstances were they to take life'.

The rest were to go to St Comgall's primary school, a red brick edifice rebuilt in the 1920s which already had a place in the footnotes of republican history, having been set on fire by republicans after it was used as a billet for British forces in 1920. St Comgall's was in a good strategic position, situated on Divis Street at the point where it curved and commanding a fine field of fire over the riot area.

By the time one IRA unit reached Cupar Street the sight of the burning buildings made their instructions irrelevant and they began firing down the road towards the police cordon and the Protestants beyond. The sound of gunfire forced the police and the crowd to take cover. One man broke from the Protestant ranks during a burst of shooting, ran down the street, staggered and fell. When rescued by two policemen under covering fire from a sub-machine-gun he was found to be uninjured but drunk.[1] The IRA squad opened up again in Conway Street as the police mounted a charge to drive back the Catholics. The RUC fired back, first with a volley over the heads of the crowd, then for effect. Altogether five people – three Protestants, one Catholic and one policeman – were wounded in the exchanges.

Shortly after midnight IRA men were also in action near Dover Street. Despite the fact that the Catholic crowd had been rioting continuously for several hours, they still had some fight left and when the shooting began were resisting an attempt by police, aided by a Protestant mob at their back, to drive them into Divis Street. As the crowd fell back, shots were heard coming from the direction of Gilford Street, opposite the mouth of Dover Street. Herbert Roy, a 26-year-old Protestant who had been peering round the corner of Dover Street, fell dying, struck in the chest by a single .38 bullet. Three policemen were wounded.

The shots had been fired into the mouth of Dover Street because it seemed that the police and the Protestants were on the point of breaking through into the Catholic enclave along Divis Street and attacking it. They also had the effect, however, of convincing the RUC that the insurrection their intelligence reports had led them to expect had at last started. Their response was to deploy three Shorlands – heavy, wheeled, armoured personnel carriers with .30 Browning machine-guns. They were grotesquely over-powered for use in a built-up area, capable of shooting through walls and designed for sustained fire. The Shorlands set off down Divis Street, creating panic among the Catholics. Paddy Kennedy, the Stormont Republican Labour MP for Belfast Central, was drinking in a pub in Albert Street, a little way from the riot area:

> There was a bang on the door and Brendan shouted out 'We're closed!' Then a woman's voice was heard saying she was Mary so-and-so and could she have a half a bottle of wine for her Jimmy who had been shot in the leg. We brought him in and his leg was pissing blood. At that stage I realised that the lid had come off. I went up to the top of Percy Street and it was all quiet. People had disappeared. I walked up to some lads hanging around the corner and told them to get off the streets because people were getting shot. Just then a Shorland armoured car came flying up the road. We crouched in the doorway. They stopped at the corner of Northumberland Street and gave a quick burst of fire, then drove off. I went down into the Loney [a small grid of streets around Leeson Street, containing a relatively high number of republican sympathisers] where men were gathering and told them to go home. What was frightening was that it was tracer bullets that were coming over. You could actually see them coming across from the Shankill Road like fireworks.[6]

The police thought they were under fire from the Divis Flats, and the Shorlands fired several bursts towards them. One of the bullets cut through the wall of number 5 St Brendan's Path and killed nine-year-old Patrick Rooney as he lay in bed. Paddy Kennedy went to the flat when he heard what had happened.

> When I got there they were taking the young lad out into the ambulance. There was a pause in the firing. The mother was hysterical and was taken next door. Mr Rooney took me upstairs to show where the bullet had come through.

There was a lot of gore and grey matter on the wall. He was saying: 'Isn't it terrible for the wife to come in and see that?' I said, 'You'd better try and clean that up.' So he went down and came back up with a saucer and a spoon and he started scraping his child's brains off the wall.[7]

Kennedy scaled the Divis Tower, the tallest block in the complex, and looked down. In Dover Street, Percy Street and Beverley Street, the Protestants were at work setting fire to Catholic houses. Families were struggling down Divis Street, weighed down by their possessions; some of them, he was surprised to note, were being helped by the 'B' Specials. The firing had temporarily stopped. The drivers of the Shorlands were taking a breather. 'I could see them getting out of their vehicles. They were in their shirt sleeves and smoking, and drinking from crates of beer that had come out of the Arkle Bar [destroyed by fire earlier in the evening]. They were talking to civilians, the Shankill Road hard men.'

Kennedy made his way to St Peter's pro-cathedral, the large Victorian parish church of the Falls next to the Divis Flats. In the presbytery he telephoned the RUC's headquarters at Knock, in South Belfast, and spoke to Robert Porter, Minister of Home Affairs, who had stationed himself there with the Prime Minister, James Chichester-Clark (later Lord Moyola), who had replaced Terence O'Neill in May that year, and the Minister of Development, Brian Faulkner.

I said, 'For God's sake, will you stop the shooting!' I was getting quite emotional at this stage. And he replied: 'You realise the whole town is in rebellion?' He said that at that moment Donegall Pass police station was under heavy machine-gun attack. I thought: 'My God, what is happening?'[8]

Porter's reaction was an indication of the confusion that reigned in Belfast and of the panicky mood of the police. Donegall Pass was more than a mile from where the rioting was taking place and at no time in the disturbances was it under threat.

111

The appearance of the Shorlands had frightened off many of the Catholics and left the Protestant looters and arsonists to operate freely. Around 1.30 am a mob of about 200 had decanted into Divis Street and was throwing petrol bombs at Catholic homes and at St Comgall's primary school opposite. Earlier, a group of six IRA men and three 'civilians' had taken up position inside the school grounds to fight off any attempt to burn it, and to block the way to St Peter's which the Protestants were rumoured to be planning to attack.

> We were without weapons or direction [said a young IRA man who was present]. All we had were a few gallons of petrol and we started making petrol bombs in the school grounds and moved up to the railings to use them for cover. There was a lot of firing coming from the loyalist side. We spent an hour at the wall, hoping weaponry would arrive and throwing petrol bombs. Eventually we spotted about seven elderly men moving into the back of St Comgall's, men we knew were from the Forties.[9]

The new arrivals were mostly well-known middle-aged republicans, some of them 'Forties men' who had been interned during the war. They were armed with a Thompson machine-gun, a .303 rifle and four pistols and they took up positions on the roof of the school behind a brick pier above the main entrance, and inside the school on the first floor. There, for the next hour and a half, they kept up a stream of fire into the streets below, only leaving when their ammunition was exhausted. Hospital records show that eight Protestants may have been hit by fire from the school. In the folklore of West Belfast, the St Comgall's school action is generally believed to have saved the area from even greater destruction. This, however, was regarded as the IRA's sole creditable act of the evening. For decades they had passed themselves off as the defenders of the community but for most of the night of 14 August they were nowhere to be found.

In Ardoyne, popularly supposed to contain a strong IRA presence, they played no part in the defence of the area when rioting broke out. The question of what had gone wrong there was to loom large in the bitter post-mortem that took place after the riots. The McMillen camp claimed they had anticipated serious trouble in the area (which had been the scene of incessant squabbling, fighting and intimidation in the preceding months) and issued a few of the precious stock of weapons to the Ardoyne unit, only to take them back when it became clear that they had no intention of using them. According to the Ardoyne unit, McMillen and his men had stripped them of the guns a few days before the violence broke out in order to protect themselves.[2] The bitterness of the subsequent split, with accusations of cowardice and incompetence flying from all sides, produced many similarly imcompatible versions of the events of those days.

The violence in Ardoyne on the night of 14 August followed the pattern established elsewhere in the city. Crowds began to form in the side streets about 8.00 pm, with both sides spoiling for a fight. At 10.30 the first petrol-bomb flew from the Catholic ranks and burst among the police. An armoured Humber was summoned and smashed through the Catholic barricades, closely followed by the Protestant mob who set fire to Catholic shops, pubs and homes.

What defence there was of the area was mounted by a group of ex-servicemen armed with shotguns which they fired at the police. The RUC replied with an undisciplined fusillade of revolver and sub-machine-gun fire which killed 47-year-old Samuel McLarnon as he sat in his front room in Herbert Street, and Michael Lynch, 28, who was walking innocently along the road. Ten others were injured, eight by police bullets and two by shotgun pellets. All were Catholics. An indication of the state of police nerves was shown when officers fired over the heads of a group of youths in the grounds of the Holy Cross girls' school, several hundred yards from the scene of the riots. On hearing the shots policemen in the Crumlin Road assumed they were under fire and began shooting wildly into the grounds of a neighbouring Catholic church. There must have been many occasions during the night when the sound of gunfire in a built-up area was taken by the police and the Protestants as an attack on them by the Catholics.

At dawn on Fridiay 15 August the Catholic residents in the streets abutting the Protestant areas began evacuating. They carried televisions, budgerigars in cages and standard lamps or piled their possessions into handcarts and lorries hijacked for the purpose, and headed for the new estates of Andersonstown on the south west of the city. Tom Conaty, a local businessman who had gone to collect a relation from the Divis Flats, remembers people leaving their homes, boarding them up and begging and crying for lifts'.[10] Each side's perceptions of the other's intentions had become so warped that the Protestants believed that the Catholics were clearing the decks for a further attempt at insurrection that evening. By 4.30 that morning the Commissioner of Police for Belfast, Harold Wolseley, had decided that his men could no longer cope. He asked for the Army to be deployed. At 12.25 that afternoon, after being approved by the Northern Ireland cabinet, the request was made to the Home Office in London. The communication, signed by the Inspector General of the RUC, Anthony Peacocke, left no doubt as to whom the police believed to be responsible for the violence and destruction of the previous two nights:

I have to inform you that, following the violence in the City of Belfast last night, renewed clashes are occurring at this time, 11.30 am, 15 August 1969. The Commissioner has informed me that all immediately available police have been committed but that he is unable to separate the rioting crowds and has had to fall back to defend his police stations. In the circumstances outlined, I now request further assistance of forces under your command in Belfast City. Information is to hand from a reliable source that an infiltration of members of the Irish Republican Army is about to commence from Eire into Northern Ireland. It is the intention to escalate the degree of control over inward bound traffic and to this end assistance in the form of patrols by armoured cars is also requested. The information

114

indicates that the infiltrators will be armed and the support of mobile armoured units, which I cannot supply, would be of material assistance in countering these subversive activities against the Government and people of Northern Ireland.[11]

The briefing given by Wolseley to the incoming commander of 39 Brigade, Brigadier Hudson, was equally colourful. It contained intelligence reports that the IRA were lying in wait in the evacuated Catholic houses north of Divis Street; that they were roaming in the grounds of the Royal Victoria Hospital in the Falls Road; and that they had taken over the operating theatre there.

In fact, by the early morning of the 15th, the Belfast IRA was exhausted and on the defensive. At 4.30 the police commissioner, as well as requesting help from the Army, had ordered the detention of six well-known Belfast republicans under the Special Powers Act. They included Billy McMillen who was arrested at home where he was snatching a few hours sleep after organising the IRA actions through the night. Jim Sullivan was left in command. As daylight came on, he gave orders that the quartermaster was to pull in all weapons and that all the men were to go underground. He had a wounded man who had been hit by a shotgun blast on his hands and arrangements were made to get him over the border into the Republic for treatment. His next task was to communicate with Headquarters to lay hands on more guns. His usual contact with the Headquarters' staff was through Sean MacStiofain, the director of intelligence. At the first news of the rioting MacStiofain had moved nearer to the border and taken over a farmhouse in Navan, from which he planned to mount attacks into the six counties. He claimed later that his unit 'was the only unit ready to take military action in the North'. In fact, its activities were confined to an attack on an RUC station at Crossmaglen in South Armagh on Sunday 17 August, which fizzled out when a hand-grenade lobbed at a van failed to detonate the explosives packed inside.

The morning after the rioting the adjutant drove to Dundalk

and telephoned MacStiofain's headquarters. He was told to wait where he was and that weapons would be delivered to him. Several hours later they had still not appeared. Anxious to return to Belfast before evening, he gave up and headed north. When he arrived back in Belfast that evening he found the British Army deployed along the Falls Road. He tried to get to his home but was stopped by a soldier of the Royal Regiment of Wales and told he could go no further. An argument broke out and a crowd gathered. In the confusion he was able to slip past and into his house. Rumours had been growing all day that there would be trouble that night in Clonard, the grid of Catholic terraces that extends into Protestant territory to the south of the Shankill Road. The IRA man with responsibility for the area, Frank Card (also known by the Gaelic version of his name, Proinsias McCartt) had been one of the six republicans arrested that morning. The situation was saved by the appearance of Billy McKee. McKee, a veteran of the Belfast IRA of the 1940s, had left the movement after being ousted by McMillen and was a focus for the republican malcontents in the city opposed to the Goulding leadership. Other veterans had also 'reported back', including Joe Cahill, another 'Forties man'. McKee was told to go to Kashmir Road, which runs into Cupar Street, the dividing-line between the two communities, and take charge. By the time he got there the rioting was well under way. Fighting had broken out in mid-afternoon with many of the Protestants drunk on liquor looted from Finnegan's pub. Drink had been an important factor in the violence of the previous three days. A policeman observed of another crowd of Protestant rioters that day: 'My assessment . . . was that between drink and hatred they were practically insane.'[12]

The news of the Army's arrival had caused the police virtually to abandon any effort to keep the peace. The Army, though, had misunderstood the sectarian geography of West Belfast and ignored Clonard, imagining the flashpoint would be along the Falls Road. The Protestants were left with a free hand. McKee and his handful of men, armed only with shotguns and .22 sporting rifles, were unable to prevent the mob breaking through. By early evening they had set fire to most of Bombay Street and also houses in Kashmir Road and the Catholic side of Cupar Street. The Protestants were also armed. At about 4.00 pm 15-year-old Gerard McAuley, a member of Na Fianna Eireann, the youth section of the IRA, was helping Catholics evacuate their homes in Bombay Street when he was shot through the heart by a bullet fired from the Shankill Road. The Provisionals honour him as the first volunteer to die in the conflict.

The police had also withdrawn from Ardoyne. Before leaving for Dundalk the adjutant had assigned each of his four staff officers with responsibility for an area of the city. Ardoyne was left to John McGuigan, in theory the IRA district commander, but he seems to have played little part in the events of the 15th. During the afternoon a group of Catholic men met to discuss the defence of the area. A collection of shotguns, sporting rifles and at least one automatic was mustered. By late afternoon there were sporadic clashes and shooting incidents all over the district. In one, a 48-year-old Protestant, David Linton, was killed by a shotgun blast in the face.

Calm did not finally descend on Belfast until Sunday. It was, as Lord Scarman noted, 'the quiet of exhaustion'. Seven people had been killed in the rioting and about 750 injured. At least seventy-two Catholics and sixty-one Protestants had suffered gunshot wounds. (The reluctance of Catholics to seek hospital treatment means the true figure is unascertainable.) The Catholics had suffered most: 1,505 Catholic families were forced out of their homes by burning, damage or intimidation, against 315 Protestant households. Of the 275 buildings destroyed or requiring major repairs as a result of rioting, 83.5 per cent were occupied by Catholics.

In the space of a few days an atmosphere had been created in which an armed, rebellious organisation could prosper. After Mass at Holy Cross Church in Ardoyne on Sunday 17 August, Father Marcellus Gillespie told the Scarman tribunal, a meeting of residents was held in a local school. The demand was for guns. '(I) did not agree with guns and

117

(said) that they should not have guns, and they accused me of being a cheek-turning fool.' Father Gillespie also testified that after the meeting had broken up, some residents 'raided the houses of people who were supposed to be IRA men by repute and found nothing, and after the riots they called the IRA, the ' "I ran away" '.[13]

CHAPTER SEVEN

The Birth of the Provisionals

The events of August had shown beyond any doubt that the
IRA was incapable of protecting the Catholics of Northern
Ireland. This did not stop Goulding from issuing a press notice
on 19 August claiming that 'units of the IRA are active all
over the North . . . ready to take every action necessary in
the defence of Catholics and the liberation of the North.' In
Derry, republicans pasted copies of the statement on walls
around the Bogside. They were quickly ripped down.[1]

The events of August had torn the last shreds of credibility
from the IRA's claim to be a secret army. Goulding in Dublin
had offered to provide protection for the demonstrations called
by NICRA around the Province on 13 August to take the
pressure off the Catholics in Derry. In Newry and Armagh,
however, volunteers sent from the South withdrew when
they encountered patrols of RUC men and 'B' Specials. In
Dungannon, where three people had been shot in disturbances
on the night of 13 August, Catholics were strongly opposed
to any intervention by the IRA for fear that they would only
be escalating the violence in which the republicans would
inevitably come off worse. The IRA role in the Newry
disturbances was equally unpopular with most of the local
Catholics. The republican-dominated Citizens' Action Committee's reponse to NICRA's call for diversionary demonstrations was to barricade the RUC in the town barracks to
prevent them being moved to Derry. This move precipitated
the resignation of the 'moderates' from the committee. The

police station was ringed with lorries while two local republicans, Sam Dowling and Joe Campbell, harangued the crowd, who threw petrol-bombs at the barracks. Next morning most of the crowd, which had never been more than a thousand strong, had melted away and the police were able to break out, causing the remaining demonstrators to flee in two trucks for Omeath, a few miles away across the border, pausing on the way to burn a customs hut.

In Belfast the IRA's inadequate and inflammatory reponse to the riots had not inspired much confidence either. When Joe Cahill arrived in Ballymurphy, a Catholic estate on the edge of West Belfast, to organise its defences he was chased away. 'It took ten days of going up there and being seen off before they accepted that I was sincere,' he recalled.[2] Cahill was one of many republican veterans who had lapsed into inactivity after the advent of the Goulding leadership and who returned to offer their services as a result of the riots. Most of them were in their forties and fifties, and had played a part in the IRA escapades in Belfast in the 1940s or been imprisoned during the border campaign. They included Seamus Twomey, a bookmaker, Billy Kelly, a seaman, and his brother John, a successful engineer. Political and personal differences between the old guard and the returnees were temporarily forgotten in the urgency of the hunt for guns. The IRA was convinced that the cessation of violence that followed the arrival of the Army was only temporary.

On the morning of Saturday 16 August, Jim Sullivan, a veteran republican who had played a leading part in the events of the previous two nights, called a meeting at a house in Leeson Street situated in the 'Pound Loney', a small grid of streets in West Belfast that contained a relatively high number of republican sympathisers, to organise the search. The following day, four groups set off from the city to various parts of Ireland with the intention of meeting up forty-eight hours later in the Southern border town of Dundalk. As there was no central record of where the arms dumped in 1962 were located, the searchers had to rely on the memory of local volunteers. In one case, the local activists in County Tyrone ended up dispatching a courier to a Belfast prison to find out where an arms dump was located.[3] Cahill scoured County Longford and County Westmeath, where he turned up 'the strangest collection of weapons you ever saw. Only about a third of them were serviceable but we took the lot. The thought was that if you have a man manning a barricade with what looks like a working gun then it is a defence weapon.'[4] When they met up in Dundalk they had scraped together seventy-five guns: a few Thompsons and stens, some .303 rifles and the rest shotguns and .22s. Cahill and his companion, Danny Burke, who was later shot dead in a pub in Andersonstown, drove unmolested across the border with the weapons in the boot of their Ford Cortina. The same excavations were going on all over Northern Ireland and the border counties. A woman civil rights activist from Newry remembers spending a moonlit night in a Monaghan farmyard resurrecting a rifle buried in the 1950s and polishing up the bullets. Sullivan recalls that 'every Tom, Dick and Harry was looking for weapons — people who for many, many years would have turned their heads away if you had put a collection box in front of them'.[4]

In Dublin, Goulding had managed to locate a supply of automatics which were dispatched North, and sporting guns and shotguns were bought from sympathetic gunsmiths south of the border with money provided by Catholic businessmen. The RUC and British Army patrols along the border were soon to discover the impossibility of policing all the myriad farmtracks and tiny lanes that bisect the border, or of carrying out a thorough search of the stream of farm trucks bearing the potato and hay harvest back and forth. The IRA passed with their occasional cargoes of rifles and ammunition undisturbed.

The harmony imposed on Belfast republicans by the crisis did not last long. The old guard were dismayed by the IRA's showing during the riots and some, like Cahill, believed that the loss of face the movement had suffered had dealt a terminal blow to its credibility with the Catholics. They were also fired with the indignation of the vindicated. For years they had been warning Goulding of the consequences of a military run-down and events had proved them right. Sullivan and his supporters were less disturbed by the IRA's lack of military preparation than by the disastrous effect of the violence on progress towards Catholic and Protestant working-class solidarity. None the less, it was Sullivan who took the lead in organising the Catholic defences once calm had returned. On 16 August he founded the Central Citizens' Defence Committee (CCDC) to co-ordinate the responses of those areas still behind the barricades erected during the violence to keep the Protestants and the police out. Defence associations had sprung up all over the city as a result of the fighting. The central committee was made up of about thirty delegates from the Catholic enclaves of the city: Andersonstown, Ballymurphy, Falls, New Lodge and Ardoyne in the west of the city; the Markets area in the centre; and the isolated Short Strand district situated on the banks of the Lagan in East Belfast and completely surrounded by Protestants. Most of the delegates were ordinary men with standing in their areas, but republicans were strongly represented and the local clergy was also there in force. Inside the Falls barricades, Sullivan and his supporters did their best to reap some political advantage from the situation, publishing a newspaper and broadcasting over Radio Belfast. A forty-strong police force patrolled the streets and in an effort to reduce drunkenness the pubs were shut at 8.30 pm.

Perhaps the most painful experience for republicans in the post riot period was the response of the Catholic population to the arrival of the Army. A Leeson Street publican remembered them 'coming into my bar with their faces coloured, with their little tin hats with camouflage on. I served them and they left their guns and bayonets up against the counter when they went off to the loo.' The soldiers, as newspaper photographers and television cameramen lavishly recorded, were met with friendliness and endless cups of tea. A NICRA statement declared that the people of the Bogside and the Falls Road were not prepared to allow the troops to be withdrawn. When Joe Cahill saw the treatment the Army was receiving on the Falls Road, 'it brought tears to my eyes. Here was the enemy, the instigators of what had just happened in the country and the people were collaborating with them . . . people were glad to see them because the IRA had betrayed them.'[2] In Derry, Sean Keenan's assertion that 'the British are the enemy', according to Eamonn McCann met with 'incredulous horror' by the moderates who had taken part in the defence of the Bogside.

As the days went by and relations with the Army stayed cordial, the reasons for maintaining the barricades seemed less compelling. In mid-September Sullivan announced that there were plans in hand to prevent any attempt to remove the barricades by force, but several of the larger ones had already been dismantled earlier in the month after negotiations between Sullivan and the Army.

They went up again in the Falls at the end of September after Catholic houses were attacked by Protestant crowds. The overall success of the Army in holding the Protestants off impressed the CCDC and early in October it announced that all barricades would be removed voluntarily provided the Army could guarantee the protection of the area. Four days later a hundred barricades in the district were dismantled and the committee agreed to allow military police in to patrol. It was little wonder the Catholics of West Belfast were so well disposed towards the Army. For the first time in their lives they were being treated to the sight of men wearing the Queen's uniform wading in with vigorous impartiality to crowds of rioters whose political and social creed was rooted in blind 'loyalty' to the Crown and whose emblem was the Union Flag. Protestant fury with the direction events were taking reached a climax on the weekend of 10 October when the government of Northern Ireland announced its acceptance of the Hunt Report which recommended the disbanding of the 'B' Specials. Crowds on the Shankill Road chanted 'Paisley is our leader', waved flags and shouted to the bemused soldiers 'Englishmen go home . . . we want the "B" Specials'. On Saturday night after the pubs had closed, a mob marching to the thud of a giant Lambeg drum set off down the hill towards the Catholic-inhabited Unity Flats where a screen of policemen was stretched across the road. Loyalist snipers began firing towards them and Constable Arbuckle of the RUC fell dying. A company of Light Infantry was moved in to clear the rioters and at one o'clock in the morning the order was given to return fire. Two Protestants were killed in the shooting.

According to Joe Cahill the disturbances saw a rare example of the cross-sectarian co-operation so wished for by the Goulding camp. Some loyalist leaders approached the IRA with a proposal to join forces to expel the 'Brits'. If the venture succeeded, the republicans could have the Six Counties minus Belfast which would be a free port ruled by loyalists.

The Army's firm handling of the affair gave a further boost to their credentials with the Catholics. The CCDC gave its permission for the RUC to resume patrols in the Falls. Sullivan's role in liaising with the Army to remove the barricades and reopen West Belfast to the Army and police provided more ammunition for his detractors among the old guard, who regarded the barriers as essential for Catholic protection given the lack of sufficient firearms. Having failed to defend the community in August, the Belfast leadership was now attempting to expose it to danger once more. Sullivan does seem to have behaved with remarkable moderation during his chairmanship of the CCDC, given the opportunities that the post presented for political agitation, and shown a carefree attitude towards the sensibilities of the hard-liners. When the Inspector General of the RUC, Anthony Peacocke, resigned, Sullivan was involved in the decision to invite his English successor, Chief Constable Sir Arthur Young, to address the CCDC at their usual meeting-place above the Long Bar in the middle of republican Leeson Street, with his deputy Frank Lagan:

I went up in a car to Springfield to bring Young down to the meeting [said Tom Conaty, a businessman and the Andersonstown delegate of the CCDC]. You had to walk up a dusty staircase to get to the room where we met and it was hung with photographs of the McMahons, a family who had allegedly been murdered by the RUC. He walked into the room – you could hardly see the walls for cigarette smoke — a big fellow, well over six foot. And when he walked into the room, I don't know why it was, but every man got up and applauded.[5]

Such episodes hardened the suspicions of the traditionalists about Sullivan's intentions. The first clear indication of a split in the ranks of the Belfast IRA came only a week after the end of the fighting, on 24 August, when a group opposed to Goulding's leadership met in West Belfast. The Belfast contingent included Joe Cahill, Billy Kelly, John Kelly, Seamus Twomey, Gerry Adams, Leo Martin, Jimmy Drumm, Jimmy Steele and Billy McKee. Daithi O'Connaill, MacStiofain's ally in the internal sniping against the leadership, was also there.[6] The participants decided to remove Sullivan and McMillen as quickly as possible and work on replacing the Dublin leadership with 'traditional' republicans.

Four weeks later they were presented with the opportunity for a putsch. On his release from prison Billy McMillen called a meeting of his supporters in a hall in the Lower Falls for 22 September. After half an hour only three people had turned up, evidence of the IRA's chronic unpunctuality rather than a reflection of McMillen's standing. He was on the point of dismissing the meeting when the door crashed open and sixteen armed men walked in. They included Steele, McKee, the Kelly brothers, and Twomey. John Kelly and Billy McKee announced that Sullivan had failed to protect the local population and that they were taking over. According to McMillen's account he replied that he had no intention of handing power to men who had left the movement five or more years before, and then pointed out that an internal squabble at such a time was both absurd and self-destructive — it benefited only Stormont and the British.[7]

The plotters agreed to a compromise where McMillen retained his command but six of the McKee faction were drafted on to the 'staff'. 'Belfast would cut off communications with Dublin for three months and the £3,500 that the unit had in its coffers — donations from Catholic businessmen — would not be used for 'relief supplies', as the donors had genuinely or euphemistically stipulated, but for guns. If after three months the Dublin leadership had still not altered course, then Goulding and the leftists would be removed and replaced by traditionalists and a separate Northern Command set up to exercise autonomous control of the IRA in the Six Counties. The movement's programme would be cleansed of socialism. At the same time the dissidents decided that as a gesture of protest Belfast would not send any delegates to the extraordinary Army Convention which had been called by Goulding for November to discuss the abstention question.

Despite the compromise and McMillen's temporary retention of the leadership, the small republican community in Belfast was drawing into separate, hostile camps. Phil McCullough recalled that at one point, 'McMillen told one volunteer that if he joined McKee he would be guilty of treason and under army standing orders the penalty for treason is death. We told McMillen that we would follow the McKee faction simply because he had proven his readiness to defend the people.'[8]

The coup attempt was later used as key evidence to support the Goulding faction's belief that the split was a conspiracy engineered by the Irish Fianna Fail Government. Their motive for doing so, the thesis ran, was to neutralise the threat to the Southern state posed by the IRA's new radical policies by replacing the leadership with a conservative faction. The traditionalists would get guns and money for a defensive campaign in the North in return for a promise to stay out of politics and military activity south of the border. The theory gained some acceptance because of a series of meetings that took place between IRA men, Fianna Fail officials and politicians and businessmen who supported the party throughout the late summer and autumn of 1969. The ambivalent attitude of the Irish Government during the period and the continued silence of many of the key protagonists about their role in the affair have meant that the conspiracy interpretation of the split is still believed by many of the Goulding camp's survivors today.

The Irish Government, led by the unobtrusive figure of Jack

Lynch, had been thrown into a panic of indecision by the events of August. Lynch had been in the forefront of the tentative rapprochement between Dublin and Stormont that had gone on in the sixties. His instinct, once the initial August crisis had passed, was to avoid confrontation with Stormont and, beyond that, Britain. But the riots had released a flood of adrenalin into the bloodstream of Irish politics which refused to abate. The suffering of the Catholics in Derry and Belfast aroused anger and frustration south of the border and awakened, albeit momentarily, latent republican sympathies. These feelings were particularly prevalent among Fianna Fail supporters, by history and tradition the 'greener' of the two main parties. Lynch was under pressure not only to come to the aid of the beleaguered Catholics, but also — from some quarters — to use the extraordinary events to advance the party's stated ambition of dismantling the state of Northern Ireland.

The reluctance of the main protagonists in Lynch's government, including Lynch himself, to discuss the events of the period has meant that much of what is known about it is still based on the testimony of Captain James Kelly, an intelligence officer in the Irish Army. Kelly had gone to Derry 'out of curiosity' while on annual leave the day before the rioting began; then he travelled to Belfast where he made a tour of the city with a family friend, the ubiquitous Paddy Kennedy, MP. On his return to Dublin he reported on the situation to his superiors and was instructed by the army director of intelligence, Colonel Michael Heffernan, to maintain his contacts with the North. Kelly returned to the North early in September and travelled extensively. In Derry he saw Sean Keenan; in Belfast Jim Sullivan and local politicians. 'Everyone, without exception, was demanding that the Dublin Government do something to support them . . . the universal message I got from everyone was that they needed arms and they needed them straight away.[9]

Kelly was also left in no doubt that the Irish Government was expected to help. The Catholics' hopes had been raised by Lynch's pledge not to 'stand idly by', broadcast during the riots. In the event, that is what he did. Irish troops had been moved to the border, but to man relief camps for the refugees who streamed to the South from Derry and Belfast rather than for any military purpose. The rumour of an impending invasion had certainly prompted the republican assault on Newry police station on 13 August. 'We thought it was all over and the North was going to be liberated,' said Margot Collins, a civil rights activist in the town.

Kelly conveyed the requests to Heffernan and his reports were passed on to Jim Gibbons, the Irish Minister for Defence. Kelly's superiors were concerned about what use any arms supplied by the South might be put to, especially the prospect that they might be used by leftists and republicans to mount an anti-British insurrection. He was instructed to find out. As he had by now become a familiar figure to British intelligence in the North he decided to hold a meeting of the main representatives of the Citizens' Defence Committees at Bailieborough in the border county of Cavan, to discuss their needs. Heffernan gave his approval and Kelly was given £500 to cover the cost. The meeting was held on 6 October in a hotel in the town. Among those present were Sean Keenan from Derry, Jim Sullivan and Billy Kelly from Belfast and representatives from each county in the North.

The participants ate and drank well. According to one present, 'There was no talk of a united Ireland or striking a blow for freedom, it was simply a matter of getting guns . . . and [those present] were prepared to accept any conditions to get them. As far as I was concerned I was prepared to take what I could get out of the Fianna Fail Government and cut their throats at the same time.' Like the rest of the Official IRA he came to regard the meeting as an elaborate intelligence-gathering exercise by the Irish Government, designed to explore the feasibility of subverting and neutering the IRA.

Afterwards Kelly reported that he was satisfied that the guns would only be used for defensive purposes and the search began for a means of supplying them. As it turned out, no guns were ever to reach the Catholics in the North as a result of the meeting. What it led to, however was the trial in 1970 of the then finance minister, Charles Haughey, and the agriculture minister, Neil Blaney, and Kelly himself on charges of conspiring to smuggle arms and ammunition into the country illegally. All involved were acquitted.

The bold posture struck by the Irish Government during the rioting did not last long. In the face of the political and military realities of the situation, Lynch's initial bravado dwindled. When the trouble began he had ordered the Army to begin work on a possible invasion strategy. According to Kelly, plans were prepared at Army Headquarters in Dublin for an occupation of parts of County Derry and County Down. Kelly himself had been consulted as to which IRA personnel in the North might be of use: 'It was an essential part of [the plan] that they knew who their friends were in the North − if they went in who would be likely to help them, and if they could have on the ground people who might even be armed to assist them.' To this end the Government tacitly authorised the Army to give small arms training to a group of Catholics at a camp at Fortnaree, just over the border in Donegal.

Despite the fact that work was still being done on the plan in February 1970, it quickly became clear that it would never be acted on. Training at Fortnaree was halted after a Dublin newspaper made inquiries about the activities there. Government policy towards the North degenerated into the unco-ordinated consideration of how they could get arms to the Catholics in the North for their self-protection without being found out. Irish officials were already operating a nudge-and-wink policy towards the smuggling of guns destined for the North. A ship found with arms on board off Dublin was freed after it was declared that they were 'supplies for the Irish Army'. According to Kelly's account, 'various arms [were being] collected everywhere and one of our reasons for getting involved officially was to bring this under some control from a Government point of view and have it organised.'

The potential embarrassment to the Government from private arms-running initiatives was graphically illustrated by an episode, related by Kelly, shortly after the Bailieborough meeting. John Kelly of the Belfast IRA was contacted by an anonymous source in London who told him that he had guns for sale. Ignoring warnings from Captain Kelly (whom he had met during one of his intelligence gathering trips North), he flew to Britain accompanied by a friend, the brother of an Irish cabinet minister. At Oxford Street underground station they were met by a small, dark-skinned man who introduced himself as Captain Malcolm Randall, a former British Army officer. To explain his rather surprising willingness to sell arms to Irishmen he revealed that he was of Arab origin and no longer had any sympathy with his former comrades. They agreed to meet him again the following evening. On leaving the station John Kelly noticed at street corners and bus-stops a succession of men and women speaking furtively into two-way radios. The friend telephoned Captain Kelly in Dublin who urged them both to come home immediately. The friend took the advice but John Kelly stayed on long enough to arrange a further meeting with Captain Randall, this time in Dublin. At the next encounter at the Gresham Hotel, he offered Kelly not only a consignment of arms at a bargain price but also the benefit of his expertise in guerrilla warfare. When three members of the Belfast IRA who were with Kelly heard of the affair they suggested that they should appear to go along with Randall's training offer but shoot him as a spy later. Captain Kelly intervened and pursuaded them against it. Kelly claims that contacts he had with the British Special Branch later confirmed that Randall was indeed a British agent.

The Irish Government's difficulties over supplying the North seemed to be solved when a surplus consignment of old-fashioned but serviceable Irish Army Lee-Enfield rifles was put up for sale. It is alleged that Jim Gibbons ordered them to be taken off the market and held for distribution to Catholics in the Six Counties if needed. The idea was dropped, however, when it was pointed out that the arms could be traced back to Dublin.[9]

A further, indirect, way of arming the Northern Catholics opened up in the autumn of 1969 when, according to Captain Kelly, the Government sponsored a fund to alleviate the

130

hardship of victims of the troubles. An account was opened at the Allied Irish Bank in Baggot Street, Dublin, which accrued about £100,000 in government and private donations. Authorisation to draw from the bank was restricted to a leading Belfast Catholic politician and John Kelly of the IRA. Most of the money was used for the stated purpose but, according to one republican, the Belfast IRA were able to 'con them out of a few thousand quid' before the split, some of which was undoubtedly spent on guns. The fund was also used, Kelly alleged, to fund the arms-buying trip that landed him, John Kelly and Charles Haughey, Fianna Fail finance minister, in the dock. The last two were acquitted.

It was an extraordinary time when conventional citizens did extraordinary things. A non-republican member of the Belfast CCDC remembers travelling to Charles Haughey's mansion at Kinsealy just outside Dublin with a priest and a lawyer to seek funds for families made destitute by the troubles. 'We said we wanted money and he just said "How much?", We said, "Twenty-five thousand pounds" and he immediately wrote out a cheque. If we had asked for double I'm sure we would have got it.'[10] The money was later administered by a Catholic diocesan fund.

The urgency with which the Catholics in the South regarded the position of their co-religionists in the North meant that in 1969 men of unassailable probity found themselves sitting down with men who were shortly to become notorious, in circumstances that would very soon look sinister. Given the fractious historical relationship between the IRA and the 'traitors' of Fianna Fail, it was unsurprising that some republicans should come to regard themselves as the victims of this ill-lit drama.

In fact, the division of the republican movement had been ordained long before 1969. In quiet times, with give and take on both sides, the habitually bickering traditions of revolutionary socialism and romantic physical force nationalism could just about get along under the same roof. Faced with a crisis of any dimensions, the union was bound to fall apart. The events of August 1969 merely accelerated a process that had begun

131

with the attempts by Goulding and his supporters to modernise the movement. The theory of a government-inspired conspiracy to remove the dangerous leftists of the new IRA and replace them with the manageable stooges of the old tradition was characteristically fanciful and vain. There was scarcely any evidence in 1969 that the Goulding camp's political strategy was making significant progress in the South nor that it had any potential to do so. Even if it had, Lynch and his government had much more immediate preoccupations than the neutralisation of a minor political nuisance.

In the autumn of 1969 the traditionalist faction in the Belfast IRA, of which Billy McKee was now the leader, had made it clear that they no longer felt any allegiance to the Dublin leadership. They made a half-hearted attempt to seize control of the organisation from within when McKee approached Sullivan with a proposal to join forces to overthrow Goulding before the Army Convention met in December and install Sullivan instead.[4] He declined the offer. Sullivan and McMillen found themselves in a humiliatingly supine relationship with the men they were supposed to command. The compromise that they had been forced to make with McKee in September in order to retain nominal control forbade any contact with Dublin and McMillen was forced to communicate with Goulding in secret. Antipathy to Goulding and, especially to Johnston, who was painted as a sinister, atheistic *eminence grise*, was widespread not just inside the Belfast organisation, but elsewhere in Ireland, particularly in the West and the border counties.

The leadership's unwillingness (and in material terms inability) to respond to appeals for arms during the approach to the August riots and its feeble showing during them spread the conviction that changes at the top were now essential. This had been forcefully demonstrated by a group of volunteers who threatened Goulding with death after he ordered back the few men who had been moved up to the border during the disturbances. According to Ruairi O'Bradaigh, Johnston did not help matters by persisting with an infuriatingly theoretical approach to the situation during Army Council discussions. 'At one meeting in the autumn Johnston said: "Now it's important to realise that we don't have a revolutionary situation here. What we have is an opportunity for education." With that, Goulding seemed to lose patience and he said: "Look here, Roy. We were caught out once. If we're caught out again the people will rise up and destroy us." I felt, my goodness, maybe we're getting sense at last but it was only a passing thing.'[1] The disillusionment felt over the leadership's performance was but the culmination of a long series of snubs and grievances suffered by the conservative, militarist, Catholic wing of the movement. The Goulding leadership had shown itself to have little patience with dissenters on the right. The controversy over the leadership's decision to drop the 'sectarian' tradition of saying a decade of the rosary at IRA commemorations produced angry protests among the Kerry IRA and Sinn Fein members, and when it persisted with the ban there were mass resignations. After the split, Kerry became a Provisional stronghold.

Early in 1969 the executive of Sinn Fein disbanded the Sligo branch after it refused to allow members of the Connolly Youth Movement (the youth wing of the Communist Party) and the Labour Party to take part in the Easter Parade. The Goulding group also made enemies of the women's branch of the movement, Cumann na mBan, barring them from using republican premises and threatening them with disbandment when they objected to marching with the Connolly youths at the 1969 Bodenstown Wolfe Tone celebration. Added to the disenchantment felt over the leadership's commitment to end the policy of abstentionism it was clear that a decisive confrontation was approaching.

Goulding's main enemy inside the Army Council was Sean MacStiofain. Before August their dislike of each other had been constrained by the need to maintain unity. After the riots, on MacStiofain's part at least, it was given full rein. He had signalled his rebellion by carrying out the attack on the Crossmaglen RUC station in contravention of Goulding's orders. After August he had been put in charge of a fund to raise money to buy arms for the North but after hearing that Goulding planned to use half the money to pay the salaries of more full-time political organisers, 'I . . . told [the subscribers] to hold on to their money for the time being, explaining my reasons. Later I was able to approach them again, and they were to be very generous to the Provisional Army Council.'[11]

MacStiofain's affection for Goulding had taken some time to sour. By now he was portraying Goulding behind his back as a stooge of the marxists and a poseur; a man who had spent the day filming with a British television company in the Dublin Hills 'while the people of the Bogside could hardly see each other in the fighting for gas and smoke.'[12]

Those of MacStiofain's characteristics that irritated Goulding and his supporters recommended him to other elements in the movement. His incoherent, God-fearing brand of socialism was shared by many. Reluctance to move with the times and abandon abstentionism was not regarded as a vice in an organisation in which rigidity of thought and refusal to compromise were admired and honoured. Indeed, until this point in its history the IRA had owed its existence to its continued opposition to a state of affairs – the partition of Ireland – that the vast majority of their countrymen, North and South of the border, had long ago accepted. Realism had never counted for much in the republican movement. As MacStiofain and the traditionalists correctly understood, if they abandoned militarism, if they ceased to regard the eradication of the border as the immediate and vital aim, then they might as well consign the IRA to oblivion and continue as just another far left political party.

To Goulding and his supporters this was an admirable end. For the preceding seven years they had been struggling to cut republicanism free of its historical impedimenta. They no longer wanted to be a *movement*, with all the outmoded clutter that that entailed. They wanted to be a *party*. For that reason the division, when it came, was as much the wish of the Goulding camp as it was of the traditionalists. Their vision of a proletarian socialist state where religion was a matter of utter irrelevancy had been a frail enough concept before the August riots. The events in Derry and Belfast squeezed it to the point of extinction. To take the path that MacStiofain and the Belfast old brigade were urging would finish it all together. If either faction was to survive, the movement would have to divide.

There was a strong resemblance between the fate of republicanism and the fate of unionism as a result of the civil rights agitation and its aftermath. Goulding's efforts to modernise and compromise were parallel with Terence O'Neill's attempts to come to terms with the ancient curse of sectarianism, to integrate Northern Ireland Catholics into the state and to dissolve some of the suspicions between Ulster unionists and the Republic. Both policies aroused the anger and opposition of the atavistic elements in their camps, and both traditions divided. 'Ironically, perhaps,' Philip Beresford wrote, 'the principal architects of both splits, Paisley and MacStiofain, had the same fanatical belief in the "traditional" virtues of the old Unionism or Republicanism and both led similar abstemious lives, devoting their energies entirely to their respective political or military fields.'[13]

The opportunity for matters to come to a head was provided by the report of the joint IRA-Sinn Fein Committee, commissioned at the 1968 Sinn Fein ard fheis to examine the policy of abstentionism and the question of forming a National Liberation Front with the tiny (and Communist) Irish Workers' Party and other leftist groups. The report had been delivered in March 1969 but was not due for consideration by the Army Council until October. MacStiofain (who had been a member of the convention) made a last attempt to persuade the leadership to shelve the report, but the effect of his appeal was diminished when he lost his temper and began banging the table. In October the Army Council (now enlarged from its traditional seven members to twenty) endorsed by twelve votes to eight the report's recommendation that in future republicans should recognise the assemblies of Leinster House, Stormont and Westminster if elected.

By the time the special IRA convention met in an isolated

village on a wet night in the middle of December to consider whether or not to grant their approval, most of the traditionalists assumed that the event was a foregone conclusion. Belfast did not bother to send any delegates. Afterwards there were accusations of vote-rigging. The number of delegates sent by anti-abstentionist Tyrone would have required a membership of several hundreds in the country, a very unlikely figure, according to O'Bradaigh. A group of MacStiofain's supporters was mysteriously never collected. The actual vote, taken on a show of hands, is disputed. There was a clear majority, however, in favour of a National Liberation Front, and for recognising Westminster, Stormont and Leinster House (the Irish parliament). After the vote, according to O'Bradaigh, 'MacStiofain got up and told them: "You are now no longer in the IRA . . . we no longer regard you as such and we will take no further part in these deliberations." '

After years' fighting to reunite Ireland the movement had now voted to participate in the institutions that divided it. O'Bradaigh's attitude was characteristic of the traditionalists: 'I was having no part of any constitutionalism and I was not going to see the republican movement subverted and turned into something that was contrary to its nature,' he said. 'What was it all about since 1922? Why not accept the bloody Treaty in the beginning and be done with it?'[1] Security considerations meant MacStiofain and his supporters, who numbered at least twelve of the fifty or so delegates, had to sit through the elections for the new Army Executive before they were able to leave.

MacStiofain remembered the meeting as a curiously subdued affair after the passion of the preceding months. 'Goulding himself showed no hostility. After the convention he asked me what I planned to do in the coming year. I think he knew well enough, but I wasn't forthcoming. "Well," he said, "I hope you'll have a talk with me before you do anything." '[14]

MacStiofain left the meeting and was driven straight to Belfast, where he addressed a meeting of IRA men. The support of the Belfast units was vital if the new organisation was to stand any chance of survival. MacStiofain was perhaps the only member of the GHQ staff to have any standing in the city. In his role as director of intelligence he had, unlike most of his Dublin colleagues, made frequent visits there in the 1960s and his efforts to get guns to the north during the year had raised his stock with the old guard. By the end of the meeting, the twenty men present had agreed to work with him to set up a new organisation in the North and to attend another Army Convention. A few days before Christmas, the core of the new IRA met in a small town in the Irish Midlands. Apart from the Belfast men there were the delegates who had voted against abandoning abstentionism, and those who had been excluded. Their first act was to repudiate the proposals passed at the earlier Convention and to reaffirm their allegiance to 'the thirty-two County Irish Republic proclaimed at Easter 1916, established by Dail Eireann in 1919, overthrown by force of arms in 1922 and suppressed to this day by the British-imposed Six County and Twenty-six County partitionist states'.

They elected a Provisional Executive of twelve which then withdrew to elect a Provisional Army Council of seven. The nomenclature, with its echoes of the 1916 rebels' Provisional Government of the Irish Republic, reflected the delegates' belief that the irregularities surrounding the extraordinary convention called by Goulding rendered it null and void. Any decisions it took were revocable. They proposed to call another convention within twelve months to resolve the leadership of the movement. Until this happened they regarded themselves as a provisional organisation. Ten months later, after the September 1970 Army Council meeting, a statement was issued declaring that the 'provisional' period was now officially over, but by then the name had stuck fast.

The delegates voted unanimously for MacStiofain as chief-of-staff. The other members of the Army Council were Ruairi O'Bradaigh; Daithi O'Connaill, quartermaster; Sean Tracey from County Leix, training officer; Leo Martin, Officer Commanding the Six Counties; Patrick Mulcahey of Limerick, secretary to the HQ staff, and Joe Cahill. There was still a final constitutional formality to be undergone before the divorce was absolute. For abstentionism to be properly cast aside required a two-thirds vote at the Sinn Fein ard fheis, which was due to be held in January 1970. Before the conference a curious ritual took place. Members of the Provisional Army Council made a pilgrimage to the Mayo home of Tom Maguire, a former commandant general of the IRA and the last surviving republican member of the 1922 Dail. In the eyes of his visitors, this old man represented the legitimate government of Ireland. Maguire judged that it was the Provisional Army Council that retained the deeds to the republican tradition, and obliged them with a press statement declaring that the convention had 'neither the right nor the authority to pass a resolution to end abstentionism.'[15] (However, when Maguire declared sixteen years later that the move to abandon abstentionism in the South ran counter to republican teaching, the Provisional leadership chose to overlook his judgement.) The ard fheis was held on 11 January in the Intercontinental Hotel in Dublin. When the resolution to end abstentionism was voted on it was carried, but without the majority necessary for it to become the policy of the movement. Undaunted, Dennis Cassin, a delegate from Armagh, hit on the device of proposing a vote of confidence in the Goulding leadership, thereby unconstitutionally manoeuvring Sinn Fein into tacit acceptance of the decisions taken at the extraordinary Army Convention of the previous month. As Goulding addressed the delegates through one microphone MacStiofain seized the other and announced that Goulding no longer represented the IRA and that to support him would be a breach of the Sinn Fein constitution. He declared his allegiance to the Provisional Army Council, urged the delegates to follow him, and left the meeting accompanied by about one-third of the 257 delegates to reconvene the conference at a hall in Parnell Square which had already been hired for the occasion.

CHAPTER EIGHT

Defenders

Shortly after the drama at the Intercontinental Hotel, the Provisional Army Council met for the first time to consider its strategy. It seemed to MacStiofain that the situation in the North could only get worse. The Protestant power structure was beginning to fall apart. In the aftermath of the August rioting various reforms had been imposed on Stormont by Westminster that undermined the foundations of the unionist state. The most significant had been the decision to disband the 'B' Specials. They were to be replaced by a new integrated force of Catholics and Protestants, the Ulster Defence Regiment (UDR) who would come under the control of the British Army. To the Army Council it seemed that the anger and resentment aroused among working-class Protestants by removal of the 'B men' would exacerbate the tensions between the modernists in the Unionist Party who accepted the need for reform and the reactionaries. MacStiofain also believed that there was a growing threat that loyalist extremists might attempt a coup.[1] One way or another, the Army Council concluded, a resurgence of Protestant violence was only a matter of time, probably during that summer's marching season.

It was in this context [wrote MacStiofain] . . . that IRA strategy had to be determined . . . it was agreed that the most urgent priority would be area defence. All our energies would be devoted to providing material, financial and training assistance for the Northern Units. The objective was to ensure that if any area where such a unit existed came under attack, whether from Loyalist extremists or British forces, that unit would be capable of adequate defensive action. The army council also decided that as soon as it became feasible and practical the IRA would move from a purely defensive position into a phase of combined defence and retaliation. Should British troops ill-treat or kill civilians, counter operations would be undertaken when the Republican troops had the capability. After a sufficient period of preparation . . . it would go into the third phase, launching all-out offensive action against the British occupation system. It was also agreed that selective sabotage operations would be carried out at the discretion of the national and local leadership, in the Northern areas concerned.[2]

Early in the New Year, the Special Branch of the RUC was receiving reports that the reconstruction of the Belfast IRA was well under way. An IRA informer passed an account of a meeting held by the Andersonstown unit of the Provisional IRA in a private house on Sunday 8 February. 'The Andersonstown company is an active service unit and requires its members to be in good physical condition,' he reported. 'They have been training in full battledress in Casement Park a number of nights a week.' Most of those attending were new recruits and they were treated to a lecture on Irish history by Jimmy Steele as well as some practical advice. If arrested they were to 'say absolutely nothing and refuse to recognise the court . . . Steele was asked why Gerald Maguire was allowed to recognise the court on 22 January and he replied that a court of inquiry would be convened and it was possible that Maguire would be disciplined . . . When questioned about weapons Steele said that prior to that time they had £1,500 but that the money had been used by communist-inspired elements for educational purposes but now they had plenty of arms. Liam O'Neill suggested that everyone be issued with a personal firearm . . and that the arms used for training new recruits should be the auxiliaries' weapons because the active service unit's guns were too good for them.'[3] The same source mentioned that profits from the Felons' Club in Milltown (a republican drinking club) were being used partly to finance the auxiliaries' support duties and partly for a central fund. Another informer told the Special Branch that units had been directed to find sites for the manufacture of petrol bombs. Another said that if trouble broke out at a forthcoming civil rights march on 21 February, 'the IRA would be there to protect marchers and attack the Protestants . . . missiles had already been stored for the purpose and a supply of missiles would be brought up from the South in a few days time,' adding that 'the Provisional Army Council have issued a directive to increase intelligence on members of the Ulster Volunteer Force [an outlawed Protestant paramilitary group] and the "B" Specials who retain arms at home.' Yet another 'extremely well-placed source' was predicting in January that the split in the movement was now irrevocable and the Provisionals would emerge as the stronger of the two.

Most of the IRA members in Belfast had sided with MacStiofain. By his calculation, nine of thirteen units had offered their backing by the time of the 'caretaker' Army Convention, shortly before Christmas. According to Billy Kelly, one of the founders of the Belfast IRA, by January all but two of the units had voted to opt for the new leadership after hearing the case put to them by a representative of each side[4] and even Jim Sullivan, who remained loyal to Goulding, estimated that only one in four of the city's republicans followed his example.[5] Just how many men these units represented was unknown, even to those at the heart of the organisation. Jim Sullivan calculates that there were nominally between 100 and 120 declared members of the IRA in Belfast at the time of the August riots. Of these perhaps half were activists, the hard-working core of the organisation involved in the day-to-day drudgery of keeping the movement alive. The remainder were social republicans who had suffered for the cause but who had now more or less retired, apart from appearances at commemorations and social gatherings. Many of these would have returned to the active list after the August riots.

Added to and overlapping this were the auxiliaries, a reservoir of between 300 and 500 republican supporters, generally in their middle years, who could be relied on to run a message or hide a gun in a time of crisis. After the riots they received some basic arms training and were loosely organised under the direction of Joe Cahill to patrol the Catholic areas and man the barricades. Sullivan's figures contradict Billy Kelly's 200 nominal IRA men in the city in August. All in all, a calculation that there were some 500 people in Belfast who felt themselves bound in spirit or by declaration to the IRA is not far from the truth. The confusion over figures is partly a result of the IRA's self-deluding regular army structure. If you persist with the brigades, battalions and companies operated by the old IRA during the War of Independence then it is necessary to have the personnel to man these phantom columns. The result was inaccurate and padded membership lists. Even MacStiofain, not one to massage the figures downwards, admitted that at Christmas 1969 he was in command of 'an organisation that was only a nucleus. Outside Belfast the battalions were very much paper battalions. The strength of a company varied from 12 to 40 volunteers.'[6]

The initial reason for using this grandiose terminology was to underline the IRA's claim to be the legitimate force of the state. According to Tom Barry, the legendary commander of the West Cork brigade of the IRA, which at the peak of the war against the Black and Tans had numbered about a thousand men, the intention had never been to imitate a standing army formation. 'Battalions, companies and sections were of unequal sizes and strengths,' he wrote. 'The organisation was elastic, based on the factors of population and terrain, and no attempt was ever made to form units on an establishment basis as in regular armies. This was important as it allowed for the development of a fighting machine under changing conditions and growing enemy pressure.'[7]

Although the split in Belfast had been overwhelmingly to the advantage of MacStiofain, the Official IRA (as the Goulding faction had gratifyingly been designated by the newspapers) was still able to increase its membership and strengthen its organisation in Belfast. The most authoritative study of the arithmetic of the split calculates that by March 1971 there were twelve Official IRA companies or Republican Clubs (the organisation's political manifestation in the North) in Belfast, with one each in Andersonstown, Ardoyne, Ballymurphy-Whiterock, Beechmount, Clonard, Markets, New Lodge-Unity Flats, Short Strand and Turf Lodge.[8] Of these, the Officials only regarded the Markets and the Lower Falls, where they had three units, as areas of real strength.[4]

During 1970 there were fourteen Provisional units and Sinn Fein branches formed in Belfast covering all the afore-mentioned districts with the exception of Short Strand and Turf Lodge. The split in Belfast had been in the making for months and when it came it was swift and decisive with the two sides quickly settling down into mutual recrimination and hostility. Outside the city the division was less sharp. The factions drifted apart. The rioting had been much less traumatic for Derry republicans than it had for those in Belfast. The defence of the Bogside by and large had been successful, and the small group identified with the IRA through the Connolly Republican Club could take pride in having played a prominent part in the victory. The republican tradition, such as it was in the city, was heavily imbued with socialism. In the late sixties republicans had been allies of the radicals in the local Labour Party and collaborated with them on a number of stunts to draw attention to housing injustices, so that most of the activists were philosophically drawn to the Officials.

Older men, like Sean Keenan, went to the Provisionals. He had in any case already been expelled by Goulding for his association with *Voice of the North*, the newspaper founded with Fianna Fail money after the riots, and in the eyes of the Goulding group another element in the Government conspiracy against them. In February 1970 the Pearse branch of Provisional Sinn Fein was founded, with Neil Gillespie as secretary. In its inaugural statement it cited opposition to the left-wing leanings of the leadership and the abstention issue as the reason for its establishment. Interest in the inner wranglings of the movement was so slight in the city that newcomers to the IRA often had only a hazy idea of the nature of the split or indeed that a split had taken place at all. Martin McGuinness started off by joining the Official IRA in October 1970, unaware that the movement had split. Later the Derry Official IRA were visited by Seamus Costello who told them that the movement was 'undergoing reorganisation'.

Outside Belfast and Derry the Provisionals initially failed to make much headway. In Newry the most senior and active republicans stayed with Goulding and it was not until September 1970 that the Provisionals opened a Sinn Fein branch in the town. In Armagh the Republican Club lost a few defectors but continued to expand. The Strabane Republican Club and IRA unit remained loyal to the Officials through 1972. In Tyrone the Republican Club's executive denied there was any split in the movement and pledged support for the Officials. In many of these areas, particularly the border lands, which had been spared the violence that had affected many of the towns in the Province, the Officials benefited from the republicans' relative lack of urgency in making up their minds. Although their sympathies probably lay closer to the Provisionals they were reluctant to take a decision. In Mid-Ulster they would turn out in equal numbers to marches organised by both sides.[9] But the Officials' success in holding on to much of the movement's membership in the countryside and in the small towns was by and large irrelevant — the centre of events was Belfast, and there the Officials were being eclipsed.

By the end of January 1970 the rival wings had arranged themselves into a rough fighting order. Billy McKee was in command of the Provisionals, with Seamus Twomey as his adjutant, Leo Martin intelligence officer, Sean McNally quartermaster, Tommy O'Donnell finance officer, Sean Murphy training officer and Albert Price controlling the auxiliaries. The Provisionals, who now styled themselves the Belfast Brigade, divided the city into three battalion areas. The first Battalion area stretched from the Upper Falls and extended north to cover the Ballymurphy Estate and west to the council developments of Andersonstown. The Second Battalion operated in the terraced streets of the Lower Falls and Clonard as well as the Divis Flats. The Third Battalion covered the Catholic outposts of Ardoyne and the 'Bone', marooned off the Crumlin Road, and the Short Strand, across the Lagan to the east.

McKee was regarded as a disciplinarian by his men. He was single, slightly-built and mild-looking, a passionate Catholic who took Communion daily and expected his subordinates to be similarly devout. This attitude endeared him to some sections of the West Belfast clergy who promoted the claims of the Provisionals with their parishioners over those of the alleged atheists in the Officials. According to Paddy Kennedy, 'he was in the mould of the old IRA. If he gave you his word he would honour it. If you talked to him he listened and he responded. He was an extremely good-living man but in the end he regarded republicanism as a more important religion than anything else.'[10] Some of the younger element found his piety irksome. One former IRA man who was 17 in 1970 remembers him as 'a Bible-thumper. You couldn't do this and you couldn't do that and everybody was expected to go to chapel and go to confession.'[11]

Unlike McKee, Seamus Twomey, his number two, looked the part — a hard, monosyllabic former bookmaker's shop manager. Jimmy Steele was put in charge of publicity and in the months before his death in the summer of 1970 set the early tone of the Provisionals' newspaper, *Republican News*. It was written in a florid, romantic style. News stories were doggedly set in a historical context so that a report of the deaths of two civilians at the hands of the Army in the July 1970 issue began, 'The ghost of General "Butcher" Maxwell, the General Officer Commanding British troops in Ireland in 1916 is again hovering over Ireland.' The text was enlivened with stirring songs and poems. The staff of the Belfast Brigade were all veterans who had been imprisoned or interned for the movement in the 1940s. For most of them, republicanism was in their genes. Joe Cahill had a characteristic background. He was born in 1920 in Divis Street, Belfast, the son of a jobbing printer who did work on behalf of IRA prisoners, and a republican mother. He joined up, he claimed, as a reaction to the poverty and mass unemployment he saw in the thirties. The hunger marches and rioting over the fifteen shilling a week 'outdoor relief' payments resulted in a brief *entente* between Catholic and Protestant workers and in the forties there was even a Protestant company in the Belfast IRA, led by John Graham from the Antrim Road. In 1942 he had been sentenced to life imprisonment for his part in the shooting of a policeman for which another member of the group, Tom Williams, was hanged. He was released in 1949 but interned during the border campaign. After he was freed he dropped out of the IRA, only returning after the August riots.

For the Officials, Billy McMillen retained command with Jim Sullivan as his adjutant and Joe McCann commanding the men in the Markets area, a patch of terraced slums just south of the city centre. The decision of individuals as to which side they joined was complicated by personal and family loyalties. Sullivan and McMillen were powerful and respected men in the areas they lived in, local patriarchs who were looked to for advice. Sullivan — small, ginger and bespectacled — had shown his leadership qualities and initiative by the way in which he set up the CCDC after the riots and the firm and cool manner in which he ran it. The success of the Officials in hanging on to the Lower Falls is more a tribute to his personality than to the popularity of his political message. McMillen was a similarly unimposing figure, 42 years old when the troubles broke out, a chubby, chain-smoking bachelor. Like many of the pre-1969 membership of the movement, his republicanism was in his blood and, like many Belfast republicans, he claimed a link with James Connolly, the great Irish socialist revolutionary who organised the Irish Citizen Army, from the first decade of the century when he had lived on the Falls Road, organising the linen workers into a trade union. His mother, he boasted, had run messages for him. He joined the IRA at 16 and was interned in Crumlin

146

Road jail in 1956. McMillen was an exotic by the standards of the Belfast IRA, a physical force man who had been converted to Goulding and Johnston's way of thinking, 'Representatives used to come down from Dublin and tell us to form Republican Clubs, get involved in tenants' associations, trade unions − all this jazz. We resisted it tooth and nail! We used to spend hours at meetings trying to conjure up ideas and excuses as to why we shouldn't become involved in this type of political activity and to tell Dublin GHQ why they were wrong . . . The funny part of it was that the more we sat down to try and convince ourselves that GHQ was wrong the more we saw that the policies were in fact the correct ones.'[12] After the riots the idea gained ground among the traditionalists that McMillen had deliberately misled them about the number of weapons that were available, and there was more bitterness over the clandestine links he had maintained with Dublin after he had agreed, under duress, to break off relations.

Some were torn between their political instincts and the family tradition. According to Sullivan, Gerry Adams was the only one of the politically-inclined activists to have joined the Provisionals after the split, a disappointment for him and McMillen. Adams had impressed them with his enthusiasm for housing agitation and other activities dear to the heart of Dublin. Sullivan believes that his decision to go with the Provisionals was dictated by pressure from his family. Adams was a republican aristocrat. His father, Old Gerry, was imprisoned in the forties and his mother was a member of one of Belfast's leading republican clans, the Hannaways, and he could go one further than McMillen − his grandfather had been a political associate of Connolly's in his days in the Falls Road. Neither family had involved itself much in the movement in the sixties and all sided with the McKee faction when the division came. Adams himself 'didn't feel very emotional about the issue.' He had grave doubts about the competence of the Goulding faction, but was also unimpressed by the 'Johnny-come-latelys' who had deserted the movement in the sixties. In Adams' area, Ballymurphy, the issue was decided

147

democratically. Sullivan and McMillen were invited up to put their case to a forty-strong gathering of republicans. Adams spoke against them. The meeting voted overwhelmingly in favour of the Provisionals.[13]

On the other side, the McCann clan, and their relations by marriage, moved en bloc into the Official camp. Joe McCann's brother Denis was interned as an Official in 1972. His brother-in-law Anthony Dornan joined the Officials in the Lower Falls and stood as a local government candidate in the 1973 elections. Another brother-in-law, Bobby McKnight, a veteran republican who stayed active through the sixties, also sided with McMillen and Sullivan and took over as commander for a period while McMillen was on the run in the South.[14]

Some families split. The McGuigans, the best known republicans in Ardoyne, divided: father and son joined the Provisionals while mother, who was a friend of Sullivan's, and two other sons stayed with the Officials. In view of the anger Goulding and his supporters had generated in Belfast by their feeble performance throughout 1969, it is remarkable that the Officials' organisation and support in the city held up as well as it did. But they were fighting a rearguard action. In the competition for the loyalties of the newcomers to the movement, who began to pour in as the New Year began, they were hopelessly impeded by their political outlook. The influx of young Catholics to the IRA had not begun in earnest until the turn of the year. In the months after the riots Billy Kelly calculates that each company in the city was receiving only five to ten new recruits each month. This was a reflection of the low esteem in which the organisation was held, but also of the Catholics' confidence that the Army was willing and able to protect them.

As 1970 progressed, this belief was to wither. Throughout January, the Army's preoccupations remained fixed on the Protestants who were still in a truculent and resentful mood over the reforms that had been forced on Stormont by Westminster and they were easily provoked into violence. In January a rumour that the Tricolour and the Red Flag were

148

flying over Unity Flats sent a mob surging down the Shankill Road where they were confronted by a phalanx of paratroopers and dispersed. In the four nights of rioting that followed troops on several occasions robustly thwarted the Protestants' attempts to break through into Catholic streets with boots, fists and clubs. The trouble was that the Army was equally tough when it came to dealing with Catholic mobs. The inevitable confrontation came on a Tuesday evening at the end of March. Despite the appeals of local politicians the authorities had given permission for a band of Junior Orangemen to march through a predominantly Catholic area on its way out of the city. By the time they returned a crowd was waiting for them. About seventy troops of the Royal Scots regiment moved in to keep the sides apart and were met with a shower of rocks and petrol-bombs. The action that followed, unspectacular though it was by the standards of the time, instantly won a place in the anti-British folklore of Northern Irish Catholicism. The troops fired tear gas which drifted into the houses of the Ballymurphy estate, choking young and old indiscriminately. Men armed with hurley sticks tried vainly to drive the canisters back into the Army lines. Soldiers with blackened faces and beating an intimidating tattoo on their plastic riot shields charged into the crowds, dragging out every young man they could lay their hands on. They smashed down doors and yelled abuse.

There was further rioting the next two nights. Shots were fired at the Army and barricades went up. On the third night in Ballymurphy troops pushed a Catholic crowd back into the Estate and were followed in by a Protestant mob who tore down a Tricolour. The disturbances were punctuated by desperate attempts by Catholics to restore peace. Vigilantes were seen trying to restrain the young rioters and seizing milk bottles to stop them being used for petrol bombs. Cardinal William Conway, the Catholic Primate of All Ireland, and a native of the Falls Road, urged his flock in West Belfast to reply with 'a dignified silence' in the face of provocation and condemned the violence as the work of 'a few irresponsibles'. It had not taken long for the Catholic Church to declare its hostility to the IRA. Historically it had enjoyed a complicated relationship with republicanism. The United Irishmen had been denounced by the hierarchy but supported by 'croppy priests', such as Father John Murphy of Wexford who led his parishioners against the British. The Easter Rising was condemned by individual bishops, but in common with the rest of Ireland the Church's attitude altered with the executions of the rebel leaders, and in the years before the treaty it had issued statements backing Ireland's right to self-determination.

During the Civil War the Church was firmly on the side of the Government and the pulpits rang with denunciations and threats of excommunication. IRA men were asked in the confessional 'if they would stop the campaign against the lawful government of the country. If the answer was "no" then they were refused absolution'.[15]

When the riots of August 1969 had broken out, Cardinal Conway had issued a statement rejecting the hypothesis that the trouble had been caused by republican insurrectionaries and blamed instead 'mobs equipped by machine-guns and other firearms'. Conway believed that violence in defence of the Catholic areas had been justified, but that this justification had disappeared with the arrival of the British Army.

The belief that the Army was somehow on the Catholics' side had faded fast. To remove any lingering doubts about the Army's intention to behave with heavy-handed impartiality, the General Officer Commanding Northern Ireland, Sir Ian Freeland, issued a warning that anyone seen with a petrol bomb in future was liable to be shot dead. The Provisionals responded with a pledge that they would shoot a soldier for every Irishman shot by the Army. The original confrontation with the Orangemen had been the work of the local IRA unit anxious to signal that coat-trailing triumphalist displays by the Protestants would henceforth be met with an aggression.

The fight with the Army had not been planned for, but the outcome was gratifying. Ever since the troops arrived, the Provisionals had been insisting that the Army was the enemy and warning against fraternisation, which even as late as Christmas the inhabitants of West Belfast had largely ignored. The experience of CS gas (it was the first time it had been used in Belfast, though 1,000 cartridges had been fired in the Bogside in August), riot clubs and soldierly abuse was to make the Provisionals' argument for them and act as an effective recruiting sergeant. The tear gas proved particularly effective in manufacturing resentment. It burned the throat, stung the eyes with blinding tears and produced undignified spasms of retching and nausea which sometimes lasted for days. Many of those who went on to take up guns cite their first experience of tear gas as the moment their alienation from the State became complete.

In the argot of the IRA the men and women who joined the movement as a result of the August rioting are known as 'Sixty-niners'. In fact newcomers did not begin to join in earnest until 1970. The average recruit was in his teens or early twenties, male, working-class and probably better-educated than his counterpart in Britain. In West Belfast he would probably have been taught by the Christian Brothers, an order legendary for discipline: at St Mary's in the Glen Road, with 1,200 pupils the largest school, at St Peter's, St Thomas's or St Paul's. The Catholic school curriculum, and its Protestant counter-part, tends to see the world from the cramped perspective of Northern Ireland with a pro-Irish or pro-British flavour. Lessons proclaimed the merits of Irish culture and Ireland's record of producing and exporting saints and savants to the less enlightened corners of the world, notably England. It would not have been surprising if many children had left school with a lasting sense of injustice mingled with a feeling of vague superiority. It would be equally unremarkable if these impressions were not reinforced every day by the routine snubs and unfairnesses that were part of life for Catholics under the Stormont regime.

All this worked to the advantage of the IRA. So too did an inherited sentimentality and tolerance towards the organisation expressed in rebel songs and stories. None the less, most of the Sixty-niners were not propelled into the IRA's arms by any great belief in republicanism; usually it was an experience or series of experiences at the hands of the Army, the police

151

or the Protestants that left them with a desire to protect them-selves in the future and also to get back at the state.

Many, as in the case of someone we shall call 'Sean Donnelly', had no republican antecedents. His grandfather was a Protestant and his cousin joined the RUC in 1967. On the night of 15 August he

> saw the police leading the Protestants on to the Falls Road. I started to throw stones and then petrol bombs to try and keep them out. I was rioting all night. In the morning I called on my mother. I was crying. I believed that thirty or forty of our people had been slaughtered. My mother took me home to our house in [a predominantly Protestant area] and left me there. I was covered in petrol and stinking of the stuff.

Whether the neighbours noticed or whether it was the climate of the times, the Protestants around began parading past his front door with Union Flags and shouting sectarian taunts. Two days later he moved back to the Falls Road with his wife and two children. A little later the Northern Ireland Prime Minister, James Chichester-Clark, came to visit a school in the district where troops were billeted. 'Me and some others chased him. My ma was annoyed with me. I said, "We're chasing those black [Protestant] bastards who shot our people out." She said to me, "Sure your cousin's a policeman." I said, "I'll chase him out too." '[16]

Donnelly first went to a meeting of the CCDC which he found 'full of middle-class types who seemed to think that the Brits were acceptable — the lesser of two evils'. During the autumn he was a regular at any riot that was going, hanging round the flashpoints in the Lower Falls, Durham Street and the Catholic junction with ultra-loyalist Sandy Row in the expectation of some trouble. Early in 1970 he felt that

> I had gone as far as could with rioting. It seemed to me that the people needed and were calling for something more, to give them confidence and morale because they felt so

slaughtered. I never thought of joining the Stickies [the Official IRA]. I felt that the Provies wanted to get the gear and that was good enough for me.

In the old days the ideal recruit would already have served an apprenticeship in Na Fianna Eireann, the republican boy scout movement founded by the formidable Countess Markiewicz to counter the 'pernicious' influence of Baden-Powell. (By 1971, instead of knot-tying and animal spoor recognition, its members were most often to be found planting bombs, running messages and acting as look-outs for snipers.) Newcomers' backgrounds were examined for evidence of criminality. Recruits were then lectured and tested on Irish history, political education and security procedures. There was time for them to reflect on whether they still wanted to join. If the answer was yes, there was arms and explosives training, a course on the IRA constitution and army orders, and finally an induction ceremony. This would usually be held in a member's or sympathiser's house, with as much ceremony as the circumstances allowed. The new recruits would be called to attention in Irish ('Paráid, Aire!') in front of the local commander and his staff. They would raise their hands and repeat the IRA declaration, the oath having been abandoned in the 1920s because of objections by the Catholic Church to oath-bound secret societies: 'I . . . promise that I will promote the objects of Oglaigh nah Eireann to the best of my knowledge and ability and that I will obey all orders and regulations issued to me by the Army Authorities and by my superior officers.' The recruit was then assigned to a company.

'Jack McShane' from Ardoyne, who had joined some months before, also had a mixed background. His maternal grandfather had been in the British Army and was wounded in the Second World War. His father was a republican, who was imprisoned during the 1940s, and every Easter the family would hang the green, white and orange Tricolour out of their window. In 1966, aged 15, he was approached to join Na Fianna Eireann, where he received lectures on republicanism and was told 'that one day we might be expected to take up arms. At the time, though, that seemed pretty remote.' During 1968 the meetings virtually stopped because of lack of interest and only ten youths were attending regularly. 'McShane' had been alarmed by the talk of Protestants in North Belfast, where he was working as a heating engineer, on the approach of the marching season as they 'spoke of the "B" Specials and what they were going to do to the Taigs [Catholics]'. When the riots of August came, the Fianna played no part but 'McShane' joined the other young rioters and shortly afterwards joined the Ardoyne IRA which later sided with the Provisionals.

'If the Catholic Church had been giving out guns at that time,' he said, in a variation on a much quoted remark, 'everybody would have been joining the priesthood.' For the vast majority of the 'Sixty-niners', the Provisionals were the obvious choice. From the outset McKee and his men pumped out a simple, potent signal. In the first issue of *Republican News*, an article headlined 'The Work That Lies Ahead' declared:

> It is the duty of every Republican to assist in the build up of a strong effective movement of resistance to British interference in Irish affairs . . . There must be an effective well co-ordinated disciplined rational struggle for freedom and National re-unification . . . We must state and re-state that the natural and lawful unit for deciding the national issues is the people of All Ireland and not any section in the Six Counties, political parties or individuals who state otherwise must be relentlessly condemned and discredited.

Elsewhere in the paper there were the ritual references to the 'Gospel of [Wolfe] Tone in seeking to unite all our people, Protestant, Catholic and Dissenter' and a denunciation of 'the monster of religious bigotry'. There was also a stirring poem which must have puzzled most of the anorak-wearing, shaggy-headed teenagers it was meant to inspire:

> Men of the North, Thraldom who scorn
> Never shall bend the knee

Defiance we throw at the old foe
Freemen we wish to be

But the overall message was clear enough — that Ireland's problems would only cease with the removal of every trace of British power and the destruction of the six-county state. The Officials' policies by contrast seemed to most of the young brick and bomb throwers to be illogical to the point of treachery. One of the greater acts of folly committed by the Dublin leadership before the split had been to issue a statement declaring that the removal of Stormont and the substitution of direct rule from Westminster would be an undesirable development. This made good sense in view of their belief that a rooted British presence would delay the dawn of the cross-sectarian proletarian revolution that they were working towards, but in the climate of the times it seemed to many in the North that the last strands tethering the Goulding camp to reality had been cut.

The Officials stuck doggedly to the letter of their political prescription. They continued their involvement in the civil rights movement and came to dominate the executive committee. Initially at least, they tried to avoid confrontation with either troops or Protestants. Jim Sullivan's reaction to the Ballymurphy rioting of March had been to call on the crowds to disperse. Throughout 1970 the Belfast Officials persisted with Robin Hood gestures designed to dispel Protestant prejudice; agitating against development proposals, organising squats in unoccupied houses and at one stage hijacking buses and forcing the crews to operate them free as a gesture against a proposed fare increase.[17] None of this met with any notable success. Even the members seemed bored and meetings and rallies were sparsely attended.

New recruits who had joined in the expectation of some action often grew disillusioned with the low priority given to violence. In Derry Martin McGuinness's decision to leave the Officials after a few months was partly prompted by reports that members had been trying to blow up electricity pylons in the area with four ounces of gelignite. He and some companions, including Phil O'Donnell, took off on their own but being short of resources approached the Provisional leader in the city, Sean Keenan. Keenan was suspicious of them at first and told them they would not receive any weapons until they had joined the organisation. Eventually, a meeting was arranged between McGuinness, then still in his teens, Sean MacStiofain and his adjutant Daithi O'Connaill in Donegal and thereafter a supply of guns began to arrive.

McGuinness was impressed by the Provisional leadership's commitment to defending the Catholics against any repetition of the events of 1969 and the aggression they showed towards the Army and the RUC. He found MacStiofain a forceful and disciplined character. At the outset, however, the Derry Provisionals were poorly equipped, small in number and disorderly. The core of the organisation had been three middle-aged republicans, Joe Coyle, Tommy McCool and Tommy Carlin. They were all killed in June 1970 along with two of McCool's children when a bomb went off prematurely at his house in the Creggan. The remnants of the Carlin group continued to operate independently of McGuinness and his companions until internment was introduced in August 1971. The most experienced activist was Phil O'Donnell, a tough ex-British Army paratrooper who passed on his military training to the younger members.

Despite McGuinness's impatience with the methods of the Officials they remained the bigger and more effective of the rival wings until spring 1972.[18] Even in their most Utopian flights the Goulding group had retained a place for the use of violence in the Official's philosophy, but in a spare and considered way. In Belfast Sullivan and McMillen were faced with a great dilemma. If they struck a more aggressive attitude they would destroy whatever feeble links they had managed to forge with the Protestant working people in the city. If they remained passive they risked losing their remaining support among the Catholics to the pugnacious Provisionals. Both men felt bitterly that they were being forced into a competition of violence by their rivals. They were convinced, for example, that the Ballymurphy riots of April had to a large extent been provoked by the Provisionals and that the bombs they had been planting in shops and factories since the start of the year (there had been forty-four explosions by the end of June, almost all their work) could only antagonise the Army and inflame relations between them and the Catholics. They also accused the Provisional leadership of accepting into a movement that had always made such great play of its high ideals scores of youths whose main motivation was a desire for revenge against the Protestants and the police. After the split Sullivan claims the Officials stuck to the same stringent recruiting policies as always and that the Provisionals 'unfortunately went for quantity instead of quality with the result that without a shadow of doubt they finished up with a bunch of young lads who were in it just to fight Prods'.[5] Some of the local population of West Belfast were less than impressed by the quality of the new organisation:

When you heard who the new officer commanding the Provisionals in our district was you had to laugh [said a Falls Road businessman]. Many of them were the scum of the area. They had the political awareness of Glasgow Celtic football fans . . . The Officials were sharper, more decent, a better type of person.[19]

The bickering and mutual denunciation came to a head at Easter. Sullivan suggested a joint parade to mark the great day. McKee rejected the idea. The Officials went ahead with their own parade and were denounced for promoting confusion and bad feeling. In the Short Strand a few weeks later there were fistfights when Provisional IRA men tried to prevent Officials from selling their publication, the *United Irishman*.

As always in the IRA, personal differences quickly degenerated into murderous hostility. At the end of April a Provisional unit fired thirteen shots at a group of Officials in Andersonstown. Their target was Billy McMillen who was slightly wounded in the attack, revenge for his alleged 'knee-capping' of one of their men. The Officials responded by trying to kill Joe McCann. Some families who supported the

Provisionals in the Lower Falls took threats against them seriously enough to move out. A peace was patched together by the CCDC but it lasted only a few weeks and by mid-May there was more shooting in the Lower Falls.

Two events in summer ensured that the squabble developed into a full-scale feud. On Saturday 27 June fighting broke out between Catholic crowds and an Orange parade that passed by the edge of Ardoyne. During the trouble that followed three Protestants were shot dead. The news spread rapidly over the city and loyalists in East Belfast began burning houses in the Short Strand, the 6,000-strong Catholic enclave entirely surrounded by Protestant streets on the east bank of the Lagan. The news of the attack prompted McKee personally to undertake the defence of the district in an encounter that has become a republican legend. He and four or five other Provisionals took up positions in the churchyard of St Matthew's, a tall, steepled Victorian edifice overlooking the quarter, and spent the entire night sniping at the Protestant attackers. They killed three and McKee was wounded in the battle. Henry McIlhone, a volunteer from the Third Battalion (which had responsibility for Short Strand) who took a particularly vigorous role in the defence, was shot dead by a loyalist. According to one of those who took part, 'afterwards we had a feeling of victory, a feeling that revenge is sweet, but also of expectancy that this really was the start of something'.[20]

The Officials had characteristically mixed feelings about the episode. The vision of McKee and his men holed up in a Catholic churchyard blazing away at the Protestant hordes was about as far as one could get from the image of republicanism they were trying to project. Their action would also have the likely effect of bringing the Army down hard on the Catholic areas. On the other hand the Army had failed to provide protection for the Catholics whereas the Provisionals had come forward, something the local clergy and the CCDC were prepared to acknowledge when they invited the defenders to a thank-you tea.

On the Friday after the disturbances the Army mounted a retaliatory search, not among the back-to-back terraces of the

Short Strand but in a house in Balkan Street in the Lower Falls, the heartland of the Officials. There, as an informer told them they would, they discovered locked in a shed nineteen weapons all belonging to the Officials. The man of the house, however, had disappeared. The presence of the Army attracted a crowd of stone-throwers. Sullivan went about urging his men not to react, reasoning that the weapons had already been lost and there was no point in risking a further search and the discovery of the rest of their guns. One of the Officials present heard the sound of explosions, nail bombs (crude gelignite and shrapnel devices) thrown, he says, by the Provisionals:

> We heard the order issued for the British Army to move in and a decision was taken by the IRA that night to fight. The way we looked at it we were not going to put up our hands and let them take the weaponry. We didn't want the confrontation but we couldn't surrender.'

At the height of the fighting that evening the Army had 3,000 troops in the area supported by armoured vehicles and helicopters. At 10.00 pm, with a full-scale riot under way, the Army General Sir Ian Freeland ordered all the residents to stay indoors and a house-to-house search began. Sullivan had eighty or ninety men at his disposal. As the troops moved from street to street they came under a continuous barrage from rifles and automatics. In returning fire the troops killed four civilians and injured sixty and one man died after being run over by a Saracen armoured car in the Falls Road. The soldiers behaved with a new harshness (the result, it would be said later, of a conviction among the commanders that the new Conservative Government would back them to take a harder line) axeing down doors, ripping up floorboards, disembowelling chairs, sofas, beds, and smashing the garish plaster statues of the Madonna, the Infant of Prague, and Saint Bernadette that adorned the tiny front parlours.

A fog of CS gas, the product of some of the 1,600 canisters fired during the weekend, wafted around the terraces. The account of a Falls bar-owner gives some idea of the mixture of fear and surreal farce experienced by the inhabitants. He went out to remonstrate with some soldiers whose presence outside his pub was attracting the attention of rioters.

I went over to the soldier and told him to fuck off because my window might be broken. He told me to 'get back in or I'll shoot your fucking head off'. I was aghast at that. The curate from St Peter's pro-cathedral told me later that they weren't ordinary soldiers, they were Paras. My brother took me back into the pub and I started to shout 'Time!' The next thing there was a bang. The soldiers had disappeared and there was a hole in the ground. Somebody had thrown a hand-grenade. Everybody ordered carry-outs and headed for home. I locked the bar that night and took the TV set home with me. Later on as I was listening to the news I began to worry if the bar was all right so I rang the number and a British voice answered. 'The bar is secure,' the voice said, 'it has suffered no damage.' I went back the next day and I could not believe my eyes. The curtains were flying in the air, the antique mirror and the radio were smashed and the side door was broken in. All the drink had gone. The place was flooded because the beer taps had been left running. Then Gerry Fitt arrived with an NBC TV crew and stood up there in the bar and was interviewed.'[19]

When the search was complete the Army had rooted out fifty-two pistols, thirty-five rifles, six automatic weapons, fourteen shotguns, a hundred home-made bombs, a grenade, 250 pounds of explosives, 21,000 rounds of ammunition and eight two-way radio sets. According to the mythology of the Official IRA, the Provisionals deliberately ignited the violence by throwing hand-grenades during the rioting, then withdrew to leave the Officials to the mercy of the Army. The small Provisional unit in the area only fired a few rounds before leaving and there is no evidence that the units in the Clonard, which borders the Lower Falls to the north, did anything to come to the aid of their fellow republicans. Despite this, it was the Provisionals who reaped the benefit in the shape of more recruits.

The ill-feeling the incident (known as the Falls Curfew or, rather melodramatically, as the Rape of the Falls) provoked was added to the list of the Officials' grievances. By the end of the year there was more trouble. Once again it started off with brawls between the rival sellers of the *United Irishman* and the Provisionals' newspaper *Republican News*. At one point some Officials captured a teenage *Republican News* vendor and dropped concrete blocks on his hands.[10] The newspapers kept up a continuous barrage of mutual abuse, with the Officials ridiculing the Provisionals as rosary-rattling gangsters and the Provisionals painting them in return as communists and cowards.

In January 1971 both sides met to set up an arbitration procedure to try to minimise the friction, and a three-man neutral committee was established to adjudicate in disputes. The feud had developed beyond this stage. In the spring of 1971, the Provisionals wound the conflict to a new pitch by moving on to the offensive and actively seeking out soldiers to shoot. Sullivan and McMillen once again found themselves having reluctantly to struggle to retain their military credentials, goaded by the impatience of the younger recruits and by the insults of the Provisionals. When the Provisionals attacked British soldiers who were carrying out an arms search in Clonard, the Officials joined in, only to be rewarded with the jeers of the Provisionals who accused them of pitching up when the battle was practically over.[21] The Provisionals also claimed that their men in the Lower Falls had been warned not to fire on British Army patrols in the district, and issued a counter-threat that they would shoot Officials if any Provisional was harmed. Ironically, it was an attack by the Officials on troops billeted in the Henry Taggart Memorial Hall in Ballymurphy, on Friday 5 March, that brought the feud to a head.

The action was an independent operation set up by the Officials' unit in the area. According to one of the men who took part in the raid, the Moyard volunteers, unlike

161

their leaders, were 'nuts about fighting the Brits'.

> The Paras were in the Henry Taggart at that time. They
> just had sentry-boxes and weren't protected. There were
> 15 of us attacking that night and all we could hear were
> the screams. At one time the Brits tried to get out. They
> opened the hall door and stood there in the lights, ready
> to run but our guy with the Remington jumped into the
> middle of the road and blasted them. The sentry-box was
> a wooden one and he just cut that to ribbons.

This uncharacteristic aggression infuriated the Provisionals.
Ballymurphy was their territory and they claimed to have 200
members and auxiliaries there. The following day they captured the Officials' commander in Ballymurphy and pistol-
whipped him. This did not deter the Officials, who that evening
attempted to ambush the Paras as they left on patrol but were
driven away during an exchange of shots in which two of the
unit were wounded. During Sunday there was a series of
shootings, kidnappings and beatings, each outrage provoking
a counter-measure. On Monday evening a team of eight
Provisionals moved into Leeson Street looking for Jim Sullivan
and Billy McMillen. Sullivan they found in a pub, accompanied by his wife. Perhaps in view of her presence they
declined to shoot him there; but they sprayed the place with
petrol and set it alight. Sullivan and the rest of the clientele
escaped with their lives. The Provisionals moved on to another
pub, the Cracked Cup, where McMillen was drinking with
his cronies, and shot it up, again without harming their targets.

At some point McKee dispatched his men around Belfast
to round up at gunpoint as many of the Officials as they could
find and hold them hostage in houses around the city. Paddy
Kennedy and a number of local priests worked frantically to
get both sides to negotiate.

> McKee was threatening to execute them all and he was
> certainly capable of doing it. I went round all the houses
> they were being held in that night with Jim Sullivan in a

car to see the poor bastards, to plead with their captors to let them go. There were a lot of guns around and the Provos were getting very emotional about it all, asking 'Why should these fuckers be released?'[10]

The Officials' reaction was to gather some weapons and go after the Provisional team that had tried to shoot their leaders. At the same time McMillen ordered the assassination of eleven Provisional commanders in the city. They found the raiding-party in a house in Cyprus Street, in the middle of the Lower Falls, surrounded the place and called on the inhabitants to surrender. After an hour and a half one of the Provisionals, Frank Card, decided he had to leave to go to the other side of the city and Charlie Hughes, the commander of D Company in the Lower Falls, stepped outside the door to check that the coast was clear. As he did so he was illuminated by a street-lamp, presenting a clear target for one of the Officials waiting outside who promptly shot him dead.[22] The death of Hughes cooled the Officials' blood. He was young and daring and only two days before had led an attack on an Army communications and observation centre. He was popular with the local people and respected by both wings of the movement. Even the Officials grudgingly agreed that he and his unit had at least offered some assistance during their battle with the Army during the arms searches of the previous year.

This time the clergy and some neutral peace-makers were able to negotiate a ceasefire. McMillen had sent orders to halt the assassination squads. In one instance the message was too late. Early on Tuesday morning Tom Cahill, Joe's brother and a prominent Ballymurphy Provisional, was in the middle of his milk delivery round when he was approached by three armed men. As he realised what was happening, he scrabbled in his milk float for his pistol and magazine (kept separately in the mistaken belief that the possession of one or the other alone would not constitute an offence) while the men fired several shots into him, wounding him severely.[3] The local Provisionals who ran to help him managed to remove his gun before the police arrived, but not the cartridge clip, with the result that the unfortunate Cahill was later sentenced to two years for possessing ammunition. Such was the mood of sobriety in the wake of Hughes' death that the ceasefire survived the incident. The desire to avoid a revival of the vendetta was heightened by the Army's evident enjoyment of the events of the previous few days. While Leeson Street had echoed with the noise of Officials and Provisionals shooting at each other they had stood aside, issuing a press release stating that they would not interfere unless innocent people were hurt.[23] Both sides decided to bury their quarrel. The obituary notice of Charlie Hughes in *Republican News* diplomatically suppressed the precise circumstances of his death. For the time being both sides concentrated their efforts against the Army.

CHAPTER NINE

'This is War'

During 1970 the IRA campaign proceeded much as the Army Council had planned at the start of the year, with a steady succession of bombs aimed at 'economic targets'. There were 153 explosions in all, few by the standard of what was to come but enough to bring about a dramatic transformation in the day-to-day life of Northern Ireland. Visiting the centre of Belfast or of any town of any size in Northern Ireland now involved a tedious series of checkpoints, body-searches and vehicle searches. This was the effect the IRA had been aiming at. One of the purposes of the bombings, as Joe Cahill explained, 'was to spread the enemy's operations. In the early periods the British Army was able to cordon off ghetto areas and concentrate on them. The business areas and the loyalist areas they could leave alone, because there was no activity there. The IRA came up with the idea of bombing commercial targets to force the enemy to deploy more outside the ghettoes and draw them away. It was a defensive measure if you like.'[1]

By MacStiofain's thinking, the next stage of the campaign was for the IRA to move from defence to retaliation, and finally to take the offensive. In practice, according to one commander in Belfast, the IRA found it was 'responding to events rather than operating a planned campaign . . . The move to the offensive was not premeditated. It grew that way when the Army was given a free hand after the election and decided to get stuck into the Taigs [Catholics].'

The replacement of the Labour administration by a Conservative Government under Edward Heath in Britain in May 1970 was widely expected by Catholics to result in a relaxation of restraints on the behaviour of the military in Northern Ireland. In fact the Army's increasing toughness during 1970 was a product of frustration rather than deliberate policy. Since the disarming of the RUC (one of the post-riot reforms, soon rescinded), the Army had been charged with policing all rioting. By the middle of the year it was under attack both from the Catholics and Protestants of the ghettoes for its brutality and from Unionist politicians for its timidity and restraint.

The Army's perception of the situation, almost from the outset, had been that a purely military solution to the problem was impossible. Brigadier (later General Sir) Frank Kitson, the British Army's leading expert on counter-insurgency and a veteran of the Mau Mau emergency in Kenya, as well as Malaya and Cyprus, arrived in the Province in September 1970. He believed, as most senior officers did, that the traditional military response of simply restoring order and returning power to Stormont's own security forces was not feasible.

> The Army recognised that the trouble had arisen because there were injustices being perpetrated over the republican community. They thought that to merely knock the thing underground and wait for it to pop up in five years was a silly way of doing business, so they tried a totally different idea, which was to keep the two sides apart, try and put right their grievances and everyone would live happily ever after.[2]

Kitson believed that the main enemies of this policy were the IRA and the Protestant extremists, who saw any improvement of the Catholics' position as a diminution of their own. The Army's task, he believed, was to 'wean the Catholic population away from the terrorists' by a process of 'de-escalation and attrition':

> The de-escalation part was to influence the population to

166

support the moderate government line against the extremists of their own sort, by trying to explain and by trying to take direct action like community relations projects. The IRA's aim was the complete opposite. Attrition was arresting the actual extremists. That was our aim but the legal situation didn't give us a very good chance of actually getting the people who were directing the violence. It gave you the opportunity of arresting somebody who was taking part in a riot or a shooting incident but not the leaders, so in the end the IRA were making more headway than we were.

The legal difficulties facing the Army revived thoughts of reintroducing internment without trial, Stormont's traditional tool against republicanism. But, for the time being, most senior officers believed that the negative effects on the military's relations with the Catholics outweighed the benefits.[3] Kitson felt that the Army's difficulties were compounded by the fact that the 'Protestant community was always leaning on us'.

It would often be desirable, since the aim was to get the moderate Catholic population to support us, to turn a semi-blind eye to an incident and not pursue someone who had done something because if you did it would give them [the IRA] the opportunity to produce a riot. But if he had just come out of a Protestant area where he had just shot some-one or blown something up then the Protestants would go absolutely mad and say the security forces were not dealing with things, and start shouting and throwing their stuff around and if you were lucky you could get them to start throwing their stuff at you, and have an 'Us v Prods' thing. What you were trying to avoid at all costs was a 'Prods v Catholics' thing because that gave the IRA another leg up and they could say to the Catholics, 'You need us. We are your only defenders.'[2]

Whatever the military's good intentions, incidents like the 'Falls Curfew' and the house searches that were now a regular part of life in Catholic areas were steadily eroding the initial goodwill towards the military, and carrying the seeds of republicanism, which even in Belfast had been confined to a narrow clique, into what had hitherto been barren territory.

The Catholics' disenchantment was compounded by the slow pace of reform. Stormont was still alive and functioning in its old, obdurate style. In July 1970 it passed a law setting six-month mandatory sentences for anyone arrested on the scene of a riot, a measure which the Northern Ireland Attorney General Basil Kelly admitted would inevitably give rise to 'harsh cases'. At the end of July Freeland's threat that rioters were liable to be shot on sight was finally acted on when 19-year-old Danny O'Hagan was killed with a bullet through the chest during a riot in the New Lodge Road in North Belfast. On 11 August the IRA retaliated, not in Belfast but in Crossmaglen, down in South Armagh.

A Provisional unit operating out of Navan, in the Republic, planted a booby-trapped car in an obtrusive position on one of the roads leading out of the town. Two officers who arrived from the barracks to inspect it wrenched open the car door and were blown to pieces. This act of revenge produced at least some equivocation in the minds of local people, for afterwards a crowd of some sixty Catholics knelt near the shattered car and recited the rosary. Despite this action, the Provisional leadership in Belfast and Dublin were in no hurry to begin mounting attacks on members of the security forces and the two unfortunate RUC men were the only uniformed victims of the troubles in 1970.

One reason for holding back was that the shortage of weapons continued to be a problem for both wings of the IRA until autumn 1970. Many a new recruit returned from training to find no gun available and so resumed rioting duties. Arms had been arriving from America since the start of the year but initially they formed only a trickle. They came in threes and fours, packed in false-bottomed cases in air and sea freight, or smuggled in by Irish-American sympathisers among the aircrews that stopped over at Shannon Airport. There were IRA supporters aboard the *QE2* and in late 1971 seven rifles and a grenade were discovered in a search of the vessel when she docked at Cork Harbour. Most of these weapons were elderly. There were Thompsons, dubbed 'rattleboxes' because of the din they made, which had retained a place in the IRA's affections since they first arrived in Ireland at the tail-end of the civil war in 1922, despite the fact that they were heavy, slow-firing and prone to jamming. Many of the guns were of Second World War vintage, like the M1 Carbine and 'greasegun', the standard American infantry sub-machine-gun which, when fitted with a silencer, was known as the 'spitting dummy'. There were Garand semi-automatic rifles, bolt-action Springfields and Lee-Enfields, thousands of which had been sold to American dealers as hunting rifles when the US Army modernised its infantry weapons in the late fifties. This motley arsenal was augmented by the odd standard NATO issue SLR stolen from the British Army. Finding ammunition posed a formidable difficulty. Almost every weapon was of a different calibre. The Thompson took a .45 bullet, the M1s and Garands .300 and the Lee-Enfield .303.

The first attempts to assemble a large shipment of identical weapons and ammunition had had mixed results. In the spring of 1970 John Kelly, the Belfast Provisional, negotiated a delivery of 500 pistols and 180,000 rounds of ammunition from Vienna to Dublin airport, but they were useless for the long-range sniping of urban guerrilla warfare. The situation changed in August with the arrival of a huge consignment of weapons from America. It had been put together by five Irish Americans from Philadelphia (who were later prosecuted) and took them six months to organise. The weapons were mostly Armalites, which could have been designed specially for the Provisionals' needs. They were light — seven pounds — yet had adequate stopping power, and were easily concealed when equipped with a folding butt, fitting, it was frequently claimed, into a box of cornflakes. The IRA's long (though now superseded) affection for them dates from this period. So far 420 guns from this shipment have been recovered.[4]

Paying for the guns was difficult. The initial willingness of Catholic businessmen to contribute money for the defence of their co-religionists had worn off with the emergence of the Provisionals, and by the spring the IRA was forced to appeal at a republican rally in Milltown cemetery, West Belfast for funds to buy arms. Their difficulties were eased to some extent by donations from Saor Eire, a tiny far-left republican splinter group which had parted from the movement in the sixties. In the spring of 1970 its members began a series of ideologically inspired robberies. On 7 May, for example, they made off with a £14,000 payroll being delivered in Strabane, County Tyrone. It was not long before the Provisionals adopted this method of fund-raising themselves.

To manufacture bombs required no such elaborate effort. Industrial explosives like gelignite were relatively easy to steal from the limestone quarries of the Glens of Antrim and from the reservoirs under construction in Fermanagh and Tyrone. Later, when the gelignite supply dried up, IRA 'engineers' discovered that it was a simple matter to mix up a bulky but highly destructive compound from a fertiliser sold all over the island. In line with the IRA's tactic of destroying 'economic targets' and property of a symbolic nature, such as council offices, electricity pylons, broadcasting transmitters and anything connected with the military or the police, the first bombs to be made were incendiaries.

In Derry they invented the Durex bomb. Sulphuric acid, sealed in a phial of candlewax, was placed inside a contraceptive sheath which in turn was placed in a large, thick envelope with a quantity of sodium chlorate, an explosive chemical used as weedkiller. The bomber walked to the target, placed the package and squeezed the phial to release the acid which ate through the sheath and ignited the chemicals. It is said that when Sean MacStiofain was asked while visiting the North to transport some contraceptives back to the South for use in training sessions he refused on the grounds that they were immoral objects.

The success of the military in defusing bombs (nearly a third of the 1,022 devices planted in 1971 were neutralised) led to the development of the anti-handling device. The initial model was crude but devastating, an arrangement using a salt-cellar and a small ball-bearing which when dislodged by a sharp movement fell to complete a circuit and detonate the explosive. It claimed its first victim when a soldier tried to disconnect a bomb left outside an Orange hall in Castlerobin, near Belfast. Bomb-testing was often a matter of the crudest empiricism. The device that killed Michael Kane, a young father of five who was blown up while attempting to destroy an electricity pylon in Belfast, was exploded by a timer based on a simple clothes-peg. It caused the Provisionals to suspend further experiments in that direction.

McKee and his staff never attempted at any point to formulate a long-term strategy to conduct the new campaign. Their response had been a return to IRA traditional practices. According to Cahill no formal decision was taken over the legitimacy of shooting soldiers – 'military targets were always on'. By opening up on the Army they were simply resuming hostilities against anyone in the Queen's uniform in a war that they had never declared over. To Cahill and his middle-aged comrades the violence was as justifiable as that used by their predecessors against the Black and Tans. The parallel was frequently alluded to. The IRA in 1919 had concentrated on eroding the morale and will to fight of the British Army through a succession of tangential encounters – ambushes, assassinations, the planting of mines. They were also encouraged, as MacStiofain had been, by the success of nationalist guerrilla groups in Cyprus and Kenya in ending British rule and this initially coloured their political thinking. Despite the marked differences in political situations, the Provisional IRA felt that in time they could do the same.

Another reason for holding back, apart from their lack of military preparedness, was the fact that the Provisionals were unconvinced that they had sufficient support among the Catholics of Belfast to sustain them in a campaign. The repeated warnings issued by the IRA during 1970 against fraternising with the Army showed that the Catholic alienation from the military was far from complete. As late as May 1971 an article in *Republican News* under the headline 'We Repeat — Don't Fraternise!' observed that

> the people of Ardoyne have been provoked, ill-treated and intimidated almost beyond human endurance. They were given the 'full treatment' by the British Army. Yet according to press reports a deputation from the district wasted three hours recently with a British Army officer who had requested 'co-operation' from the local residents . . . It is important that we realise that the British soldiers in the Six Counties are part of the armed forces controlled by the British Government.[5]

To press the point home the Provisionals had, since the autumn of 1970, been taking measures against those who befriended the soldiers. Housewives who persisted in giving out cups of tea found their homes daubed with slogans. Young girls foolish enough to socialise with off-duty squaddies had their heads roughly razored, the traditional punishment for *collaboration horizontale*, and were tied to lamp-posts with badly-lettered placards announcing their crime around their necks. The new volunteers claimed to find this work distasteful, but they did it all the same.

The Provisionals were quick to take for themselves the role of the moral guardians of the ghetto. On a Sunday morning in January 1971 four young men were tarred and feathered in front of a curious congregation making their way to Mass in the Falls Road. A statement by the republican press centre warned that in future the IRA would be taking responsibility for stamping out crimes like drug-peddling and burglary. In October 1970 an editorial in *Republican News* denounced the opening in Belfast of the Paradise Club under the Army's auspices:

> A discotheque they call it. A place of iniquity would be a better description. The blatant display of sex slogans — 'Viva Sex' being one, the life-sized paintings of scantily-clad girls . . . all these and more do nothing other than

172

confirm that the Paradise Discotheque is only following a long-established British Army practice of assuring its soldiers easy access to pleasure at the expense of the local girls.

Despite the hazards a surprising number of romances were forged between Catholic ghetto girls and the soldiers. The sister of Danny Morrison, who became the publicity director of Sinn Fein, married a British soldier who used to drop by at the family home in the Mid Falls while on patrol.[4]

The Provisionals' strictures were disingenuous to say the least. During 1970 and up to February 1971 Billy McKee, Frank Card, Leo Martin and Liam and Kevin Hannaway had been meeting senior Army officers in the mutually convenient role of 'community leaders' to discuss the policing of the ghetto and particularly how to control rioting in the Ballymurphy area, which the IRA was unable to control. There was nothing secret about the meetings. The local battalion commander would visit one or other of the five every few days in his home or in the pub.[6]

According to 'McShane', the leadership actively held volunteers back from attacking the Army. After the Falls Road Curfew, he said 'we wanted to go out and shoot Brits but we weren't allowed to.' As well as the concern of McKee and his staff about the consequences for themselves and for the Catholics if they launched a proper shooting campaign, it is clear that the vital consideration was the reaction of local people. By the late summer of 1970 the Army had undoubtedly made itself unpopular in West Belfast, but not to the point where the Catholics wanted them dead. 'There was no way at that time that the IRA could have shot Brits or policemen,' said Danny Morrison. 'They couldn't have sold it. The reaction of people would have been "God Almighty, did we produce people who are capable of doing that?"'[7]

None the less, a process was under way by which the perception of a significant proportion of the population of the ghettoes would eventually coincide with that of the Provisionals and they would come to see the Army as their enemies. The

IRA's plausibility as defenders of the community was enhanced by the change in the role of the CCDC. During 1970 it had gradually become a spokesbody for the Catholics rather than a defensive organisation. For them to have carried on as such would have required the indefinite extension of the atmosphere of fear and high drama that brought them into being in the first place. With the arrival of the Army, these conditions were only intermittently reproduced. And as 'Sean Donnelly' found when he attended a meeting of the CCDC, most of the respectable types who belonged were content in the end to leave things to the military, though they continued to issue denunciations of the Army's tendency to search the Catholic quarters while sparing the Protestants. As a result, then, a significant section of the working-class Catholic population of West Belfast began looking to the IRA for protection. When Dr William Philbin, the Catholic Bishop of Down and Connor (the diocese covering Belfast), gave a sermon in Ballymurphy in January 1971 condemning violence, declaring that members of secret organisations were not bound to obey immoral orders and in fact were 'bound to disobey them and have no more to do with the organisations which issue such orders,' a group of Ballymurphy women marched to his house to protest.[8] None the less a smaller number of Catholics expected the Provisionals to avenge brutalities committed by the soldiers, and according to Joe Cahill 'we were always under pressure to hit back. After [O'Hagan] died people were asking "When, when, when?" '

The attacks on soldiers began in earnest at the start of 1971 though individuals had taken pot shots before that, in defiance of the leadership's wishes. On 3 January, a foggy Sunday, an RUC patrol making its way through Ardoyne was fired on by an IRA sniper. A month later, troops searching houses in the Clonard district were confronted with a crowd of angry women and girls and a riot broke out. That evening the IRA opened up on Army posts in the Crumlin Road, and in an unusual extension of their normal operations, at Cadogan Park, a genteel stretch of the South Belfast suburbs. The following day the Army called a press conference at which Major

General Anthony Farrar-Hockley named five men — Billy McKee, Frank Card, Leo Martin and Kevin and Liam Hannaway — as having been behind the recent rioting, the same men who had been secretly meeting with the military. He went on to defend the arms searches and declared that they would go on despite the opposition. There were more army raids that evening and Ardoyne and Clonard were sealed off with road-blocks; and there was rioting in the city throughout that evening and the following day.

The Army's uncompromising tone was partly caused by a belief that a showdown with the Provisionals was now inevitable. Farrar-Hockley had received an intelligence report from the Army Headquarters at Lisburn, ten miles south of Belfast, which predicted that at long last a full-scale shooting campaign against the Army was being discussed.[6] In theory taking the decision to kill soldiers was not necessary. According to 'McShane', 'there was no question that we would eventually go on the offensive. It was just a question of when the time was ripe.'[9] Approval to do so had been granted at the start of 1971 by the Army Council in Dublin, in the belief that the Catholics were sufficiently alienated by the Army's behaviour to tolerate the escalation in violence.

Once the news came through there was considerable rivalry among the Belfast units over who would be the first to be blooded. On the night of Friday 5 February 1971 there was serious rioting in Ardoyne. A Saracen armoured car was hit by a nail-bomb and its petrol tank set on fire. In the panic that followed the troops shot a young Sinn Fein stone-thrower, Barney Watts, dead. One of the Ardoyne IRA men decided to go for help:

> I went up to the 'Bone' [a small Catholic enclave off the Crumlin Road] to ask James Saunders, who was the OC [Officer Commanding] there to open up a second front. His last words to me were 'I'll do my best' and a few hours later he was dead. Then I went down to New Lodge to get them to do the same. Billy Kelly wasn't there so the

quartermaster, Billy Reid, was prevailed upon to do it. At first he didn't have the gear but then a Sterling appeared and a blast bomb as well. At one stage he was going to throw the bomb because he didn't have the experience [to use the sub-machine-gun] but then he took the Sterling and emptied the magazine at the soldiers.[10]

Reid hit and killed Gunner Robert Curtis, a 20-year-old with the 94th locating regiment of the Royal Artillery, who became the first soldier to die since the Army was called in. Reid, 23, a keen cyclist and boxer, was to survive another three months. On 15 May he was part of a team that ambushed a mobile Army patrol in the centre of the city and was killed in the ensuing shoot-out. His comrades noted with superstitious awe that he died in Curtis Street.

The day that Gunner Curtis died the Provisionals lost their first member to a British Army bullet. James Saunders, the OC of the 'Bone', a 22-year-old bakery worker from F Company, was shot dead in the Old Park area of West Belfast. Catholics from the 'Bone' had been fighting with Protestants from Louisa Street and both sides had gunmen backing them up. As Saunders was exchanging fire with loyalist gunmen he was shot by a British patrol — from behind, according to Provisional legend. These deaths were followed by a new wave of rioting on Sunday and Monday with the Army coming under fire in Leeson Street, Ardoyne and New Lodge, where an Army scout car crushed a five-year-old girl to death. In the following days the thud of IRA bombs began to grow familiar around the city, twelve on the night of 9 February, eight in the Falls Road in the early hours of Saturday.

The notional guidelines to spare civilian lives began to be forgotten or ignored. A woman bringing a child home from school was seriously injured by a gelignite bomb. IRA units outside the city joined in the destruction. In County Tyrone five men in a Land-Rover driving up to a BBC transmitter on Brougher Mountain were blown up and killed by a landmine. In Holywood, County Down, an explosion shattered a pub, injuring nine people. On the night of Saturday 27 February alone cars and buses were burned in the Markets area of Belfast, two policemen were shot dead when the Provisionals opened up on a joint patrol at Alliance Avenue, and more policemen were injured by gunfire in the Glen Road and by a bomb placed at the door of Ligoniel police station. The attack at Alliance Avenue had been deliberately set up by A company of the Third Battalion who fired a garage to lure the patrol there.

In these first few weeks of 1971 the Provisional IRA arrived at its destructive maturity. They began to appear openly in distinctive kit, a makeshift uniform of army surplus combat jacket and beret or balaclava helmet. It immediately took on a symbolic power. Women dressed in camouflage jackets and berets to demonstrate over the arrests of republicans and thirty women paraded in berets at a meeting to protest against the Special Powers Act.

The inability of McKee and his staff to control the offensive against the Army was demonstrated by an incident on the night of Tuesday 9 March. In the lull following the Leeson Street feuding between the two wings, which resulted in the death of Charlie Hughes, three Provisionals from the Ardoyne, including a prominent member, Paddy McAdorey, went drinking in Mooney's Bar in the centre of the city. There they got into conversation with three young off-duty soldiers of the Royal Highland Fusiliers, Joseph McCaig, 18; his younger brother John, 17; and 23-year-old Douglas McCaughey. One of the Provisionals had been in the British Army, so conversation was easy. After a while they moved on to another pub before the IRA men suggested that they go to a party where they promised there would be women. The group crammed into cars, and drove west through the city climbing the hill towards Ligoniel. On a deserted stretch of road high above Belfast the Provisionals stopped and the three Fusiliers climbed out, still clutching half-empty beer glasses, to relieve themselves at the verge. As they did so their companions shot each of them in the back of the head. The two brothers were found lying on top of each other. McCaughey was propped up by the embankment, his beer glass in his hand. Despite the fact that two of the perpetrators were later questioned about the murders, no one was ever charged. The two who were interrogated went on to make reputations as enthusiastic killers. McAdorey survived a few more months before being shot dead on 9 August in a fight with troops in Jamaica Street in Ardoyne.

Revulsion at these assassinations caused the Provisionals to issue an immediate denial of responsibility. The action had breached the IRA's rules of engagement concerning soldiers which stated that they should only be attacked when on duty. There was something particularly repulsive about the way the young Fusiliers were tricked to their death by promises of a good time. It was only a couple of years before the technique was in use again. In March 1973 four NCOs were persuaded by some girls to attend a 'party' in the Antrim Road. When they arrived three of them were shot dead and the fourth seriously wounded. From the outset it was clear that the rules governing the conduct of the campaign, solemnly laid down by the GHQ in Dublin, were infinitely elastic and anyone breaking them had little cause to worry about disciplinary action.

The Fusiliers' killers received no punishment and their actions were put down to an excess of enthusiasm. But the Provisionals retained a brutal code of discipline for offences that threatened themselves. From the outset 'touts', as informers are called, could expect death if they were proved or strongly suspected of passing information. The Provisionals had carried out their first execution in January 1971. The victim was John Kavanagh who had ignored warnings to avoid contact with the police, and who was sentenced in his absence by an IRA 'court'. They picked him up as he was walking to work one morning, drove him down to the banks of the Blackstaff — an industrial sink that winds through the back streets of West Belfast — and made him kneel on the ground. A hood was placed over his head and he was shot, first through the left nostril, then through the back of the head. This practice was later modified to a single bullet in the back of the head.

The arrest of McKee on 15 April 1971 released the final

restraints on the new recruits who had been pressing for action. He was picked up with Frank Card and charged under the Explosive Substances Act. He was replaced at the instruction of MacStiofain and O'Bradaigh in Dublin by Joe Cahill, a less remote figure who was inclined to give the volunteers their head. The politicians who operated at the perilous conjunction between the Provisionals, the ordinary Catholics and the State had been able to do business with McKee. Cahill was something else. He appeared unreflecting, indifferent to the rapid escalation of violence. Paddy Kennedy felt that with McKee's passing the last chance of keeping the Provisionals under control had gone. 'If he had remained the bombing campaign would never have properly got off the ground.'[11]

That spring, 'Sean Donnelly' gave up his job as an electrical engineer and turned his skills to manufacturing bombs. Later in the year he was promoted to engineer of the First Battalion after Terry McDermott − another electrician − was killed, blown up by one of his own bombs when planting it, complete with an anti-handling device, at a Lisburn electricity substation. In Belfast there was plenty to do. By the middle of the year the city was routinely thrown into chaos by incendiaries.

By 7 May there had been 136 explosions in Northern Ireland, more than one a day. The day after this statistic was released fifteen incendiaries were found in Anderson and McAuley's, Belfast's answer to Harrods, and thirteen in the Co-op. The following day another six were found. Only a few of these devices actually caught fire, but by next month the Provisionals were having more success and bombs planted over a weekend in several stores in the city centre went off, gutting one large shop completely. The violence was now being augmented by the Officials. The propaganda successes and popularity with young Catholics that the Provisionals were winning with their aggressive tactics forced Goulding and his colleagues into a rather stagey belligerence.

In July, MacGiolla announced that their policy was now 'defence and retaliation', in effect bringing them into line with the Provisionals' decision to start shooting soldiers. The first

179

ambush in Belfast had already taken place on 22 May, independently of Dublin, when a patrol of Royal Green Jackets went to help a patrol of military police who were being stoned by a gang of youths in the Markets. The youths fell back to a prearranged position where Joe McCann and a group of Officials were waiting for the soldiers. In the ensuing fight a 25-year-old corporal, Robert Bankier, was killed when a bullet severed an artery in his thigh, fired, it is believed, by McCann. The Provisionals did not take long to extend their range of targets. In March the offices of the Official Unionist Party in Glengall Street were blasted with gelignite and later three sticks of gelignite were found in the garden of William Craig, the former Minister of Home Affairs at Stormont and a Unionist hard-liner. Their attacks suggested that another republican convention was about to be breached. Non-sectarianism was theoretically a fundamental principle of republicanism and this inevitably imposed restrictions on what violence could be regarded as legitimate. In the border campaign care had been taken to attack only members of the RUC or the 'B' Specials. The fact that most of these men were Protestants was dismissed as irrelevant. They were wearing the uniform of an occupying force. The Wolfe Tone philosophy, that Irishmen were Irishmen whether Protestant, Catholic or Dissenter also ruled out attacks on Protestant civilians or Protestant politicians. The activities of the Provisionals against loyalist mobs such as in the battle around St Matthew's Church in the Short Strand in June 1970 could be rationalised as self-defence. Cold-blooded and deliberate attacks on Protestant politicians and Protestant individuals was another matter.

During the summer of 1971 a succession of attacks began that could only be construed as sectarian. Just before midday on Monday 24 May, as the first drinkers were assembling in the Mountain View Tavern, a pub frequented by loyalists at the top of the Shankill Road, a bomb was thrown at the building. Several people were seriously injured in the explosion, which was denounced by the Officials as the work of 'sectarian bigots'. In an earlier attack a bomb was placed

180

in a hardware shop in the Protestant Albert Bridge Road, setting fire to a flat upstairs and killing the mother of John McKeague, Chairman of the Shankill Defence Association and organiser of the loyalists during the August 1969 riots.

The non-sectarian principle meant little to many of the new recruits. Indeed some of Donnelly's intake 'joined because they hated Protestants', although he says that 'this feeling later wore off'. The actions of the Protestant murder gangs in the following years ensured that sectarian assassinations became part of the Provisionals' routine activities. The older republicans like McKee were sensitive to charges of sectarianism and *Republican News* frequently carried fraternal messages addressed to 'Our Protestant Irishmen' pointing out the great tradition of Protestant republicanism, starting with Wolfe Tone and the United Irishmen, to which Belfast in particular had generously contributed.

Cahill's period as Officer Commanding the Belfast Brigade lasted from April 1971 until shortly after his internment in August. It was, he felt, 'a nice, smooth run. The thing dovetailed nicely. Operations came on tap. There was a slow build-up and there were no great problems and it was fairly clean.'[1] At this point, he says, there were about a hundred active service volunteers with another thousand in a supporting role. Armed with a .45 pistol and virtually untroubled by the police or the Army (after August 1970 he had moved house and neither the RUC Special Branch nor Army Intelligence knew where he lived) he made the rounds of the city. 'I made a practice of visiting all the areas every day and if I didn't then the second-in-command would do it for me.' Every day there would be a staff meeting at a different 'call house', usually in the Andersonstown area, loaned by a sympathiser, where operations were discussed and planned. Cahill claims that the director of operations of each company was in constant consultation with him over proposed attacks, none of which he ever recalls rejecting, and that strict criteria were observed in each action. Snipers, for example, were meant to engage the enemy in open ground and when there were no civilians around. The prime target was the Army but the RUC would do. A snipe was generally a solo effort (unlike the three-man operations that the Provisionals later favoured) with a single shot being fired before making off. Cahill prided himself on going along on the odd operation.[1]

The attacks on policemen and soldiers grew more and more reckless. In May an IRA man flung a suitcase full of gelignite into the joint RUC-Army post in the Springfield Road in Belfast, injuring twenty-two people and killing an Army sergeant who threw himself on to the bomb in an attempt to protect some children. A few weeks later a duffle-bag stuffed with gelignite was thrown over the back wall. The homes of two senior Special Branch men were wrecked by explosions. By the middle of July, ten soldiers had been killed since the start of the year. To 'Donnelly' and his fellow young Provisionals, ambushing soldiers was regarded as preferable to merely planting bombs:

> Initially you would be satisfied with a good bomb but then you realised that to be effective you must stiff more Brits − that is the attitude − to the point where the Brits leave. Obviously you have to bear that objective in mind, otherwise you would become psychopathic. I don't see the man, only the uniform. It seems to me that it is just a job that has to be done and someone has to do it.[12]

The First Battalion's 'first big job' of 1971 was an ambush in Andersonstown. A group of them crouched behind a low brick wall in Shaw's Road and opened up with a Garand carbine on a Paratroop patrol as it passed along the Andersonstown Road. One of the Paras was killed. 'Donnelly' remembered it as 'a great morale-booster. The Paras were a rough bunch.'[12]

In Derry the violence was much more subdued. The Army's behaviour had not provoked the same reaction as in Belfast and IRA activity was correspondingly limited. Before July only one soldier had been injured in a shooting incident. This relative quiet ended with the shooting of two Catholic youths, Seamus Cusack and Desmond Beattie. According to Martin

McGuinness, the incident marked the 'rejection of the British Army and the establishment of the republican base in Derry'.[13] Cusack was shot in the early hours of Thursday 8 July during the fourth successive night of rioting in Derry. He was bundled into a car and driven over the border to Letterkenny Hospital in Donegal, where he subsequently died. The decision − which may have cost Cusack his life − was taken because both the local people and republicans felt that if captured, the Army would attempt to charge Cusack with a terrorist offence. In fact neither he nor Beattie, who was shot in the inevitable riots that followed later in the day, were members of the IRA. The Provisionals in the city retaliated with their first determined engagement against the Army. A group armed with Thompson sub-machine-guns opened up on soldiers in Bishop Street, hitting one of them in the head. The Army post at Bligh's Lane came under repeated attack.

The deaths had a dramatic effect on IRA recruiting. The Army's claim that Cusack had been aiming a rifle and Beattie had been about to throw a nail-bomb were believed by no one. Three days after the deaths, Maire Drumm, a member of the Sinn Fein executive, told a mass rally organised by the Provisionals in Derry: 'It is a waste of time shouting "Up the IRA!" The important thing is to join.'[14] Eamonn McCann noted that 'afterwards applicants formed a queue.'[15]

In Belfast a soldier on guard duty was shot dead by a sniper. A statement issued by the Provisionals took responsibility for the killing and warned that 'further retaliatory action' would be taken for the 'murder of two citizens of Derry last week'.[16]

Since the reappearance of the IRA, pressure had been growing to bring out the traditional weapon against outbreaks of republican violence − detention without trial. The Northern Ireland Prime Minister, Brian Faulkner, who had replaced James Chichester-Clark in March, had initially been opposed to the introduction of internment, but was eventually convinced of its value by hard-liners in his own cabinet. Internment had been invoked repeatedly by both governments in Ireland since the island was divided in 1922. The Official IRA came to believe that the junior home affairs minister at Stormont, John Taylor, had played a crucial part in resurrecting it, and made an attempt on his life, the first time in the conflict when republicans had tried to assassinate a politician. Taylor recalled:

I was back home in Armagh City that day in my father's office. I normally parked my car at the front door but that day I couldn't get into my usual place because it was taken by a car with a Southern Irish registration number. I said 'It's very odd,' but thought no more about it.

Normally I would leave the office about 5.00 pm but on that particular day . . . it was about 5.30 when I came out. I went round the corner, got into the car and turned on the ignition. There was an almighty roar that made me think that I had been booby-trapped and a bomb had gone off and my left leg was paralysed immediately . . . my left leg was full weight on the accelerator and the engine was roaring like mad and I couldn't in any way release it. I had lost all power . . . Then I realised that I wasn't bombed at all but that I was being shot. At that stage blood was gushing out and I collapsed back into the seat with the result that out of the seventeen bullets only seven went through my body. Five went through my head and jaw and the other ten went past my nose and through the far door and that was it. I didn't see who shot me. I didn't feel any pain but I was certainly nearly unconscious.[17]

The assassination team was in fact led by Joe McCann but the Officials' intelligence was wide of the mark. Taylor, although an enthusiast for internment, was on holiday in Europe when the decision was taken and had only learned the news when driving home from Dublin airport.

Although Faulkner was persuaded that the time for internment had come, the Army was less convinced. Neither the Commander of Land Forces, General Sir Harry Tuzo or the Chief of the General Staff, Sir Michael (later Lord) Carver was against internment in principle and 'felt it was bound to come'.[3] But they were extremely cautious about the timing and the width of the operation. Brigadier Frank Kitson felt that 'if it had been done at the right moment and for a good reason and in the right way, then it might have been extremely beneficial. You could have even used internment to cheer up the Protestants while seeking a major concession on the Catholic side — getting rid of Stormont — and introducing direct rule.'[2] The chief danger in the Army's eyes was that if the operation was badly conceived it would provoke yet more hostility among the Catholics and increase support for the IRA.

The violence that followed the shootings of Cusack and Beattie in Derry on 8 July 1971 supplied the clinching argument in the debate. At a cabinet meeting on 3 August at which Tuzo repeated the Army's misgivings, Faulkner insisted that internment would have to come now. After a long discussion in London the Prime Minister, Edward Heath, agreed.

The probability that internment would be introduced had been in the air since 1970. It required no elaborate legal preparations. The legislation to detain without trial already existed in the shape of the Special Powers Act.

Republicans had begun a pre-emptive campaign, predicting its introduction at the start of 1971, and there had been rallies in the summer to protest about it in advance. Both IRAs were alerted to the fact that something was on the way on 23 July when the Army raided houses all over the Province and detained 110 men for questioning. Almost all of them were connected to the Official IRA or the Republican Clubs and in Belfast only two Provisionals were arrested. One theory for the onesidedness of the raids was that the Army believed that the Officials possessed lists of their rivals, which they needed in order to carry out the main operation, which would be aimed at the Provisionals.[18] The Provisionals were further alerted to the impending swoop by a woman sympathiser who worked for the Government of Northern Ireland at Stormont. Forty-eight hours beforehand, Joe Cahill and Sean MacStiofain travelled around the Province warning every unit of Provisionals that internment was imminent.[1]

Operation Demetrius, as the Army codenamed it, went into action at 4.00 am on Tuesday 10 August. In the Belfast ghettoes men were dragged from their beds half-clothed, roughly bound with plastic twine and bundled into vans to be driven away to Girdwood Barracks in the north of the city.

Much of the initial operation was inept. Of the 342 men arrested around the Province 116 were released within forty-eight hours. Among those trawled in were ancient and long-retired republicans, youthful revolutionaries from the People's Democracy, trade unionists, respectable middle-class civil rights activists, a drunk picked up at a bus stop and several people held on mistaken identity. A number of people on the Army list turned out to be dead. The squad who called at the Leeson Street home of Billy McMillen found he had already departed so they arrested the editor of the *United Irishman* who was staying there. John McGuffin, a republican lecturer who was among those picked up, estimated that of the original number seized only 150 were connected with the IRA. 'Of the 160 men in Crumlin [jail] no more than 80 had anything to do with the IRA and of these only four were senior officers [none of them the top men].'[19]

Because of the Officials' political activities their identities were better known to the authorities and, proportionately, they suffered more losses than the Provisionals. On the Official side, McMillen, Sullivan and McCann had all fled by the time the Army came for them, McMillen to Dundalk where he lay low for several months, much to the derision of the Provisionals. Of those held, most were involved primarily on the political side of the organisation, chairmen of local Republican Clubs or members of the area executive committees. In Belfast almost every leading Provisional IRA member escaped the net, and by their own account only fifty-six volunteers were held in the whole Province.[20]

The Provisionals' brigade, battalion and company leaders had either left the city or moved to another house for they virtually all survived the round-up. Since the start of the year the Provisionals had been organising a skeleton force that could keep the organisation going if internment took a swathe out of the ranks. These members were nicknamed 'unknowns', 'Sixty-niners' with no republican background and therefore less likely to be known to the Special Branch and less in danger of being picked up. For the same reason the 'unknowns' were forbidden to take part in operations inside their own areas and would move to another part of town to shoot or bomb.

In Derry they were less fortunate. The arrests removed nearly every active Provisional in the city, including Sean Keenan and Phil O'Donnell, leaving only three or four members. The control of the organisation, such as it was, passed to a little-known middle-aged republican named Griffin, but after a fortnight MacStiofain intervened and gave the command to Martin McGuinness.

Part of the reason for the overall failure of the operation was the quality of the Army's information. They were operating with a list supplied to them by the RUC Special Branch. At some levels the Special Branch's intelligence was excellent. Throughout the sixties a high-ranking informer in the IRA in Dublin fed them a stream of accurate reports of the impending split.[4] As Brigadier Kitson found when he tried to improve the flow of information to the soldiers on the ground, there was a strong reluctance on the RUC's side to part with it. The Chief of the General Staff Sir Michael Carver also felt that the police had 'pushed up the list to the large number they produced and were encouraged to do so for Stormont's political reasons.'[3] Despite the claim by the Army and the Northern Ireland Government that the operation had seriously hurt the IRA, most senior Army officers regarded it privately as a disaster. Kitson 'said very quickly afterwards that this was done at the wrong moment in the wrong way for the wrong reasons. But that wasn't much help. You've got to get the right people but instead they arrested the people who weren't really important.'[2]

That the exercise was a failure was swiftly and dramatically illustrated within hours. In the next thirty-six hours, seventeen people were killed, and in Derry and Belfast hundreds of houses were destroyed by fire. In the Catholic areas of Belfast crowds hijacked buses and cars and turned them into burning barricades from behind which they stoned and petrol-bombed the police. Behind and among them the Provisionals and Officials, acting for the most part without commanders, combined forces and kept up a steady fire against the troops.

In Ardoyne, where the crack of roof slates on the burning houses alternated with the sound of small-arms fire, Paddy McAdorny, the leading Provisional in the area after the removal of Francy Maguigan and Pat Mailey (two of the few senior members to be lifted), was shot dead while firing on an Army observation post. Later his body was laid in state in the Holy Cross primary school, complete with IRA military guard of honour. The following day at nightfall a squad of Officials led by Joe McCann took over Inglis's bakery in the Markets in an attempt to tie down the Army to let remaining IRA men escape, and opened fire on the soldiers from behind blazing bread vans. The encounter produced one of the few photographs to convey the excitement for a young man of belonging to the IRA at that time. McCann is romantically silhouetted in front of a flaming vehicle, an M1 carbine in his hand.

In Derry the raw recruits that had been drawn to the movement after the shooting of Cusack and Beattie were pushed into action. McGuinness had far more volunteers than he could arm. Within ten days two of them were dead — Eamon Lafferty who had been an energetic participant in civil rights agitation and the defence of the Bogside in 1969 but had remained a 'non-aligned republican' until internment; and Jim O'Hagan, a young newcomer.

The Army continued to insist that internment had been a success. Five days afterwards they gave a press conference in Belfast claiming that a major defeat had been inflicted on the IRA and that troops in the past few days had killed between twenty and thirty men with as many wounded. The figure was grotesquely exaggerated. At that stage only two Provisionals had died in the post-internment fighting and no one from the Officials. By the end of the following day, however, the Army had lost three.

* * *

In the months that followed the IRA men who had gone on the run drifted back to their old haunts. Many of them were picked up and removed to the huts at Long Kesh and Magilligan or the prison ship HMS *Maidstone*, a 33-year-old warship moored in Belfast Harbour. By then the point of the operation had rebounded. The IRA was, on the whole, very satisfied with the outcome. Internment had brought it enormous benefits. The militancy of the young men of Derry, Belfast and an increasing number of rural areas was deepened by the experience, to the point where some of the Provisional leaders believed that a full-scale encounter with the British forces was now feasible. More significantly they had been handed an endlessly productive mine of propaganda. Internment succeeded in uniting the IRA's fiercest enemies inside the Catholic community behind them and lent some credence to their claims to legitimacy. Politicians, from the newly-formed Catholic party, the Social Democratic and Labour Party (SDLP), such as John Hume and Gerry Fitt, both implacable opponents of physical force republicanism, announced a campaign of civil disobedience against internment. In Derry 8,000 people took part in a one-day protest strike. The ghettoes united in a rent and rates strike. The sentiment of the Catholic working class instantly found its way into a classic rebel song:

> Armoured cars and tanks and guns
> Came to take away our sons
> But every man will stand behind
> The men behind the wire.

The editorial in the *Republican News* could scarcely suppress a triumphalist tone.

Faulkner must go and with him the whole Stormont regime. Now is the time for a vast united effort to flatten the tottering edifice. It is afflicted on all sides from within and without . . . It is therefore imperative that in this, our finest hour we stand united to face what may be the most repressive period in our history. Faulkner's 'olive branch' has already been rejected by our people. He has nothing left to offer us but the iron fist. It is our duty to make every hour count in our preparation for it.

The Republican Movement must be assured of the willing co-operation of all our people. Political strife is meaningless now. The nation must take precedence over the party. The die is already cast. 'This is War.'

CHAPTER TEN

After Internment

Following the introduction of internment, whatever notional restraints remained on the activities of the Northern units were removed and the Army Council sanctioned an all-out bombing campaign. In addition MacStiofain declared that from then on, all members of the RUC and the UDR, the 8,000-strong supposedly non-sectarian force which had replaced the 'B' Specials, were liable to be attacked, whether or not they were on duty or in uniform. Their crime was that they had helped the British Army in the mass arrests, behaving brutally on occasion, it was alleged, and had contributed intelligence concerning republicans to the British forces. In fact, attacks on policemen had already begun long before Dublin gave its official sanction. As well as the two policemen killed at Crossmaglen following the shooting of Danny O'Hagan in July 1970, some members of the Belfast Third Battalion in February 1971 had lured Special Branch detective Cecil Paterson and a fellow officer into an ambush by setting fire to a garage in Belfast and shooting them both dead when they turned up to investigate.

The Northern units responded to the exhortation to step up the campaign with great enthusiasm. Every index that measured the violence rose with sickening abruptness after internment. Before 9 August there had been only eleven soldiers killed in Northern Ireland in 1971. Afterwards there were thirty-two. The UDR, previously unscathed, lost five. As usual it was the civilians who suffered most. Only seventeen had been killed in the seven months before internment. In the five months that followed ninety-seven were shot or blasted to death.

The Army calculated that by the end of the year the IRA had fired 17,400 rounds at them and thrown 1,531 nail bombs. On the weekend of November 27-8 they carried out nearly a hundred attacks, shooting soldiers, blasting buildings and burning customs huts.

In Ardoyne 'McShane' found that after internment 'everything was geared to setting up operations and carrying them out, from when you got up in the morning to when you went to bed at night.'[1] The death of Paddy McAdorey meant that Martin Meehan was the leading Provisional in the area. There were now seven companies, and young men who had previously avoided the organisation were clamouring to join. In several cases sons of families who had emigrated to England and Australia returned to offer their services. Meehan wanted 'action, action, action. He couldn't get enough operations his way.' The daily routine for company members was to turn up at a call house, pick up a weapon and ammunition from the tiny armoury of two Armalites and a sub-machine-gun allotted to each company, then set off in pairs, usually by car, to cruise the narrow streets in search of a target. Meehan's instructions were vague. Little planning went into the operations. They were simply under orders to engage any troops who entered the district, an event which was now routinely announced by vigilant housewives clattering dustbin lids in warning.

The encounters between soldiers and Provisionals were brief and confused: an initial burst of shots as the IRA unit opened up on the patrol, a hesitant exchange of fire as the soldiers scrambled for cover and frantically sought the source of the shooting, and then silence, punctuated by the squawk of the radio as reinforcements were called, while the Provisionals hastily pulled back into the ghetto. These clashes were costly for the security forces. In the six weeks after internment the Green Howards lost six men in Ardoyne. Of the twenty members of the Provisionals' Third Battalion who were killed in the twelve months after internment, however, only five can be said to have died in a straightforward gunbattle.

For most of them death came unanticipated, overtaking them while they travelled to a 'job' in the back of a van, fiddled hesitantly with the unaccustomed *materiel* in a ghetto parlour, or crouched in a shop or office doorway nervously priming the device. Premature explosions accounted for the deaths of twelve Third Battalion members in 1972. Of the 106 IRA men and women who died between 1969 and 1973, forty-four were blown up by their own bombs, though this is hard to discover from the Provisionals' roll of honour. The already ambiguous designation 'explosion' placed next to their names in the early death lists has since been changed to the even more opaque 'killed in action'.

On 21 February 1972, for example, four members of the Belfast Third Battalion set off to plant a bomb in the east of the city. In a van were Gerard 'Dinger' Bell, a 20-year-old plumber and according to his official obituary a 'mild-mannered young man with a distinctive, infectious laugh [whose] spare time was mostly spent playing football and handball or just having a crack with his friends on the street corner'; Robert Dorrian, a 31-year-old roofer and a father of four sons, one of whom had been run over and killed by an Army jeep; Joe Magee, 31, a steel-fixer with three children who had been intimidated out of his house in a Protestant area of East Belfast; and Gerard 'Nailer' Steele, a 27-year-old bachelor whose spare time was spent 'playing handball up against the gable wall of Anderson Street or in the betting shop at the corner of Clyde Street.'[2] Why they didn't place the bomb at its 'economic target' was never established — the speculation was that they were scared off when an Army patrol moved into the area. As they drove along the Belfast ringroad the bomb exploded, killing them all instantly.

This was only the first of a series of multiple 'own goals', as the security forces termed the incidents. On 7 April three Third Battalion youths, none of them older than 18, were blown up in a premature explosion. The following month four more were killed in the Short Strand when the bomb they were preparing went off. The self-inflicted carnage was partly caused by the crudeness of the devices. Despite experiments with timing devices removed, copied and studied from washing-machines and other household appliances, most of the units relied on old-fashioned fuse-detonated devices, 'smokey joes' as the IRA called them, which gave the planter a matter of minutes to depart before the explosion. For this reason, most of them were set at night. By 1972 the supply of industrial gelignite was running short and the IRA were forced to experi-ment with uncertain recipes using fertiliser.

The horrifically high chances of accidental destruction did not seem to act as a deterrent. Some of the young Provisionals were frenetically active. Joseph Fitzsimmons, 18, was the sixth child in a family of eighteen. His grandfather had been an IRA man in the thirties. He left school at 15 and worked as a labourer for a fruit merchant. In 1969 during the riots he turned up at the barricades and then joined the Fianna. During the gunbattle around St Matthew's in the Short Strand he ran ammunition to McKee and his men. Shorly after internment he was arrested following a riot and given six months' imprisonment. He was released on the morning that 'Dinger' Bell and his companions were being buried and spent his first hours of freedom delivering Mass cards carrying the sympathies of the republican inmates of the Crumlin Road jail to the men's families. Then he reported back to the Provisionals. In the next few weeks he was wounded by an Army patrol who came across him while he was planting a bomb in the city centre. A little later he managed to wound himself while clearing his gun after an exchange of fire with some British troops. Within several weeks he was dead, killed in a premature bomb explosion in the Short Strand.

In the west of the city, according to 'Donnelly', it was 'open season. You had bombings, shootings and snipings — it was part of our daily routine.' In one week 'Donnelly's' company carried out six bank and post office robberies. By 1972 these were everyday occurrences in the Province and a routine source of IRA funds. Before the troubles began bank raids, wage snatches and hold-ups, the staples of serious crime, were virtually unknown in the Province. In 1971 there were 437 armed robberies in Northern Ireland with £303,787 stolen. In 1972 there were 1,931 which netted £790,687.

As always, some volunteers were keener than others. There were those whom the activists derided as 'office hours republicans' and in 'Donnelly's' company most of the mayhem was the work of six or seven men. Some who joined up in the post-internment flush found that their initial enthusiasm did not survive the first sight of blood. 'McShane' found that 'quite often shooting someone dead would decide them to leave. They couldn't stomach it. Their recruitment had been based on emotionalism. They didn't really know what they were letting themselves in for and after they'd shot someone they couldn't live with their consciences.'[1] 'McShane' found that after a shooting 'the feeling was not of joy', though this was far from a universal reaction.

You would rather not do it but you felt you had no alternative. When the reports of the shooting came through on the news and the facts about his wife and family emerged you felt annoyed with yourself. But most volunteers got it into their minds that it was the uniform and not the individual that was being shot. This was pointed out to you at every opportunity at lectures to try and prevent you from getting emotionally involved. They told us that the Brits themselves had been conditioned in a similar way to terrorise and beat people and not to see them as people at all.

Many others found the experience of war exhilarating, especially those who took part in rural operations. One spoke of 'being so excited after a job that we shot the wee birds in the wires as we drove back from it'. Another, after a shooting, of 'feeling like eating a big dinner you felt so excited afterwards'.[3] Eyewitnesses to the assassination of a school bus-driver and part-time UDR man in 1984 described how his two killers whooped with joy as they escaped on a motorcycle. Some found the excitement addictive. 'McShane' observed that it was difficult for Meehan to persuade any of the activists to take on responsible staff jobs and that 'people were happier going off shooting. Someone would have to be asked four or five times before they would agree to be operations officer.' Certainly politics was a minuscule part of most people's motivation. 'Volunteers were reacting to their hatred of the Brits and the RUC and the feeling that they stood between us and a united Ireland. We never thought of politics. It was only when we went into jail that politics was discussed.'[1] Units were jealous of their reputations and competed with each other, encouraged by the brigade and battalion leaderships. Each battalion held a weekly meeting where the unit commanders would give a progress report.

In Derry the IRA led a freer existence than their colleagues in Belfast. After internment the Creggan and the Bogside had been sealed off to the Army and the police by barricades, and inside the no-go areas of Free Derry, as the locals called it, the Provisionals and the Officials were able to operate openly, patrolling the street with weapons on display. They had their own recognised headquarters, in the Provisionals' case a house in the Bogside. By the start of the year there were about a hundred Provisionals operating inside Free Derry. According to one of the commanders,

> There were gunbattles almost nightly, and you ate and slept with your gun by your side. Our lifestyle was that you would start out at about eleven in the morning, picking up the pieces from the night before, then organising, getting supplies and planning. It was a question of living from day to day, working from eleven in the morning to six the following morning then falling off to sleep for a few hours in a safe house. After 9 August I never slept at home. Shooting was a way of life. You did not go to dances or pubs. It was your life — shooting and looking for the Army. People became very close. Eating and sleeping together, fighting and dying together.[3]

The Provisionals in Derry operated in isolation. They had virtually no contact with either Dublin or Belfast. The few weapons in their arsenal they had obtained for themselves. There were only twenty to go round, mostly Thompsons and Sterling sub-machine-guns with a few Garands and Lee-Enfield 303s though at one point they laid their hands on a bren gun. The Lee-Enfields were prized for their accuracy. One, fitted with a telescopic sight, was nicknamed 'Jude' after the patron saint of lost causes, and was credited with killing eight or nine soldiers. Most of the Provisionals' energies went into single-shot sniping operations – and because flak jackets had yet to be introduced they could operate effectively at a range of 200 or 300 yards – but there were also full-blooded engagements with as many as fifteen Provos attacking an Army look-out point or patrol.

On one occasion a team of fifteen men and women placed a landmine on the Letterkenny Road, detonated it as a security forces vehicle approached and opened up with Garands, .22s and shotguns. The ensuing gunbattle lasted one and a half hours and ended, not unusually, with no casualties on either side. The amount of cover afforded by the townscape and the generally poor shooting of the Provos, meant that many rounds could fly without anyone being hurt. The Derry Provos campaign had more dash than the fighting in Belfast. On one occasion Martin McGuinness heard that some of his men were pinned down in a gunbattle with the Army, again in Letterkenny Road, and rounded up some volunteers to drive across town to relieve them. A full mile from the shooting their van was hit twenty times and they were forced to stop, unload the bren from the back and return the Army's fire.

The compact, clannish nature of Derry made it easier to impose some discipline on the organisation. Martin McGuinness was a natural leader. Despite the fact that he was barely 22 he had an unobtrusive air of authority. He was handsome, and he was willing to take as many risks as the most active of his men. He planned the campaign with care and even the British Army respected his military capabilities; 'excellent officer material' according to a Royal Marine major who fought him during those months.[3] McGuinness had no republican antecedents. His conversion took place during the 1968 rioting when he was among the young petrol-bombers and stone-throwers at the Bogside barricades.

His father was a pious man, a Nationalist (as were most Derry Catholics), a constitutionalist and conservative who disapproved of republicanism's violent and socialistic creed. In late 1969 McGuinness and some friends had broken into a local school, Saint Columb's, and stolen some sulphuric acid for acid bombs. A cleaner alerted the priest, Father Mulvey, who went to the school with McGuinness's parents and caught them red-handed. He was severely rebuked for the escapade. Father Mulvey, a patriarchal figure to Catholics in Derry, became a leading opponent of the IRA and frequently denounced them from the pulpit. Later he and McGuinness were to clash repeatedly on the question of the morality of violence. Despite this incident McGuinness had a respect for discipline and the teaching of the Church.

His sense of discipline probably saved many lives in 1972. During the year the Provisionals succeeded in reducing the centre of Derry to rubble without killing civilians. McGuinness's men and women were under instruction to abort any bombing mission if there was the slightest threat to innocent people, and to leave through the police and Army checkpoints with the explosives, even at the risk of arrest and imprisonment.[4] Even so, they 'managed to bomb the city centre until it looked as if it had been hit from the air'. The bombings became a bizarre spectator sport with crowds gathering to watch the flash, the rolling smoke, the stately subsidence of another shop or office. They blew up the Guildhall, the symbol of the Protestants' political dominance for so long. They celebrated the 12th of July with the biggest offensive to date, blasting Waterloo Place in the city centre with 500 pounds of explosive.

There were two points to the bombing in McGuinness's eyes. In the first place, it hurt the British economy because the government had to pay millions of pounds in compensation to the victims. Secondly, it tied down the Army and kept them fully occupied with clearing the streets of people while they attempted to defuse a device, then more often than not clearing the streets of debris. That meant that they could not 'attack' the ghettoes and Free Derry remained sealed off to the troops. The Provisionals became the sole representatives of the IRA in Derry following an episode that dispelled most of the popular sympathy for the Officials. In May they 'tried' and executed a 19-year-old British Army soldier, Ranger William Best, who had foolishly returned to his parents' home in the Creggan. The following day 500 women marched to the Officials' headquarters in Meenan Square. This was the second ghastly blunder the Officials had made. In February a unit had placed a bomb outside the officers' mess of the Parachute Regiment in Aldershot, in reprisal for Bloody Sunday. It killed five cleaning women, a Catholic chaplain and a gardener. These events shook the already half-hearted commitment of Goulding and the Official Army Council to violence and on 29 May 1972, nine days after Best's death, they declared an indefinite ceasefire. However, their statement contained an important condition: 'The only exception to the general suspension of armed actions is the reservation of the right to defend any area under aggressive attack by the British military or by the sectarian forces *of either side*', a clear reference to the fact that the murderous dispute with the Provisionals had only been temporarily shelved.

In Belfast the volunteers lived an enclosed existence, spending most of their time inside the small grid of streets that made up the unit's area with the occasional foray into the middle of town to snipe or plant a bomb. They had practically no contact with their fellow Provisionals in other parts of the city and most of them knew the brigade's commanders only by reputation. Until the ceasefire was announced in 1972, Dublin had no relevance to their lives at all. Their drive was maintained by the rhythm of killing and counter-killing. Families frequently suffered disproportionate losses, as the desire to avenge one death, wounding, beating or imprisonment drew a son or brother or sister into the movement. Gerald McDade of the Third Battalion joined the IRA in March 1970. Four days before Christmas and six weeks before the birth of his first child he was shot by British soldiers as he ran away after being stopped for questioning during a raid on an Ardoyne club. His brother James had emigrated to Birmingham with his wife and two children. He joined the IRA in England in September 1972 and became involved in the bombing campaign on the mainland. On the night of 14 November 1974 he was placing a device at Coventry telephone exchange when it exploded prematurely and killed him.

By now the violence had also spread to the countryside and particularly to the border areas. Initially, to the young Catholic men and women who lived along the frontier in South Down, South Armagh and Fermanagh, the television images of burning Belfast streets and stone-throwing mobs were 'as remote to us as what was happening in Vietnam'.[5] In South Armagh in particular, the Catholic population felt little identification with the State, 'the black North' as they called it, and looked southwards for their links. Catholic teenagers in Crossmaglen regularly crossed the border to the dance-halls and bars of Dundalk and Castleblayney for their Sunday night entertainment.

At the same time there was an ingrained nationalism among them that was sympathetic to the IRA. South Armagh had seen fighting during the War of Independence and the exploits of the local IRA unit under the command of Frank Aiken, who later became Minister for Foreign Affairs, were still recounted by the older men. A favourite story concerned an episode in June 1921 when King George V came to Belfast for the state opening of the Stormont parliament. The IRA derailed a train which they mistakenly thought was carrying the king, and succeeded only in killing four guardsmen and all the horses on board.

The area was the scene of intermittent incidents during the border campaign, with the occasional destruction by the IRA of a transformer or a telephone box. Down the years there were always a few republicans around to keep the tradition alive. Every Easter, in the graveyard of St Patrick's, Crossmaglen, James Daley and Tommy Lucky and a few other elderly IRA men would gather to hoist the Tricolour over the grave of Barney Morris, shot dead in 1922 just south of the village. The young, crossing the border for a night out in Dundalk, were exposed to the sentimental republicanism of the Northern 'Fifties men' who had fled Belfast after the start of the border campaign and had been living in the town ever since.

Both groups frequented Mark's bar, a traditional pub behind the courthouse where local musicians pounded out patriotic airs on Saturday nights. When the rioting of summer 1969 broke out, however, no one had the means or the desire to go into action. As the situation worsened in Derry and Belfast in the late summer of 1970 however, Armagh men began to travel South for arms training in the secluded countryside in the Inniskeen and Dungooley areas of Monaghan and Louth, some of it provided by former British Army soldiers who had joined up in the 1960s. But they were still without the expertise or equipment to carry out their own operations unaided. By the autumn they were starting to receive arms and advice from the growing number of IRA fugitives who had fled from Belfast and were now living alongside their counterparts from the fifties in and around Dundalk.

For a brief time Dundalk took on a little of the tawdry glamour of a frontier town. IRA men on rest and recreation brawled and drank their way around the clock. On one celebrated occasion a disgruntled Provisional watching the racing on television at the Imperial Hotel shot up the screen when his horse trailed in last. The military adventures of the Dundalk IRA — 'the long rifles' as they were fancifully styled by the locals — were equally wild. On one occasion in January 1972 Martin Meehan and six others who had fetched up there from Belfast took up position on a hill overlooking the South Armagh border and began a gunbattle with a British Army patrol that lasted ninety minutes, expending hundreds of rounds of ammunition but failing to produce a single casualty. This did not prevent Meehan later telling a newspaper reporter that the British had been 'squealing like pigs'. Even the Dundalk gardai, who were inclined to avoid confrontation whenever possible, were unable to ignore the incident, especially as

201

Meehan and Clark were boasting about the exploit in the Dundalk bars that evening. All seven were duly arrested and sent to Dublin for trial. For the first twenty-two months, the war still seemed like a dangerous but exhilarating game to many in the border areas. This attitude was drastically transformed by two events in the summer of 1971: a shooting incident fifty miles away in Belfast on 7 August and the introduction of internment two days later.

Harry Thornton was a driver from Tullydonnell near the border. He had been driving vehicles for some engineering contractors who had returned from England in the 1960s to lay pipes as prosperity began to grow in the area and more homes were supplied with running water. On the morning of 7 August Thornton and his friend Arthur Murphy were working in Belfast. As they drove their old van past Springfield Road police station the engine backfired. A soldier on sentry duty panicked and opened fire, shooting Thornton dead. Murphy was dragged away and beaten so badly that his interrogators later delivered him to hospital. The incident jerked the Catholics of South Armagh out of their insularity. It was, as one local man saw it, 'an attack on the herd. Thornton worked with fathers and sons all over South Armagh. Everyone identified with him.'[6] Two days later internment descended on South Armagh.

Three weeks later two British Army ferret scout cars strayed over the border into County Louth while on patrol and were soon surrounded by an angry crowd who set fire to one of the vehicles. The patrol limped back towards the North but the local IRA had been alerted and were waiting for them. As the patrol moved past McArdle's shop, a few miles south of Crossmaglen, they opened fire, killing a soldier. The attack was the first major operation to be carried out by the local South Armagh unit of the IRA.

Thornton's death and the internment drove a number of previously indifferent Catholics into the Provisionals' ranks. In South Armagh, soldiers had arrested a mild-mannered schoolteacher, Kevin McMahon, who came from a staunchly republican family but with no connection with violence, changing the attitude towards the IRA of the hundreds of people who knew him from indifference to approval overnight. Among those who joined the IRA was Michael McVerry, a neighbour of McMahon's. McVerry was generally regarded as indifferent — even hostile — to republicanism. One story had him berating a youth who was trying to sell copies of the *United Irishman* on the church steps. His prime interest seemed to be the local Gaelic football club, Dorsey. Immediately after McMahon's arrest, McVerry joined the local IRA unit. Within a couple of months he was leading it. He became a byword for enthusiasm, taking part in every available operation, even after he blew a hand off in an explosives accident. McVerry had an instant aptitude for guerrilla fighting. Under his leadership the mining of the local lanes and roads began in earnest. The initial devices were milk churns, packed with explosive, buried in culverts under the tarmac and detonated at a safe distance by a command wire, often hidden under the newly turned sod of a field ploughed to order by a friendly farmer.

As a result of the IRA operations in South Armagh the Army abandoned road patrols altogether and troops were inserted by helicopter. In 1972 the units were supplied by GHQ in Dublin with rocket launchers to add to their arsenal, and they began a morale-boosting series of full-scale attacks on the security forces. McVerry was a sharp propagandist and sometimes took tape recordings of gunbattles that were later played at fund-raising hooleys in the United States. It was on one of these actions that he was killed. On 15 November 1973 he led a bomb and rocket attack on the police barracks in Keady in County Armagh. The police returned fire and he was hit in the stomach. His companions drove him across the border to St Mary's Hospital, Castleblayney but he was dead by the time they arrived. According to the security forces he had personally killed more than twelve of their members.

The IRA border units showed a daunting capacity for innovation and subtlety, especially in military technology. In 1974, working from radio devices used for controlling model aeroplanes supplied by GHQ, they perfected the remote control bomb. These devices worked on the same principle as a remote television channel changing switch. The bomb was fitted with a radio receiver tuned to a certain frequency. When a signal was sent to it by a transmitter tuned to the same wavelength, the bomb exploded.

The first success was on 13 August 1974. A four-man marine patrol arrived to staff an observation post on top of Drumuckavaal Hill overlooking the border. The IRA had previously identified the post and buried a 100-pound charge underneath it. The unit waited for the patrol to settle in, then pressed the button on the device eight times, sending a radio signal that detonated the mine. The post erupted, killing two marines and seriously wounding the others. The remote control technology was passed on to other IRA units and was used in Tyrone.

The South Armagh Provisionals' success was in part due to their relationship with the Catholics in their area of operations. Their activities did not arouse the same uneasiness as those of their counterparts in the cities. It seemed to most border Catholics a relatively clean war. To many of them, anyone who wore the Queen's uniform was eligible for attack, whether he was a private soldier from the south of England or a Protestant farmer who happened to be a part-time member of the UDR. The IRA in the country had less to fear from informers than their comrades in Belfast and at the same time could rely on local people to gather intelligence, such as passing on details of troop activities, or for the loan of a shed or a car.

At the start of 1972 the Provisional IRA was buoyed up at every level, from the leadership in Dublin to the rawest recruit in Ballymurphy or the Creggan, by the highest volume of support the Cathlic population north and south of the border had given them since 1922. There were great variations in its depth and warmth, from grudging acceptance of a regretful necessity through romantic indulgence (growing in strength the further one went from the violence) to outright backing, and as the IRA knew from their history, this new regard was likely to wane as quickly as it had grown.

Internment had created the climate of sympathy. Repeated house searches ensured that the level of resentment against the Army stayed high. In mid-November the Army reported that they had searched 2,500 homes in the previous four weeks and arrested more than 400 people. Whatever open or covert sympathy the Army felt towards the Catholics (and at the outset they certainly felt a considerable amount) had worn off by now and they regarded both sides with the same hostility and contempt.

Ill-feeling towards the military was stoked up by a stream of allegations of torture and rough treatment of internees. Fourteen of them, it transpired, had been selected as guinea pigs in a series of sensory deprivation experiments in which they were hooded, deprived of sleep, food and drink and subjected to constant unidentifiable background humming ('white noise') intended to disorient them further. It was a scientific attempt to get the men to co-operate in their captors' intelligence gathering, without the Army and the RUC having recourse to more traditional methods of persuasion. The case was later sent by the Irish Government to the European Court of Human Rights which found Britain guilty of 'inhuman and degrading' treatment of the internees. Such incidents were fully exploited by the Provisionals and MacStiofain was keenly aware of their importance in the propaganda war.

The IRA's efforts to portray the British Army as a brutal and repressive occupying force were helped considerably by the events of Sunday 30 January 1972, Bloody Sunday as it soon came to be known. Late in 1971 the Civil Rights Association had re-emerged from relative obscurity to organise an anti-internment march in Derry, in defiance of a Stormont ban on all marches which had been in operation since the introduction of internment.

This decision caused the British Army to focus on the question of what was to be done about Derry. Up until then it had concentrated its efforts in Belfast, a policy in keeping with Stormont's and Westminster's general view that while

Belfast could be successfully dominated by the Army, Derry, with its two-thirds Catholic majority, could not. The increasing activity by the IRA in the summer of 1971 had led the Army in the autumn to draw up plans to re-establish themselves in the no-go areas of the Bogside and the Creggan Estate, but these had been dropped because it was felt that the troop levels needed to hold the areas would be politically unacceptable. As late as 17 January, thirteen days before Bloody Sunday, an Army brief advised that 'the policy in Londonderry is to play the Creggan and the Bogside in the lowest key possible . . . it is the intention to keep Derry out of the headlines.'[7] There was, however, a strong determination to crack down on the activities of the Catholic youths of Derry, for whom rioting was now an established and relatively risk-free recreation. By the Army count there were about 500 young 'hooligans' disturbing the peace almost daily.

In the consultations that took place between the local police, commanded by Chief Superintendent Frank Lagan, and the Army over the policing of the march it rapidly became clear that they disagreed fundamentally on how the demonstration should be handled. Lagan believed that the best chance of avoiding trouble lay in allowing the demonstrators into the city centre, if necessary photographing troublemakers and picking them up later. The Army was convinced that if the march was allowed out of the Bogside the IRA would use it as a cover to snipe at troops. Violence, they felt, was an inevitability, due to the inability of the organisers to control the actions of the hundreds of riot-hardened Catholic youths who were bound to turn up (a view shared by the organisers themselves).[8] They concluded that if the march was contained inside the Creggan and the Bogside it would not be challenged but if they strayed outside and into the city centre the Army would confront them. The Commander of Land forces in Northern Ireland, Major-General Robert Ford, who was under pressure from Stormont to take a firm hand with rioters, saw in the march the opportunity to teach a lesson to the unruly Catholic youths of Derry.

The Army order for the operation stated that an arrest force was to be deployed and 'launched in a scoop-up operation to arrest as many hooligans and rioters as possible'.[9] The First Battalion of the Parachute Regiment was drafted in to reinforce the existing troops in the city and to act as the arrest unit. They were chosen because they were available, experienced and had a reputation for toughness that caused Belfast streets to empty on their appearance, a reputation the Army hoped had spread to Derry. This same reputation caused some Army officers to doubt the wisdom of deploying the Paras in what was clearly a delicate situation. Only a few days before, they had confronted a civil rights march on the sands near the newly opened Magilligan prison, a short way east of Derry, and broken a number of heads — causing a frisson of anticipation among the demonstrators when they assembled on the cold, sunny afternoon of 30 January.[10]

The mood was good-humoured enough when the march began. A local general practitioner, Dr Raymond McClean, who had gone to the march felt that 'the atmosphere was so relaxed and cheerful that I decided to leave all my equipment in the car at Creggan as it did not seem as if there would be any casualties to treat'.[11] McClean believed at this point that the march had no hope of getting into the city centre and that when challenged by the Army there would be some minor rioting but that the bulk of the demonstrators would move off peacefully to hear speeches at Free Derry corner in the Bogside, having registered their protest. This prediction of the afternoon's developments was partly shared by the Army. Their intention was, once the march had been stopped at William Street, to wait for the peaceful demonstrators to break off from the rioters, then move in and seize the hooligans.

Both predictions proved correct. Once the march reached the Army barriers confining them to the Catholic areas and blocking their route to the city centre, the organisers turned away and the bulk of the marchers followed them, returning towards the Bogside and leaving a crowd of young Catholics at the head of the march to throw missiles at the soldiers, who replied by firing CS gas canisters and plastic bullets into their ranks. Eventually, after an exhortation to hurry things up from General Ford who was accompanying the Paras, Brigadier Pat McClellan

207

was satisfied that the peaceful marchers had separated out from the hooligans and gave the order for the Paras to go in.

According to the Army, the troops then came under fire. Whether this was real or imagined, they began shooting *con gusto*. Altogether 108 7.62mm rounds of bullets were fired into the crowd. As the paras' **SLR** rifles were welded to fire only in the single shot mode, this could hardly be explained by a few panic-stricken bursts of automatic fire. The casualties were dragged into the small houses of the Bogside while Dr McClean and a team of first-aiders did what they could while waiting for the ambulances to arrive.

> In the first house [he wrote] I found Michael Kelly who had a bullet wound just to the left of his umbilicus. I could not find any exit wound. Michael was already dead when I examined him. Lying beside Michael was Jim Wray. He had two entry gun-shot wounds on the right side of his back. He had an exit wound on the left side of his back and another larger exit wound at his left shoulder. Jim was also dead . . . I went next door where I found William McKinney lying on the floor. He had an entry bullet wound over his right chest and a jagged exit wound in his left chest . . . he was pale and shocked and extremely calm. He said to me . . . 'I'm going to die, doctor am I?' I lied a bit and said, 'You have been hit badly but if we can get an ambulance and get you to hospital quickly I hope you will be alright.' I saw Father Mulvey in the hall and asked him to see William, which he did. I stayed with William until he gradually lost consciousness and died.[12]

The Army had killed thirteen men, seven of them under 19, in the shooting and wounded thirteen others, one a woman. Soldiers who were there still maintain that they heard the sound of Thompson fire before the Paras opened up. The men leading the Derry IRA at the time are equally insistent that no IRA action took place that day. Almost the entire membership of the Derry units, McGuinness included, was on the march and the likelihood of being arrested or searched meant that none of them were armed.[4] Before the march the organisers had been given assurances by the IRA that there would be no violence on the day. Even if the Army had been fired upon it was hard to justify the indiscipline of the soldiers' response. None of the men hit was wanted by the security forces. The official Widgery Report on the shootings found that the Army had been fired on first. But it remained unconvinced that any of the dead were armed or had been throwing nailbombs.

In the Republic of Ireland, Bloody Sunday brought reactions of anger, horror and disgust. The Paratroopers' actions had been 'unbelievably savage and inhuman', said the Premier, Jack Lynch, and called a national day of mourning to honour the dead. When that took place, three days after the slaughter, demonstrators burned down the British Embassy while the gardai (Irish police) looked on.

Elsewhere in the world the reaction was curiously muted. In America, Irish American politicians such as Senator Edward Kennedy condemned the 'senseless and terrible new sacrifice' and asked: 'Can anyone now doubt that the presence of British troops is compounding the violence instead of contributing to peace.' The liberal *New York Times*, however, strained to give Britain the benefit of the doubt, declaring that the provocation to the troops had been deliberate and great. 'To many,' it concluded, 'it would be rank injustice if Britain were now to dissolve the Stormont government that has enacted so many of the reforms demanded by Ulster Catholics and impose direct rule from Westminster.'[13]

By the time those words were written, however, Stormont was already on the road to extinction. Bloody Sunday had not been Stormont's fault. Although the Government of Northern Ireland possessed nominal responsibility for law and order, the decision to send in the Paratroopers had been entirely the Army's. None the less, Stormont was the casualty of the affair. After Bloody Sunday Prime Minister Edward Heath decided that the Government of Northern Ireland should be relieved of its law and order powers, a decision that, if implemented, as Brian Faulkner was later to remark bitterly, would have reduced Stormont to the status of a county council. One way or another, Sir James Craig's 'Protestant parliament and Protestant state' was about to be eclipsed.

CHAPTER ELEVEN

Fighting and Talking

Despite its crucial role in the history of the troubles, the IRA
had remained on the sidelines of political developments. There
were several reasons for this. Since the first year of the troubles
the IRA leadership had been too preoccupied with prosecuting
the 'war' to devote much time to its political strategy. They
had given little consideration to the reforms, resignations and
improvements that had followed on from August 1969. By the
spring of 1972, two Northern Ireland Prime Ministers had been
propelled from office by the pace of reform. Almost everything
that the civil rights marchers had agitated for had been, or
was on the point of being, granted. The Provisionals' response
to the announcement of each reform had been merely to reject
it as insufficient, irrelevant and insulting.

It was easy for the IRA's enemies in Stormont, Westminster
and Dublin to dismiss them as representing only themselves.
From time to time some event or catastrophe — such as the
introduction of internment or Bloody Sunday — would throw
the IRA and the constitutional nationalists of the SDLP together
but these conjunctions of interest rarely lasted. The republican
tradition of doctrinal purity and exclusivity ruled out any long-
term coalition with outsiders. In any case, the Provisionals
and the SDLP were enemies fighting over the same political
territory. For this reason the SDLP usually fared worse than
'Brits' or unionists in the republican press, portrayed as 'slaves
and lickspittles' who had failed to grasp the essential lesson
when dealing with the British — that they only respected might.

211

By the spring of 1971 the Provisionals' war machine was running sufficiently smoothly for MacStiofain, O'Bradaigh and O'Connaill to devote some time to a political blueprint. They had originally intended to unveil it in the summer but the moment was delayed by the introduction of internment[1] and their proposals were eventually revealed early in September. They formed two parts: the conditions on which the IRA would cease hostilities, and the Provisionals' vision of the future of a thirty-two county state. The five-point peace plan called for the immediate cessation of the British forces' campaign 'against Irish people', the abolition of Stormont, a guarantee of non-interference with a free election to establish Dail Uladh (an Ulster regional parliament), a new governmental structure for the entire country, the release of all 'political prisoners', tried or untried, in Britain and Ireland and compensation for all those who had suffered 'as a result of direct or indirect British violence'.[2]

The IRA's political plans had never drawn the line at simply removing the border. In their eyes the twenty-six-county state was as contemptible and ripe for demolition as Stormont was, but prescriptions for the form the new model should take had varied over the years. The structure unveiled in the Provisionals' proposal was primarily the creation of O'Bradaigh but was enthusiastically endorsed by MacStiofain and O'Connaill.

Ruairi O'Bradaigh was the most academic of the Provisional troika. He had a solidly middle-class and relatively cosmopolitan background, with a Swiss Protestant maternal grandmother who moved to Belfast and later to Armagh and Donegal. His mother had been at University College, Dublin where she joined Cumann na mBan (the women's section of the IRA) before moving to Longford in the Irish Midlands and marrying O'Bradaigh's father. He too was a republican. O'Bradaigh remembers as a child the hanging of two IRA bombers, Barnes and McCormack, in Birmingham jail on Ash Wednesday 1940. 'Before my sister and I went out to school my father stood by the clock and when it struck nine he said: "Go down on your knees and pray for two Irishmen who are gone into quicklime graves." '[1]

O'Bradaigh followed his mother to University College, Dublin and returned to Roscommon to teach and to join the republican movement. Despite his unpromising appearance he turned out to be an enthusiastic, and by the low standards of the IRA at the time, efficient operator. In the fifties he was elected to the Army Council, led the daring but unsuccessful Arborfield arms raid in England, and commanded a 'column' in the opening burst of the border campaign when he took part in an attack on the Derrylin RUC station. In the 1957 elections in the South he had been elected to the Irish Parliament as the Sinn Fein member for Longford-Westmeath but abstained from taking his seat. He was imprisoned in The Curragh camp but escaped along with Daithi O'Connaill and ended the campaign on the run, as IRA chief-of-staff. Throughout the wrangles of the sixties he had retained a foot in both camps. He was more sympathetic than MacStiofain was to Goulding's attempts to modernise the movement's political thinking and was in favour of the fish-ins and housing demonstrations. Yet at the same time he had a strong traditionalist streak, faithful to abstentionism and militarism. This traditionalism was lavishly expressed in his contribution to the Provisional policy for Eire Nua (New Ireland).

Eire Nua regarded the parliamentary system, like almost everything British, as an unsuitable importation for Ireland's needs. Instead, it proposed a federal arrangement, based on the four ancient Provinces of Ireland: Ulster, Munster, Leinster and Connaught. As much power as possible would be vested in the hands of regional parliaments, with the central government restricted to the duties of diplomacy and defence. This offered an ingenious solution to the Ulster problem. Dail Uladh (Parliament of Ulster) would cover the historic nine counties of the Province: the original partitioned six of Antrim, Armagh, Derry, Down, Fermanagh and Tyrone, plus their neighbours to the south and west, Cavan, Monaghan and Donegal. The restoration of the three counties would even up the demographic odds against the Catholics and answer the Protestants' objection that absorption into an all-Ireland state would mean the loss of political power and their cultural and religious identity.

The IRA announced the proposals on 5 September. It said that if the British Government accepted them within four days the Provisionals would reciprocate by suspending military operations. Rejection of the proposals would 'leave the IRA with no option but to intensify its campaign of resistance to British military rule in Ireland'. Showing a proper sense of protocol and occasion, MacStiofain 'travelled across Dublin that night to take the proposals personally to the British embassy in company with a leading member of the movement from County Armagh. As we approached the embassy we were stopped by a Special Branch man from Dublin Castle. On telling him, we had business there we were escorted to the door, where an official accepted the communication and assured us that he would hand it on to the ambassador.'[3]

The Provisionals' offer was hopelessly unrealistic. The British Government had from the outset stated its refusal to 'negotiate with terrorists', and while the Provisionals were justified in not taking it at its word there was nothing to suggest that the moment was ripe for talking. The prospect of anyone taking the document seriously was diminished by the extensive nature of the demands. A British government of whatever political hue could hardly discuss, for example, the abolition of the Southern Government, as the IRA proposed.

The proposals received a gratifying amount of coverage in the media, but met with silence from London. Despite the failure of this initiative, the leadership let it be known privately that they were interested in establishing an informal line of contact with the British Government. In the autumn, the independent Unionist Stormont MP Tom Caldwell had been approached by a journalist and asked if he was prepared to act as go-between. Caldwell consulted the General Officer Commanding Northern Ireland, Sir Harry Tuzo, who advised him against it. In November he was again approached by a journalist and asked if he was interested in meeting with Roy Johnston from the Officials. Again Caldwell sought advice, this time from Howard Smith, the United Kingdom's representative in Northern Ireland and in charge of intelligence co-ordination between the police, the Army and the intelligence services. According to Caldwell, Smith said, 'Look, Tom, the feeling in London is this: If you do talk, and we would like you to talk, you're not doing it on behalf of the British Government, you're doing it off your own bat and take the consequences.'[4]

The meeting took place a few days later in the pleasant Dublin suburb of Ballsbridge. Johnston was courteous but uncompromising. A truce would only be called if the Government agreed to end internment, withdraw troops to barracks and announce a timetable for the reunification of Ireland. Details of the meeting were duly reported back. In January 1972 Caldwell met Labour Party leader Harold Wilson in his office in Westminster and told him about the encounter. Wilson told him that the meeting was useful but that he was 'talking to the wrong guys', as the Officials had played only a small part in the violence. Caldwell told Wilson he would choose his time and he did so. 'I made my decision to talk to the Provisionals on the Sunday after the Abercorn bombing, Sunday 5 March. I met O'Bradaigh and MacStiofain', said Caldwell. He eventually concluded he had gone as far as he could go with Whitelaw and Wilson, having talked to the IRA. On the afternoon of Saturday 4 March the Abercorn restaurant in the middle of Belfast was packed with women and children taking a respite from shopping. At 4.30 a bomb exploded without warning, killing two women and injuring another 130 customers, some of them horribly. Two sisters out shopping for a wedding-dress had both their legs blown off. The reaction of the Belfast Brigade was to deny responsibility, a position that has been maintained to this day, and an elaborate attempt was made to blame Protestant extremists instead. In fact the atrocity was the work of the First Battalion who did not leave enough time to phone a warning when setting the bomb.[5]

The twin horrors of Bloody Sunday and the Abercorn could not stop the Provisionals edging towards the negotiating table. Since Bloody Sunday, the demise of Stormont was accepted as an inevitability. The question now was what was to be put in its place. The British Government's strategy saw the removal of Stormont and the substitution of a more equitable form of rule as one of their key weapons in the fight to deprive the IRA of support and sympathy. As MacStiofain saw it, the Provisionals had to make their own initiative if they were not to be frozen out by the 'climate of acceptance' that Stormont's abolition would create among the Catholic population and the Catholic politicians of the SDLP for the Heath initiative.[6] With this in mind, before the Abercorn bombing, he had cast another fly on the waters by announcing a new set of terms which the Army Council would accept as the minimum for calling a cessation of hostilities. The offer was a revision of the terms of the previous September. The demands for compensation and for non-interference in the elections to Dail Uladh had been dropped. The new terms were a withdrawal of British troops in the North from the streets to barracks as a prelude to eventual evacuation; acknowledgement by the British Government of the right of the Irish people to determine their future without interference; the abolition of Stormont; and a total amnesty for political prisoners.

Six days after the Abercorn incident the IRA made a further gesture of encouragement with the offer of a seventy-two-hour ceasefire intended to 'demonstrate that the IRA was under effective control and discipline'.[6] The Army Council knew that some parts, at least, of the British political establishment were prepared to countenance talking to the Provisionals. Late in February the revised truce terms had been conveyed to Harold Wilson by Dr John O'Connell, a Labour member of the Dail. Wilson, while indicating that no British Government could agree to the terms, agreed to meet 'friends of the IRA'. The encounter took place on 13 March just as the seventy-two-hour ceasefire was drawing to a close, while Wilson was visiting Dublin to take part in a television programme. They met at Daithi O'Connaill's home. The 'friends' turned out to include O'Connell, Joe Cahill and John Kelly, the Belfast Provisional. MacStiofain decided not to attend, he said later, to spare Wilson from charges that he was conducting top-level negotiations behind

216

Prime Minister Heath's back. Merlyn Rees, the Labour spokesman for Northern Ireland, who was present, found them 'hard men who talked and looked like soldiers. They thought solely in terms of military victory. There was no sign of compromise.'[7]

Cahill thought Wilson was 'disappointed that none of us took a drink.'[8] 'Their line was: "You tell us how to get out. You make it easy for us to get out." It was pointed out to them there there was no easy way. They had to pack up and go.' The Labour team also expressed fears that what was happening in Northern Ireland might spill over into mainland cities. The meeting broke up at midnight with Kelly saying that it was too late to continue talking of a truce. Time was up and operations were already under way. Cahill thought it had been 'a waffling session. To me it had been a complete waste of bloody time.'

A few weeks after the resumption of hostilities there was another bloody debacle. A Provo unit hijacked two cars and drove them into the centre of Belfast packed with explosive. One of them went off in Lower Donegall Street next to a crowd which had been moved there following a report that there was a bomb in the street next door. Six people were killed, including two policemen, and nineteen people seriously injured. The kind of 'effective control and discipline' that the Belfast units were under was demonstrated in a characteristic incident of Wednesday 22 March: a group of men drove a car into the Great Victoria Street railway station and ran off shouting a warning that it would explode in thirty minutes. It went off fifteen minutes later, injuring sixty and blowing the roof off the station and most of the windows out in the neighbouring Europa Hotel.

On 24 March, Stormont finally fell. Two days previously, Heath had summoned Brian Faulkner to London to tell him that he wanted Stormont's powers of law and order transferred to London and a start made on phasing out internment. When Faulkner refused to accept the loss of security powers, the Government announced that Stormont stood prorogued for one year, a euphemism that fooled nobody, and that all Northern Ireland's executive and legislative powers, including control of the courts and the security forces, would now be transferred to the United Kingdom parliament. Heath also created the new office of Secretary of State for Northern Ireland, with William Whitelaw as its first holder. Heath knew that his terms were unacceptable to the Unionists, but the abolition of Stormont was the necessary precondition of any sort of political solution to Northern Ireland that embraced the Catholics. Bloody Sunday had only hastened its demise. The handling of the demonstration had been entirely the responsibility of the Army. In the aftermath, to avert the criticisms, it had been convenient to put some of the blame for the catastrophe on Stormont. Much was made of the 'muddled relationship' between the Army, commanded by London, and the police, who were still controlled by the Northern Ireland Government. While Stormont continued in existence it retained a say in the handling of military operations and it always favoured the use of maximum force. Heath's decision had also been swayed by a change in the Army's assessment of the military situation. The IRA's spring bombing campaign caused General Sir Harry Tuzo to alter his prediction that the IRA could be defeated by the end of March and to argue instead that the IRA could not be contained while law and order powers remained in Stormont's hands.

The abolition of Stormont, though a persistent demand of the Provisionals, did not impress the Army Council, which issued a statement rejecting the package and pledging its determination to carry on. The IRA thereafter claimed the credit for having destroyed it. MacStiofain wrote later that 'I have yet to meet a single person who ever thought that Stormont fell for any other reason than the armed struggle of the Republican movement'.[9] This was a great over-simplification. Stormont fell ultimately because of its own inadequacies and vices and because the arguments for keeping it alive ran out. The IRA widened the cracks and highlighted the flaws by constantly heaping up the burdens it had to carry. If the Government of Northern Ireland had been equitable and efficient, there would have been no need for the civil rights movement and no possibility for the IRA to re-establish itself in the climate of violence the civil rights campaign provoked. As it was, the IRA's achievement had been to deepen and spread the violence as they took the part of the defenders of the ghettoes against the Army.

The death of Stormont seems to have made little impression on the Belfast units. Most of them had reached the stage when the mere abolition of the unionist state was not sufficient grounds to give up violence. The Army, the police and the Protestants were still there. A nominal change of authority altered nothing. MacStiofain called a meeting of the COs and some of the staff officers of the Northern units together with members of the IRA Executive, the Army Council and the GHQ staff at a Southern seaside resort in early April. He recorded that the weekend ended 'on a note of complete unity. The way to lasting peace in Ireland was not through any colonial compromise imposed by England, but on the basis of the simple, clear proposals we had spelled out, with the English acknowledging the right of the Irish people to determine their own future without foreign interference.'[10]

The speed of the rejection was an indication of the leadership's confidence that there was a much bigger prize waiting to be won. MacStiofain was becoming increasingly convinced that the British were prepared to enter some negotiation. His view was reinforced by a number of portents from across the water. He was particularly encouraged by public opinion polls which by September 1971 were showing that fifty-nine per cent of the population wanted the troops brought home, and by the opinions of left-wing pundits like Paul Johnson, then editor of the *New Statesman*, who was calling for the Army to be withdrawn.

By the middle of the year the military was under greater strain than ever before, with sixty-nine soldiers killed since the arrival of the Army. The introduction of the car bomb in March had proved a devastating and demoralising development for the soldiers, the police and the citizens of Derry and of Belfast particularly. The credit for its invention was subsequently given to Seamus Twomey, who had taken over from Joe Cahill shortly after internment. (Cahill was forced to flee South after appearing in a triumphant news conference designed to show that the big swoop had failed to net the Provo leadership in the city.) Twomey was highly enthusiastic about the device. In fact the car bomb seems to have been invented in response to the problem of self-inflicted injury and death caused by existing bomb practices. IRA engineers had discovered the recipe for a powerful explosive mixture that required only fertiliser and other readily available ingredients (gelignite was now in short supply). The drawback was that much larger quantities were needed. In discussions in Belfast about how best to solve the transport difficulties, the notion of making the car itself into a bomb was born.[8]

As well as taking much of the risk out of setting explosions car bombs were less labour intensive. Rather than struggling to the site of the explosion with a device − with all the attendant dangers of being caught − one man could drive it into position in the boot of a stolen car and saunter away, indistinguishable from the crowd. And they posed huge difficulties for the security forces. The authorities tried sealing off traffic from city centres and setting up check-points, which stretched the resources of the security forces even further and failed to halt the bombings. For the civilian population every parked vehicle became an object of suspicion and much time was wasted 'defusing' harmless cars.

This development was compounded by an increase in all the other Provo operations. During May 1972 alone the Army logged 1,223 engagements and shooting incidents. In June more deaths and injuries were inflicted on the troops than in any previous month in the campaign.[11] The Army ceased to speak with any confidence about the defeat of the IRA and Brigadier Kitson had revised his initial prediction that the situation would be resolved by 1975. Now he suggested that the emergency could continue until 1980.

The need to get into negotiation with the British was

sharpened by the suspicion that the Provisionals' military successes could not last. The military initiative was in the hands of the IRA but they were not having it all their own way. For one thing, the one-sided seventy-two-hour truce announced in March had given the security forces an opportunity to move in and seize important operators, something that rankled with MacStiofain who felt that the authorities were not playing fair. They were helped by the new intelligence methods championed by Brigadier Kitson and based on his experiences in British post-colonial campaigns. Despite a lurid reputation with left-wingers, Kitson's methods were fairly commonsensical. He believed in the acquisition of as much low-grade intelligence as possible so as to construct a complete image of the personnel, structures and behaviour of the IRA. He was devoted to technological developments: he planted men in secret observation posts in the ghettoes and in the countryside and with cameras and electronic surveillance equipment they built up a picture of the organisation which was then passed on to the RUC.

More alarmingly, by the spring of 1972 the attitude of the Catholics to the IRA was changing. The abolition of Stormont had enhanced the attractiveness of the constitutional politicians of the SDLP who on 26 May urged those who had withdrawn their support for public bodies in protest over internment and other actions of the old regime to return to their positions, declaring, 'it is time for a positive response to Mr Whitelaw'. They also announced that they would be seeking meetings with leaders of the Protestant community to 'demonstrate our determination to create community reconciliation.' The sympathy the IRA had gained after internment was wearing off, dissipated by the bombings. Apart from the hideous carelessness that produced the Abercorn and Lower Donegall Street bomb massacres there were weekly, painful, frequently fatal acts of recklessness and impetuosity that generated mounting anger and resentment in the ghettoes.

In the month of May alone a woman in Andersonstown was wounded when troops were fired on by a sniper. As the

221

soldiers were helping her into the ambulance eight more shots were fired at the patrol.[12] A few days previously, a girl of 13 had been killed in Ballymurphy during an exchange of fire between IRA men and troops. On 29 May a 12-year-old girl on holiday from Liverpool was shot and later died when the IRA opened up on an RUC patrol in the Oldpark Road in West Belfast, and the same day a 70-year-old woman was hit in another shooting incident in the area. The car bombs continued to take a toll of the innocent. On 26 May a 64-year-old woman out doing her shopping was killed by an explosion in Oxford Street, Belfast. The Catholic inhabitants of the ghettoes, particularly the women, were increasingly reluctant to accept the apologies offered by the IRA after such incidents. Even in the most strongly republican areas of Derry and Belfast there was an incoherent but heartfelt longing for peace.

In April a group of Andersonstown women sought a meeting with MacStiofain after a 39-year-old woman had been killed in an hour-long gunbattle started by the Provisionals, to tell him that they wanted the violence to stop. MacStiofain's response was given the following day at the Easter republican parade in Derry, when he declared that any truce would mean that 'the fight of this generation will be lost and the suffering you have seen over the last three years will have to be endured again'. He appealed to the women to continue their support for the IRA and ended: 'Concession be damned: we want freedom.'[13] This did not stop the protests. In Andersonstown a few days later there was another meeting organised by a middle-class peace group, Women Together, which was disrupted by women IRA supporters led by Maire Drumm, who climbed on to the platform and harangued the audience. Later in the month the Belfast CCDC announced that nearly 50,000 people had signed a 'call for peace' and a local priest, Father Murphy, and a businessman, Tom Conaty, said they hoped that the Provisionals would respect the wishes of the people and stop bombing and shooting. There was more unrest in Derry where the Citizens' Central Council, a group of 'moderate' Catholics, held talks with the Provisional leaders and told them that hostilities should be ended.

The Provos' pious declarations of support for law and order inside their own communities were clearly regarded with profound scepticism by many Catholics, as an incident on 14 April showed. A crowd of a hundred women marched into the Creggan Estate after a £30,000 wage roll was stolen from a Derry shirt factory and demanded that the IRA give the money back. Both Officials and Provisionals denied involvement in the robbery. The killing of Ranger William Best and the bombing of the Parachute Regiment's headquarters at Aldershot provoked a wave of anger and revulsion among the inhabitants of the Bogside.

The Officials' campaign had been, as far as the leadership was concerned, a half-hearted affair. They had consistently opposed the Provisionals' commercial bombing campaign on the simple grounds that the people it most damaged were the Irish working class, and had restricted their activities to defensive shootings at members of the security forces, with mixed results. In their Army Council statement at the start of the year they had declared that 'it has never been and is not now our intention to build a movement to launch a purely military campaign against the British forces in the North. We have seen the failures of past campaigns based on military action only and have set our faces against such campaigns which are doomed to failure.'[14] Goulding had wanted to cease operations after the collapse of Stormont but had been constrained by the militancy of his men in the North. The death occurred in April of the leading Official in Belfast, Joe McCann, shot down by the Paras as he walked through the Markets after he was identified by Special Branch detectives. In deference to the high feelings the killing provoked, Goulding was obliged to give a fiery graveside oration which delayed a ceasefire further. After it was finally declared, the Officials ceased to pose a serious threat to the security forces.

The Provisionals had tried to make political capital out of Ranger Best's death, ordering the Officials out of the Creggan and the Bogside, but it was clear that the local people made little distinction between the activities of the rivals. These demonstrations against violence were regarded with an exasperated incomprehension by the leadership and their responses to the calls for peace were heavy-handed and doctrinaire. After all, what was meant by 'peace'? As MacStiofain saw it,

All wars have to end sometime and there could be several outcomes to the present situation. One, the colonial position would remain unchanged, which is what Craig [the Unionist hard-liner] and his friends wanted. Two, the old structures would be reformed, but of course with no real changes. This was what Faulkner wanted. Three, a neo-colonial set-up would emerge if the new Northern assembly and a Council of Ireland functioned, as visualised by the British. This is what the SDLP [the successor to the old Catholic Nationalist Party, founded in August 1970] and the Dublin politicians wanted. Fourth, a free Ireland restored to its natural territorial and economic unity was what *we* wanted. Certainly the sacrifices and suffering of revolutionary war can never be justified by mere reform.[15]

The reaction of the Provisionals was to listen to representations by their working-class supporters and to dismiss those of the middle classes or the more unsympathetic clergy as unrepresentative, cowardly or self-seeking. But the uneasiness in the ghettoes and the agitation for a truce gave a further impetus to MacStiofain's desire to speak to the British. The departure of the Officials meant that the Provisionals were the sole exponents of republican violence. MacStiofain felt under pressure from 'churchmen, the media, opinion makers, everyone . . .'[16] to declare a ceasefire.

Early in June two senior Derry Provos came South to put a proposal to him. They suggested that the Provisionals should hold a press conference in Free Derry and offer to suspend operations for a week if Whitelaw would agree to meet them.

The initiative cast the Provisionals as the peace-seekers, and the Government, in the IRA's eyes would suffer a propaganda reversal if they refused it. If they accepted it, then the

Provisionals' credentials as a political force would be greatly enhanced. The fact that the proposal had sprung from two hard-liners also endeared it to MacStiofain who was highly protective of his uncompromising reputation. When the scheme was put to the Army Council they backed it unanimously and word was sent out to the units that an important development was in the offing.

The offer was put on 13 June and rejected the same day by Whitelaw, who said that he could not respond to 'an ultimatum from terrorists'. The following day, however, the initiative's fortunes were boosted by two SDLP politicians, John Hume from Derry and Paddy Devlin from Belfast, who announced that they felt that the proposals were sincere and called on Whitelaw to meet the IRA. They then travelled to Derry where they met MacStiofain and O'Connaill. The Provisionals outlined their demands: before talks could begin, republican prisoners would have to be granted the status of political prisoners; an independent witness who was not a politician should be present; any meeting would have to take place somewhere other than Stormont; there should be no restrictions on the team the Provisionals nominated, and that it should include Gerry Adams, currently detained in Long Kesh but not yet formally interned.

Hume and Devlin then put the proposals to Whitelaw. To the surprise of the Provisionals he acceded to everything but the request for a third party witness (though this was later granted). The extraordinary swiftness with which political status was surrendered was a reflection of the British Government's concern over the hunger strike that forty republican prisoners led by Billy McKee had been conducting in the Crumlin Road jail in support of their demand that they be treated as prisoners of war. Whitelaw was convinced that McKee was approaching death, an impression reinforced by alarmist rumours in Belfast.[5] A few days after the meeting Whitelaw announced some improvements in the prison regime for republican and loyalist prisoners — the right to wear their own clothes and receive more visits and food parcels — that amounted to *de facto* recognition of political status, and the thirty-day hunger strike was called off. Adams was released from prison into the custody of Devlin, now armed with passes to negotiate the road-blocks. On 20 June Adams and O'Connaill met with two of Whitelaw's representatives to discuss the terms of the truce. The Provos insisted that it must be bilateral with the Army stopping all arrests, raids and searches. On 22 June the Irish republican publicity bureau issued a statement announcing that the Provisional IRA would cease offensive operations from Monday 26 June. Whitelaw coyly responded in the House of Commons that afternoon by saying that the Army 'will obviously reciprocate'.

The negotiators had agreed that the meeting between Whitelaw and the Provisionals should take place ten days after the truce went into effect and would be kept secret. MacStiofain was anxious to dispel any impression that the Provisionals were negotiating from a position of weakness and instructions were issued to all units to continue bombing and shooting up to the deadline. A British Army sergeant was shot dead in the Short Strand five minutes before the truce came into being.

MacStiofain spent some of the remaining time talking to trade union officials and lawyers, wise in the ways of the powerful, who advised him about the negotiating gambits he might expect to meet in London, where it had been agreed the meeting would take place.

On Friday 7 July the Provisionals' team was flown by helicopter from Derry to Aldergrove airport outside Belfast where they boarded a Royal Air Force plane for London. Earlier that morning two British Army officers in plain clothes who had been out drinking were found wandering around the Bogside and were taken hostage by the Provos as an insurance against the negotiators' safe return. No one said much on the flight. Martin McGuinness joked with Seamus Twomey about his fear of flying. They were a mixed crew. From the national leadership were Sean MacStiofain and the gaunt and introspective Daithi O'Connaill. Ruairi O'Bradaigh had fallen foul of MacStiofain, who believed he was conspiring against him, and was left behind. McGuinness was there to represent Derry, and Twomey, Gerry Adams and Ivor Bell, Belfast. O'Connaill was regarded as the Provisionals' theoretician, and was intended as the main intellectual strength on the team. The inclusion of Adams and Bell was a surprise to the security forces.

Adams was only 23 years old. By the autumn of 1971 he had taken over as the commanding officer of the Second Battalion in Belfast and had also joined the Belfast Brigade staff as second-in-command or adjutant to Twomey. His republican connections had ensured that he had an immediate position in the organisation. He was intelligent and energetic and quickly established himself as a planner and organiser rather than an active volunteer. Bell was Adams' deputy in the Second Battalion and they were close friends. He had been active in the border campaign and afterwards left to work in England. He was the antithesis of the old-fashioned republican and an unlikely ally for Adams, a drinker and womaniser nicknamed 'the Heathen'. He was also on the Brigade staff, and was at one stage the operations officer.

In London they were taken to a house in Cheyne Row in Chelsea on the banks of the Thames, the home of Whitelaw's junior minister, Paul Channon. As usual when meeting with British politicians, the Provisionals gravely declined the offer of drink. MacStiofain's puritanical streak was offended by the opulence of the surroundings and the fact that none of the accoutrements of high-level negotiation − writing paper, water jug, even the proverbial conference table − had been provided. He was slightly mollified, however, when Whitelaw pronounced his name with the correct Irish inflexion.

There was little to negotiate on. The Provisionals had already decided that they would only be satisfied with one outcome. A week previously there had been a meeting in Dublin chaired by MacStiofain to discuss the IRA's position. According to McGuinness 'We basically agreed that the only purpose of the meeting with Whitelaw was to demand the declaration of intent to withdraw.'[17] MacStiofain opened the proceedings with a repetition of the Provisionals' demands: the recognition by the British Government of the right of the people of Ireland acting

227

as a unit to decide the future of Ireland; a declaration of intent to withdraw its troops from Irish soil by 1 January 1975; and an amnesty for political prisoners. After some exchanges over Bloody Sunday it was decided that Whitelaw would bring the Government's reply within a week. In the meantime the truce would continue without a deadline. According to McGuinness, Whitelaw at one stage offered to produce a formula that would offer a new British position on the matter of withdrawal and reunification, which would be put to them at a meeting in Belfast a week later. On the whole, though, he 'quickly realised that there was nothing in the talks for us. They just wanted to buy time for the truce.'[17]

MacStiofain was keen that the truce should hold for as long as possible. It was the vital element in the sub-strategy he had planned. His intention was to convene a conference of Irish organisations of all political and religious denominations to discuss the North. Unless there were Protestant representatives the exercise would be worthless. The longer the truce held, the greater the chance of involving them. Any progress towards calling the conference would make it more difficult for Whitelaw to reject the Provisionals' demands completely.

Within forty-eight hours of the end of the meeting, all these considerations had become academic. The atmosphere in the Province had been tense for days, despite the existence of the ceasefire. Barricades had gone up in the loyalist areas and there was an outbreak of sectarian intimidation. In the Rathcoole area of Belfast, Protestants forced all 300 Catholic families to leave the estate. Some displaced families were allocated by the Housing Executive to houses on the Lenadoon Estate in West Belfast, vacated by Protestants who had left the district. On Friday afternoon the loyalist paramilitaries of the Ulster Defence Association (UDA) intervened saying that they would burn down the houses if Catholics occupied them. The Provisionals pressed the Army to install the families, otherwise they would do so themselves. By the following day Lenadoon had turned into a symbolic and crucial test for the IRA of the Government's sincerity concerning the truce. On Saturday Twomey, and another leading Belfast Provo, Seamus Loughran, held talks with Army officers in Lenadoon to try to resolve the matter. On Sunday there was another meeting. Twomey gave the Army until 4.00 pm to move the Catholics in. During the afternoon troops turned away a van carrying the Catholics' furniture, fearing a confrontation with a gang of UDA men who had gathered behind the Army lines. A Catholic crowd of about 3,000 began to stone the soldiers and they returned fire with rubber bullets and CS gas. Seamus Twomey announced that he considered the Army had violated the truce, and a gunbattle was shortly under way. MacStiofain was angry and bitter. An attempt was made to contact Whitelaw but he was unavailable, and at 7.00 pm MacStiofain officially declared the truce over. Whitelaw responded by accusing the Provisionals of having manufactured the Lenadoon incident. Shortly before midnight six bombs exploded in the centre of Derry.

Given the charged atmosphere and the mutual hatred and hostility between the Army and the Provos it was extremely unlikely that the truce would have lasted very long. As always, MacStiofain was haunted by the prospect of a repetition of the events of August 1969 when the IRA had earned the contempt of the ghetto population. Any aggression by the Army had to be responded to: 'There was no option. If our units had been ordered to stand aside, the consequences would have been disastrous. The IRA would have lost the defence initiative and all credibility with the people.'[16] It was this fear, rather than the prospect of alienating the Catholics by indiscriminate violence, that fuelled MacStiofain's thought processes.

The chances of any political progress resulting from the talks were equally slim. The Provisionals' cast of mind left no room for manoeuvre. The marginal shifts, which were all the British could realistically offer, would have been contemptuously rejected by MacStiofain and his men in their triumphant mood. They had bombed their way to the conference table only to find to their disgust that they were still expected to negotiate. For Republican leaders of the IRA who were present it was a formative experience. 'I learned in two hours,' said Martin McGuinness, 'what Irish politicians still haven't learned; that the British don't give easily.'[17] Both resolved that from now on there could be no question of an end to the violence until the ink on the treaty of withdrawal was dry.

CHAPTER TWELVE

Bloody Friday

In 1972 the IRA had enjoyed an influence on politics unparalleled for fifty years, and unthinkable only three years before. They had done nothing with it. The nature of the organisation saw to that. Its philosophy was all or nothing. In republican thinking, compromise equalled betrayal. That conviction was the IRA's strength and weakness. It sustained it in the lean years and crippled it in the good ones. The encounter with Whitelaw confirmed in the minds of all who took part the wisdom of that attitude. The IRA had been straightforward in negotiation. The British had replied in 'doublespeak and diplomatic jargon'.[1] Afterwards, politics was once again shoved to the margins of the Provisionals' preoccupations. The only remaining option was to resume the campaign, as MacStiofain promised, 'with the utmost ferocity and ruthlessness'.[2] In the coming years the violence was to become darker and more incoherent, its aimlessness reflecting the political sterility and intransigence of the leadership. The commanders in Dublin and Belfast had interpreted the fact that the British Government had agreed to see them as a sign of weakness. Once the fighting resumed they were anxious to make sure that their own involvement in the talks evidenced no such slackening of will.

The events of Friday 21 July were designed to demonstrate this. Bloody Friday, as it immediately became known, was the most concentrated burst of violence yet perpetrated by the Belfast IRA. It was planned by Twomey, assisted by Bell and a leading Belfast Provisional who is now a senior member of Sinn Fein. During the day they placed twenty-two bombs in the city centre, mostly hidden in cars. All the Belfast battalions were involved but members of the Third Battalion planted the bulk of the devices (fifteen).[3] Shortly after lunch, in the space of an hour and a quarter, they went off one by one. Panic-stricken crowds massed in the middle of the streets. Roads out of the city were blocked with fleeing drivers. A crowd who took shelter in the Oxford Street bus station after hearing a warning that there was a bomb on the Albert Bridge nearby were blasted by an explosion that killed six of them including two Welsh Guards and two teenage boys.

Initial reports said that eleven people had been killed but the figure was later reduced to nine. The confusion had been caused because many of the bodies were dismembered. The Provisionals immediately accepted responsibility for the explosions and indignantly insisted that they had telephoned warnings about each bomb's position an hour or half an hour beforehand to three separate organisations. What they did not say was that they had telephoned a large number of hoax warnings as well.[3] There was little public remorse. MacStiofain's reaction was to construct a rambling and fantastic case to show that the warnings had been deliberately ignored to discredit the Provisionals.

Until now Whitelaw had resisted pressure from the Army to move into the no-go areas of Free Derry, on the grounds that it would alienate the Catholics at a crucial time when the Government was trying to win their confidence and involve them in the new, equitable machinery that was being planned to replace Stormont. After Bloody Friday, the Army's case was unanswerable. Ten days later, in the early hours of the morning, armoured cars, tanks and bulldozers ringed the Creggan and the Bogside and began nudging away the barriers that had stood for the best part of a year. The pitched battle the Army had prepared for never took place. The IRA had long since taken the decision not to stand and fight, only too aware that such a gesture would be suicidal. Most of the sixty or so hardened activists had fled over the border to Donegal after being alerted to Operation Motorman, as it was codenamed, by the build-up of armour in the area. McGuinness stayed behind but was able to slip through the security checks in disguise and join them.[3]

On the same day, in the village of Claudy, twelve miles outside Derry, three car bombs went off killing six people and wounding two more who subsequently died of their injuries. No warnings were given. This time the IRA vehemently denied responsibility, though the security forces believe it to have been an IRA unit operating independently. The bombings and killings could not disguise the fact that the failure of the ceasefire and the disappearance of Free Derry were serious setbacks. The existence of a republican mini-state inside the North was good propaganda which the leadership exploited to the hilt, going up there frequently for press conferences and displaying it to journalists and camera crews as an example of the symbiotic nature of the IRA's relationship with the people. Losing it dispelled the notion that the Provisionals still held the military initiative. By the autumn of 1972 the victory which had been trumpeted in the Belfast Provisionals' new year address seemed a long way away.

There was no immediate lowering of morale. Republicanism was steeped in failure. Indeed, it sometimes seemed that it was nourished by it, so that every setback merely reinforced the 'old, indefatigable obduracy'.[4] Before the truce, however, the bombers and gunmen had a goal in sight. They were driven by the thought that one more explosion, one more dead soldier might prove the fatal act that broke the British will to stay. After the truce and after Motorman, this conviction grew less sustainable.

By the late summer it was clear that the Provisionals' military ascendancy was over. They began to come under increasingly painful pressure, not only from the Army, who had started to use more ruthless and unconventional tactics, but from a new quarter: the loyalist paramilitaries. In August 1971 a leaflet had appeared in the Protestant terraces of Sandy Row, Shankill and East Belfast announcing the formation of a new organisation, the Ulster Defence Association. The inaugural statement portentously declared:

> Being convinced that the enemies of the Faith and Freedom are determined to destroy the State of Northern Ireland and thereby enslave the people of God, we call on all members of our loyalist institutions and other responsible citizens to organise themselves *immediately* into platoons of twenty under the command of someone capable of acting as sergeant. Every effort must be made to arm these platoons with whatever weapons are available.[5]

The founders of the UDA had manned the barricades of the Protestant ghettoes during the rioting of 1969 and 1970. Their re-emergence as a quasi-military group was caused by the belief that after internment the Protestant areas would come under attack by Catholic crowds and the UDA's initial function was intended to be defensive. Later, though, the mood changed. The collapse of Stormont and news of the IRA's talks with Whitelaw convinced them that the Provisionals' campaign was on the point of driving the North into the hateful embrace of the South. The conviction that Westminster was on the point of betraying the loyalists was widespread in Ulster in 1972. It was the force behind the Vanguard movement founded by William Craig, the former Stormont home affairs minister, shortly before Stormont was prorogued. Inevitably it drew its inspiration from the past, and members were pledged to an updated version of Edward Carson's 1912 Covenant, binding them to Ulster's defence. Craig made an effort to invest the organisation with some totalitarian chic, arriving at the first rally in Lisburn in February 1972 in a motorcycle sidecar accompanied by uniformed bodyguards and calling on the 7,000-strong crowd to raise their hands three times and shout out 'I do!' if they agreed with his message. But it was hardly Nuremburg.

As the collapse of Stormont approached, the rallies increased in size and the language of Craig grew more threatening and violent. In a speech to the Monday Club, a right-wing pressure group attached to the British Conservative Party, he declared: 'When we say force we mean force. We will only assassinate our enemies when we are denied our democratic rights.' Four days before Stormont finally fell he told Unionists at Newtownbreda, 'the great majority want no political juggling. The course is pretty clear – liquidate the IRA.'[6] This was an accurate reflection of the feelings of the combat-jacketed men from the Shankill and Sandy Row who stewarded the Vanguard marches and the monster rallies.

As 1972 progressed the murder gangs, dormant for six years and for forty before that, reappeared in Belfast. It was clear from the outset that they were not concerned whether or not their victims were members of the IRA. It was enough that they were Catholics. The pattern for the killings had been set in 1966 when 'Gusty' Spence and two other Shankill hard men operating under the banner of the UVF had murdered a young Catholic barman as he left a pub in Protestant West Belfast early one morning. This shoddy act was intended both as a warning against a sell-out to the South to the supposedly liberalising regime of Terence O'Neill and as a caution to the leaders of the Belfast IRA, who in the imagination of the UVF planned an uprising to coincide with the fiftieth anniversary of the 1916 Easter Rising. On the whole, the Shankill Protestants were repelled by Spence and his companions. By 1972, however, the threat to the Protestant state and fear of the IRA were much more commonly felt.

The killings began in earnest in April and May. On 20 April, just before midnight two men went into the Arkle Taxi office at the bottom of the Crumlin Road and asked for a cab to Ardoyne. By this stage taxidrivers would only drive at night to parts of town inhabited by their co-religionists so the men were sure of getting a Catholic. The driver was Gerald Donnelly. Once inside the car the men produced guns and directed him to a street off the Crumlin Road. At the inquest a woman told how she had heard a car draw up at midnight and the sound of what sounded like a man being beaten followed by a noise she took to be a car backfiring (revealing a highly optimistic nature, given the times). When she

235

investigated she found Donnelly bleeding to death from five bullet wounds in his chest. He had no connection with the IRA.

In other cases a mere rumour was enough to condemn a man. Bernard Moane, a 46-year-old drinks firm representative, was approached by three men in a bar on the Shankill Road in May and taken to the Knockagh Monument, a beauty spot in the hills north of Belfast. His three kidnappers drank his samples and then warned picnickers to move off because 'we are going to fill a chap in'. Moane was made to lie on the ground, murmuring according to witnesses: 'Ah, no, boys.' Then he was shot three times in the head. Moane was believed to be connected with the assassination of James Elliot, a lorry-driver and member of the UDR executed by the IRA whose booby-trapped body was dumped on the border after he had been held for two days. Again there was no evidence that Moane had any IRA connections.

The Belfast IRA had a long tradition of defending the city's Catholics from assassinations of this sort. Indeed, it had been the organisation's main function during the reign of terror of the murder gangs in the twenties and the sectarian riots of the thirties. When the killings started up, the Army Council in Dublin had sanctioned the use of retaliation. In effect this amounted to authorising revenge killings. Realistically, the IRA could offer little protection to the random abductions and executions carried out by the UDA, the UVF and the other loyalist splinter groups. The only effective tactic was to convince the loyalists that their campaign was futile by engaging in random killings in return.

On 30 June an innocent Catholic barman was beaten up and executed in the early hours of the morning in a children's playground off the Shankill Road. Within twenty-four hours two Protestants were assassinated in reprisal. David Fisher and Hugh Clawson, both in their thirties, were wandering back from a UDA-owned shebeen when they were intercepted near the Catholic area of the 'Bone' off the Crumlin Road. Their bodies were found the following afternoon by children at play on some nearby wasteground. They had been shot in the head and the neck.

With each killing and reprisal the horror seemed to deepen. In July a resident of Cliftonville Road in North Belfast called the police after he saw three men staggering into the city waterworks in the early hours of the morning with what appeared to be a body. Later that day the badly beaten corpse of David Andrews, a simple-minded Protestant who worked as a porter in the Belfast City Hospital, was discovered. An asthmatic, he had left his sister's house, where he was supposed to be spending the night, to return home for some tablets he had forgotten.

Many of the Protestant killings were conducted with a particular gruesomeness. In the early hours of 12 July four Protestant men, one with 'UDA' written in ink on the back of his hand, broke into the home of Sarah McClenaghan in Oldpark Road in North Belfast. She was a middle-aged Catholic widow with three children. With her were her son David, who was 15 and mentally retarded, and a Protestant lodger, David Titterington. The intruders were armed and three of them were masked. They began by demanding to know where the guns were hidden. Mrs McClenaghan's truthful assertion that there were no guns had no effect. The men interrogated their captives about their religion. Titterington frantically explained that he was a Protestant — he even produced his Orange sash to prove it — and that Mrs McClenaghan was too. It was to no avail. He was taken to the attic and made to kneel. Before he could be shot the gunman was called downstairs and Titterington escaped through the skylight.

In the living-room the leader of the men, Trevor Hinton, returned to the subject of religion. He asked the boy what church he went to and receiving an ambiguous reply asked him to bring the family prayerbook. The simple youth returned not only with a Catholic missal but with his mother's rosary beads as well. That sealed his fate. Mrs McClenaghan was ordered to take off her clothes and Hinton raped her. Then the two were taken upstairs and ordered to lie on the bed.

237

As David was shot Mrs McClenaghan flung herself across him to shield him from the bullets, but she was too late to save him. She was hit in the thigh and hand. The men fled thinking them both dead, but Mrs McClenaghan survived to give evidence against the four in court and send them to jail. Such endings were the exception rather than the rule. Most of the sectarian assassinations of the period went unpunished.

The loyalist killings frequently had an element of ritual to them. They took place late in the evening when the participants had drunk themselves into viciousness. One practice was known as 'rompering' where groups of up to twelve men would gather to kick and punch — 'give a few digs' — to their usually innocent victim, at leisure in a backroom or garage, before shooting him. One, a middle-aged, inoffensive night-watchman, Thomas Madden, was found dead with every inch of his body covered with small stab wounds. There had to be a theoretical justification for this ghastliness. Usually it was that the body in question was either connected to the IRA or could give intelligence about IRA activities and personalities. In this the loyalists were either deliberately or stupidly mistaken. Virtually none of the victims were members of the organisation.

To a certain extent the loyalists aped the IRA. They justified their violence with a political motive. To emphasise their distance from common criminality they adopted, like the IRA, a military structure and discipline. When special category status for political prisoners was introduced to the jails by Whitelaw they eagerly took advantage of it. In prison agitations in Long Kesh and the Crum loyalists and republicans often made common cause. There was even a grim camaraderie, evidenced by the letter sent by 'Gusty' Spence to the widow of Joe McCann after 'Big Joe' was shot by the Paras:

My Dear Mrs McCann,
    I would like to tender to you my deepest and profoundest sympathy on the tragic death of your beloved husband, Joe.
    There are those who would find it strange to hear from someone such as myself but I can assure you that whilst

your husband and I may have been opposed to each other in politics we shared that common bond that is known only to those who fight their own respective corners to the best of their ability. He was a soldier of the Republic and I a Volunteer of Ulster and we made no apology for being what we are or were. Joe once did me a good turn indirectly and I never forgot him for his humanity and even though I never got the chance to thank him personally I am almost sure that he knew how I felt and that I was grateful to him.[7]

The last sentence is thought to be a reference to an episode when two members of the UVF wandered into McCann's fiefdom, the Markets, but were released unharmed on his word.

The Provisionals were less concerned than Officials like McCann were about such gestures of non-sectarianism. The loyalist assassinations had landed them with a role they needed if they were to maintain their credibility as the defenders of the Catholic community, yet simultaneously did not want. Generally the IRA assassination squads were much less active than their loyalist counterparts; and at least some of the reprisals were carried out by Catholic vigilantes with no IRA connections. There were 300 civilian deaths in 1972 of which 122 were classed as assassinations. Of these, forty were Protestants and eighty-one Catholics.

Assassinating Protestants in reprisals – 'stiffing' them in Provo slang – was a retrograde step. The organisation was back to where it had been in 1970. This realisation was reinforced by the fact that in the two years following Motorman the British Army was for the first time on the offensive. In 1973 Tuzo was replaced as the Northern Ireland commander by General Sir Frank King. King believed that too many troops were being deployed in Derry and along the border, where they served as easy targets for IRA snipers and mine-layers.

The crucial area was Belfast. Throughout 1973 King moved troops into the city. He shared Kitson's enthusiasm for immersing the companies on the ground in the minutiae of the lives of their opponents. Company commanders were encouraged to concentrate their resources on building up a complete intelligence picture of the IRA. They cut down on the old garrison tactic of patrolling and switched resources to covert operations. Teams were deployed in observation posts hidden in attics and stayed there for days on end, reporting the movements of the Provos by radio. Much of the new surveillance activity was carried out by plainclothes military intelligence teams who cruised the ghettoes in suitably battered cars, posing as civilians, and set up phoney businesses, including a massage parlour, as a means of infiltrating the community. One of their most ambitious efforts was the Four Square laundry, which plied its trade in West Belfast, travelling the streets in an armour-plated, radio-equipped van collecting washing from house to house, picking up information and testing clothes for signs of explosives or gunpowder. When the IRA learned of its activities the van was ambushed on the Twinbrook Estate and the driver killed. This new informality spread to all areas of Army operations. In May 1973 the occupants of a passing car in Andersonstown machine-gunned five men, killing one of them. At first it was assumed that it was the work of a loyalist gang, but it later emerged that an Army plainclothes squad was responsible.

The Army information service deliberately set out to disrupt internal IRA morale. They would frequently announce that an arrest had been the result of information from an informer when it had not, or put an exaggeratedly high figure for the haul in a robbery, often resulting in a spate of punishment shootings as the Provos meted justice to the imaginary miscreants.[8]

The IRA was also hampered by legal changes which increased the chances of their arrest and conviction. At the end of 1972 one of the British law lords, Lord Diplock, visited Northern Ireland at the invitation of William Whitelaw to consider how the legal machinery of Northern Ireland could be adapted to deal with terrorism. One of the main concerns was that military ignorance of the law meant that offenders were often set free on legal technicalities. In his report, published on 20 December 1972 and immediately accepted by the Government, Diplock recommended a simplified form of arrest that enabled suspects to be locked away on the word of a soldier. He also urged that in cases involving weapons possession, the onus of proof should be shifted to the defendant. Confessions should be considered admissible in court unless it could be proved that they were obtained through torture. The most significant change, however, was the introduction of juryless courts. The justification for this was that juries and witnesses were being intimidated. By 1972 any means were considered justified by both the IRA and their loyalist counterparts to subvert the courts. In January, the IRA had murdered a Protestant bus-driver in East Belfast who was due to give evidence against three Short Strand Provisionals accused of the relatively minor offence of hijacking a bus. 'Unless the state can secure [witnesses'] safety,' Diplock wrote, 'then it would be unreasonable to expect them to testify voluntarily, and morally wrong to compel them to do so.' The anger that the new system provoked among republicans was a testimony to its effectiveness.

The IRA were also being increasingly hard-pressed by the Army. As Army intelligence improved, the chances of arrest for a Provisional increased. The more experienced of them now ran considerable risks with every operation they carried out. They either persisted and courted arrest and a long prison sentence or they stopped active service. In Belfast the better tacticians began to be removed from the streets with morale-sapping regularity. Gerry Adams, who had succeeded Seamus Twomey as Belfast Brigade commander, led a pimpernel existence after returning from the London talks, commanding his men from a succession of safe houses and keeping constantly on the move. He was eventually picked up again early in 1973 and interned in Long Kesh. He was succeeded by his friend Ivor Bell who survived until early 1974 before being arrested. He in turn was succeeded by Sean Convery, who lasted only a few weeks before being captured in March 1974. His successor, Brendan 'Darkie' Hughes, survived only until 10 May when he was arrested and sentenced to twenty years in prison. The result was that the fighting fell on the shoulders of younger volunteers, many of whom were no longer motivated by the prospect of victory but by a vague pressure exerted by family and friends that it was their duty to fight. The IRA was forced to throw its net wider to gain recruits. The camaraderie and attention to internal discipline and security evident in the pre-truce units began to fray and slacken, with the result that many of the young volunteers were only in action for a short period before being locked up. Between April 1973 and April 1974 no fewer that 1,292 people were charged with terrorist offences.

When, later, the Government moved away from special legislation (such as the interim custody orders which enabled soldiers to arrest and detain) in favour of normal criminal methods there was little respite. In January 1975 the RUC set up a new Crime Squad entitled to plunder the Special Branch intelligence files which had previously been jealously guarded by the branch, partly in order to preserve their empire and partly to protect their sources. A network of collators was set up to bring together disparate pieces of information previously held in isolation around the various departments of the RUC and the Army, an elementary move that resulted in a continuing flow of convictions.[3]

South of the border the IRA was also suffering. The early, wary tolerance that the authorities had shown towards the IRA in the wake of the August 1969 rioting did not last long and official hostility towards them grew in proportion to the violence of the campaign. In the spring of 1972 Irish premier Jack Lynch had announced the reintroduction of Part Five of the Offences Against the State Act, the Republic's own anti-republican legislation which was as harsh as the Special Powers Act in the North. Under its provisions suspected terrorists could be convicted on the evidence of a senior Garda officer in a juryless court presided over by three judges.

These measures did not surprise republicans, who complained bitterly that, lauded as patriots one minute, they were designated criminals in the eyes of the state once emotions had subsided. The IRA had a complicated relationship with the Free State. The fact that the Republic was Irish and Catholic did nothing to diminish the IRA's contempt for its government and institutions. If anything, it intensified it. On the other hand, the Republic was the IRA's hinterland for its campaign in the North, providing it, at various times, with an operational base for launching attacks over the border, a landing-point for weapons and explosives, a refuge when life in the North became too hot, and a relatively hospitable climate in which they could oversee the organisation's operations. Despite the gradual shift of power and action to Belfast over the period, the IRA's administrative headquarters remains in Dublin, and most of the most important gatherings take place there.

However much hatred it might feel towards the government of the Twenty-six Counties, there were overwhelming reasons for not provoking the anger of the authorities. For most of the time, Army Order Eight, a long-standing IRA instruction forbidding military activity south of the border, has been rigorously applied (though in the early eighties, desperately short of funds, the Army Council sanctioned a number of kidnappings that resulted in confrontations with the Gardai and police).

Each Irish government was faced with a similar dilemma when considering how to deal with the IRA. They were confronted with an organisation whose ideology was as hostile to the Irish state as it was to the British. Self-interest demanded that they move against it. On the other hand, the extent of latent sentimentality about the IRA among the Irish people made a case for caution. Shortly after the announcement the Gardai launched a series of raids, arresting Ruairi O'Bradaigh, his brother Sean, who was the Sinn Fein director of publicity, and Joe Cahill. All these were charged with membership of the IRA and immediately launched hunger strikes, a tactic agreed by the leadership six months before. They were each released for lack of evidence, in Cahill's case not before he had gone twenty-three days without food.

One November Sunday MacStiofain was picked up in the early hours as he was being driven around Dublin Bay by

243

Joe Cahill. He was charged with IRA membership. With characteristic bravado, he announced that he was not only on hunger strike but on thirst strike as well. To MacStiofain's undoubted satisfaction, his ordeal made him the centre of attention. At the hearing at the special court he was accompanied by a doctor and his whispered responses through parched lips could scarcely be heard by the judges. During the proceedings a patriotic young lorry-driver dramatically flung a handful of coins towards the bench and shouted 'British traitors!' before being ejected from the court. Back in Mountjoy MacStiofain had a string of important visitors, including Dr McQuaid, the former Archbishop of Dublin, who gave him absolution. As his condition worsened it was decided to fly him to the military hospital at The Curragh camp, the South's main army base thirty miles outside Dublin. In his delirium, MacStiofain imagined that the Irish authorities were plotting to deliver him up to the British and claims he lashed out at the helicopter pilot in an attempt to crash the aircraft. At the hospital he was brought a form expressing his objection to being intravenously fed if he fell into a coma. He refused to sign it, insisting that it be retyped in Irish. As MacStiofain slipped towards oblivion there were large antigovernment demonstrations in Dublin, and troops stood by in the expectation of trouble. A republican priest, Father Sean McManus, who had visited MacStiofain frequently, warned him on the tenth day without food or water that he would probably die within twenty-four hours and pleaded with him to abandon his fast and avert the bloodshed that would follow his death. At last MacStiofain agreed, but not until three IRA prisoners had been brought in at his request to witness his condition.

MacStiofain was only too aware of the effect this compromise would have on his standing in the movement. The whole point of these strikes was that you got your way or died. Last-minute changes of heart devalued the tactic as a political weapon, and hardened the authorities' resolve to sit things out in future. In an attempt to retain some dignity from the episode MacStiofain maintained his hunger strike, though the water he was now taking was bolstered with glucose. On this regime he soldiered on for the rest of his fifty-seven day fast until the leadership intervened and ordered him to stop.

This episode finished MacStiofain. His authority, built on a reputation for toughness and dedication, was severely bruised by his failure to see the fast through. His brusque manner, towering self-regard and humourlessness ensured a good supply of enemies ready to spread scurrilous stories about the exact extent of MacStiofain's ordeal. It was rumoured that his survival during the hunger and thirst stage of the fast was not unconnected to the fact that he had been taking hourly showers in the prison. But in the end his fall from grace was not so much the result of abandoning the hunger strike as refusing to accept the orders of the IRA officer commanding the republican prisoners in Mountjoy prison in Dublin. IRA discipline demands that any prisoner, no matter how high-ranking, is reduced to the status of volunteer once he is imprisoned and is required to submit to the jail hierarchy. MacStiofain refused to do this. Most republicans regarded him as 'an egomaniac'. Martin McGuinness who was the IRA adjutant in The Curragh camp at the time (he was captured in the South when he fled over the border after Motorman) said: 'He thought everyone in Dublin should be dancing attendance on him. He served a purpose up until 1972, but it was clear by then that he had no long-term future in the movement.'[1] When he emerged from prison he was reprimanded and removed from his position as chief-of-staff. Most cruelly of all, republican publications began to refer to him as John Stephenson.

While MacStiofain was in prison Joe Cahill had taken temporary command of the IRA. He was replaced in March 1973 by Seamus Twomey, whose reign was interrupted three months later when he was arrested by the Gardai and jailed for three years for membership of the IRA. In October, while he was exercising in Mountjoy prison in Dublin, a helicopter bearing an IRA rescue team alighted in the yard and took off again with Twomey and two other leading republicans, Kevin Mallon and J. B. O'Hagan, on board. Legend has it that a bemused guard cried 'Shut the gates!' as the helicopter climbed into the sky. Twomey resumed his command (which had been held in his absence by a little-known republican from Tipperary, Eamon Doherty, who was himself arrested shortly afterwards and charged with membership) and was not recaptured until 1977. Such exploits provided a welcome boost to morale.

Joe Cahill was arrested in March 1973 when the West German-registered cargo ship *Claudia* was intercepted by the Irish Navy in Waterford Bay. On board were five tons of arms, which had been loaded in Tripoli, a donation from Colonel Gadhafy towards the 'anti-imperialist' struggle in the North. The Libyans made the original approach to MacStiofain. After his imprisonment they asked to deal with Cahill, by now a familiar media figure.[9] Cahill believes that the German skipper of the vessel had been in touch with British intelligence from the start. He noticed the presence of a submarine on radar on the return voyage but was assured that it was probably only a Russian vessel on exercises. It now seems that the *Claudia* was trailed by a Royal Navy submarine until she was in Irish waters, when the authorities could move in. The loss of the shipment, which contained general purpose machine-guns, Kalashnikov automatic rifles, sub-machine-guns and grenades was, according to Cahill, 'a disaster. At that time the sources of weapons in Ireland had dried up and we needed to look further afield. The IRA depended on those arms and we believed that this was a new market. We pinned a lot of faith on those particular weapons and it took the IRA a long time to get over it.'[9]

One successful importation was the RPG-7, a small Russian-manufactured rocket which was used all over the Province from late in 1972. Its propaganda value was highly prized by the Provisionals and staged photographs of hooded men lurking in hedgerows became part of the output of the republican publicity bureau, painting a romantic, if rather inaccurate, picture of the IRA's *modus operandi*.

From 1973 onwards the IRA's military fortunes entered a long and continuous decline. Since then, the numbers of deaths, bombings and shootings fell steadily. In 1972 the IRA killed 103 soldiers, seventeen RUC men and police reservists and twenty-five members of the UDR. In 1973 the number of soldiers killed fell to fifty-eight with thirteen RUC and eight UDR men. By the end of 1974 only twenty-eight soldiers had died, fifteen RUC and seven UDR men, and in 1975 only fourteen soldiers and sixteen RUC and UDR men were killed.

In Belfast the Provisionals changed their tactics. The revulsion caused by Bloody Friday persuaded the Provisionals gradually to abandon the car bomb. In any case it was dawning on even the slowest volunteer that bombing 'economic targets' was not having the desired decisive effect on the British exchequer. As a result of the many arrests and the increased Army presence, prolonged engagements with the Army faded out and were replaced with single-shot sniping. These were one- or two-man operations. Great emphasis was put on avoiding capture, the importance of a good 'run back' or escape route from the sniping point and the use of 'dicks', schoolchildren who acted as scouts and look-outs. The IRA training manual, the 'Green Book', advises:

In order to set up a sniping operation it must be well planned beforehand. In your Coy. [company] area you should have a wide range of positions to choose from. It is not feasible to run to a call-house [safe house] or move every time a patrol is spotted, too much can go wrong eg dangerous positioning, run backs not planned. A lot of positions are given away sometimes due to negligence on Vols. parts. They make operations look obvious to civilians by acting suspiciously in and around positions, by leaving empty shells behind after operation [sic] IO [intelligence officer] will gather all possible intelligence needed for the operation. This will include lay-out of district, times and strengths of patrols etc. When this is gathered the IO will pass the information on to the ASU [active service unit] who will decide what tactics to adopt for the operation.

When position is picked you will have your weapon in a standby house nearby where you will have safe and easy access to your position. All Vols will be fully briefed before operation eg snipping position [sic], run back, dumping of weapons etc. The sniper will be of experience and fully trained on all weapons in the Coy. A Vol. should be capable of proper sighting, be able to clear stoppages, proper gas regulating. When a patrol is sighted near your position the sniper will move into his firing . . . position [which] should command a clear view with all available cover being used to its fullest. Scouts will be on hand to warn him of any other immediate danger (eg other patrols) All Vols. on operations must wear gloves and also hoods in so far as circumstances will allow. The sniper and coverman will take up positions and will sight on his target. When preparing to fire, pull butt of weapon into shoulder, relay your breathing, don't pull at the trigger, squeeze it gently. When ready to fire hold your breath for a second or so as to avoid any unnecessary movement.

After operation retreat on your run back . . . it is good practice to have a secondary plan of escape in the event of any unforeseen difficulties with your main plan. After reaching your base give weapon to QM [quartermaster] who will prepare it for dumping. All local units should be familiarised with the General Search and follow up tactics of the Army . . . It will be your own speed and efficiency that will enable you to vacate that area before the enemy has time to mobilise.

CHAPTER THIRTEEN

Bombing Britain

In 1972 the growing realisation that the campaign in the North alone was not going to drive the British out of Ireland revived interest in the idea of extending the campaign to Britain. The tactic was not new in the history of republicanism, and the IRA's operations in Britain had produced mixed results. Memories of the IRA's ineffectual 1939 campaign which ended with the execution of Barnes and McCormack and the various bungled arms raids of the fifties were still fresh. But there was another precedent which did encourage optimism. Following the failure of the Fenian rising in 1857, there was a sensational incident that gave rise to the belief in some republican quarters that one bomb on the mainland was worth a hundred in Belfast. On 13 December 1867 a group of Fenians blew up the wall of Clerkenwell prison in London in an attempt to rescue a comrade, Richard O'Sullivan Burke.

It was a bloody debacle. The explosion killed twelve Londoners and blinded, maimed and disfigured thirty more. Burke was not freed, but the outrage had a more dramatic consequence. The Irish question, which had hovered in the wings of British political life for so long, was thrust into the centre of the stage. Fenian violence, as Gladstone noted, had persuaded the British public 'to embrace in a manner foreign to their habits in other times, the vast importance of the Irish controversy'.[1]

The idea of bombing Britain had been discussed informally

at various times since the start of the current campaign but little was done about it until June 1972 when the Army Council met in a hotel at Black Rock, near Dublin. The meeting was chaired by MacStiofain who had come to the conclusion that 'sooner or later there would have to be a drift to another area to take the heat off Belfast and Derry'.[2]

The original plan was highly ambitious. MacStiofain talked about sending over a wave of 'sleeper' units to find jobs and merge into the local community. When ordered into action, they would strike at factories and military instalments, opening a new front and diverting troops away from Ulster. A Belfast Provisional was given the task of recruiting a large number of serious, sober 18 to 24-year-olds for the task. In the end the operation never materialised. A team sent over on reconnaissance was arrested shortly after it returned. It had already reported that bombing units would have great trouble sustaining themselves in Britain for any length of time, and the plan was shelved.

It was not until early in 1973 that the Army Council gave its formal approval for action in Britain. There were good reasons why the leadership had hesitated from taking this step. Until the summer of 1972 there was still hope of a political accommodation with the British Government. Furthermore, there were considerable logistical difficulties involved in extending the campaign to the mainland and a high risk of failure.

By the start of 1973, however, the attitude of the leadership had changed. The talks with Whitelaw had reinforced their view that the British would only be driven into serious negotiations by force. The destruction the IRA was wreaking in Belfast and Derry was clearly not having this effect and the threshold of violence would have to be raised.

The aim of the British campaign, Daithi O'Connaill was to state later, was to 'strike at economic, military, political and judicial targets', and to bring home to the British Government that the consequences of 'the war being waged in their name in Ireland' would be felt at closer quarters.[3] But it was also designed to re-engage the attention of the British public, just as the Clerkenwell bomb had. Bombing Britain, the IRA leadership hoped, would generate a gathering weariness with the problem of Northern Ireland which would translate into pressure on the British political parties to pull out.

There was one event scheduled for the spring of 1973 which made the IRA particularly anxious to push the Irish question into the faces of the British public. After Stormont fell, the Conservative Government sought to reassure the Protestants that their future was secure within the United Kingdom through the means of a 'border poll'. The Northern Ireland electorate was to be asked the questions: 'Do you want Northern Ireland to remain part of the UK?' and 'Do you want Northern Ireland to be joined with the Republic of Ireland outside the UK?' Whitelaw solemnly announced that the wishes of the majority would be respected. The effect, as nationalists angrily pointed out, was to fix, immutably it seemed, the Unionists' veto on change in Northern Ireland. Both the SDLP and the republicans urged their followers to boycott the poll, so that when the outcome was announced, 97.8 per cent of those voting were in favour of maintaining the UK link.

The day of the poll, the Army Council decided, would be a suitable time for a violent demonstration that whatever the outcome, the IRA intended to continue its campaign until the British had withdrawn. The security forces believe that the plan eventually put into action was suggested by Jimmy Brown, a tireless 26-year-old from Belfast who had been arrested in November 1972 and imprisoned in the Maze on an interim custody order. In jail he developed appendicitis and was moved to the Lagan Valley Hospital on the southern edge of Belfast. While he was recuperating in a private ward guarded by two policemen, he was visited by two young women. Meanwhile, ten armed men took over the hospital reception area, and four of them moved on to Brown's room. When they arrived the two women disarmed the police guards and the whole party left, taking Brown with them.

According to police informants, Brown then went on the

run in Belfast, using the name John Clancy. He was involved in at least one shoot-out with the Army and received a wound in the process. While at large, he produced a plan for bombing targets in London and chose the personnel to carry it out. They included 22-year-old Dolours Price, and her 19-year-old sister Marion (the two women, the police believe, who helped spring Brown from hospital), a young student, Hugh Feeney, and Gerard Kelly. They were all members of the Belfast Brigade and had volunteered for the mission. They were chosen for their intelligence and respectable demeanour. The Price sisters were training to be teachers and thus, the planners believed, unlikely to attract attention.

The Provisionals would come to look back on the first British bombing as an amateurish operation. About three weeks before the attacks were due, the Belfast IRA hijacked four cars at gunpoint. They were resprayed, fitted with false number-plates, packed with explosives, detonators and timing devices and driven to Dublin.

There were eleven in the team, all of them young and relatively inexperienced. The youngest, Roisin McNearney, a typist and member of Cumman na mBan was only 18. On 5 March the first group, commanded by Feeney, left on board the ferry to Liverpool taking two of the cars; the second group under Marion Price left the next day. The team met up again in London, and the night before the bombings stayed in a number of different hotels in Pimlico. That morning, Dolours Price had flown in from Dublin to take charge of the operation. In the evening, while the others went to reconnoitre their targets or to the pub, she and her sister went to the Royal Court Theatre to see a play called *The Freedom of the City*, in which a group of Catholics stage a take-over of the Derry Guildhall. The following day the group rose before dawn and ferried the cars from the underground carpark in Dolphin Square to their targets. A Ford Corsair was parked outside the Metropolitan Police headquarters at New Scotland Yard. Another was driven to the Central Army Recruiting Office at Great Scotland Yard, Whitehall. A third was parked at the British Forces Broadcasting Services building in Dean Stanley Street, near Smith Square, and another outside the Central Criminal Court at the Old Bailey. By 8.30 am they were all in place, with the bombs in the back seats set to go off at 3.00 pm, and the team set off to Heathrow airport to fly back to Dublin. The Metropolitan Police had received an unspecific warning that an attack was on the way the day before, after a tip-off from a highly-placed IRA informer was passed on by the RUC. It was not long before the Corsair outside New Scotland Yard was attracting attention. A policeman noticed that the fixing holes on the number-plate did not correspond to the bolts securing it. Explosives experts were called in and the bomb was defused. At the same time the alarm was raised at ports and airports. At Heathrow the team were all set for their departure when the message came through. Three of them were already on the plane before being called back for questioning. All but one of the team was arrested.

After the discovery of the Corsair, there was a frantic search of the capital. At 2.50 Marion Price was being questioned at the airport. According to the detective who interrogated her she looked at her watch and smiled. Six minutes previously, the bomb at Great Scotland Yard had exploded. At 3.00 pm the Old Bailey device went off. The Dean Stanley Street bomb was discovered, however, and defused. One man died and 180 were injured in the blasts.

The mission had mixed results. The IRA had lost the Price sisters and their companions but they had also demonstrated that they could hit the institutional heart of Britain. The explosions had produced a satisfying howl of anger from politicians and the press, but there was no sign of the hoped-for clamour for withdrawal from the British public. The IRA were to learn that as a means of changing public opinion, bombing was hopelessly inefficient and counter-productive, though this never diminished the appetite for mainland operations.

Apart from creating a popular movement for withdrawal British bombing operations were also supposed to demon-strate the IRA's potency and strength of will. Bombing was a deeply incoherent way of conveying this message. The population reacted with incomprehension and stoicism. Although polls regularly suggested that most people were in favour of a withdrawal from Ireland, this sentiment was never translated into a political issue. After the capture of the Price sisters, the Army Council decided that 'in and out' jobs were too dangerous and revived the original plan for sleeper units. In future, IRA teams would have to stay put and carry on an intermittent series of attacks, going to ground after each bomb. The next IRA team acclimatised themselves before starting operations. In three weeks in August they planted nine bombs around the Midlands. A police bomb disposal expert was blown up and killed while trying to dismantle a device. In London they planted a series of small incendiary and booby-trap bombs in big stores — including Harrods — stations and stock exchanges which injured twenty people. In September a bomb exploded in Chelsea, injuring five.

Early in 1973 control of the mainland campaign had been taken over by Brian Keenan, a highly intelligent and efficient Belfast man noted for his left-wing views. The units were supposed to integrate themselves into the Irish expatriate community in London and the big cities, then wait for orders from the Dublin headquarters. Contact would be maintained by couriers, mostly women, who would forward directions and money.

In February Keenan asked Peter McMullen, a former Paratrooper who had defected to the IRA, if he would go to England and reconnoitre a series of targets. Keenan's idea was to attack industrial and military bases over the whole of England, from chemical plants and oil refineries to barracks. McMullen was to identify them and pass the information on to a courier who would notify the unit chosen to carry out the attack. That way, the theory ran, knowledge of the entire IRA network would be confined to a small circle. In the end, as so often with the organisation's activities, events were to turn out differently and McMullen ended up being involved in the bombing himself. At the end of February he took a ferry to Liverpool, faintly disguised in heavy brown-rimmed spectacles and carrying an American passport in the name of William Joseph Pekar Jr.

He went to a house in Bootle and met a man named 'English Joe', a Mancunian who had taken up the republican cause while living in Ireland. Joe was a sleeper and McMullen initially found him 'quite bright'. Joe was less impressed with the IRA. He had been given only £25 a month to live on and after six weeks in position had barely had contact with the courier. He and McMullen moved to a cheap flat in Liverpool and McMullen assumed the unlikely identity of a land speculator, an occupation which would explain his site-inspection activities. On one of his trips around the region he dropped in on his parents who lived in Skelmersdale, Yorkshire, narrowly missing the police who were looking for his brother. Eventually, he decided on Claro-Deverell Barracks, a Royal Engineer depot in Yorkshire, as a suitable target. He informed his courier and requested a shipment of commercial gelignite for the job. It duly arrived from Dublin concealed behind the door panels of a Ford Cortina.

McMullen constructed three timing devices from clocks bought from Woolworth and made three bombs. On the morning of 26 March, he and Joe walked through the camp, planted the bombs and 'walked out of the camp, like two guys going on leave'.[2] When the devices exploded at seven o'clock the only casualty was a canteen manageress. The pair were approaching Manchester when they heard the news. 'We said, "A good job done, a good job." Then we drove back to the flat and went out and celebrated. We went to a disco that night.'

Shortly beforehand, a bomb planted in a coach carrying soldiers up the M62 motorway had exploded killing nine soldiers as well as a woman and her two children. It had been placed there by a visiting IRA team from Belfast, armed with intelligence supplied by sympathetic Irishmen living in England. It soon became clear, however, that relying on the Irish community was fraught with risks. By the early seventies every pro-republican organisation had been thoroughly infiltrated and scrutinised by the Special Branch. It was for this reason that Sinn Fein, despite considerable pressure, never allowed its British supporters to open overseas *cumanns* (branches).

This lesson had been learned by the time a new active service unit arrived in Britain in the summer of 1974. Four of its members were to become notorious as the Balcombe Street gang. Unlike their predecessors they were all Southerners, an indication of the extent to which the Northern units were suffering from arrests and internment. At the core of the group were Joe O'Connell, Eddie Butler, Harry Duggan and Hugh O'Doherty.

O'Connell, the leader, arrived in London in August 1974 and was joined two months later by Butler and Duggan. The team adopted an unobtrusive lifestyle, taking separate flats in Fulham and working-class districts of North London, where the high population of Irish immigrants made them relatively inconspicuous, avoiding the pubs and especially the company of their fellow Irishmen. Each month they received money from Ireland delivered by two female couriers. O'Connell's unit was prodigiously energetic. During the year they were at large they averaged about one attack a week. Ostensibly they were under instructions from Dublin but difficulties with communications meant that they had a fair degree of autonomy. Furthermore, Brian Keenan was now off the scene, serving a twelve-month sentence in the Republic until the end of July 1975. A few months after his release he came to London to brief them, staying with Hugh O'Doherty at Crouch Hill in Hornsey, a shabby North London suburb.

The team began striking in the autumn of 1974. They bombed pubs frequented by soldiers and blitzed institutions symbolic of the British establishment: Brooke's Club, the Army and Navy Club and Harrow School.

They set themselves a huge range of targets. Documents found after police raided their flats listed fifty-eight MPs, and thirty judges, as well as leading businessmen, royal aides and military chiefs. MPs, Margaret Thatcher and

Airey Neave, the Conservative spokesman on Northern Ireland (later blown up by the Irish National Liberation Army), were candidates for assassination. The closest they came was a bomb which exploded harmlessly at the Belgravia residence of the Prime Minister, Edward Heath. Another of their intended victims was Hugh Fraser MP, but the bomb they planted outside his house killed an innocent and eminent passer-by instead, Professor Gordon Hamilton Fairley.

The unit's aim was to generate panic in the Establishment. Ross McWhirter, a vigorous right-winger who had offered a reward for the gang's capture, was shot dead on his doorstep. They felt it would be particularly demoralising to attack the 'ruling class' while they ate, and so chose West End hotels and restaurants as their targets. It was while on a reckless action to shoot up Scott's restaurant in Mayfair (for the second time) that the police finally caught up with them. After a car chase through the West End they ran into a block of council flats in Balcombe Street, Marylebone and took a middle-aged couple hostage, only surrendering after a six-day siege.

The group had a shifting membership. Each man had a strictly defined role. O'Connell gathered intelligence, plotted the attack and made the bombs; Duggan planted them; O'Doherty was the look-out; and Butler stayed in the background until needed. By the time of their capture they had been responsible for six murders. On 10 February 1977 at the Old Bailey they were sentenced to more than thirty years each.

The IRA bombing teams were under a general instruction to avoid killing 'innocent' civilians, but the indiscriminate nature of their tactics had been obvious from the start. The clumsiness of the bombing campaign reached its nadir on Thursday 21 November 1973, when an IRA team blew up two pubs in the centre of Birmingham on a night when they were packed with young people, killing twenty-one people and injuring 162. The bombs were planted by members of the Birmingham branch of the IRA which had been recruited from Northern Irishmen living in the West Midlands. This unit had been active during the year planting bombs and incendiaries in stores in April and July. In the July explosion, at a seventeen-storey office block, the police had had time to clear the area. On 5 August seven men had appeared in court charged with conspiracy to cause explosions. The week before the July blast, James McDade, a member of the unit, was killed when a bomb he was planting outside a telephone exchange in Coventry exploded prematurely.

On the evening of 21 November two IRA men walked into the Tavern in the Town, a pub in the Rotunda complex in the heart of Birmingham, and placed a bomb in a duffle-bag under a bench seat. In the Mulberry Bush they put the bomb by the telephone. A third man was positioned nearby. As soon as he saw the bombers pass he was to telephone a warning to the offices of the *Birmingham Post* and *Evening Mail*. In the event, both the telephones that had been earmarked earlier in the day were out of action and it was ten minutes before he could find another one. When the warning was finally delivered it was hopelessly vague, referring only to the general location rather than the specific pubs.

Within hours of the attack the police had picked up six men, Patrick Hill, Hugh Callaghan, John Walker, Richard McIlkenny, Gerard Hunter and Billy Power. All were from Northern Ireland but had been living in Birmingham. Five of them were captured as they boarded the Heysham-Belfast ferry. After three days' interrogation four had signed confessions saying they had planted the bombs. At their trial all six pleaded not guilty and claimed that the confessions had been extracted by beatings. They were all sentenced to life imprisonment. Soon afterwards, Daithi O'Connaill announced that an IRA internal inquiry had found that none of the six was a member of the republican movement. The inquiry did not establish, however, whether any member of the IRA was involved in the bombing.

The truth as to who was responsible for the killings has yet to emerge. Subsequent journalistic inquiries suggested two things: first, that the forensic evidence suggesting that some of the six had handled explosives shortly before their arrest was so dubious as to be inadmissible; and second, that beyond reasonable doubt, other men, who are still at large, played a major part in the bombings. According to the MP and journalist Chris Mullin, the main participants in the bombings were four IRA men, none of whom were ever brought to justice.[4] Mullin found that the bombs were actually planted by a young man who had joined the IRA in Birmingham in the summer of 1973 while still in his teens and an older man who remained in the IRA after the atrocity and who now lives in Dublin. Mullin claims, convincingly, that he has tracked down and interviewed all four men, who were alive and well and living in Ireland. The RUC certainly take the view that the chief culprit was never brought to justice. They privately identify the organiser of the attack as a Dubliner, born in July 1947, who joined the IRA while living in Birmingham. He disappeared at the time of the explosions, returned to Dublin and resumed his IRA activities. In September 1976 he was sentenced to three years' imprisonment for membership and possession of weapons, ammunition and explosives.

As a result of the efforts of Mullin and others, an appeal based on new evidence was finally brought before the Court of Appeal in the Autumn of 1987. The court heard from expert witnesses that the traces found on some of the men which had originally been analysed as evidence that they had been handling gelignite could have come from playing cards (the men had been playing cards shortly before their arrest) or cigarette packets. The three judges, led by Lord Lane, the Lord Chief Justice, preferred the original interpretation.

As to the appellants' claim that they had been beaten, the judges noted that the original jury had rejected this charge and pointed out that if the men had been ill-treated this would have been apparent at their first remand appearance.

They also dismissed the evidence of two former policemen who said they saw violence against the prisoners as unworthy of belief. Lord Lane concluded, 'the longer this has gone on, the more the court has been convinced that the jury was correct.'

There is also strong evidence that the men and women imprisoned for bombing pubs in Guildford and Woolwich in October and November 1974, killing seven and injuring ninety-two, were wrongly convicted. Paddy Armstrong, Gerry Conlon, Carole Richardson and Paul Hill were all sentenced to life imprisonment for the attacks.[5]

In the summer of 1975 Conlon, Armstrong (his friend from St Peter's school in Belfast) and Armstrong's English girlfriend Carole were all living in London. During the day the men worked on building-sites or lay around drinking, taking drugs and listening to music. Later, on a visit to Southampton, Conlon bumped into another old boy of St Peter's, Paul Hill. Of the four, only Hill had any serious connection with the IRA. He had been involved in the abduction and shooting of a former British soldier who had been 'tried' and executed as a British spy, but had fallen out with the Provisionals after a gun he had borrowed from an arms-dump went missing and he had come under suspicion of being an informer. Hill understandably gave a sanitised version of these events to his old friends.

Conlon had joined the Fianna in 1972 but had been beaten up and thrown out for his persistent drunkenness and drug-taking. In the summer of 1974, the four made up a dissolute coterie. Ten days after the Guildford bombs went off, Conlon returned to West Belfast on a visit. While out drinking with some IRA acquaintances he mentioned that he had renewed his friendship with Hill. The IRA seemed very interested in this news. Within a few weeks, Army intelligence passed to the Guildford police, who were still searching for a lead, information from a Belfast informant that Hill had been involved in the attack.

The intelligence carried some peculiar details — such as the fact that Hill had a new tattoo — which could only have been known to Conlon. Conlon's stories about Hill, it appeared, had been played back to military intelligence.

Who had done this? Could it have been the IRA, anxious to punish Hill and divert attention from the real culprits? Within a month of the tip-off, Hill was arrested. Within a short time he had confessed to the bombings and named a host of friends and acquaintances as his accomplices, inventing a few for good measure. He has subsequently given an explanation for doing so. He was confused, and worried about his girlfriend. In desperation he calculated that if he made up a confession that would not stand up in court, the police would let her go and he would ultimately be released. But faced with Hill's denunciations, confused and tired by the police interrogation, the others fell into line.

According to their solicitor, Alasdair Logan, the bombings were carried out by the Balcombe Street gang. O'Connell, Butler and Duggan admitted to being involved in the Woolwich pub bombing immediately after their capture. The three, together with Brendan Dowd, later gave detailed statements to Logan describing the attack. Dowd and O'Connell also confessed to the Guildford bombings, painting an intimate picture of the operation. These confessions were used in the Guildford four's appeal in October 1977, but the judge merely found that Dowd and O'Connell had been accomplices and upheld the convictions. (The case is currently being reviewed at the request of the Home Secretary, Douglas Hurd.)

After the capture of the Balcombe Street four the campaign became more desultory. There was a brief experiment using second and third generation Irishmen but they were found to be hesitant and unreliable, which the planners in Dublin put down to a lack of commitment due to the absence of first-hand experience of the violence in the North.[6]

Bombing Britain had failed to move British public opinion in the way the IRA had hoped for, and it had not noticeably undermined the will of British governments to maintain the Union for as long as the Unionists wanted. That did not stop the campaign from continuing. From now on its purpose was mainly symbolic, though its results would prove none the less murderous for that in the coming years.

CHAPTER FOURTEEN

On the Sidelines

The great question that followed the fall of Stormont was: What was going to replace it? During the summer of 1972, Whitelaw struggled to bring all the angular elements of Northern Irish politics together to discuss the future government of Ulster. After the utter failure of the July 1972 meeting with MacStiofain and his men, the IRA was consigned to the sidelines. Whitelaw conceded almost immediately that the talks had been a serious mistake. For one thing, there had been nothing to discuss. There was no item in the IRA's list of ultimate objectives on which it was prepared to concede an inch. For another, events like Bloody Friday and the Claudy bombing meant that any further contact was politically unacceptable.

On the Catholic side, Whitelaw now concentrated on winning over the SDLP who had persisted in a boycott of talks with the British Government imposed after internment. On the Protestant side, he pitched his efforts at Brian Faulkner, the last prime minister of Stormont, and the moderate Unionists grouped around him. At the end of 1972 the Government published a Green Paper which canvassed a number of options for the shape of a new political framework for Northern Ireland. The British Government's strategy was shaped by the principle that any concession to one part of the community would be balanced by a similar concession to the other. To soothe the Protestants there was a promise that Northern Ireland would remain part of the United

Kingdom for as long as a majority in Ulster wanted it. To please the Catholics, there was the proposal that the minority would have a guaranteed share in the executive power of a new government. Finally, the package would have to have the overall approval of the Government of the Republic of Ireland.

The loyalists of Ian Paisley's Democratic Unionist Party (DUP) and William Craig's Vanguard were predictably opposed to the suggestions. Brian Faulkner, however, was coming to terms with the fact that there would have to be some sort of accommodation with the constitutional nationalists of the SDLP if a significant degree of self-government was to be retained in Ulster. The Unionists had never wanted their own parliament, rightly regarding it as a device whereby the British could keep the Northern Ireland problem at arm's length. After the fall of Stormont they had come to regard a devolved assembly as 'the only effective obstacle to a unification of Ireland against their wishes'.[1] Faulkner was prepared to concede increased influence and human rights guarantees to the nationalists. But he was not immediately prepared to agree to power-sharing.

Nor was there any immediate enthusiasm on the SDLP side for rushing into a new Northern Ireland executive, even one where they had a guaranteed stake in power. After Bloody Sunday, John Hume, the Derry SDLP leader, had declared that the feeling among the Catholics of the Bogside was 'It is a United Ireland now or nothing.' For a while it had been possible to believe, as the IRA had, that the British had been wearied by events in Northern Ireland to the point where they were contemplating leaving. Entering a new Northern Ireland parliament, even one balanced in the Catholic's favour, would only prolong the British connection. The Green Paper's reiteration of the sanctity of the wishes of the majority (later forcefully, if onesidedly, expressed in the March 1973 border poll) tended to undermine the illusion that the British were about to depart.

When the Government published a White Paper on 20 March 1973, with specific details of a new Northern Ireland Assembly, the SDLP gave it a cautious welcome. The proposal was for a seventy-eight-member parliament, elected by proportional representation, which would in turn choose a prime minister and cabinet, which would include a proportion of members from the leading opposition party. The executive would have limited powers for the moment and control over the security forces would remain in London. The paper also recommended a Council of Ireland which would act as a link between the Government of Ireland in the South and the new Assembly in the North. Faulkner gave his backing, believing that a rejection would 'seriously endanger our position as citizens of the United Kingdom'.[2] On the positive side, the necessity for the SDLP to accept the wishes of the majority in the matter of the border if they were to take part in the new government would, he believed, increase the security of unionists. At the elections for the new assembly the SDLP won nineteen seats and Faulkner's Official Unionists twenty-four. Together with the non-sectarian Alliance Party, they began discussing the establishment of a coalition government. The final shape of the new power-sharing executive was established at the Sunningdale conference, held at the British Civil Service's training college in Berkshire early in January and attended by the British and Irish Governments.

The final communiqué started with an affirmation by the Irish Government and the SDLP which reiterated their aspiration for a united Ireland, but only by consent. It went on to set up a Council of Ireland made up of representatives of the Dail and the new Assembly which would study a number of non-contentious matters of mutual interest, such as agriculture and trade and industry. It was also agreed to establish a joint law commission to look at ways of improving legislation both in Britain and Ireland to combat political violence.

The IRA was severely discomfited by Whitelaw's political initiative. The official line was that the new Assembly would establish a 'Northern Free State' and there were frequent public predictions that it would never work.[3] Privately, the leadership was deeply concerned about the support that the agreement was generating for the SDLP. As O'Bradaigh saw it, 'the SDLP was able to grow more and more and claim that they had a mandate from the nationalist people and that the IRA was only carrying on a military campaign with no political dimension to it'.[3]

At a meeting of the Ulster Sinn Fein executive O'Bradaigh had warned, 'we shall have to gut them before they gut us'. The question was how to do it. The IRA had little to offer in the way of an alternative. O'Bradaigh's beloved Eire Nua policy had failed to generate much debate inside the ranks. Indeed, most volunteers had only the dimmest idea of what it was. The movement lacked proper political machinery. Provisional Sinn Fein at this time was an organisation for those too old or too timid to bear arms and its activities were limited to agitation and propaganda against the governments North and South and the security forces. Both Sinn Feins had campaigned against Ireland's entry into the EEC, believing, with slightly puzzling intensity, that joining the Common Market would deepen Ireland's economic dependence on Britain. Political activity in the South was hampered by the fact that Sinn Fein was banned from the airwaves.

O'Bradaigh felt that the only way to combat the SDLP was to oppose them in elections and register in an uncontrovertible way the level of IRA support. The idea of contesting elections, however, was extremely unpopular in a number of republican quarters. The Northerners on the Army Council — particularly Twomey and Cahill — regarded political activity as a distraction while the war was still being bitterly fought, and believed that the emphasis should stay on violence. There was also opposition from Belfast republicans, notably Maire Drumm, acting president of Sinn Fein when O'Bradaigh was imprisoned again, who added the argument that the risk of humiliation was too great.[3] Sinn Fein and the Army Council therefore voted against fighting the 1973 district council elections in the North and did not take part in the June 1973 election for the new Assembly. O'Bradaigh made another effort to persuade Sinn Fein to fight the 1974 British general election, even going so far as to send nomination papers to a number of candidates in prison but again he was overruled.

On the face of it, the IRA was about to be swamped in the tide of moderation and non-sectarianism flowing from Sunningdale. On 1 January the new executive was sworn in at Stormont Castle, a stone's throw from the old seat of Unionist power. Faulkner noted an atmosphere of 'comradeship and trust'.[4] The aura of optimism could not disguise the fact that Faulknerite Unionism was a minority taste among Northern Irish Protestants. And only five weeks after the new Assembly began sitting, Edward Heath, beset by the miners' strike, called a general election on the issue of trade union power. The SDLP had implored him not to, believing that 'the vibrations resulting from an electoral defeat of the power-sharing parties . . . could shake the Executive apart'.[5] In the election of 28 February the anti-Assembly parties, who had formed an electoral pact under the banner of the United Ulster Unionist Coalition (UUUC) won fifty-one per cent of the votes and eleven of the twelve Northern Ireland seats at Westminster.

This result strengthened the will of the enemies of power-sharing, particularly the Protestant workers from the engineering shops and factories of the Lagan valley who provided the hard core of loyalist opposition. The element of Sunningdale that aroused most fear was the Council of Ireland, which seemed to many Unionists to be, in Faulkner's phrase, a 'massive Trojan horse'. This belief was not ill-founded. According to Paddy Devlin, the SDLP's head of the executive's health and social services department, the party's aim at Sunningdale had been to establish all-Ireland institutions which would 'produce the dynamic that could lead ultimately to an agreed single State for Ireland'.[6]

Faulkner's confidence was severely dented by the election results and in an effort to appease unionist opinion he worked frantically and in secret to get the SDLP to agree to a watering-down of the Sunningdale commitment to a Council of Ireland. Before any accommodation could be reached, the assembly of the UUUC proposed a motion calling for a complete renegotiation of the Sunningdale agreement in the light of the election outcome. Without revealing that elements of the accord were under further discussion, the executive countered with an amendment calling for the commitments entered into at Sunningdale to be honoured. When the debate eventually took place on 14 May the UUUC was defeated, as the make-up of the Assembly ensured it would be.

By now the loyalists had opened up a new front outside the assembly. A few days before the vote, a previously disregarded group called the Ulster Workers' Council (UWC) urged the Assembly's members to 'vote cautiously in the crucial issue of Sunningdale', and threatened a strike should the vote go the wrong way. Faulkner and the SDLP had taken little notice. There had been strikes by the Loyalist Association of Workers (LAW) in 1973 that had come to nothing and rebounded on their organisers. But the UWC was a more complicated and threatening organisation. It was a coalition of loyalist trade unionists, politicians and paramilitaries, with clearly defined political aims – the abandonment of Sunningdale and new elections for the Assembly – and a clear idea of how to achieve them. Unlike LAW they did not set out to be a mass organisation but concentrated their efforts on the Province's key utilities and industries, particularly the power stations. Where they had no support they used intimidation.

By the afternoon of the first day of the action, 15 May, gangs of men in paramilitary uniform were out on the streets erecting barricades and threatening those who carried on working. By the second day, employers' representatives reported to the executive's economic council that ninety per cent of their employees had failed to report for work. As the days went by Northern Ireland's power grid was steadily shut down and by Monday 20 May Ulster was at a standstill. The following day the UWC announced it was imposing an embargo on petrol and oil. In some towns, movement in and out was only permitted with UWC-issued passes. By Thursday, Derry was without a gas supply.

The executive believed that their best chance of defeating the strike was a joint military and political initiative. On Wednesday, after a long wrangle with the SDLP, Faulkner announced that the full implementation of the Council of Ireland would be postponed. The concession only encouraged the loyalists to press for total victory. As the executive had no control over security, the military initiative would have to be made for them. The Army, had held back from the outset, arguing that dealing with a civil strike was the responsibility of the police and that their intervention would only provoke trouble. At various points during the strike it was suggested that the Army move in to run the power stations, but they lacked both the expertise and the co-operation of middle management personnel that would make it possible.

By Monday 27 May Faulkner decided the situation was hopeless and there was no choice but to open discussions with the strikers, as his own backbenchers were now demanding. The SDLP members of the executive did not agree. Nor did the new Labour Secretary of State for Northern Ireland, Merlyn Rees, when he was approached the following day with a suggestion that a mediator should be appointed. Faulkner resigned, to be followed shortly by the rest of the executive. Faulkner and his colleagues mostly blamed the British Government for their downfall. Rees was portrayed as vacillating and weak, incapable of taking an early decision to deploy the Army, which would have crushed the strike at birth. But the scale of the strike and the depth of support for the aims of the strikers meant that there was little the soldiers could have done.

The Irish Government blamed the IRA for the executive's fall, claiming that continuing violence had been the cause of this 'massive sectarian backlash'. The truth was that fear of the Republic moved the strikers more than fear of republicanism. The deference that the British and moderate unionists had shown towards Catholic aspirations, and which had led to power-sharing, was largely conditioned by the climate of violence created by the IRA. In the drama itself the IRA played only a small part, providing the noises off.

Towards the end of the year, the Army Council was offered another chance to reopen contact with the British Government. Despite the lingering bitterness over the encounter with Whitelaw, there were pressing reasons why the idea of a ceasefire was attractive. The IRA was tired, directionless and increasingly unpopular in the ghettoes. Even Seamus Twomey, who led the initial opposition to the idea, conceded that 'as an army you could not fight forty-eight hours a day. In the end we simply thought it would be useful. It would be an opportunity to regroup and revamp the movement and build up the army. Also it was time to give ordinary people and volunteers a rest.'[7] The opportunity to re-establish links was provided by an energetic and voluble clergyman, the Protestant Reverend William Arlow, the Assistant Secretary of the Irish Council of Churches. Returning home from an international church conference on Northern Ireland in Amsterdam, he was approached by one of the participants who had republican connections and asked if the Church could arrange a similar conference in Ireland involving the paramilitaries.

The contact put him in touch with Maire and Jimmy Drumm in Belfast who passed on the idea to the leadership, who agreed to meet a delegation of Protestant churchmen. Arlow assembled a distinguished cast including the Church of Ireland Bishop of Down and Connor, Dr Arthur Butler, the Clerk of the Presbyterian Assembly, Dr Jack Weir, and the Secretary of the British Council of Churches, Dr Harry Morton. They met at Smyth's Village Hotel at Feakle in County Clare on 9 December 1974. The IRA team was led by Ruairi O'Bradaigh and Daithi O'Connaill, and included Seamus Twomey, Seamus Loughran (the IRA's Belfast commander), Maire Drumm, Kevin Mallon and Billy McKee.

The encounter was given an added urgency by the Birmingham bombings the previous month which had killed nineteen young people and wounded 182 in two pubs in the city centre. The IRA had denied responsibility for the atrocity. Arlow's intention was to make a rational appeal to the IRA to call off the campaign, pointing out that 'the more people that were shot and bombed on the Protestant side the less likelihood there would be of a united Ireland, and the difficulty of any political movement on the part of Britain as long as the military campaign went on'.

He had mixed feelings about the meeting: 'I thought I was going to meet a group of mindless monsters because that is how the media was projecting them at the time.'

We met informally the night before in the hotel and somebody said 'Lets have a drink,' so we all drifted off towards the bar. I think there was only one person on our side who didn't take a drink. We were astonished and a little bit embarrassed when most of them declined to take alcohol. McKee and O'Bradaigh explained that there was no discourtesy meant. They were just temperance men and that gave me pause for thought. We got talking and one of them said he wanted to see an end to the military campaign. His children were up and coming and nearing the age when they would be caught up in it. He didn't want them to go through what he had gone through.

[Twomey said] he went back to the area where he lived and was astonished to discover what was happening. Young people had been running wild, creating a nuisance, especially for old people late at night. They were caught up in drink, they were caught up in drugs and he suddenly thought to himself 'Why don't the police do something about this?' and then he remembered that he had been one of those who had helped to drag the police out of the area and he said 'Well now, is this the kind of new Ireland I'm fighting for?' and the answer was 'It isn't' . . . And when they started to talk in these terms, men concerned about

270

their children and men concerned about their church, then I began to see that these men were not the monsters I thought them to be.[8]

The churchmen had drafted a theoretical government proposal which they thought might satisfy the IRA's preconditions for a ceasefire. It was a vague document containing only one clause of any substance, which declared that 'contingent upon the maintenance of a declared ceasefire and upon effective policing, HM Government will relieve the army as quickly as possible of its internal security duties'. Discussion of the document was interrupted by the news that the Garda Special Branch were descending on the hotel, and the IRA fled. A few days later, however, they delivered their reply. They would agree to a total ceasefire if the British Government agreed these terms: the establishment of a constitutional assembly elected by voters North and South of the border, to draft a new all-Ireland constitution which provided for an Ulster parliament; a commitment to withdraw from Ireland within a year of the new constitution taking effect; and an amnesty for political prisoners. It was the old formula with Eire Nua tacked on the top. As a declaration of good faith, however, the Army Council declared a temporary cessation of activities from midnight 22 December 1974 to midnight 2 January to give the British time to consider. The vote was 5-2, the two Northern representatives opposing the ceasefire.

This was a considerable concession. The mainland bombing campaign was in full swing. O'Connaill revealed to Arlow that the IRA had been planning to bomb the London underground in Christmas week when the trains would be packed with shoppers, but was now prepared to suspend the operation.[8] Arlow communicated this to Rees, who issued a statement that if there was a cessation of hostilities then there 'would be a new situation to which the British would naturally respond'. Rees, by his own account, had no intention of negotiating with the IRA. His immediate political objective was to set up a constitutional convention in which

271

the Northern Ireland political parties could attempt to invent a workable political machine to run the Province. To do this it was desirable that the level of violence be reduced and Northern Ireland returned as near to normality as possible. Part of the normalising process was to be the phasing out of internment and the release of the remaining detainees from the prisons, and the abandonment of special legislation to attack the IRA. The legislation would be replaced with normal criminal procedures, a policy which would mean the end of the political status won by McKee and the rest of the Crumlin Road hunger-strikers in 1972.

Rees's task was to balance the two aims. If the IRA could be persuaded to lower the level of violence in return for a quickening of the pace at which detention was phased out, then the chances of a political reconstruction of the Province would be improved. He was anxious to avoid the impression that direct negotiations were taking place with the IRA. However, officials were authorised to maintain contact with representatives of Sinn Fein (which he had deproscribed the previous year in the hope that this might promote the IRA's political activity at the expense of its military effort). At the same time, he reduced the size and frequency of Army patrols and continued to release detainees while desisting from signing any new interim custody orders. These improvements could continue, he stated repeatedly, if there was 'a genuine and sustained cessation of violence'.[9] The IRA responded on 2 January by extending the ceasefire for a further fourteen days. The Army's touch in the ghettoes grew still lighter. They now avoided 'screening' inhabitants or searching their homes. After Rees reported his progress to the House of Commons on 14 January the IRA replied with a more aggressive statement complaining that Rees's report had contained nothing about their peace proposals and adding a list of diverse grievances (including the refusal of prison authorities to grant compassionate parole to IRA men over Christmas), before announcing that the Army Council could not 'in conscience' renew the ceasefire order. The door was left open to further talks in the final paragraph, however, which affirmed their willingness to 'engage in worthwhile talks with the appropriate authorities to secure peace and justice in our land'.

Rees had formed a low impression of the intelligence of the Sinn Fein representatives his officials were talking to in Belfast, the main one being Jimmy Drumm, a republican old-timer, and felt that this factor may have contributed to the breakdown.* He authorised his men to seek contacts higher up the organisation. Further developments were halted in December when a Catholic boy was shot dead by loyalists in South Armagh and the IRA bombing campaign was renewed around the Province. Rees's response was to 'fire a warning shot over the heads of the hawks' on the Army Council by signing some interim custody orders. Then in a speech in the House of Commons on 5 February he spelt out what was on offer if the ceasefire was resumed: there would be no actions by the security forces which could be interpreted as harassment by the civilian population; there would be no more interim custody orders and internment would be phased out; the use of screening, photographing and identity checks would be ended; gun permits would be available for potential victims of assassination; the Army would be slowly reduced to peacetime levels and ultimately withdrawn to barracks, to be replaced by the RUC. In return, the IRA would have to end all offensive operations, including sectarian killings, beatings and knee-cappings, as well as giving up buying guns and explosives and mounting robberies.

This seemed to the IRA to be a bargain. Despite Rees's assurances that the security services would still relentlessly track down wrongdoers, the terms suggested a considerable lessening of the pressures of recent months. In the three weeks up to the 13 January forty-five people had been arrested and charged with hijacking, murder and firearms offences and a further thirty-four were charged with similar crimes in the few days before Rees's speech. The offer

---

* Merlyn Rees interview with the authors, November 1984.

also held out the prospect of the IRA establishing themselves openly in the ghettoes. In order to monitor the ceasefire, Rees envisaged a number of incident centres, to maintain contact between his office and the Province's likely flashpoints. On 9 February the Army Council announced that 'hostilities against the Crown forces will be suspended from 6.00 pm, Monday 10 February 1975'.

CHAPTER FIFTEEN

Ceasefire

The period ushered in by the ceasefire marked the Provisional IRA's darkest hours since its inception and brought it the closest it has yet been to collapse and defeat. During the next eighteen months, the violence previously directed towards the security forces was funnelled inwards into internecine feuding, sectarian murder and gangsterism. The current leadership of the movement regard this period with superstitious dread, an age of decadence in which republicanism lost its way and was led to the edge of the precipice by the cunning of the British. To Danny Morrison, who was then a volunteer in Belfast, it was a 'disaster'.[1] According to Martin McGuinness, it was 'the most critical stage in the last sixteen years and if changes had not taken place in the short time then the IRA would have been defeated'.[2]

The leadership had gone into the ceasefire with mixed motives and no clear idea of what they could gain from it. At best, they believed (for this was a stubborn illusion) that the British willingness to bargain, albeit at a distance, signalled an intention to withdraw. At the least it was an opportunity for the movement to rest and rethink. It even appeared at first that there were valuable gains to be made. Rees had pledged himself to ending internment and emptying the cages of Long Kesh of the remaining detainees. The establishment of the incident centres gave the Provisionals a quasi-official representative status in the community and Sinn Fein set up shop in a Government-funded office in the Falls Road, to the equal

275

annoyance of the SDLP and the unionists. Furthermore, there was something about Rees's courteous and decent manner that suggested it would not be difficult, with a little shaking, to extract further concessions from the Government. Rees's behaviour throughout 1975 encouraged the illusion that the IRA were getting the best of the bargain.

After the collapse of the power-sharing executive Rees moved with surprising rapidity to mount another attempt to construct a political machine to run Ulster. Power-sharing had failed because most Unionists had disliked it. Rees's idea was to create a body to allow the Northern Irish political parties to produce their own system of government. The means he chose was a constitutional convention of the parties elected by proportional representation, to consider, as the government White paper announcing it said, 'what provision for the government of Northern Ireland is likely to command the most widespread acceptance throughout the community there'. Rees believed that it was essential for the level of violence to be suppressed for the convention to have any chance of success. The ceasefire was an essential element in his plans. For this reason it survived in spite of numerous breaches and the British bombing campaign.

To the volunteer on the street, as well as to the leadership, the ceasefire seemed good news. 'To the men on the run it was like being demobbed [said one]. There was no interning and as long as you weren't caught red-handed you didn't go to jail.'[3] By the time the consequences of Rees's strategy dawned on the IRA there was little they could do about it. To a large extent the history of republicanism in the subsequent years is the history of the consequences of the ceasefire. At the end of the decade the emotional energies of the movement switched to the prisons, the scene of a life-and-death struggle to regain lost ground. The middle-aged Southerners who had entered the near-fatal agreement were discredited and ultimately removed, to be replaced by the young Northerners who run the IRA today. And the idea that the IRA would ever agree to any cessation of hostilities that was not bound in hoops of steel to a British withdrawal from

Ireland was eradicated for the foreseeable future.

Rees's aim was 'to create the conditions in which the Provisional IRA's military organisation might be weakened. The longer the ceasefire lasted, the more difficult it would be for them to start a campaign again from scratch and in this period of peace I hoped political action would be given a chance.'[4] His assessment of the atrophying effects of military inactivity on the IRA is shared by Martin McGuinness who returned to Derry from jail to find the ceasefire in place. As the level of operations dropped so did morale and numbers, leaving him with inferior material to 'restructure' − the reason the units had given for pursuing the ceasefire in the first place. McGuinness believed that 'good operations are the best recruiting sergeant'.[2]

Rees's plan was to link the release of detainees to the level of IRA violence. If they behaved, the flow was brisk. If they did not, it slowed to a trickle or stopped. The leadership of the IRA seemed to be mesmerised by this process and oblivious to the importance of a parallel operation which was taking place. The purpose of ending internment was to replace it with a new set of anti-terrorist laws as close to the normal criminal code as the situation allowed. Instead of merely picking up IRA men and throwing them into open-ended incarceration on the word of an Army officer, as was the case with the Selective Detention Orders, Rees wanted them arrested charged and tried in the usual way (albeit in an unusual, juryless Diplock court).

The unionist and Conservative opposition to this apparently permissive and indulgent behaviour, which was the necessary corollary to the strategy, may have blinded the IRA to the ultimate result − that when the cages were empty there would be no more special category status. The change in the law would have removed from the convicted bomber, sniper or driver the standing of a prisoner-of-war and lowered him or her to the level of an ordinary criminal.

The ending of political status had been foreshadowed in the Gardiner Report, the result of an independent inquiry commissioned by Rees to examine anti-terrorist legislation in

Northern Ireland, published in January 1975. It stated that special category status had been a serious mistake and recommended all prisoners found guilty of any crime after 1 March 1976 be treated the same as any apolitical prisoner in the United Kingdom. The report drew immediate condemnation from both republicans and loyalists, and a Sinn Fein spokesman threatened a mass hunger strike. But the ceasefire went ahead anyway.

Rees moved slowly, reluctant to announce the order to end special category status -- because the new cellblocks started in 1973 and appropriate to the criminal status of the new generation of IRA men at Long Kesh (shortly to be renamed the Maze) had yet to be completed. When the news was finally given in the spring of 1976 there was rioting, providing the IRA with a suitable point to break off their by then desultory and barren links with Northern Ireland Office (NIO) officials, and effectively marking the death of the ceasefire. The first prison protests did not begin, however, until the end of the year.

Rees had constructed elaborate machinery to keep the IRA leadership engaged. Face-to-face meetings were out of the question as the official line was that no negotiations were taking place: the IRA had declared a unilateral ceasefire, the Government had responded. In order to maintain the peace it was important that there should be good communications between the sides. The incident centres were staffed twenty-four hours a day by civil servants who had permission to call Rees at any time if they felt the situation warranted it. Some, such as the Newry centre, were barely used at all. The IRA in South Armagh never accepted the ceasefire. At the Derry centre, however, there were about 1,600 contacts between the IRA and the NIO officials. In Belfast Sinn Fein officials regularly drove over the Lagan to rendezvous with NIO officials at Laneside, a house on the shores of Belfast Lough, which Rees maintained for informal contacts with all the factions, parties, and self-appointed political advisers who thrived during his period of office. There was also, according to O'Bradaigh, a confidential channel of communication between the NIO and the IRA in Dublin, which they could use for 'off the record' discussions.

Inevitably, both sides have differing recollections of what was being talked about. By Rees's account, the matters under discussion were largely the state of the ceasefire and the progress being made to free internees, though the conversation frequently strayed into political areas, such as the elections to the constitutional convention, which met in 1975 to consider political models for Northern Ireland.[5] The IRA, however, were under the impression, at least at the outset, that the ground was being prepared for withdrawal. O'Bradaigh believed that the talks were an adjunct to the constitutional convention, part of an attempt to devise structures for post-occupation Ulster. This was certainly the impression conveyed to the volunteers, though couched in generalised terms.[6]

The effect of the ceasefire on the units on the ground was to allow the Army to build up and the IRA to run down. During that period the IRA's energies were turned to morale-lowering and destructive feuds with the remnants of the Officials and the Protestant paramilitaries of the UVF and the UDA.

The origins of the revival of the feud with the 'Stickies' (Officials) were as much personal as political. The Official IRA had suffered a further halving as a result of another internal dispute. Once again the same issues divided the organisation, aggravated by the same rivalries, enmities and accusations of chicanery endemic in republican politics. Ever since the Officials' ceasefire in 1972 a faction inside the organisation had held out against the leadership's anti-militarist stand. A few activists in the North had never accepted it, and there were occasional reports of freelance military operations carried out by the dissidents. Furthermore, at the end of 1974 the leadership decided in favour of Workers' Party councillors taking the council seats they had vacated in protest after internment − a betrayal of the internees in the eyes of the rebels. In late 1974, after Goulding's leading opponent, Seamus Costello, was expelled from the movement, they broke away completely and formed a new Trotskyite republican party, the Irish Republican Socialist Party (IRSP), and later a new force to augment it, the Irish National Liberation Army (INLA). In Belfast, one third of the Officials' remaining strength defected to the IRSP, including some of the more impressive members, like Ronald Bunting, the Officials' commander in Turf Lodge and Ballymurphy and son of Major Bunting, one of the leaders of the loyalist gangs who had harassed the People's Democracy civil rights marchers.

The Official IRA could see history repeating itself. Once again the organisation in the city was going to be reduced to insignificance by the birth of a more militant and ruthless rival and it was not going to make the same mistake twice. A decision was taken to strangle the IRSP at birth. Four assassination squads under the command of Billy McMillen were set up to deal with the dissidents.

The Officials came off worst. In the spate of shootings, woundings and murders that took place in the spring of 1975 they lost three members, including McMillen, while only two IRSP men were killed. The situation was complicated by other considerations. After the demise of Joe McCann and the announcement of the ceasefire, the Officials had sunk into gangsterism. Bunting's stated reason for going was that most of the Belfast organisation's energies were taken with running a shebeen racket.[7] According to one former member,

They were robbing town and country – they were robbing every place they could get their hands on and they were beating people up who were dissidents in the movement. In 1972 I was picked up and brought to a maisonette in [North Belfast]. First of all they binded my hands round my back and feet and blindfolded me. They said that I was letting the Provies in on what we were doing, secrets and anything else, and keeping company with them and as far as they were concerned I wasn't going to join them and this was a lesson so that I wouldn't. So I ended up with a couple of broken ribs out of that and a tooth kicked out and I couldn't see for about a day or so.[8]

The attackers later emerged as founder members of the Belfast IRSP.

The sympathies of the Belfast Provisionals were with these new rebels. They shared a desire for action and a hatred of the Official leadership in the city. Some Provos who were annoyed by the constraints imposed by the ceasefire went off and joined them. Others, with no soldiers to shoot at, joined in the feud on the INLA side. In this they were encouraged by the leadership. The old justification − that the Officials were communists − was wheeled out to justify the resumption of hostilities. In late 1974 Billy McKee had emerged from jail to take control again of the Provisionals. His predecessor had been Seamus Loughran, a Sinn Fein member with no military experience who had taken little interest in operations, a marked contrast to his predecessors, Brendan 'Darkie' Hughes (arrested in May 1974) and Ivor Bell. McKee's enmity towards his old adversaries was undiminished. In the autumn of 1975 an order was given to assassinate the 'Stickies', and on 29 October the Provos struck the first blow, killing one Official and wounding another fourteen. The vendetta was carried out with a mixture of callousness and stupidity. A group of Provo gunmen broke into a house in Beechmount Pass. Like many who found themselves in this situation, their intended victim tried to hide under the bed. In the shooting his six-year-old daughter was killed. Another unit went looking for 'Stickies' in Bagan's bar on the Falls Road. Finding none they blew up the bar.[6]

The Officials were efficient at fighting back. By the time the quarrel had ended eleven men were dead, at least seven of them Provisionals. The truce was forced on the two sides by popular pressure. On 12 November gunmen shot and killed the chairman of the Falls Taxi Association, the fleet of black London cabs that shuttles Catholics around West Belfast at rates that compare favourably with public transport. Although the firm was controlled by the Provisionals, the chairman had no formal connection with them. The cab-drivers blocked the Falls Road in protest and demanded that the feud end. The following day it was called off.

The IRA ceasefire had not proved much of a respite for the population of the Catholic ghettoes. In the spring of 1975 the loyalists started another spate of killings. Catholics and Protestants continued to be killed at random throughout 1974 (159 were murdered in the first nine months) but the announcement of a truce and the old fears it revived led the murder gangs to intensify their activities. With little else to distract them, the IRA reciprocated enthusiastically. On 5 April, for example, loyalists placed a bomb in a bar in the New Lodge district. It went off early in the evening killing two Catholics. A few hours later there was an explosion in the Mountainview bar on the Shankill Road which killed five Protestants.

The most notorious killing was in the countryside. Early one morning in July the five members of an Irish pop group, the Miami Showband, were driving along a road in County Down after an appearance in the town of Bannbridge when they were stopped by what seemed to be a UDR patrol. It was a familiar experience to anyone travelling the roads of Northern Ireland. The uniformed men were in fact members of the UVF. Two of them placed a bomb in the back of the bus, apparently primed to blow up as the band unwittingly drove away, thereby proving to the world a dearly-held loyalist contention — that showband members from the republic ferried guns and explosives for the IRA. But the bomb went off prematurely, triggered by the 'static' residing in their loud-speakers, according to forensic experts, killing its carriers. The remainder of the gang machine-gunned three of the band members to death before making off.[9]

Next month the IRA retaliated. A team lead by Brendan 'Bik' McFarlane planted a bomb in the Bayardo Bar on the Shankill Road, killing five people. McFarlane was a respected man of strong political convictions, who went on to command IRA prisoners in the Maze after Bobby Sands' death before escaping to Holland in 1983 where he was later recaptured. Today McFarlane's involvement is frequently cited by the Provisionals as evidence of how far they had sunk. Some idea of the motivations and calibre of volunteers at the time is given by the testimony of Kevin McGrady. McGrady, an unemployed butcher, took part in three murders and a number of shootings in 1975. In 1976 he went to England, and from there to Holland where he joined an American Christian sect, Youth With a Mission. In January 1982 he returned to Belfast to expiate his crimes and turned Queen's Evidence against his former comrades; he is the only 'supergrass' to have given himself up voluntarily. He was also anxious to clear the name of his brother Sean whom he claimed had been wrongly convicted for murder, and doubt was cast on some of his evidence. In conveying the flavour of the times, though, he is a reliable witness.

I joined the Provisional IRA when I was about 18 because I felt there was a threat to the Catholics from the Protestants. My first involvement was an attempted murder on the Ormeau Road. I drove a car up from the Markets. [My companion] got out of the car and rang a doorbell. He then shot the person who answered the door. I don't know the name of the person who was shot but I believed he was in a Protestant paramilitary organisation.

The next thing I was involved in was the murder of Ernie Dowds [a 21-year-old Protestant shipyard worker]. I stole a van from Norton Street and drove it up the Ormeau Road. There was another man with me in the van. He got out and waited for Dowds to come along. Then he shot him. I didn't see it, I just heard the shots. I believed Dowds to be in the UDA and to be involved in a number of murders in the Ormeau Road against Catholics.

The next thing was an attack on a bar in a street in the Markets. There was an attack two days in a row. I drove the car and the man in the car with me opened fire on the bar with a pistol. It was a pub used by the Official IRA.

I was also involved in the shooting of Stevenson. I was told to go to the corner of a street in the Markets and watch out for the British Army. He was being held somewhere. It was dark. [Stevenson] walked with a guy up the street to the junction of the street beside St Malachy's. The fellow said to him, 'If you say anything this is what you are going to get.' The guy had a gun in his hand and then he shot Stevenson. I think he shot him in the head.

Another time was when I was in the Short Strand. I was told to drive a car. I was told to drive to a house in the Short Strand. I stopped there and three people got out. I think it was around midnight. One of them had a hood over his head. All three got into the car and I was told to drive to the Markets. I drove to the junction of Houston Street and Albert Street. I stopped the car and all three men got out. I started to drive away and as I was doing so I heard shots.

Such was life in the IRA in 1975. In December the last of the internees was released and the Government no longer saw much point in maintaining links with the organisation. In November Rees announced that the incident centres were to be closed down. With that the IRA gradually returned to the offensive. The ceasefire had been a highly elastic notion for much of the period that it operated. More people were killed in 1975 (247) than in 1974 (216). As early as August the mainland campaign had been revived and there were bombings and shootings in England throughout the autumn. None the less, violence never returned to the level of the pre-truce years. From then on the number of explosions and shooting incidents has gone into erratic but definite decline: 1,902 shootings in 1976 compared with 382 in 1982; 766 explosions in 1976, 113 in 1982.

Long before the ceasefire finally hobbled to an end it — and its architects — were coming under bitter attack inside the movement. During the feuding Gerry Adams smuggled a letter out to the Belfast Brigade from Long Kesh, where he was serving a sentence for attempted escape after being picked up again and interned in 1973, demanding to know what was going on.[6] Adams and the younger republicans like Danny Morrison and Tom Hartley were concerned that the spate of internecine killing would be used to the British advantage — to justify the ending of special category status by presenting the IRA as on the one hand a mafia-like organisation, and on the other a sectarian murder gang.

Morrison and Hartley achieved a significant coup by using their friendship with the old republican Frank Card, a confidant of McKee's, to oust Sean Caughey from the editorship of *Republican News* and install themselves in his place. Caughey was a solitary figure, a supporter of O'Connaill and O'Bradaigh's political ideas and a passionate advocate of Eire Nua, a subject aired at tedious length in the paper's columns. According to Morrison, it was learnt that he was planning to carry a statement from a Catholic defence association threatening to blow up Protestant schools if attacks on Catholics continued. His departure followed soon afterwards. Under Morrison and Hartley the tone of the paper altered sharply. They used it as a platform to attack the regional policy at the core of Eire Nua. A new columnist appeared with the pen-name 'Brownie', who regularly out argued the case for developing the movement's vestigial political senses in support of the 'armed struggle'. Brownie was Gerry Adams, who had been invited to contribute to *Republican News* by Danny Morrison. Between them they used the paper as a vehicle to promote their ideas and to defeat those of O'Connaill and O'Bradaigh.

After the ceasefire the authority of O'Bradaigh, O'Connaill and McKee went into a long decline. It did not take long for a general feeling that the ceasefire had brought nothing to grow. The British were still there and the IRA was weaker. What was more, they were about to lose probably the single greatest propaganda victory of the campaign, the winning of prisoner-of-war status. The stock of the critics — notably Adams and McGuinness — rose sharply. Within a year of the ceasefire ending, military control of the organisation slipped from the Southerners' hands as the units of the Six Counties formed themselves into a virtually autonomous Northern Command. In one sense this was merely the regularisation of what had been the real situation since the campaign started in earnest. The units in Belfast, Derry and rural Ulster had bombed and shot at will — with Dublin's imprimatur being sought only in exceptional cases — so that in many cases the first O'Bradaigh, O'Connaill and even

MacStiofain heard of spectacular operations was when they turned on the radio.[10] The advent of Northern Command underlined the fact that a long-standing republican anomaly was at an end. From its birth, the IRA had been dominated by Southerners. Republicans from the territory at the heart of republicanism's *raison d'être* had never had the representation in the decision-making councils of the IRA that their importance merited. This imbalance was now reversed.

CHAPTER SIXTEEN

Other People

From the outset the Provisional IRA purported to be representing 'the people'. By this they meant the working-class Catholics of Northern Ireland. It was a necessary claim to make if they were to sustain their self-image as freedom fighters. But until they began contesting elections there was no reliable measure of the extent to which Catholics approved of what was being done on their behalf. The republicans of the North, as we have seen, were for a long time extremely wary of putting their popularity to the test in an incontrovertible way. This caution was justified. As long as the IRA's energies were dedicated mostly to violence, their relationship with the community they sprang from would be exploitative, intimidatory and underlaid with contempt.

Even in the blackest and most destructive passages of the IRA's history, sectarian loyalty meant that there was always a large enough reservoir of sympathy and support in the North to ensure its survival. It had always been able to rely on men and women who had no formal connection with the Provisionals but were willing to help, to the extent of acting as accomplices. Many of the operations carried out by the IRA in Northern Ireland involved the complicity of ordinary Catholics. At its lowest level, it was a matter of seeing nothing and hearing nothing. More seriously, it could mean the loan of a car or a lorry. Frequently it was more sinister. The IRA's intelligence sometimes came from sympathisers working in administrative jobs. IRA spies in tax and social security offices passed on much useful material, the home addresses of policemen, for example, or personal information about members of the loyalist paramilitaries. Part-time members of the RUC or the UDR were particularly vulnerable to betrayal by workmates. In the late summer of 1981 Tommy Montgomery, a worker in Gallaher's cigarette factory in Belfast and a reserve constable in the RUC, was at his machine when a girl working alongside him called his name. When he turned round there was a flash: the girl had taken his picture. After a while he became suspicious and asked to be given the photograph, but was continually put off with excuses. Eventually, after two months, she handed it over. A Belfast court later found that she had taken the picture at the request of the IRA who had inquired about reservists working at the factory. Montgomery's life was spared because the IRA team chosen to assassinate him decided that he had been tipped off. Others offered more passive assistance; an elderly woman who allowed her home to be used as a base by the Ardoyne IRA described to the police how she returned one day to find some sinister bundles in the back room and a group of men sitting and talking. 'I knew they were in the IRA and so I turned and went out . . . When I saw the black plastic bags in the house I knew they were guns.' However, she was at pains to point out that she was never intimidated.

But such open co-operation was rare and usually a degree of intimidation was necessary. It did not need to be heavy-handed. Few of the witnesses whose houses were taken over for sniping attacks or whose cars were borrowed for assassinations were threatened. The knowledge of the fate of police informers was enough. On hearing the radio news Francis Murphy, a postman whose coat was used to disguise the killer of a part-time UDR man who worked at Belfast Zoo, 'knew immediately that my coat must have been used in the shooting', but told detectives 'youse know the position up there yourselves about reporting anything to the police. I was frightened.'[1] The extent of intimidation shows that the IRA is generally tolerated rather than admired in the ghettoes of Belfast and Londonderry.

Over the years, there were a number of occasions when anger against the Provisionals burst through the crust of acquiescence. Outrages against civilians produced regular protests in Derry and Belfast in 1971 and 1972, mainly led by women. The Provos took little notice of them, relying on the inevitability of a counter-outrage by the security forces to restore the balance. The usual attitude of the leadership towards criticism from the Catholic community was irritation or authoritarian contempt. When a 17-month-old girl was shot dead in an exchange of fire between the IRA and the Army in Belfast in August 1971, Ruairi O'Bradaigh explained that this was one of the hazards of urban guerrilla warfare. Often the IRA derided the protesters as middle-class outsiders and enemies of the republican movement.

The most visible popular expression of revulsion against the IRA (though not the most successful – the Derry women who caused the Officials to call a truce after the shooting of Ranger Best have that honour) came at the end of the freakishly hot summer of 1976. The incident that gave rise to it was a minor one in the long catalogue of IRA violence against civilians. On the afternoon of 10 August, Anne Maguire was out walking in the sunshine with her four children in Andersonstown, West Belfast, when a speeding car approached, pursued by a convoy of British Army vehicles pouring fire from their gun slits. The driver, Danny Lennon, a member of the Andersonstown IRA and a friend of Bobby Sands, was shot dead, and the car slewed into the group, badly injuring Mrs Maguire and killing three of her children. The grief and the anger the incident provoked was summarised by Anne Maguire's sister, Mairead Corrigan, on the television news that evening when she broke down weeping. Betty Williams, another Belfast Catholic, was so moved by this that she contacted her and together they formed the Women's Peace Movement. They were both working-class and Catholic. Corrigan was an organiser for the church women's lay organisation, the Legion of Mary, and regularly visited prisoners in the Maze.

The Peace People, as the organisation came to be known, was described by Bernadette (Devlin) McAliskey as 'an explosion of female rage'. On 14 August 10,000 people joined a peace march in Belfast. A week later there were 20,000, and a further 20,000 at a rally in Dublin. Protestants began to join in. The phenomenon was seized on by the media as an indication of hope and Corrigan, Williams and Ciaran McKeown (the other founder of the movement) became international figures.

The IRA was complacent, but as the movement gathered pace became alarmed. In West Belfast marchers were stoned and organiser's houses daubed with threats. As the success of the Peace People continued — with fund-raising visits to the United States and the award of the 1976 Nobel Peace Prize to Williams and Corrigan — the alarm turned to hatred. The republican press attacked the 'hypocrisy' of the movement in failing to condemn the security forces with the same vigour as they did the IRA. In October that year Williams and Corrigan issued a statement in which they said 'we do not equate the vicious and determined terrorism of the republican and loyalist paramilitary organisations with the occasional instances when members of the security forces may have stepped beyond the rule of law . . . Until the Northern Ireland community themselves evolve their own new community institutions and form of government, then the RUC and other security forces are the only legitimate upholders of the rule of law.'[2] This frankness was unwelcome in the ghettoes. When they later went to urge Catholics to pass information about the IRA to the security forces their credibility was further impaired. To republican sympathisers in the Catholic areas this was asking them to breach a religiously observed convention against informing. No matter how unpopular the IRA might be in the community, voluntary information reaching the police about their activities was virtually non-existent. The 'confidential telephone' established in the early seventies through which citizens could leave anonymous messages about paramilitary activities was a failure. As Gerry Adams pointed out, it is impossible for the great majority of Catholics to see the IRA in the same terms as the authorities and the Protestant population did. IRA members are 'Mrs Smith's daughter or young O'Connor down the street. The child you brought to school or went to their wedding. It's not staff officer Paddy Maguire. It's Mrs Maguire's boy.'[3]

By the end of 1977 the Peace People had begun to slide into obscurity. The movement was contemptuous of conventional politics and its activities soon settled down to the organisation of mixed religion camps and attempts to start up small, non-sectarian businesses. Its demise was hastened by internal squabbling and by 1980 the founders had left. None the less, it succeeded for a while in scaring the Provisionals. The venom they felt towards it is reflected in the rejoicing that took place over its demise, recorded in the official death notice of Danny Lennon. 'While the treacherous pro-Brit antics of this organisation were soon exposed and discredited,' wrote the anonymous obituarist, 'the self-sacrifice and heroism of young IRA volunteers like Danny Lennon shall be written into the history books and looked upon as a source of strength by the new generations of Irish men and women in a free republic.'[4]

Concern over the Peace People did not make the IRA any more sensitive to community feelings. In June 1978, for example, they executed Paddy McEntee, claiming he was an informer. McEntee was a postman from Crossmaglen where he was well known and well liked. His family denied the charge. At his funeral several hundred people turned out to walk behind the coffin in defiance of the IRA.

The brutal nature of the IRA's 'policing' operations was another cause of resentment. The casual beatings and kneecappings that car-thieves, drug-users and petty criminals of the Catholic quarters could expect from IRA vigilantes were clearly much harsher punishments than they would receive at the hands of the RUC, an irony that never seemed to strike the Provisionals. These methods gained a surprisingly high degree of approval among the Catholic working class. It was rough justice but it was better than none, and the victims of it were often thought to have got what they deserved. On rare occasions, though, local people were moved to intervene. In October 1977 a group of residents in Clonard, West Belfast stopped IRA men dropping concrete blocks on the limbs of a slow-witted local teenager. The Provisionals responded with a statement declaring:

> Local people in Dunmore Street interfered when a unit of volunteers was about to apprehend one of the worst criminals in the Clonard area. As a result of this interference, the lives and liberty of the volunteers was put in jeopardy. We wish to make it absolutely and emphatically clear to the people of Dunmore Street and the whole of the Clonard area that this interference will not be tolerated in the future and that anyone, young or old, male or female, who obstructs the volunteer in this work will be shot.

If the IRA was ever to become a serious political organisation, as the new leadership emerging in the North wished, such murderous arrogance would have to be curbed.

CHAPTER SEVENTEEN

Allies Abroad

When the troubles revived, the republican movement had naturally looked to America — whose shadow was to fall across events regularly in the ensuing years — for help. The IRA retained a strong belief in the ability of the United States to influence events in Ireland, a conviction shared by the British Government, which expended a great deal of effort on anti-IRA propaganda there. Since Irish emigrants began flooding into America in the wake of the famine of 1846-8 the expatriate community had provided a reservoir of anglophobic sentiment, and from the 1840s onwards the republican movement had regarded America as a potential source of money, political influence and armaments. This belief had sustained the Fenian agitation of the 1860s and American republican secret society Clann na Gael had provided guns for the IRB on the eve of the 1916 uprising. In the years of the 'Tan War', Irish emigrant groups, labour unions, the Ancient Order of Hibernians and politicians with Irish antecedents exerted pressure on Congress and on the US Government to take the part of the rebels; and they fought a hard, but unsuccessful, battle to have Ireland's right to national self-determination placed on the agenda at the Versailles conference at the end of the First World War.

To the supporters of a minority cause in a tiny country moored on the edge of Great Britain, Irish America's apparent potency was awe-inspiring. As James Stephens, the egotistical but shrewd Fenian leader, had noted this patriotism could often be merely 'a windbag or a phantom, the laughing stock of sensible men and the El Dorado of fools . . . speeches of bayonets, gala days and jolly nights, banners and sashes . . . bunkum and fulsome filibustering'.[1]

This was not how it seemed to the IRA in August 1969, however, as they contemplated their lack of funds, arms and international influence in the aftermath of the riots. Almost as soon as the immediate scrambling for guns around the island was over, it was to the US that they inevitably turned for further help.

In 1969 the US had five times as many Irish citizens as Ireland but the IRA was to find that sentimental loyalty to the republican cause and inherent hatred for Britain had weakened considerably since the start of the century. There were several reasons for this. For one thing, Ireland had had a form of independence since 1922 that satisfied most expatriate aspirations. Affection for the old country had been eroded by her decision to sit out the Second World War on the sidelines, neutral and aloof. Probably most important, Irish America had changed class. A survey carried out in the town of New Port, Massachusetts in the 1920s showed that of the Irish population as a whole, thirteen per cent were of the lower-lower class, fifty-four per cent of the upper-lower class, twenty-eight per cent in the lower-middle class, and six per cent in the upper-middle class. An examination of the third generation Irish population, however, told a different story: only two per cent remained in the lower-lower class, thirty-nine per cent were in the upper-lower class, forty-two per cent were lower-middle and seventeen per cent were upper-middle. This was upward mobility at a rapid rate. The apotheosis of this process was the election of John F. Kennedy as President. This event produced a revival of Irish-American sentimentality, but no political effect. The Northern question was an old dispute. The Kennedy generation was preoccupied with the new.

None the less, in 1969, America was clearly the best place for the IRA to look for guns, money and political support. In November, three months after the riots, Sean Keenan, the hero of the defence of the Bogside, was dispatched across the Atlantic. He was a sensible choice: middle-aged and comfortable-looking, with impeccable history of suffering for the cause. He toured the Irish centres in Boston, Chicago and New York, appealing for money publicly – and privately attempting to set up a network for the supply of arms. Even with America's lax gun laws, obtaining weapons was not a simple process. The first shipment, put together by a group of Irish-American sympathisers in Philadelphia, took six months to arrange and was not sent to Ireland until August 1970. It was of crucial importance. Until its arrival the IRA had only an odd assortment of elderly weapons, insufficient for any serious escalation in violence. The Philadelphia shipment put into their possession several hundred Armalites,* light weapons with an unloaded weight of only 6lb 11oz but carrying a considerable punch.

Initially the IRA's agents moved cautiously, buying in small quantities so as not to arouse suspicion, travelling to mid-Western gunfairs, saving the guns up and then shipping them out from an Eastern seaport to Ireland. Small consignments were smuggled in by sympathetic crews in the holds of airplanes and passenger ships. In October 1971, for example, the Dublin police found that six unclaimed suitcases were full of guns and ammunition. This discovery shut down what had been a successful conduit for weapons. Two IRA supporters in the crew had been shipping six or seven suitcases of arms on every trip. The guns were then claimed by an Irish customs agent in Cork.[2]

These operations were greatly helped by the co-operation of pro-republicans in the ranks of the longshoremen's union and the US customs. According to the IRA defector Peter McMullen, who spent the winter of 1972-3 in New York, 'the way the weapons got out was in household and office furniture. They'd strip the furniture down and fill it with weapons. Guns would go inside everything, cabinets, beds, sofas, chairs – everything'.[3] The furniture would then be loaded aboard a Dublin-bound ship sailing for New York, sealed in a container.

* The precise number is unknown but the security forces have over the years recovered 420 weapons dating back to the consignment.

New York customs presented no problems. 'Someone took care of that here and on the other side too. Telephone calls would be made to a contact in Dublin giving the date of the arrival of the container, the numbers and so forth and it would be let through customs.'[2] From Dublin the container would be driven to Dundalk where the arms would be hidden in trees, shrubs or even flower nurseries, then picked up by IRA members in rented cars. The weapons would be ferried to the North hidden under the seats of cars, often full of children and driven by women, on busy Saturday afternoons when the customs were inclined to be less diligent. Once in Belfast they were distributed by the Brigade quartermaster, then Brian Keenan.

The IRA's American allies were largely, but by no means exclusively, working-class, with a strong, inherited anglophobia and a hazy but firmly-held belief in the republicans' credentials as freedom fighters. The five who put together the Philadelphia shipment were all working-class men active in the Irish-American community of their home town. Two of them, Daniel Cahalane and Neil Byrne, were also officers of the Irish Northern Aid Committee. Noraid, as the organisation is better known, was stigmatised by the British and Irish authorities from its inception as the IRA's main fund-raising arm in America and a cover for the purchase and transportation of armaments. It was founded in 1969 by three elderly republicans: Michael Flannery, who fought on the IRA side in Tipperary in the civil war before emigrating to America, Jack McCarthy and John MacGowan. It sprang from the numerous expatriate clubs which kept alive the Gaelic tradition, cultural, social and sporting, all over America. It also had strong links with the trade unions where Irish-Americans were strongly represented, particularly the longshore workers' unions. Many IRA men who fled to America in the early seventies found work and shelter in the docks.

Flannery was an unrepentant hard-line republican who 'if asked for money in the knowledge that it was going to buy guns for the IRA would have no hesitation in handing it over',[4] and in 1982 was acquitted of charges of supplying $16,800 for the purpose of buying AK-47 assault rifles for the IRA. Noraid persisted in maintaining, however, that its purpose was merely to provide money for the dependents of IRA prisoners and victims of the troubles.

According to Martin Galvin, its chief executive, Noraid was sending $600,000 to Ireland for the first years of the conflict but in the mid-seventies this dipped to $160,000. During the hunger strikes of 1981 the figure leapt to $800,000 but afterwards fell back to $300,000.[5] The money came from donations, contributions from Noraid's 100 chapters across the US, $5-a-head dinners and the proceeds of the sale of its staunchly pro-IRA newspaper, the *Irish Weekly*, which claimed circulation of 10,000 in New York, Boston, Philadelphia, Chicago and San Francisco.

The organisation also saw itself as the IRA's chief propaganda agent in the US and claimed to have far more support than the Irish National Caucus, a rival organisation which concentrated on social issues. During the hunger strikes, Galvin appeared on numerous television programmes putting the IRA view and proclaiming its 'moral support for the IRA struggle against the British forces of occupation'.

Although Noraid undoubtedly unofficially contributed to IRA arms-buying in the US, most of the transactions were made by sympathisers with no direct connection with any of the pro-republican organisations. This became inevitable once it became clear that Noraid and the Irish National Caucus had been thoroughly infiltrated by the US security agencies, notably the Federal Bureau of Investigation (FBI). During the mid-seventies the IRA was forced to rely on criminals to obtain guns. In August 1976, for example, a Boston gang known as the Roxbury Rats broke into the US National Guard armoury at Danvers, near Boston and made off with seven M60 heavy machine-guns, which were sold to the IRA for £667 each. For a while they often featured in IRA propaganda posters and were once put on public display in 1978 in Derry during the annual Bloody Sunday commemorations. According to the RUC they were used in incidents in which ten people died and nineteen were wounded.

The IRA's main contact in obtaining the M60s was a stocky

Corsican with Mafia links and a lengthy criminal record called George De Meo. He posed as an antiques dealer but most of his income came from trading in 'offies' (off the record firearms). One of his main suppliers was a firm called B and B guns of Wilson, North Carolina. The proprietor, Howard Bruton, kept up a regular trade with De Meo for three years. Twice a year for three years De Meo would drive from New York to load up the boot of his Cadillac with high-powered rifles and what the state prosecutor later calculated as a million rounds of ammunition. None of these transactions was ever recorded, as the law demanded. When asked where the guns were destined, De Meo would reply, a court heard later, 'someplace cool and green'.[6] This trade finally ended in 1980 when guns seized in Ireland were traced back to B and B and Bruton and De Meo were fined and sentenced to ten and five years respectively.

De Meo, however, offered the FBI a deal. In return for leniency he would lead the FBI into the IRA arms-buying network. They accepted. De Meo began by making contact with a 67-year-old Brooklyn security guard called George Harrison. This unlikely figure, the FBI claimed, had been the main supplier to the IRA since the start of the troubles. De Meo introduced him to an arms dealer called John White. The pair had several meetings. Harrison seemed eager to have anything he could lay his hands on, but especially ammunition for an M79 grenade launcher and for a 20 mm cannon which was awaiting shipment to Ireland. After several small deals Harrison agreed to buy forty-seven machine-guns for $16,800. But first he had to get the money.

That evening he rang a number in the New York borough of Queens. It belonged to Michael Flannery of Noraid. Harrison, the wire tap later revealed, when talking of the payment asked Flannery to 'make it as high as you can . . . over the stated amount' to which he replied 'Yeah, yeah.'[7] Flannery and Harrison were arrested with four other Noraid conspirators, but at their trial were acquitted when the jury accepted their defence that the whole operation had been engineered by the Central Intelligence Agency (CIA).

*   *   *

The IRA also saw America as a potential source of political support. The first reactions of Irish-American politicians to the resurgence of the troubles in 1969 were encouraging: they called for a political solution in line with the Provisionals' fundamental aspirations.

As late as 20 October 1971, Senator Edward Kennedy, the most important mouthpiece of Irish-American opinion, was demanding in Congress the 'immediate withdrawal of British troops from Northern Ireland and the immediate convening of all parties for the purpose of establishing a united Ireland'. Kennedy was supported by three other senior Irish-Americans: Senator Daniel Patrick Moynihan from New York; Hugh Carey, the Governor of New York; and the speaker of the House of Representatives, Thomas 'Tip' O'Neill. On most issues they formed a united front, calling down the years, but with decreasing volume, for a thirty-two county Ireland and periodically deploring Britain's apparent unwillingness to solve the problem. In the early days, at least, the Provisionals believed that they had some friends in the political establishment. Maria Maguire claimed that Kennedy's office, and Paul O'Dwyer, a Wall Street lawyer who was a long-time activist in Irish causes, intervened to enable IRA men to get visas to visit America, after several of them, including Joe Cahill, had been barred from entry.

It did not take long for whatever chances the IRA had of presenting themselves as a legitimate political force to disappear. Their own behaviour saw to that. As the violence deepened and the list of atrocities lengthened, Irish-American politicians hastened to denounce the IRA, Moynihan condemning it as 'a band of sadistic murderers'. And the IRA failed to gain any credibility with the American political establishment because American political attitudes were also coloured by the propaganda efforts of the other participants in the drama. John Hume of the SDLP forged particularly strong links with the Irish-American lobby so that he and his party were overwhelmingly accepted as the authentic voice of nationalism in Northern Ireland. By the mid 1970s the Irish-American political establishment was actively hostile to the

IRA and its allies in the US, and there were regular appeals against donating money to Noraid. In March 1983 Edward Kennedy and his colleagues boycotted the St Patrick's day parade in New York in protest at its pro-IRA flavour and the presence of Michael Flannery as grand marshall of the festivities.

But until 1986 the IRA could still regard the US as a safe haven for men and women on the run. America had been a refuge for rebels from the 1848 uprising onwards. Several of the leaders of the border campaign had fled there in the 1950s and stayed on undisturbed by the authorities. It was inevitable that soon after 1969, IRA men should flee there again. Successive British governments sought to get the US to act against republican fugitives but the first extradition case, brought against the IRA deserter Peter McMullen, was not heard until May 1978.

McMullen had been arrested a month after arriving in the US on a false passport. The British authorities sought his extradition for his part in bombing Claro-Deverell Barracks in 1974. McMullen admitted the charge but said his offence was political, a plea accepted by the court. The magistrate based his judgement on a finding from a case in 1952, when Tito's government had sought the return of Andrija Artukovic, a minister of the Nazi client state of Croatia during the war, who was accused of murdering about half a million Jews, gypsies and communists. Artukovic argued, successfully, that his was a political crime. The case produced a durable, and remarkably liberal, interpretation of what constituted a political offence. To qualify, 'the crime must be incidental to and form a part of political disturbances. It must be in furtherance of one side or another of a bona fide struggle for political power.'

A succession of IRA men subsequently escaped extradition on the strength of this ruling, including Desmond Mackin, wanted for a shooting incident in Andersonstown, and William Quinn, who was born and brought up in Los Angeles but moved to Northern Ireland at the start of the troubles and joined the IRA. Quinn was eventually extradited and convicted with the murder of PC Stephen Tibble, shot dead in Fulham in 1975.

The British Government's view of the importance of America to the IRA was exaggerated. There was never any likelihood of the organisation attracting any significant support there and what success it did have depended on showing a false face to Irish-Americans. According to Maria McGuire, republicans on propaganda tours were instructed to 'make copious references to the martyrs of 1916 and 1920-22, the period most of the audience would be living in',[8] but to avoid any mention of socialism, or the movement's attitude to the Catholic Church. When Americans visited the republican centre in West Belfast, posters in support of international revolutionary groups were prudently removed from the walls.

The IRA regarded America primarily as a source of guns. By 1981, forty-seven per cent of the weapons recovered by the police and Army since the troubles started were of American manufacture. But America was by no means the IRA's sole supplier and so even if the American arms market ended, this would not dramatically affect the IRA's capacity to create violence.

After 1969 the IRA had begun to investigate other possibilities abroad. During the dog days of the fifties and sixties the IRA maintained a keen interest in the activities of similar separatist and nationalist revolutionary organisations overseas. There was a particularly strong fellow-feeling for the guerrilla fighters of Kenya and Cyprus, whose struggle to break their colonial ties with Britain the IRA saw as an exact parallel of their own.

Until 1969 the IRA's interest in foreign affairs was not reciprocated. The international revolutionary left was barely aware that the IRA was still in existence. Within a very short time, however, the organisation had become the object of intense interest. To the satisfaction of Sean MacStiofain, who had strong internationalist beliefs, men he had long admired from afar were by the early seventies treating the organisation seriously and with respect. Initially, however, there was some confusion about how best to exploit the IRA's new standing. On the one hand, it provided obvious opportunities to obtain guns and funds and also to spread the IRA's propaganda

301

message to a world audience. On the other, history advised that it was best to be extremely cautious before becoming involved with any organisation beyond Ireland's shores.

Republicanism's contacts with foreign powers in the past had usually finished in failure. In 1925 an IRA delegation visited Moscow to try and enlist Stalin's help. One of the delegation, Gerald Boland, told Tim Pat Coogan that 'the first question he was asked on arrival was "How many bishops did you hang?" When he answered, "None", his interrogator replied, "Ah, you people are not serious at all." ' One of the party, 'Pa' Murray, met Stalin who showed himself surprisingly well briefed on Irish affairs. To Murray's discomfiture he reeled off a list of the guns seized by the Dublin government to date. How could he be sure any Soviet supplied guns would not meet the same fate and be used as anti-communist propaganda? In the end no help was forthcoming.[9]

Another member of the party, Sean Russell, played a key role in a second initiative to raise help abroad. Russell was motivated by the republican dictum that England's difficulty was Ireland's opportunity, an attitude that allowed the professed anti-Fascists of the IRA cheerfully to contemplate an alliance with the Nazis. At the start of the war Russell was living in America where he had gone after the failure of a bombing campaign in England; he was picked up by the authorities in a precautionary swoop before the visit of George VI and served with an expulsion order. He went on the run but found that wartime restrictions made it impossible for him to find a passage back to Ireland. In desperation Russell approached the Germans for help. Soon afterwards he was shipped to Berlin where he was reunited with an old comrade, Frank Ryan, who had ended up in Germany after narrowly escaping execution after his capture by Italian troops during the Spanish Civil War where he had been serving with the Lincoln Washington Brigade. After a meeting between the German foreign minister, Joachim von Ribbentrop, and intelligence chiefs including Admiral Canaris, the head of the Abwehr, it was decided, with some misgivings on the part of Ribbentrop, to put a U-boat at the pair's disposal. The operation, codenamed Dove, left Russell free to carry out whatever action he saw fit in Ireland.

Russell never reached his homeland. A hundred miles offshore he developed acute stomach pains and died, probably of a perforated ulcer. The submarine turned back to Germany where Ryan lived out the remainder of the war in gathering obscurity and ill-health until his death in June 1944. The Germans' half-hearted attempts to set up a spy network in Ireland were equally unsuccessful, hampered more than helped by the efforts of their allies in the IRA.

With these examples in mind, the Provisional leadership was chary of becoming involved with foreign governments or organisations. But some sort of foreign operation was clearly going to be necessary to avoid relying on America as the sole source of weapons. It was also necessary, for propaganda purposes, to publicise the republican cause abroad. Later, as opportunities to strike at the British presence in the North diminished, the Provisionals would come to see abroad, and particularly Europe, as a legitimate theatre for operations against British soldiers and diplomats. These considerations determined the shape of the IRA's overseas enterprises.

MacStiofain's virulent anti-communism should theoretically have ruled out any accommodation with marxists. The Soviet Union was not anxious to strike up any relationship with the IRA. While Russian propaganda tirelessly distorted the Northern Ireland situation the state carefully avoided giving republicanism any overt support and has even on occasion condemned the Provisional IRA. However, practical considerations meant that the leadership's scrupulous attitude did not survive long and the IRA soon turned towards the Eastern bloc. Successive IRA leaderships took a pragmatic attitude towards the provenance of military hardware and support and would talk to anyone if they thought it might benefit them. According to one IRA leader, 'we don't mind where the gear comes from, as long as there are no strings attached'. This attitude produced some exotic encounters. At one point in the mid-seventies, security forces' intelligence reports claimed that there were even meetings between the IRA and Chinese communist officials.

303

The first major overseas attempt to establish an arms supply line through Europe was in 1971 when Daithi O'Connaill and Maria McGuire organised an arms shipment from the Czechoslovakian state munitions manufacturer, Omnipol. The trip underlined the dangers of operating abroad. The pair were at the mercy of shadowy and untrustworthy middle men, news of the mission mysteriously leaked to the *Daily Telegraph* and the two returned home ignominiously and empty-handed after the arms shipment — 166 crates packed with rocket launchers, machine-guns and rifles — was seized at Schipol airport near Amsterdam.

Necessity forced the IRA to continue with foreign arms-hunting forays. In the early seventies the Army Council sent several IRA men to make foreign contacts in an effort to open up a reliable supply line of weapons. The most important member of the group was Brian Keenan, perhaps the most intelligent, energetic and resourceful military operator the modern IRA has yet produced. Keenan was born in 1942 and brought up in South Derry before his family moved to West Belfast. At the age of 18, like many of his Catholic contemporaries, he travelled to England to find work, for a time in partnership with his brother as a television repair man in Corby, Northamptonshire. He came to the notice of the police when in a burst of frustration he damaged a faulty cigarette machine. As a result, they had a record of his fingerprints, which Keenan would come to regret.

After the troubles resumed, Keenan returned to Northern Ireland and with the electronic skills he had acquired in England was able to get a job in the Grundig factory in the Belfast suburb of Finaghy, where he was active in the trade union and made a reputation as a radical. Although there was no republican tradition in his family, in 1970 or 1971 he joined the IRA. Before long he had attracted the attention of Seamus Twomey and by August 1971 he was the quartermaster of the Belfast Brigade. Keenan was a singular man. He was older than most of the other 'Sixty-niners', aloof and resolutely serious. If anything this reticence enhanced his popularity and reputation, and he is still held up today as an example of republican virtues. He was articulate, well informed and — an exotic rarity among the early Provisionals — a committed marxist. His political beliefs, unlike those of the rest of the leadership in Dublin or Belfast, were of a pure and theoretical kind and had undergone little modification to take account of his Irishness or given religion. Keenan felt an unforced empathy with foreign guerrilla movements, especially the Palestine Liberation Organisation (PLO). It was natural that when the search for arms caused the IRA to think about spreading its net wider, he should be the one to organise the trawl.

Details of Keenan's movements in the early seventies are obscure. He was a very busy man. Besides travelling abroad to foster political contacts and open up supply lines he was masterminding bomb attacks in Belfast and working on the incipient British mainland bombing campaign. His most significant trip is believed to have been to Libya some time in 1972. The purpose of the journey was to obtain arms and finances from the regime of Colonel Gadhafy. The country's apparently boundless oil revenues and the impulsive nature of its leader had given it a reputation as a soft touch among revolutionary freeloaders all over the world. Keenan's initial contact was probably made through an Irish schoolteacher from County Monaghan with Sinn Fein connections, who went to teach in Tripoli in 1972.

The result was a flow of arms and money from Gadhafy that persisted for several years. In the early days of the relationship the Libyans were suspicious of Keenan and insisted that a well-known IRA figure conduct the negotiations. Joe Cahill, one of the most visible of the IRA leaders after his post-internment press conference, was dispatched to oversee the shipment of five tons of free arms on the *Claudia*. The vessel was seized off the Irish coast in March 1973. But there is no doubt that later shipments got through. By the Libyans' own account, the IRA were the recipients of generous amounts of financial aid. Gadhafy reportedly told Maltese officials in 1974 that so far he had given a total of £5 million.[10]

Gadhafy soon proved an unreliable ally of the IRA. His hazy view of the nature of the conflict was further obscured by the arrival of more Irish visitors. Gadhafy had approved of the IRA because it was 'anti-imperialist'. In 1974, however, the Provisionals found they had some rivals for his admiration. Gadhafy had reportedly been impressed by the UWC council strike of 1974 which brought down the power-sharing administration, an event which, it was claimed, reminded him of his own bloodless coup in 1969.[11] In the autumn of 1974 the UDA joined the Development of Irish Resources organisation, a small group of visionaries visiting Tripoli who wanted Libya's help in exploiting Ireland's offshore gas and oil reserves. It was founded by a Dublin businessman, Walter Hegarty, and a Northern journalist, Patrick Turley, who believed that the key to the Irish problem lay in accelerating economic development. The two had agreed to let the UDA accompany them because they shared some common ground. Since the UWC strike a powerful group inside the UDA had been arguing that Ulster's best hope was as an independent state. The most common argument against this was that Northern Ireland was not an economically viable entity. Perhaps Libyan backing could change that.

The UDA delegation, led by Glenn Barr, arrived in November and stayed at the Palace Hotel in Tripoli. Together with the resources group they had several meetings with Libyan officials, mainly centred on the possibility of contracts for the Belfast shipyard Harland and Wolff to build oiltankers. News of the UDA visit alarmed the IRA who feared that it might produce a change of heart in Gadhafy and they dispatched their own three-man delegation to Tripoli.

The UDA's embarrassment over their presence in Libya was enough to kill off the talks. Barr and his men returned empty-handed to a storm of loyalist condemnation. The UDA visit succeeded in one of its objectives, however. Apprised of the complexities of the Ulster situation, Gadhafy immediately lost interest. His interest was rekindled after the American attack on Libya in 1986. When the French customs intercepted the *Eskund* they discovered a cargo of guns and bomb-making equipment for the IRA. Irish Intelligence now believes that the IRA had already landed two or three consignments of arms before the capture of the *Eskund*.

The search for guns also took the IRA to the Middle East. In the dispossessed Palestinians they felt they had natural allies. But the PLO and its related organisations were never to prove a fruitful source of armaments. In the early seventies contacts with the Middle East resulted in the IRA laying hands on a consignment of Russian-made RPG-7 rocket-propelled grenades which probably had greater propaganda value than military worth. In 1977 the IRA managed to negotiate a sizeable shipment with Yasser Arafat's Al Fatah organisation. It included seven rocket-launchers, twenty-nine French-manufactured sub-machine guns, two bren guns, twenty-nine machine pistols and twenty-nine Kalashnikov assault rifles, along with ammunition, grenades and nearly 500 lbs of explosives. They were to be packed into two hollowed-out transformers at Nicosia in Cyprus and shipped to Ireland. The consignment never got there. Tipped off by Israeli intelligence, the transformers were seized at Antwerp and the man who had organised the operation, Seamus McCollum, a 55-year-old Liverpool Irishman, was arrested in Dublin.

On several occasions Sinn Fein representatives took part in conferences organised by Palestinians, who often showed an alarming ignorance of the facts of the conflict. When Garret FitzGerald visited the Maghreb as President of the European Council of ministers in 1975 he found that some senior members of the PLO thought the IRA was a clandestine branch of the army of the Republic, whose activities the Irish Government found it politically necessary to denounce from time to time.

Some of the IRA's foreign adventures were inspired by idealism rather than necessity. From the outset the Provisionals had friendly dealings with the Basque separatists of northern Spain who shared the IRA's enthusiasm for Celtic culture. Ruairi O'Bradaigh was particularly close to them and made a number of visits there. A liberated Euskadi (Basque land) was an element in his personal political fantasy of a Celtic federation on the fringe of Europe composed of Irish, Welsh, Scots, Bretons and Basques. On the whole, co-operation was confined to mutual expressions of support, though Maria McGuire reported that Basques had handed over fifty revolvers to the IRA in return for explosives training.

The IRA's successes during the seventies and eighties attracted emissaries from a number of foreign revolutionary organisations seeking advice and assistance. According to Joe Cahill, the IRA has received approaches from Nicaraguans, Grenadans and South African blacks in recent years.[12] Concern over security and the logistical problems of giving assistance have meant that it is mostly moral support that has been forthcoming.

On the other hand, the Provisionals carefully avoided any association with the student revolutionaries of the Red Brigades, Baader-Meinhof gang and the Red Army Faction, whom they regarded as indulgent middle-class nihilists. In the judgement of one IRA spokesman: 'We cannot afford to get involved either politically or militarily with such groups.'[13] One of the problems facing the Provisionals at the end of the seventies was that the activities of the Euro-terrorists had eroded any sympathy that might have been felt for their cause among European liberals, who once they were in close proximity to the violence tended to bracket all terror groups together.

The IRA's claim on liberal sympathies was also diminished by a series of attacks on British targets on the Continent, taking advantage of the relatively lax security to teach the British that there was nowhere they could feel completely safe. In August 1978 eight British Army bases in Germany were blasted on the same night. In March 1979 an IRA team assassinated Sir Richard Sykes, the British ambassador to the Hague, and his Dutch footman, the same day shooting dead a Belgian businessman in mistake for the British envoy to NATO. Later, on 28th August 1979, four British soldier bandsmen and eight Belgian civilians were injured in Brussels and in June 1979 the NATO supreme allied commander in Europe, Alexander Haig, was caught in a landmine explosion near Mons in

Belgium which the police believe was intended for a senior British Army officer. Up until 1987 the level of IRA activity in Europe subsided. The previous attacks were the shooting dead of a senior British Army officer at the garrison at Bielefield in West Germany (with the gun that was used to kill Sykes) and two other sniper attacks at Munster in 1980.

In the botched IRA bombing in 1987 outside a British Army base in West Germany thirty civilians were injured, among them the wives of German officers out for the night. Despite the permanent presence of an IRA cell in Germany, their guns went silent and the next continental operation was an expensive undertaking for the IRA. On 6 March 1988, just as the IRA were putting the finishing touches to what they viewed as a 'prestige' operation against the British Army in Gibraltar, their unit of Mairead Farrell, Danny MacCann and Sean Savage was wiped out by an SAS squad dispatched to Gibraltar to thwart the IRA plan. At the time of writing, a major investigation is underway inside the IRA to establish how the security forces penetrated the IRA and knew exactly when to strike. This coincides with another ongoing investigation to find the mole who supplied the SAS with the information which put them in a position to shoot dead eight of the Provisionals' most experienced operators, among them Jim Lynagh, during the attack on the Loughall police station in the spring of 1987.

CHAPTER EIGHTEEN

Northern Command

The disillusionment that the ceasefire engendered led to two critical developments. The first was that the young IRA commanders in the North subjected the organisation to a military and political overhaul. This in turn produced the second major change: the ebbing of authority away from the Southern-born, Southern-based leadership of O'Bradaigh and O'Connaill and towards Adams, McGuinness and their comrades in the Six Counties. Long before the ceasefire ended, the commanders in Belfast and Derry had decided that it had been a strategic blunder and the position of the leadership began to come under close scrutiny. Until the ceasefire the leadership's obvious shortcomings went either unnoticed or overlooked. After it, they became unavoidably obvious. O'Bradaigh and O'Connaill were middle-aged and their personal experience of fighting the British was limited to the barracks-blasting tactics of the border campaign. The Northerners on the Army Council, Twomey, O'Hagen and McKee, lived in the South and could not easily visit the North. Safely ensconced in Dublin, how much did any of them know of the realities of the front line?

The degree of control the Army Council exercised over the operations of the Northern units — and despite the multitude of breaches of the ceasefire and the perpetual disobedience of the border Provos, the events of 1975 had showed it was considerable — seemed both inefficient and unfair. The Northern volunteers did the fighting yet they had relatively little influence on the political or military direction of the movement. Some units, expecially in the rural areas, did not have any contact with the Army Council or the representatives of the GHQ staff for six months at a time. A group of leading Provisionals in the North, including McGuinness, and Bell, argued that this was an undemocratic and cumbersome way of running the campaign. The Provisional IRA's elongated command structure put a great distance between top and bottom and concentrated the bulk of decision-making powers in Dublin.

GHQ staff were the committee that carried out the planning of campaigns and acted as a link between the Army Council and Northern Command, and had responsibilities for raising money, buying arms and explosives, gathering intelligence and propagandising. Several members of GHQ staff were also on the Army Council, which was sometimes augmented by representatives of the Northern units. Links between the GHQ staff, who supervised the overall campaign, and the Belfast and Derry brigades and battalions and the units in the countryside were through representatives who liaised individually. The North was without a combined political and military voice. The younger Provo leaders proposed that to improve effectiveness the North should have its own administrative structure and more autonomy over its actions. The idea of a Northern Command was not a new one. It was a favourite notion of Gerry Adams' father ('Old Gerry') in the 1940s and had surfaced several times in the early seventies. The practical advantages were indisputable. This time the Northerners had a moral advantage — they had had no active involvement in the ceasefire. They also had powerful allies in Seamus Twomey and Brian Keenan. In the autumn of 1976 the Army Council gave its approval for a new organisation in the North and Northern Command duly held its first meeting in November 1976.

The creation of Northern Command constructed a semi-autonomous tier between Dublin and the North. It had its own officer commanding, Martin McGuinness; an adjutant, director of operations, intelligence officer, and quartermaster, just like the brigade and battalion staffs. The new arrangement meant

311

that the battalion commanders in the Six Counties had greater freedom to raise money, organise arms and *matériel* and plan operations without reference to the Army Council. The structure allowed for co-ordinated operations that struck across the whole of Northern Ireland. The first demonstration of this was a wave of incendiary attacks on hotels at the end of 1977. It led to the establishment of commando units that could operate on both sides of the border.

In effect, the commando units were a resuscitation of the old flying columns: there were three of them, operating in Donegal, Cavan, Monaghan and South Fermanagh, and Dundalk, South Down and South Armagh. The new ten-strong teams adopted the methods of the British special forces who were hunting them. In training they were expected to live off the land for a week at a time, feeding on what they could scavenge. They dressed as soldiers in camouflage jackets, patrolling the hills and fields for days on end, lying up when it was light and moving when dark, laying mines and manoeuvring their opponents into carefully laid traps. In a typical encounter in 1983 an IRA unit in South Armagh began firing at an Army patrol. Their intention was not to hit the soldiers but to drive them into the nearest cover where a bomb (operated by a pressure plate) was lying buried. In the event, the plan misfired but the bomb later claimed a victim when a soldier searching the area for booby traps accidentally detonated it.

Members of the units were nearly all countrymen whose familiarity with the land was turned into a military advantage. They lived apart, scattered around their areas, but were expected to team up at short notice. Unlike their counterparts in the active service units they were allowed to carry personal weapons at all times rather than drawing them from the quartermaster. Each man was issued with three: a rifle, a magnum pistol and a knife.

The border units' most spectacular actions took place in 1979. Shortly after 11.30 on the morning of Monday 27 August, a twenty-eight-foot cruiser, *Shadow V*, slipped its moorings and headed into the flat waters off Mullaghmore in

Sligo on the west coast. On board were Earl Mountbatten and five members of his family, the dowager Lady Brabourne, Lord and Lady Brabourne and their twin sons Nicholas and Timothy. The boat was piloted by a 15-year-old Enniskillen boy, Paul Maxwell. It headed slowly towards a line of lobster pots. To the gardai officers who were always assigned to guard Mountbatten during his annual stays at Classiebawn Castle near Sligo, everything seemed to be normal. Just as young Maxwell pulled a pot to the surface there was an explosion. The boat disintegrated. Mountbatten, his grandson Nicholas, and Paul the boatboy were killed outright. The elderly Lady Brabourne, mother-in-law to his daughter, died of her injuries the next day and Lord and Lady Brabourne were seriously hurt.

The killings caused a wave of disgust, anger and disbelief. Mountbatten was 79 years old and universally honoured. His long military career had never brought him near Ireland. As a symbol of colonial oppression he was hopelessly inappropriate, having presided over India's secession from the Empire. Bobby Sands, asked by one of the authors a year later why Mountbatten had been chosen as a target to die, replied lamely that 'he knew the problem and did nothing about it. He did nothing except to exploit Ireland and its natural resources.' The plan to assassinate Mountbatten had been drawn up by the Army Council several months previously. The killing had several purposes. First and foremost it was designed to drag the world's attention back to the Irish problem. It was also intended to give heart to the movement, recovering from a morale-draining period of arrests and convictions. Finally it was a flamboyant act of will, an indication that the IRA did not inhabit the same moral sphere as the bourgeois sentimentalists — Catholic and Protestant — who had been so outraged by the killing. In all these respects Mountbatten, venerable, revered, pre-eminent in the British Establishment's pantheon and above all *available*, fitted the Provisionals' requirements perfectly.

The remote control device that killed him had been tested for weeks on a hillside in County Louth before the bombing. The leader of the team was a stalwart of the South Armagh unit, Tommy McMahon, a 31-year-old carpenter from Carrick-macross in County Monaghan. McMahon had been explosives officer in the South Armagh unit. He had been responsible for many of the land-mine explosions of the early seventies. He was short, fat and red haired, a teetotal non-smoker whose only previous brush with the law had been in 1972 when he was briefly detained after a copy of the IRA constitution was found under his bed during a police search.

McMahon was picked up almost immediately after the blast, along with Francis McGirl, a 24-year-old gravedigger from Ballinamore, County Leitrim. McGirl was later acquitted.

Unknown to McMahon other members of the South Armagh unit were also going into action on the day of Mountbatten's death. The ambush at the Narrow Water was a routine attack conceived by the local IRA without any reference to Northern Command or Dublin. Its success in striking a blow at the Parachute Regiment, hated by nationalists since Bloody Sunday, was, as the IRA admit, largely fortuitous.

The site chosen for the action is a picturesque stretch of water at the point where Carlingford Lough widens on its way to the sea. On the Northern shore is a ruined stone lodge, the gateway to Narrow Water Castle, which sits at the side of a dual carriageway connecting Newry with the village of Warrenpoint. The southern bank, which lies in the Republic, rises steeply up to the hills of the Cooley Peninsula. The IRA plan was subtle and devastating. Several days before the attack they buried a 500-pound bomb fitted with a remote control device under the stone archway of the derelict lodge. Another bomb was hidden in a hay wagon parked by the side of the road. On the day, the IRA team lay up on the southern shore of the Narrow Water waiting for the first Army or police patrol to come by. Just before 5.00 pm a platoon of the Second Parachute Regiment appeared in convoy, two four-ton trucks preceded by a Land-Rover. As the third lorry passed the hay wagon the IRA team, using a model aircraft radio control device, detonated the bomb. The rear truck was smashed into a tangle of steel by the blast which killed six and critically wounded two of the platoon.

The remnants of the force raced to take up defensive positions, as the Provisionals anticipated, in the stone gatehouse 400 metres away. There, after a short time, they were joined by reinforcements, more Paratroopers and a contingent from the Queen's Own Highlanders led by their CO, Lieutenant Colonel David Blair. A Wessex helicopter hovered down to pick up the wounded, now lying in the lee of the lodge. As it did so the IRA exploded the second bomb. Thick clouds of dust spewed from the shattered gateway, and they opened up with automatic fire from across the loch. In all, eighteen soldiers died at the Narrow Water including Colonel Blair.

Despite these spectacular successes, the scope of Northern Command for altering the direction of the campaign was still limited. A contentious operation, such as the assassination of a politician or a bombing campaign where there was a strong risk to civilian life, would still have to be referred to Dublin for approval. The seat of power remained the Army Council, and it was not until young Northerners began to dominate that the undercutting of the Southerners became a reality.

By accepting Northern Command, however, the leadership had accepted the right of the North to a bigger say. By 1977 McGuinness had joined the Army Council and after the recapture of Twomey — as the pre-eminent military man — he became chief-of-staff. On his release from prison Gerry Adams was also elected to the Council and succeeded McGuinness as its head in 1979. It was their presence, as much as the existence of the Northern Command, that ensured that the political direction and strategy of the IRA from 1977 onwards began to reflect the thinking of the Northern volunteers.

Adams was emerging as the natural successor to the discredited regime of O'Bradaigh and O'Connaill. He had all the qualifications to lead the republican movement, as well as a sharply analytical mind and a tactical subtlety rarely encountered in the ranks of the IRA. Despite his determination to move republicanism on to a more political footing there was nothing in his rhetoric or past record to suggest that he lacked a genuine commitment to violence, although this was

315

not to stop dissidents later suggesting otherwise.

Adams was born in 1949 in the Pound Loney in West Belfast. His father had been shot and wounded by the RUC and imprisoned in the 1940s. His mother was Anne Hannaway, whose brothers were also prominent republicans and on his paternal grandfather's side could trace a republican line of descent back to the IRB. His upbringing was poor. There were ten children in the family and his father did not earn much as a builder's labourer, but he had a happy childhood which he recorded in *Falls Memories*, a lyrical memoir of the Catholic ghettoes, steeped in nostalgia for a vanished past that is shared by many of the working people of Belfast.

> I passed Harbinson's corner and memories came flooding back. Of Sundays spent tickling trout in Kansas Glen only to have our catch devoured by a great uncle whose greatness was measured not least by his relish for fresh trout. Of double-decker candy apples with coconut on top. Of being slapped on my first day at St Finians. Of pig's feet and matinees in Clonard picture house. Hopping the carts in Leeson Street. The 'reg' man and the wee man selling coal brick. The happy horse man and the refuse man.[3]

After attending primary school he passed the eleven-plus examination at his second attempt and went on to St Mary's College in West Belfast, which was run by the Christian Brothers. There he showed a keen interest in Irish language and history but no aptitude for exams. According to one of his teachers, Brother Bosang, 'he was a meditative sort of fellow, very quiet, almost taciturn. He would never show his hand. You always wondered what was going on in that little mind. He could be in the class and you would barely be aware of his existence but you knew when you looked at him that he was taking everything in.'[4]

At the age of 15 he became involved in republican politics, working for Sinn Fein when they put up a candidate in West Belfast in the 1964 election and witnessing the rioting in Divis Street when the police moved in to seize a Tricolour displayed in a shop in contravention of the Flags and Emblems Act. He recalled later:

> In the build up and aftermath of the Divis Street riots there was some awakening of national consciousness and a few of us began to query, with candid curiosity, the state of the nation. We were puzzled by our description in official forms as British subjects and wondered as we passed the customs posts on our way to Bun Beag for a summer in the Gaeltacht [the Irish-speaking area of Donegal where many Belfast Catholics went for their summer holidays] what exactly the border was. We were beginning to get a sense of our essential Irishness.

By the end of 1964 he had joined Sinn Fein and was part of a small group meeting in a dingy room in the Cyprus Street Gaelic Athletic Association Club to learn about 'Fenianism, colonialism, neo-colonialism, partition and British imperialism'.[5] Later he joined the Republican Club in Andersonstown, where the family had moved, and was appointed public relations officer. Working as a barman in the Duke of York pub in the centre of Belfast he came across communists, trade unionists and republicans. When agitation against the Vietnam war spread to Belfast he marched against it. He was one of the most energetic members of the West Belfast Housing Action Committee which opposed the building of the Divis Flats, taking part in sit-ins at Belfast Corporation offices in the city centre.

Like most young Catholics he watched with curiosity and excitement the growth of the black civil rights movement in America. '[It] not only had its obvious influence in terms of the anthem of *We Shall Overcome*,' he wrote later, 'but also in terms of its affinity with what was happening in the six counties. Courtesy of television we were able to see an example of fact that you didn't just have to take it. You could fight back, you could fight back.'[6] By the time the riots of August 1969 broke out he was already in the IRA. In its decayed state he rose quickly and, according to the security forces, was head

317

of the Ballymurphy IRA by the time he was interned in 1971. In July of the same year he had met a girl from West Belfast, Colette McArdle, and married her five weeks later. According to her, Adams 'is very romantic and understanding. He never forgets an anniversary or a birthday.' The first time they met he presented her with a rose plucked from a front garden.[7] They have a 13-year-old son, Gearoid.

In prison Adams established a reputation for intelligence and seriousness, leavened with courtesy and charm. In the cages he was a regular lecturer on republican history and politics, and would spend long hours debating the future of the movement with the younger men. 'He was very persuasive and eloquent,' said one former prisoner. 'He had great patience and when he punched a hole in your argument he would do it very dramatically.'

Adams' success has been founded on an ability to balance innovation with tradition. In prison he was regarded as an ultra-leftist, yet he was also among the most devout of the minority of Long Kesh inmates who attended Mass, and in debate would often argue that Catholicism and republicanism were easily reconcilable. The closest thing Adams had to a hero outside the republican movement was Robert Mugabe, with whom he shared a joint belief in Marx and the Catholic faith. Adams' piety earned him the cheerful derision of Ivor Bell ('the Heathen') who, with Brendan Hughes, was one of his closest friends in prison.

He had a cold and hard side to his nature. He despised the prison authorities and spurned any contact with them, delegating another prisoner to convey any communication between the two sides. According to one inmate, he was constantly assessing fellow prisoners for their usefulness to the movement once they were released, and many of the IRA staff in Northern Ireland in later years knew Adams in the Maze.

In his private life Adams was frugal and ascetic. He spent little time on personal pleasures. Most of his socialising was done with friends who were drawn from the inner circle of the movement. He rarely drinks and scarcely visits the republican clubs. He has been careful to avoid any criticism that he has grown away from his roots. He lives in a private house but it is in the heart of the ghetto in Andersonstown and the only visible luxuries are a video recorder and a stereo system. In his private life also he has stuck to the conventions of working-class Catholic life.

Adams is indisputably popular, both within the movement and among some of the Catholics of West Belfast. He is tall, with a well-tended beard and slightly prominent teeth, and dresses in respectable working-class clothes: worn but neat grey trousers, a cheap windcheater and an open-necked shirt. He can often be found in the Sinn Fein advice centre in Beechmont, West Belfast, surrounded by supplicants: young mothers with children and stout middle-aged women with varicose veins. They treat him with familiarity but respect, to which he responds with uncondescending courtesy. There is a tribal feeling to the scene. Since a Loyalist attempt on his life on 14 March 1984, in which he was shot in the neck and shoulder, he is accompanied by bodyguards and is chauffered in a bullet-proof car.

Martin McGuinness's elevation to the leadership was based almost entirely on his military record. He was never imprisoned in Northern Ireland and contributed little to the early political development of the movement, though later he grew fluent in the new terminology of republicanism. McGuinness has an appropriately military directness of manner, refined Irish good looks and startling blue eyes which convey an impression of sincerity and honesty.

Like Adams he dresses soberly, in tweed jacket, tie and corduroys, is frugal in his habits and a devout Catholic. 'If I believed that the struggle I am engaged in was wrong from the point of view of being a Catholic, I would not be part of it,' he said. 'I believe that God will understand the pressures under which we live and be a fairer judge than the bishops and the cardinals.' He is married with five children and once said that 'if my activities caused my marriage to break up I would consider the British had won.'[8]

A third important member of the new Northern leadership was Danny Morrison. Like Adams he came from a strong republican Belfast family with one uncle a famous 'Forties man' who was involved in the shooting of a gard in Dublin. Morrison had no military reputation to speak of. His talent as a propagandist, however, was formidable. After taking over *Republican News* from Sean Caughey he transformed it into a lively, well-designed and sophisticated journal, better produced than many conventional newspapers in Ireland. He had considerable charm which he used with great effect on journalists, particularly those visiting from abroad.

The ingrained republican reverence for the past meant that Adams and his supporters were anxious not to alienate the older IRA men, and the Army Council still had a number of members, such as Joe Cahill, to provide a link with the old traditions.

The critical mood that followed the ceasefire had also produced pressure for an overhaul of the Northern units themselves. The large increase in membership in the early and mid seventies had diluted the quality of recruits and distorted the IRA's structures. The nominal system of brigades, battalions and companies had grown up out of the irregular rural warfare of the War of Independence. In the early seventies, Belfast companies were sometimes fifty-strong. As the numbers swelled, security slackened. As the decade progressed it became increasingly hazardous to be in the IRA. In 1972, the worst year for violence, when there had been 10,682 shooting incidents, 1,382 explosions and 1,931 armed robberies, only 531 people were charged with terrorist offences. In 1973, when there were less than half as many shootings (5,018), 978 explosions and 1,215 armed robberies, nearly three times as many people were charged − 1,414. Even allowing for over-laps between an offence being committed and the perpetrator being charged, the pattern of the following years shows that although the level of violence generally declined, the risks of being caught increased dramatically. In 1974 there were 6,186 violent incidents related to the troubles and 1,362 people were charged. In 1975, the year of the ceasefire, there were 3,887 shootings, bombings, robberies and so on and 1,197 people were charged. By 1977 the level had fallen to 2,739 terrorist incidents, yet the number of people charged remained high at 1,318.

The attrition rate of 1977 was to a large extent a reflection of the new methods introduced during the term of office of Roy Mason, who had succeeded Merlyn Rees as Secretary of State for Northern Ireland in the autumn of 1976. Mason presided over the second stage of the process begun by Rees. 'Ulsterisation' as it was unofficially known, was the logical extension of Rees's policy of 'criminalising' the IRA. The Army were gradually withdrawn from the primary role in the campaign against the IRA and replaced by the police.

In the spring of 1976 a new Chief Constable had been appointed to the RUC. Kenneth Newman was addicted to modern methods and a vigorous believer in the doctrine that if the North was to be 'normalised' – the third leg of the Rees strategy – the police would have to be returned to the front line in the fight against the IRA. Under the Emergency Powers Act suspects could be held for seven days without being charged. The RUC took advantage of this to subject them to intensive and frequently rough interrogation. It was a development that produced immediate and potentially disastrous results for the Provisionals. Between 1976 and 1979 about 3,000 people were charged with terrorist offences, most of them on the basis of confessions obtained under interrogation. An Amnesty International report into allegations of ill-treatment subsequently provoked an official inquiry headed by an English Crown Court Judge, Harry Bennett, which found that at least some of those injured while in police custody had not inflicted their wounds themselves, as Newman had claimed. The IRA were able to derive some propaganda gains from this but the new system alarmed them considerably. The number of confessions it generated had revealed that many volunteers were unable to stand up to protracted questioning. A senior detective said 'the fact that we were able to interview them for hours on end and through the night was what broke them. On the journey down in the car, once Castlereagh was mentioned they were talking freely.'[9]

The IRA response in the North was twofold: to devise a system which would minimise the amount of information an arrested IRA man could give about the organisation; and to find a means of counteracting the RUC's interrogation techniques. McGuinness and Adams fell back on the cell system. The idea had been around for some time and Ivor Bell had written a paper advocating its introduction while incarcerated in the Maze. During 1976 McGuinness and others drew up a plan to replace the old companies with a tighter structure. Under the cell system the basic IRA unit would in theory have only three or four members, known to each other by a pseudonym and with no knowledge of the identities of their superiors. Their actions would be directed by an anonymous controller.

The cell structure made sense to the middle-class ultra-left guerrillas of the Red Brigades and the Baader-Meinhof gang but the interbred and overlapping worlds of West Belfast and the Bogside were a different matter. The large hauls of IRA men brought in by informers in the supergrass trials of the early eighties shows that in some areas, like Ardoyne, the cell system never progressed very far beyond wishful thinking. What happened there was that volunteers were now divided into largish, loosely organised companies and small active service units (ASUs). The companies did the work of the old auxiliaries, policing the ghettoes, tracking and punishing young joyriders, drug-takers and burglars and supporting the units by fetching and dumping weapons, driving getaway cars and gathering intelligence.

The ASUs, with a commander and four or five members, were responsible for carrying out military operations. The kudos of belonging to a cell, as the ASUs were termed, was considerably greater than of belonging to a company. The case of Christopher Black showed that despite the overhaul it was quite usual for any IRA man to be acquainted with twenty or thirty others. On the other hand, it seems that after the reorganisation the average member's detailed knowledge of the membership activities of the rest of the organisation was severely curtailed, and the police admit that the introduction of the cell system has dramatically strengthened the Provisionals' security. The other undoubted improvement to security was that information about the whereabouts of dumps was now severely restricted.

The IRA made great efforts to devise an antidote to the protracted interrogations. The pressure that arrested members were under was greatly eased in 1979 by the introduction of Judge Bennett's recommendations that supervision of interviews should be strengthened; prisoners should be seen by the medical officer every twenty-four hours and offered an examination; detectives should be rotated and given different duties from time to time; and, most significantly, that closed circuit television should be installed in interview rooms, and that late-night interrogations should cease.

In the early days, the standard technique on being arrested was to use an alibi. At first this practice worked reasonably well but with the mushrooming of low-level intelligence on the organisation, following the introduction of Kitson's methods and the advent of the crime squads in 1975 which had access to all available information, even the best constructed cover was quickly shredded. After 1978 volunteers were instructed to say nothing during interrogation. It was drummed into them that even when the odds seemed hopeless, silence provided their best chance. The story was often told later of an IRA man who had been caught, bomb in hand, by an Army major but refused to admit anything. When the major was later blown up and killed at Warrenpoint, the case against him disappeared.

An impression of the experience of interrogation is given by the police notes on the questioning of 23-year-old Kevin Barry Artt in connection with the murder in 1978 of Albert Myles, the deputy governor of Crumlin Road jail. After refusing to answer questions for some time, Artt learned that he had been implicated by another IRA man's statement:

> Artt continued to look at the Detective Sergeant and appeared to be listening intently to what was being said to him. Again it was put to him that he was at the Shamrock

Club on the evening before the murder, that he met two other men and that they left there in a car and went to Evelyn Gardens where they got out and went to the house and when Mr Myles came to the door was shot by him [sic].

Throughout this Artt appeared to be thinking a lot. He was asked what he was thinking and he said he was thinking what his father would say if he was sent to prison for this . . . he went on to add 'What is my wife going to think of me, she will not stand by me' . . . The Detective Sergeant asked Artt if . . . he had now reached the point where he wanted to tell him of his part and get the matter cleared up. He began to sob heavily but made no reply.

After telling the story of his involvement in the IRA Artt finally confessed to his part in the shooting. He was told to go to the Shamrock Club one night and meet other people.

I thought it was to move guns. When I went there I met two others and we were given two guns. We drove to Evelyn Gardens and we were told we had to shoot a jail warden. I did not know he was the deputy governor and I don't think the others knew.

According to the police notes, Artt then stopped and remained silent for a while. Then he broke down and sobbed heavily. He composed himself and went on.

A woman came out and the other man held her. Fuck me, I just fired at the man in the hallway. I can't remember seeing that man's face but I killed him. I have prayed many times for that man since and for his wife. Why did it have to be me? I couldn't kill a dog but I killed that man. What is my wife going to think, what is my family going to think?

Artt later claimed that his statement was made under duress, after the detectives had punched and abused him and produced a set of rosary beads for him 'so that he could pray and ask for forgiveness'.

The correct technique in dealing with interrogation was demonstrated by a 26-year-old IRA man. The police reported after four hours of questioning, 'during this interview [he] refused to speak one word. He just sat and grinned and stared at the wall and picked his nose.' When told he was to be questioned about a murder he 'made no reply but smiled smirkingly'. Several interviews later, when it became clear that he was to be charged anyway, he allowed himself to be drawn into smalltalk. The police reported that

> a conversation then took place about his football interests, namely that he played amateur football for a mixed Lisburn team in 1973/74 and now plays football and gaelic for any team that wants him locally . . . [He] was asked what he thought about the new RUC Ruger revolver. He stated, 'We never seen one.' He was asked that he must surely have seen them on policemen. He stated, 'We never looked that close.' He smiled and stated, 'That's a leader, isn't it?'

The developments that followed the truce threw up a series of new dilemmas for the Provos. For one thing, their targets were changing. Ulsterisation meant that the British Army was no longer as accessible as it was. In its place were Irishmen — the RUC and the UDR. From 1976 onwards, with the exception of the freak year of 1979, the number of deaths of local members of the security forces always exceeded the number of British Army casualties. This in turn presented the Provisionals with propaganda problems. Taken with the civilian casualties (which, again with the exception of 1979, always far exceeded military ones) it was clear that it was Irish men and women, not 'the Brits' who habitually bore the brunt of republican violence.

How were the IRA to explain this? It did not stretch the Provisionals' considerable talents for sophistry to come up with a justification.

The IRA had encountered the same problem when they had been shooting Irish members of the RIC during the War of

Independence. Then they had been condemned for shooting Catholics. They used the same argument then as in 1977. On balance, they said, the IRA would rather attack the British Army. In their absence, they were compelled to shoot their surrogates. The UDR and the RUC were members of the Crown forces. As long as they were there they would be targets and whether they were in uniform or out of it made no difference. IRA communications persisted in reporting the assassinations of part-time members of the UDR and RUC in the language of military dispatches, even when they were unarmed and at their workplace. 'A UDR soldier was shot and killed by IRA volunteers on Wednesday this week in an attack near Mountfield, County Tyrone', *Republican News* reported in March 1986. 'The soldier, a private based in Omagh Barracks was ambushed at 2.30 pm on Wednesday afternoon at a sewage works outside the village of Mountfield . . . In a statement claiming responsibility for the attack the IRA said that one IRA volunteer walked up to the UDR soldier and shot him killing him instantly.' The article also repeated a periodic warning to members of the British forces saying: 'Two months ago we warned all members of the UDR and RUC that we would be forced to execute them unless they resigned. We now repeat this warning to call on them to resign forthwith . . . On doing so they should immediately inform us so as to prevent any unfortunate casualty.'

During 1977 Northern Command decided to widen its range of symbolic targets. In February they shot dead Jeffrey Agate, the head of the DuPont Corporation's Derry division, and followed this with two more murders of businessmen in the next few weeks. This was a deliberate attempt by Northern Command to extend its freedom of action and the decision to do so was taken without reference to the Army Council. The killing of Agate provoked anger among Catholics at the DuPont plant, who went on strike for an afternoon in protest. The justification for this incident was given in an IRA press notice released through the Irish Times in March, which explained that, 'In all cases, those executed by the IRA played a prominent role in the effort to stabilize the British-oriented

326

Six County economy. That economy has never served the interests of the people. It is geared completely to their exploitation and is to the benefit of those in control. The war is not merely a conflict between republic and British forces; it is also a conflict between the interests which those forces represent. Those involved in the management of the economy serve British interests . . . Unlike British troops they are not expendable. Thus the outcry.'

The campaign was incoherent and short-lived, but it was a symptom of an important political development which had been taking place inside the Northern IRA. The Provisional IRA had been conceived in haste. The circumstances of its birth and early years meant that by the time of the hunger strikes it was politically backward, not to say retarded. The demands of the campaign meant that in the ranks below the Army Council little thought was spared for political strategy.

The political education newcomers received had much in common with religious instruction. There were history lessons, rich in examples of the persecution of republicans, a lecture on the codes and laws of the movement, and a talk on republican doctrines. Indeed, when describing their recruitment, IRA men often talk in the language of religious conversion. The republicanism of most Provisionals required belief in a particular view of the world, rather than a detailed prescription of how to change it. The political message of the early years was simple and easily remembered. The border was the problem. Who had put the border there? The British, the root of almost every evil that had afflicted Ireland since the arrival of the Normans in the twelfth century. Clearly the thing to do was to remove the British.

Like most men engaged in combat, the volunteers in Belfast and Derry and in the Ulster countryside in the early 1970s had not given much thought to the society that would succeed the peace. For many of them it was not until they went behind the wire at Long Kesh that their political education began (but the idea that all — or even most — IRA men developed political instincts in prison is an exaggeration).

The Provos had a policy but it had been designed to meet

needs of a moment now passed. Eire Nua had been drawn up in 1971 by O'Connaill and O'Bradaigh at a time when it seemed possible that the British were on the point of withdrawal. Much of the original inspiration for the crucial section on decentralisation and regional parliaments had, ironically, been provided by Roy Johnston. Eire Nua proposed a new constitution, a new governmental structure and a new programme for social and economic development. The constitution provided a charter of rights, pledging 'that we will practise tolerance and live in peace with one another in order to achieve a better life for all'. The new governmental structure envisaged a plethora of assemblies, topped by the federal government. Below this were four provincial parliaments, based on the four historic Provinces of Ireland, Ulster, Munster, Leinster and Connaught. In addition, there would be regional development councils 'to promote and co-ordinate the economic, social and cultural affairs of clearly defined economic regions'. Their members would be drawn from representatives from community councils. These were the lowest tier of government and were to be the 'keystone and strength' of the new order. The point of the system was to make government as local and self-sufficient as the modern world permitted.

By far the most important section was that relating to regional parliaments and in particular the proposal for an Ulster parliament, Dail Uladh. This was an ingenious contribution to the problem of partition, and the Provisionals' first overture to the Protestants of Ulster concerning the life they envisaged after Stormont was removed. According to the document, by creating a provincial parliament for the nine counties of Ulster (the Six Counties, plus Donegal, Cavan and Monaghan) within a new Ireland, 'the partition system would be disestablished and the problem of the border removed. Dail Uladh would be representative of Catholic and Protestant, Orange and Green, Left and Right. It would be an Ulster Parliament for the Ulster people. The Unionist oriented people of Ulster would have a working majority within the Province and would therefore have considerable control over their own affairs. That power would be the surest guarantee of their civil and religious liberties within a new Ireland.'

The social and economic programme was doctrinaire democratic socialism, tailored to Ireland's then predominantly rural economy. There would be nationalisation of 'the means of production, distribution and exchange,' plus finance, insurance and all key industries. The federal and provincial governments would control the development of agriculture, industry, the fisheries. The federal parliament would have complete control over the import and export of capital. There was to be an upper limit on individual land holdings, which were to be for Irish nationals only. Large ranches were to be taken over and turned into co-operatives. The workers would have a stake in all industry and enterprise, a philosophy which was 'native to the Irish way of life'. Private enterprise would remain but in a diminished role, excluded from the major industries.

The New Ireland would be independent of NATO and the Warsaw Pact but would foster relations with the 'smaller and neutral nations of Europe and with the countries of the Third World in Asia and Africa. We have more in common with the developing countries . . . than we have with the rich club of former colonial powers in the EEC.' Irish language and culture would be promoted.

Eire Nua was a document written by Southerners from a Southern perspective and the symmetry of its proposals betrayed its origins. On the whole they were the utopian prescriptions of an organisation that was not faced with any immediate prospect of power. In the mid-seventies, as a steady stream of politically interested ex-prisoners trickled from the jails, the policies of O'Bradaigh and O'Connaill began to come in for public criticism and then hostility. There was a feeling that the leaders in Dublin were unqualified to speak for the North. The awakening of the political instincts of the Northern volunteers had only been a matter of time. Indeed, the mystery is why it took so long. One problem was that the internees and inmates of the cages had to construct a political programme almost from scratch. The Provisionals knew what they were against — the British and the border. They were less sure about what they were for. The vague socialism espoused by the republican movement had not been clearly illuminated by the prescriptions of Eire Nua, with its heavy emphasis on agriculture (which meant little to the predominantly urban working-class volunteers of the North) and which had scarcely considered a programme to suit Belfast, with its dead or declining heavy industries.

Slowly, in the columns of Morrison's *Republican News*, a distinctive Northern political approach began to emerge. The first open doctrinal split was over an issue at the core of the Eire Nua policy — the notion of a Dail Uladh. As the authors had themselves pointed out, the addition of the three historic counties would not upset the unionists' domination of Ulster. Adams felt that the proposal's relevance had long expired. It had been suggested when it seemed the war was being won and a British withdrawal was round the corner. That was no longer the case. In any case both he and Morrison regarded the idea as hopelessly unrealistic. What was the point of extending the Protestant monopoly and swapping one loyalist state for another? It was further proof, if needed, of the Dublin leadership's remoteness from the reality of life in the North. Adams and Morrison were particularly aggrieved at the way O'Connaill and O'Bradaigh had nailed Eire Nua so tightly to the republican flagpole that a huge effort would be needed to prise it off. In 1972 at the Sinn Fein ard fheis the policy had entered the constitution. It now required a two-thirds vote by delegates to remove it. Adams felt this was 'elevating federalism into a republican principle which it patently wasn't'.[9]

The ease with which the leadership had stitched federalism into the constitution was a reflection of the nature of Sinn Fein in the seventies. Until Bobby Sands' election to Westminster in April 1981 Sinn Fein was according to Adams 'the IRA's poor second cousin' whose main occupation was selling newspapers and raffle tickets, and taking part in demonstrations on the rare occasions there was an issue emotive enough to warrant it. For most of the delegates the annual ard fheis was a passive affair, when they gathered in Dublin to renew acquaintanceships, enjoy themselves and endorse the views of the leadership. On the other hand, it had a healthy membership and at least the bones of an organisation. At least the movement had a ready-made vehicle with which to develop politically. By early 1976, *Republican News* was frequently out of tune with the official organ of the movement, *An Phoblacht*, which was published in Dublin and reflected the leadership's line.* Not everyone in the North was against Eire Nua. Seamus Loughran, sometimes OC of the Belfast Brigade, supported it. After the ceasefire his reputation, never particularly high on account of his lack of military experience and a correspondingly lukewarm attitude towards 'operations', began to be chipped away. IRA gossip, which always gave a warm welcome to a good conspiracy theory, speculated that the security forces had moved fast to remove Bell and Hughes from the Belfast leadership in order to manoeuvre the plant Loughran into the job.

The Northerners' groping progress towards their own political philosophy can to a certain extent be charted through the writings of Adams in his column (under the pen-name 'Brownie') in *Republican News*. He and the Northern progressives, as they thought of themselves, had arrived at the basic realisation that a purely military victory against the British was not possible. This may have been obvious to many at the time, not to those inside the movement. As late as March 1976, Provisional propaganda was still insisting that the withdrawal of British troops was only a matter of months or at most a year away. As long as they regarded themselves primarily as an army confronting the enemy in a predominantly military way, the IRA could be defeated. Indeed, in 1977 the IRA showed every sign that it was suffering this fate. The only solution was to build a political base to support the military

* *An Phoblacht* (The Republican) was the national organ of the movement, which since the split was published in Dublin. *Republican News* was the Belfast publication founded in the forties. They merged in February 1979 and moved to Lurgan in the North. They later moved to Dublin, as a result of repeated raids on the offices by police.

effort and substitute for it when necessary. In one Brownie article Adams had written: 'We can have countless theories, but all theories are useless unless we implement them and our republicanism serves no real purpose unless it is an active republicanism.'[10]

This new realism was given its first official airing at the annual Wolfe Tone commemoration ceremony at Bodenstown in June 1977. The person chosen to deliver it was Jimmy Drumm, husband of Maire the former vice-president of Sinn Fein, who had been murdered the previous year by loyalist gunmen while she recovered in hospital from an eye operation. The speech had been written by several people, including Adams while he was still in the Maze. Drumm had been chosen to deliver it because of his impeccable republican credentials — fifteen years in jail for the cause. As the crowd gathered in the shadow of the ruined church by the graveyard where Tone lay, they heard Drumm tell them,

> The isolation of socialist republicans around the armed struggle is dangerous and has produced a reformist notion that 'Ulster' is the issue, without the mobilisation of the working class in the Twenty-six Counties . . . The British government is *not* withdrawing from the Six Counties and the substantial pull-out of business and the closing of factories in 1975 and '76 was due to world recession, though mistakenly attributed at the time [as] symptoms of withdrawal . . . Indeed the British government is committed to stabilizing the Six Counties and is pouring in vast sums of money . . . to assure loyalists and secure from loyalists, support for a long haul against the IRA . . . We find that a successful war of liberation cannot be fought exclusively on the backs of the oppressed in the Six Counties, nor around the physical presence of the British army. Hatred and resentment of the army cannot sustain the war.

This statement contained some startling admissions. Half of the Provos' strategy of the early seventies, the bombing of 'economic targets' to drive away investment and bleed the

British exchequer dry, was now being dismissed as a waste of effort.

The shift of emphasis away from Ulster and towards the idea of an all-Ireland socialist state, and the reference to the 'mobilisation of the working class in the Twenty-six Counties' sounded remarkably similar to the conclusions of Goulding and Johnston in the days before the IRA split. According to Drumm, the speech was the result of a long period of discussion inside Sinn Fein:

> It didn't just happen overnight. At leadership level we'd spent a lot of time discussing where to go from here and there was a definite decision made; we would have to put into effect what we'd been saying for years — that we were a political organisation. We should be involved in political activities, rather than a back-up force for the IRA.[11]

There was a sharper socialist tone in the air at the Sinn Fein ard fheis four months later. The indifference the IRA had previously shown towards public opinion and to attracting popular support had disappeared. Much of the discussion was taken up with the question of how to educate the public about the mechanics of British Imperialism and to explain the role of the IRA as the vanguard of the republican movement. Eire Nua came under attack, and there was an unsuccessful attempt to remove the passages which left room for some private enterprise in the new state. On the whole the only dissent was from the traditionalists. During the summer a crop of letters critical of the new direction began to appear in *An Phoblacht*. 'It sickens me,' wrote 'Disgusted Student', 'to see republicanism being referred to in the context of Karl Marx's writings — a man who believed neither in God nor in nationalism — and I certainly see it as serving no useful purpose to compare republican beliefs with those of Lenin, whose followers torture and crucify, daily, people who dare to express differences of opinion.' The tone and the criticisms were familiar to anyone who had lived through the split.

Equally recognisable was the debate on electioneering. This

333

time the perennial question surfaced in the discussion on the EEC. Was it better to promote Sinn Fein's anti-Common Market views by contesting the 1979 elections to the European parliament, or not? The delegates could not decide. They did vote to take part in the 1979 local elections in the South where the councils were considered sufficiently legitimate and close to the people for republicans to participate in.

The election issue rumbled on through the next few years. It was another question that divided the North from the South. Despite the fact that most of the energy for the increasing radicalism of the movement was coming from the North, Adams, Morrison and McGuinness were extremely wary of the ballot-box. This was not an ideological objection — there was no question of those elected taking their seats — but a practical one. The probing fingers of the electoral process might reveal the IRA's lack of support and kill off the hesitant enthusiasm for the new direction. Feelings against involvement ran strong. At the 1980 ard fheis the delegates voted to prevent the ard comhairle (executive) from entering the local elections in the North the following year. It was possible to be a political progressive and an opponent of electioneering.

It was all very well to desire political activity. It was more difficult to know what form this should take, especially if the movement was denied the opportunity to contest elections. In the pre-Bodenstown deliberations, Drumm and the Sinn Fein leadership had hit on a vague plan to involve the party in 'various protests and activities on housing and a tenants association. Not just gimmicky stuff to get cheap publicity in the paper. We were going to try and align ourselves with the people and give them something. We were asking something of the people all the time, but we gave nothing in return. So we decided that we would have to go and work with the people, help them as best we can.'[12]

When the new direction was reiterated in a speech by Gerry Adams at Bodenstown in June 1979 there was still a distinct lack of detail as to where the political energies were to be applied.

We stand opposed to all forms and manifestations of

imperialism and capitalism. We stand for an Ireland free, united, socialist and Gaelic . . . Our movement needs constructive and thoughtful self-criticism. We also require links with those oppressed by economic and social pressures. Today's circumstances and our objectives dictate the need for building an agitational struggle in the Counties, an economic resistance movement, lining up republicans with other sections of the working class. It needs to be done now because to date our most glaring weakness lies in our failure to develop revolutionary politics and to build an alternative to so-called constitutional politics.

Sinn Fein was to discover that, initially at least, the simplest way to extend its links with other left-wing groups and with working-class non-republicans was through protests centred on their own misfortunes. Early in 1978 they took part in an 'anti-repression conference'. It was organised by the Coalisland Relatives Action Committee, which was dominated by republicans, including Bernadette (Devlin) McAliskey and the People's Democracy, still soldiering on with about 250 members and now allied to the Trotskyist Fourth International. About 500 delegates discussed the prospect of a united front against the Diplock Courts and the 'criminalisation' policy in the prisons and another conference was held in Andersonstown a month later. The proposed anti-unionist front came to nothing, however, after Betty Sinclair, a member of the Communist Party of Ireland and a NICRA stalwart, called on the Provisionals to declare a unilateral ceasefire. In one sense, republicanism had survived because of its isolationism and exclusivity and attempts to broaden the circle of its political friends ran counter to the movement's nature.

Indeed the whole business of 'going political' was laden with difficulties. The memory of 1969 was fresh in the minds of Adams and his supporters. They had no intention of making the mistake of allowing anyone to claim that enthusiasm for political action meant a corresponding distaste for violence. In 1980 most IRA members, whatever Sinn Fein might say about the matter, were still convinced of the need for a military victory. The gap between Sinn Fein's policy and the volunteers' actions had been vividly illustrated by a series of incendiary attacks at the end of 1977, the year of Drumm's Bodenstown speech.

In two weeks in December volunteers set off bombs in twenty towns in the North. Hotels in particular were badly hit as the IRA attempted to finish off what remained of the Northern Ireland tourist industry. So much for ending attacks on economic targets. On the night of 17 February three Provisionals from Ballymurphy, all experienced operators, fixed an incendiary to a window at the La Mon House hotel, in the heart of Unionist North Down, about ten miles from Belfast. It was a Friday and the bars and restaurants were packed with members of a cycle club and a dog club who were having a night out. The incendiaries were a new type, cheap to manufacture and horrifically effective. A small quantity of recrystallised ammonium nitrate and aluminium filings were mixed together and attached to gallon tins of petrol. The blast that resulted created a fireball and could be as effective as a 400-pound car bomb. The volunteers primed the bomb, drove away from the hotel and stopped at a call-box to telephone a warning. The phone had been vandalised. They drove on and were stopped by a UDR patrol. It was some time before they were waved on. By the time they reached another phone and rang the RUC, there were only nine minutes to spare. The bomb went off, flinging a sheet of blazing petrol across a crowded room and engulfing the hotel in flames in seconds. Twelve people were burned to death. Any thoughts that the republican leadership had of building bridges to the working people of Ireland were temporarily shelved.

The scale of the atrocity shocked even the IRA leadership. There was an intense internal debate. According to a member of the Army Council: 'There were varying degrees of emotionalism with some people saying, ''Just because it went wrong it doesn't mean we have to change,'' and others arguing that it must stop.' In fact La Mon caused a dramatic scaling down of commercial bombings and a tightening of discipline on operations. The Army Council met and agreed

336

that there could be no repetition of such a happening. Guidelines were laid down to each unit. They were to cut out high-risk bombings on buses, trains or hotels.' The La Mon attack was more than just a setback for Adams' political plans. Shortly afterwards he was one of those picked up in a wave of arrests that followed the killings and charged with membership of the IRA. After his temporary disappearance (the charges against him were dropped) Martin McGuinness took over as chief-of-staff.

Meanwhile, inside the Maze prison a new phase of the conflict had begun which was to dominate the coming years.

CHAPTER NINETEEN

Hunger and Dirt

By the middle of 1976 the new accommodation for the inhabitants of the Maze prison was ready for occupation. The single-storey cell blocks were, as the authorities were keen to point out, the most modern in Europe, but for the IRA prisoners who were about to enter them the move meant a drastic worsening of the quality of their lives. The H-Blocks, as republicans quickly christened the edifices, with their distinctive shape of two parallel wings linked by a connecting corridor, were a physical manifestation of the criminalisation policy. Following the Gardiner commission's finding that Whitelaw's *de facto* granting of prisoner-of-war status to the IRA had been a mistake (a judgement Whitelaw ruefully and publicly concurred with) the Government announced that anyone found guilty of any crime after 1 March 1976 would be treated in the same fashion as any ordinary convict on the mainland would be. The IRA's defence of its status as political prisoners meant that during the coming years the H-Blocks became a new front in the war against Britain.

Before the decision to end special category status, republican and loyalist prisoners had enjoyed some of the most favourable jail conditions in the world. At Long Kesh they lived inside barbed wire compounds — 'the cages' — housed in Nissen huts, which had previously served as accommodation for a Second World War Air Force base. They were damp and hard to heat but they had compensations. The cages were left to run themselves. Each one contained three huts housing about eighty men, a canteen, a shower hut and a Portakabin where the inmates could study. Internees and sentenced prisoners were in separate cages but shared the same regime. The life of the compound was controlled along loose military lines. Overall command was in the hands of the cage OC who was elected by all the men, and the huts in turn elected a leader. Each hut had a quartermaster in charge of gathering materials for escape and training, an education officer to organise lectures, and an intelligence officer. The military discipline the organisation strove to achieve in the outside world became a reality inside the cages. According to Pat McGeown, who was interned at the age of 16 and later returned to Long Kesh with special category status after being convicted of possessing explosives,

> An average day began at about 8.30 or 9 o'clock when the adjutant went round and woke people up. The next hour was spent washing and getting dressed and cleaning out the hut which was arranged on a rota. From 10.00 to 12.00 you could have either gone to education classes which were generally Irish or Irish history or to English. After dinner-time which was maybe 12.00 to 2.00 you had a fairly relaxed afternoon and activities didn't start up again until after 6.00 when you might have had a series of debates or discussions, sometimes organised on a cage basis. From then you had the freedom to do what you wanted until the next morning, read, watch TV or play records.[1]

These activities were augmented by weapons training using wooden models, explosives lectures in which the less experienced members experimented with detonators constructed from watch movements and match heads, and general tactical discussions. There were frequent parades and drills. Into this little world the prison authorities barely intruded. Prison officers entered the cages to deliver the food or to patrol at a respectful distance when the inmates took their exercise, while the British Army was confined to guarding the perimeter fence. Relations between the two sides were cordial. The governor and his men were inclined to live and let live. If it came to a confrontation, the IRA tended to emerge on top. On one occasion a prisoner who doubled as the camp barber was using the pretext of his hairdressing duties to move a pair of wirecutters, wrapped in a blanket, from one compound to another. He was stopped and challenged by a warder to reveal the contents of the bundle. The prisoner refused and bolted through the gates of the cage. The compound OC was so outraged at the warder's behaviour that he demanded that he be moved to other duties. The authorities duly complied.

In keeping with the prisoner-of-war camp atmosphere, escape was a constant preoccupation. According to McGeown, 'the principle that all prisoners worked under was that it was first and foremost your duty to get out'. In practice, most prisoners were content to leave the escaping to the more daring spirits. The most dedicated republicans tended to be the most dedicated escapers, even though the escape often made little sense in personal terms. Gerry Adams was caught breaking out of the Maze in 1974 even though his release was imminent, and was returned to serve three more years. Many of those who had done it once were determined to try again. Dingus Magee escaped from the Crumlin Road jail in 1981, was captured in the South and went on to form part of a team involved in an unsuccessful break-out from Port Laoise in 1986.

Some cages attracted a high number of determined would-be escapers. Planning was usually left to one person and a team would build up around him as the scheme took shape. Tunnelling was the usual method. In 1973 ten tunnels were dug in Long Kesh — all discovered — and there were several attempts to go 'over the wire' and to leave by the front gate in the back of the garbage truck. At the beginning warders searched for tunnels by the simple device of tapping the earth around the compounds and listening for the tell-tale hollow thump, but by the late seventies the prisoners' efforts were hampered by the prison authorities' regular aerial sweeps of the compounds with helicopters equipped with infra-red detection devices that recorded the progress of the tunnels.

The practice was to wait until the tunnels approached the wire before the authorities stepped in.

The desire to escape was partly to get back to the struggle, partly to ward off boredom and partly to enhance one's reputation. At times this impulse was in head-on conflict with the other basic objective of republican prisoners — to obtain the best possible conditions in which to do time. According to McGeown, 'there would be a lot of conflict at times between these two views . . . you're talking about a situation which may detract from your conditions and while you may have five or six people escaping you're still leaving maybe 300 people in a worse situation behind. Those things have to be weighed up and very carefully. You have people saying: "Look, first and foremost the primary aim is to have the best possible living conditions in here and you've got other people saying the primary aim is to escape and get back to the war." '[1]

As in any army there was a division between activists and passivists. In each compound in the early seventies perhaps only thirty would take part in the extracurricular discussion groups. The huts tended to break up into cliques with men from the country areas and the Belfast contingent sticking together. Occasionally there were arguments between the older and younger prisoners. In the early days the veterans were often more gaelicised than the newcomers and would constantly press the merits of Irish music and dancing when it came to evening entertainments when the younger element preferred to watch television or play pop music.

On the whole, people got on with each other. Given the lax arrangements, life could be quite tolerable. It was not long before the prisoners had assembled the materials for a poteen still. A photograph of the period shows a group of inmates waved poteen-filled mugs cheerily at the camera during a compound celebration. Despite all this, republican propaganda outside the cages persisted in presenting them as hell-holes.

There was a standard practical joke played on all newcomers. Within hours or arriving in the cages he would be told that an escape was imminent and that he had been chosen

341

to take part. It was all quite simple. All he had to do was climb into a sack which would be loosely secured with string. This would then be shifted to the gates where it would mingle inconspicuously with the rest of the garbage. At a given signal he would break out of the sack and sprint for the gates which the warders had been bribed to leave open. Warders and prisoners would gather to watch the moment when, after several hours locked in the fetal position among the camp refuse, a whistle would be blown and the eager youth would fight his way out of the sack and hurl himself at the obstinately locked exit.

The existence of the cages was not so civilised elsewhere. The loyalist compounds were torn by rivalries, some of which ended in murder. And the regimented structure could easily degenerate into bullying and cruelty, as one INLA prisoner witnessed in April 1976:

Frank Gallagher was the OC of the INLA in Long Kesh. It didn't take me long to see that he was a nutcase. He used to make up all these mad stories saying he'd heard them from Dublin and made people do all these mad things like jumping over huts and crawling round the yard. There was a bloke from Derry called Hughie Bradley and Gallagher got this thing that Bradley was meeting the Special Branch when he went out to receive a visitor. So they took him into one of the huts and they had him there from seven in the morning to three in the afternoon. The beating this guy was going through was torture. They were tying him up on the beams by his feet and blattering and beating him around the privates and all with batons and hitting him on the toes and sticking things in his hands to get him to admit this. [Eventually he escaped and] ran out into the yard. Everybody was lying around getting sunburned, and they saw Hughie running out, blood dripping all over him, squealing and crying and shouting.[2]

As a result of this, a general meeting of the INLA prisoners was called.

Everybody knew the charges were a load of balls because it was impossible. The Special Branch don't come up on ordinary visits to visit you, so there was a whole row over that. [Gallagher] asked for a vote of confidence and he promised all sorts of reforms.

The INLA prisoners kept quiet about the incident at the time because a tunnel they had been digging was just approaching the wire. Eventually, in early May, the escape went ahead. Ten men set off down the hole, and scaled the fence with grappling hooks made from chair legs and knotted towel ropes. One of them fell back into the camp and had to retreat back down the tunnel to the cages.

The UDA and UVF prisoners in Long Kesh had gratefully accepted the introduction of special category status and organised themselves along military lines in imitation of the IRA. At the time of the UWC strike in 1974 the republican prisoners were convinced that the loyalists would conspire with the warders to obtain weapons and massacre them. The camp OC, Davey Morley, was given permission to parley with the British Army major commanding the troops at the prison to discover what his attitude would be in those circumstances. Morley was told that his soldiers would not fire on any IRA men escaping from the Protestant inmates. The threat was taken so seriously that for several months each prisoner was under orders to carry a small bag containing black clothing and boot polish should a hasty night-time departure become necessary.[3]

Relations between the two sides were initially cordial enough. Inside Crumlin Road jail, where the organisations were less segregated, the IRA ruled the roost and the loyalists accepted this. Contact with them provided an excellent opportunity for gathering intelligence about the Protestant paramilitaries.

The loyalists generally talk in jail [said one prisoner]. Half of them haven't even got a clue that they are giving information away. Because the Taigs [Catholics] are in the majority, they run the jail and the screws do more or less what the Taigs tell them. The OC of the wing will talk to the loyalists and tell him, 'Look, this is the way we run things', and let him think he's getting something out of [it] when they're manipulating him all the time. There's a couple of loyalists too who maybe get peeved off in jail and aren't very happy with the UDA and they're talking to an IRA man [about someone] and say 'Sure, he's a fruit' or something, telling him things like that . . . and it's all going back and they're building up their intelligence all the time.[2]

Most of the prisoners were thrown into a black depression by the first few weeks of incarceration.

When I really sat down to think about it [said Pat McGeown] I thought, 'Well, I'm 16 now and this could go on for quite a long time. Say I got five or ten years. What would I be like when I got out?' It was a great shock. At that point ten years seemed like life itself. I would miss out on all the things that teenagers do. It was something you didn't dwell on.[1]

The thing, as all prisoners learned, was to avoid 'doing your whack hard'. Brooding about lost opportunities and rumours of infidelity merely made the days last longer.

The experience of prison finished many IRA men with the movement. NIO figures show that republican prisoners have a remarkably low rate of reconviction, between ten and fifteen per cent, compared with about sixty per cent for ordinary criminals. This is partly explained by defections, partly by the IRA practice of sparing released prisoners frontline duties. But for many the reflection and self-examination forced on them by prison had the opposite effect, deepening their commitment to republicanism and encouraging them into a more articulate expression of their beliefs. McGeown found himself moving from 'a very romanticised view of the struggle . . . kids growing up want to play soldiers or they want to play cowboys and indians and really in your teens it's an extension of that. You also have a very elitist attitude that you're doing the people a favour by fighting. Around that period I came out of that and into a more political outlook.'[1]

Political development was helped by the presence of a large number of older republicans, such as Kevin Hannaway, who were happy to pass the time in endless theoretical discussions. In prison McGeown was able to take part in debates that were 'very much deeper than you would ever have had time for on the outside. You could sit down and take things apart and question the morality of various tactics and various directions. It wasn't questioning in a pessimistic way . . . you tried to keep it as constructive as possible.' Led by the more prominent IRA prisoners, like Brendan Hughes, the one-time OC in Belfast, he was 'encouraged to look at the political problem, rather than just accept the superficial thing that all you have to do is kill enough Brits . . . that the problems were deeper.' The return of Gerry Adams to Long Kesh in 1973 made a strong impression on him:

> Gerry Adams was striking. He had a capacity to sit down and explain backgrounds; maybe for two or three hours and go through a historical situation in a very methodical way. One of the things he encouraged was that his outlook wasn't necessarily the one and that not everyone else would hold it. Rather he encouraged you to come back and question it.

Adams was badly missed in Belfast during the ceasefire. At one point the Brigade adjutant, Brian Keenan, planned a repeat of the daring helicopter operation that had whisked Twomey out of Mountjoy, to snatch Adams and Bell from the cages, but the plan was vetoed by Billy McKee, who disliked Bell.[3] Adams was not a dominant force inside the wire. He once stood against Morley in the election for the position of Long Kesh OC, but was defeated by eleven votes. Morley was eventually defeated by 'Darkie' Hughes.

Outside the prisons the demands of daily life prevented much reflection on political events; inside the Crum and Long Kesh

345

they were the subjects of lengthy seminars. The 1972 truce and the subsequent talks with Whitelaw were regarded with optimism. By the time of the fall of the power-sharing executive the prisoners' analyses of the political situation were reaching a wider audience. For example, McGeown's attitude to the Sunningdale agreement was that it would 'fall down because of the loyalist intransigence and if the British were forced to face up to loyalism they would back down as they had done continuously'. These thoughts were smuggled out and published on the front page of *Republican News*.

The prisons became a research department for the republican movement. The IRA's current strategy and its current political attitudes began life in Long Kesh. The 'Green Book' − the IRA training manual that sets out the history, rules, and aims of the operation as well as providing a series of practical lectures on tactics, security procedures and methods of standing up to interrogation − was compiled in prison in the mid-seventies and later smuggled outside where it was tidied up by Belfast Sinn Fein activist Paddy Molloy, published and distributed to the volunteers. The basic organisational change that affected the IRA in the late seventies − the breakdown of the old company-based system into smaller units − was worked out by Ivor Bell while he was in Long Kesh. In the late seventies and early eighties events inside the prison were as important as events outside and the evolution of the movement into its current shape is a result of a sequence of actions and reactions that reverberated back and forth over the prison walls.

At the centre of the drama was the question of the prisoners' status. Even under the lax regime of the cages, the IRA commanders were punctilious in pushing their demands to the limit, threatening riots and destruction if they did not get their way. In 1974 this brinkmanship was to have disastrous results. In late summer the prisoners objected to being strip-searched when they went to and from visits, a process which sometimes entailed anal examination. Messages, densely inscribed on cigarette papers and rolled into sawn-off biro barrels, regularly left the prison concealed in the vaginas of women visitors.

Other articles arrived there by this method: tobacco, miniature cameras and even guns. The small calibre pistol used in the October 1983 mass escape from the Maze was smuggled in this way, broken down into its component parts.[3]

Republican prisoners refused to accept visits for three months in protest at the searches. Eventually the argument was settled, with the authorities conceding all the prisoners' demands. Two weeks later, on 15 October, after a trivial dispute over whether Morley had the right to arbitrate in disputes between prisoners and warders, fire broke out in one of the sentenced prisoners' compounds and the word was shouted from cage to cage to start burning the rest of the camp. Some of the inmates refused to do so until they had received the order direct from Morley himself but stopped prevaricating as the wooden huts leapt into flames. The men poured from the huts, snipping through the wire (almost every compound was equipped with cutters) and assembled in the middle of the sentenced prisoners' area. There a pitched battle with the security forces who herded them on to the football field broke out. By the prisoners' account, Army helicopters bombarded them with CS gas. Some 300 of the men managed to break away and took shelter in the loyalist cages, until one of the Protestant leaders, John McKeague, negotiated a safe passage for them with the authorities.

In the morning the cages were a smouldering, sodden ruin. Most of the prisoners had escaped with what they stood up in. They were moved into the few huts that remained where, according to one prisoner, there was 'no sanitation, no hot water and a concrete floor which we had to sleep on. We were forced to break open the main sewer and place planks over it to use as a latrine.'[2] They were kept there for two months. The new location enabled them to open up a new tunnel in cage 5, one of the compounds nearest the wire. Seventy men went down it but only six made it beyond the fence. All were later picked up as they returned unerringly to their old Belfast haunts, and one man, Hugh Coney from Coalisland, was shot dead by British Army guards. The wirecutters they had used were the same to which a hapless warder had previously objected.

The aggression the prisoners had shown was a taste of what was to come. They had been understandably quicker than their comrades on the outside to sense the significance of the decision to phase out special category status. Being prisoners-of-war had enormous propaganda value. It allowed the IRA to claim that the British Government had accepted it at its own assessment — an army in revolt, with genuine political aspirations. Stripping them of this status was the first stage in the process of normalising the problem of IRA violence, presenting them as an unrepresentative group of criminals. But, at the time, this progression was only guessed at by republicans. Also, things were obviously going to be worse under the new regime. 'Doing your whack' — an intrinsic part of most IRA men's careers — would henceforth be infinitely less bearable, which could have a potentially damaging effect on the morale of the next generation of republican prisoners.

Throughout 1975 negotiations were going on between the prisoners and the NIO about the changes. Davey Morley had more than a dozen meetings with a NIO official to discuss the new development, and was even escorted outside for talks with the Belfast Brigade staff.[3] The IRA claim that at one point an offer was made of two-thirds remission on their sentences if they accepted the new regime without protest.[3]

The debate inside the prisons was complicated by personal considerations. None of those involved in the discussion in 1975 would be affected by the changes, which would only apply to prisoners sentenced after March 1976. All those with special category status were already eligible for fifty per cent remission if they behaved. A protest campaign could ruin hope of an early release. None the less, the initial response was belligerent. From the outset there was talk of a hunger strike. Pat McGeown found that 'there was this idea that if we're going to fight the removal of status then we might as well get it over with'.[1] The prisoners had before them, however, the bleak example of Frank Stagg, an IRA prisoner who had been sentenced to ten years for conspiracy to plant bombs. He had died in February 1976 on hunger strike in Wakefield prison in pursuit of political status for republicans in mainland prisons and for transfer to a Northern Ireland jail. A consensus was established that a hunger strike would only be used as a last resort. There was a feeling that this was a battle that could be won by less drastic means. Political status had been easily conceded. It could just as easily be restored.

In the end, the decision as to what form a protest should take was left to the men who would have to contend with the new conditions. The responsibility was effectively thrust on to the prisoners in the Crum who were on remand or awaiting transfer to the new H-Blocks in the late summer of 1976. The debate in Crumlin Road had gone on all summer. No one was sure what the changes would mean. One major departure from existing practice was that prisoners would no longer be allowed to wear their own clothes and would have to do prison work. It was decided that the first prisoner to take up residence in the H-Blocks would refuse to comply with these rules. This role fell to Ciaran Nugent. Nugent had been reared in West Belfast, the son of a sailor who had been decorated by the British for his service in the wartime merchant convoys. While still a pupil at St Peter's intermediate school in Belfast his best friend was shot dead beside him by a loyalist assassination gang as they stood chatting on the Grosvenor Road. Nugent was badly wounded in the attack. He had witnessed the Falls Curfew raids (Rape of the Falls) by the Army in 1970, which convinced him that 'the Brits would have to go . . . I had been attacked several times by the security forces and I felt they had no right to be in the country.'[4]

Nugent had been an internee in Long Kesh in 1975 and watched from the roof of his compound as the building took shape. He was freed during the mass releases authorised by Merlyn Rees but arrested in May 1976 and found guilty of possessing weapons and hijacking a car. In September, aged 19, after a period on remand in the Crum, he was brought to the Maze (as Long Kesh was now known) to serve the rest of his three-year sentence.

I was brought straight to the blocks. Cell 17, D wing H1 or 2. I was stripped and beaten. The screws who knew me

said, 'We are the bosses now. There are no OCs here.'
A screw said to me, 'What size are you in the waist and
what size are you for shoes?' I asked him 'What for?' and
he told me 'For a uniform.' I said, 'You have got to be
joking.' I was the only one in the H-Blocks. They dragged
me into the cell. Davy Long [one of the warders] wanted
me to compromise. He suggested I wore my own shoes and
trousers if I wore a prison shirt. I just laughed. He locked
the door. I lay on the floor all night without mattress,
blankets or anything else. The heat was reasonable in all
fairness and I slept.[4]

The first day Nugent spent naked. The second day they gave
him a blanket which he wore to take exercise. He did put on
his prison uniform once, in order to see his mother. I told her:
'You will not be seeing me for three years because to have
a visit I have to wear uniform. If they want me to wear a
uniform they'll have to nail it on my back.' Nugent kept to
his resolution. As the H-Blocks began to fill up the number
of prisoners 'on the blanket' multiplied. By the end of the
decade there were more than 200 blanket men and women in
the Province's jails.

At first the prisoners were allowed to wear their blankets
during exercise. After a while they were told they would have
to leave them in their cells. Every fourteen days the governor
would order them to wear uniform. Each time, they would
refuse and be punished with three days 'on the boards'. All
the cell furniture would be removed and the 'number one diet'
served — black tea, dry bread and watery soup.

Relations between prisoners and jailers in the H-Blocks were
bad from the outset and they steadily grew worse. When it
became clear that the Government was set on removing special
category status the leadership inside the compounds sent word
out to the IRA asking them to begin a campaign of assassination
of prison officers. In spring 1976 they had announced that 'we
are prepared to die for political status. Those who try to take
it away from us must be fully prepared to pay the same price.'

On 8 April a warder called Patrick Dillon was shot dead at his home in County Tyrone. Over the next four years eighteen prison officers were killed. Warders responded to this development in different ways. Some tried to befriend prisoners, bringing them books and comforts as insurance against assassination, urging outgoing prisoners to tell 'the lads' of their kindness. Many responded with systematic brutality, and beatings and abuse became part of the routine of the blocks.

Often the beatings were administered when prisoners left their cells to shower or use the lavatory in the central washroom. In March 1978 the situation became so bad that some prisoners refused to leave their cells. At first they were provided with wash-basins. The prisoners demanded that showers were rigged up. When this was turned down they refused to make use of the wash-basins. A grim battle of wills developed.

The prisoners now felt that a greater crisis must be provoked to resolve the issue of political status. The initial view that it would be a relatively easy matter to force the Government to change tack had given way to a belief that drastic measures were needed. The prisoners felt neglected. Protests outside the Maze in support of the prisoners were sparsely attended, and the political status issue had provoked nothing like the anger among the Catholic community that the introduction of internment had. Every night the subject would echo between the blocks as the prisoners shouted news, gossip and messages in Gaelic to each other across the 150-yard gap.

One day at the end of April a fight broke out in H-block 6 between a prisoner and a warder. As the prisoner was dragged off to solitary confinement he was badly beaten. When the news spread around the wing prisoners began smashing furniture in their cells, precipitating the arrival of the riot squads who removed all the remaining beds and lockers. In order to get them back, the prisoners had to give a guarantee that the episode would not be repeated. They refused. Thereafter they were left in bare cells with nothing but blankets and mattresses. Because they would not leave their cells the warders would not clear them. Mounds of excreta piled up. The prisoners began smearing it on the walls to make a

351

clean space where they could sleep and to dissipate the stench.

The authorities responded by breaking the cell windows and hosing in concentrated disinfectant, then herding the prisoners out and sending in rubber-suited warders with steam hoses to clean the walls. Once the prisoners were back in, the process would start again. By the summer of 1978 between 250 and 300 republican prisoners were on 'dirty protest'.

> There were times when you would vomit [said Pat McGeown]. There were times when you were so run down that you would lie for days and not do anything with the maggots crawling all over you. The rain would be coming in the window and you would be lying there with the maggots all over the place.[1]

As an attention-seeking exercise the dirty protest worked. It became a long-running news story attracting the interest of American politicians and the media of the world. The impact was increased by the release of some smuggled photographs showing bearded, lank-haired figures, blankets draped around their naked shoulders standing solemnly and defiantly in front of excreta-caked walls. The image brought to mind the mass-produced portraits of Christ that hung in most working-class Irish Catholic homes.

The Catholic Archbishop of Armagh, Dr Tomas (later Cardinal) O'Fiaich, had tried to intercede with Roy Mason on the prisoners' behalf. O'Fiaich's own nationalism, inherited from his background as the son of a schoolteacher in South Armagh, led him to take a more understanding view of the IRA than many of his bishops. 'I can see their point of view,' he told the authors. 'I don't agree with it but I can see how an Irishman can take this viewpoint.'[5] In August, after a visit to the H-Blocks, he issued a forthright condemnation of the authorities:

> One would hardly allow an animal to remain in such conditions, let alone a human being. The nearest approach to it that I have seen was the spectacle of hundreds of homeless people living in the sewer pipes in the slums of

Calcutta. The stench and filth in some of the cells, with the remains of rotten food and human excreta scattered around the walls was almost unbearable. In two of them I was unable to speak for fear of vomiting.

He noticed that morale seemed extraordinarily high.

From talking to them [he wrote] it is evident that they intend to continue their protest indefinitely and it seems they prefer to face death rather than to submit to being classed as criminals. Anyone with the least knowledge of Irish history knows how deeply this attitude is in our country's past. In isolation and perpetual boredom they maintain their sanity by studying Irish. It was an indication of the triumph of the human spirit over adverse material conditions to notice Irish words, phrases and songs being shouted from cell to cell and then written on each cell wall with the remnants of toothpaste tubes.

Nugent and the other prisoners felt the Archbishop's statement was 'a major coup' for the movement. Spirits were also buoyed by the continuing campaign against the prison staff. On 26 November, for example, Albert Myles, the deputy governor of the Maze, was shot dead in Belfast by the Ardoyne IRA.

Both the Government and the prison authorities were remarkably complacent about the political consequences of the protests. Senior NIO officials advising Mason were not particularly dismayed at the blanket protest, believing that 'as long as these guys were wearing blankets, the likelihood of their escaping was very light'. The initial concern over the dirty protest was mainly the danger of an epidemic. According to one official, 'We didn't see it in terms of what the political consequences might be',[2] though this attitude changed when the attention of politicians and the media in America was alerted and the prisoners' case was taken to the European Court of Human Rights.

With the announcement of a visit by Pope John Paul II to Ireland in September 1979 another great opportunity to attract publicity to the protest presented itself. Shortly after his election he had received an invitation from Cardinal O'Fiaich to come to Ireland for the centenary of the apparition of the Virgin Mary at Knock, a small town in County Mayo. On 12 July O'Fiaich learned that the invitation had been accepted but there were no details of the papal itinerary. As the summer advanced, the Cardinal came

> under more and more pressure to have a visit to Armagh. I didn't see it as a matter of principle but it was gradually being borne in on me by the number of people coming on the phone saying, 'Well if he doesn't come to Northern Ireland it's not worth his while coming at all.' I finally decided I would make an all-out effort, I made a list of thirteen reasons why he should come and had it brought out by a priest who I knew was going to Rome.[5]

A few days later he received a telephone call from the Vatican to say that the Pope had agreed to visit Armagh. O'Fiaich was triumphant. On 27 August he travelled to Rome to discuss the details of the itinerary. Shortly after he arrived there the news of the murder of Mountbatten and the attack at Warrenpoint came through on the radio: 'At one point it came through that there were six dead and there were ten dead and there were twelve dead . . . I could just feel the ground crumbling under my feet.'

The Pope's initial reaction was that the killings made it all the more necessary to visit the North. When O'Fiaich took a telephone poll of lay and Catholic views in Ireland that evening, though, all support for the idea had vanished. Before the attacks, the Cardinal had received the personal assurance of one loyalist leader, John McKeague, that he had no objection to a visit by the Holy Father to Armagh. Now, such was the outrage that 'the reaction might be too terrible to contemplate'.[5]

Any chance of an excursion across the border evaporated. So too did any hope that the IRA had of attracting favourable publicity for the dirty protest. Indeed, the visit was now being seen as an opportunity for a papal denunciation of republican violence that would seriously undermine the IRA's standing in the community. On 29 September, at a vast open air mass in Drogheda, north of Dublin, John Paul addressed himself in halting English to the IRA 'in language of passionate pleading'. 'On my knees I beg you,' he said, 'to turn away from the paths of violence and return to the paths of peace.'

Three hours before the Pope left Ireland a Provisional unit took over the house of a woman who had just returned from seeing him in the Republic and fired on a British patrol, wounding a soldier. The IRA took longer with their formal response. Adams and Morrison spent three days drafting it. It ignored any direct reference to the Pope's message, declaring that it had widespread support and that the British presence could only be removed by force.

This proved conclusively to those who retained any doubts that the Catholic Church had little capacity to harm the IRA. None the less the leadership continued to take the Church seriously. In times of crisis, as O'Fiaich had demonstrated in the case of the dirty protest, it could be relied on to give a sort of tribal support. Adams was careful to prevent the movement's socialism from encroaching on too many of the Church's preserves. There was never any public criticism of the Church's monopoly on the education of Northern Catholics. In fact, the Church dispensed a brand of teaching that other socialist republicans vilified as reactionary, and in an IRA state, parents would still have the right to send their children to denominational schools.[6]

Back in prison the protest was proving extraordinarily popular. Nine out of ten prisoners arriving from the Crum, where they were held after sentencing, chose to join it.

At that time the dirty protest was making a fair amount of headlines [said Pat McGeown] and people therefore reckoned it wouldn't last too long. There was an air of unreal optimism when people went from week to week saying, 'Well, they've got to move this week.'[1]

Once you were on it, it was hard to get off without losing

face. The culture of defiance and endurance from which the prisoners came made it almost impossible not to accept the challenge when the prison uniform was ceremonially proffered. In McGeown's view, 'prison life for ordinary prisoners isn't a very attractive life. The screws would always be on top of you. You would always know that you had been in prison.' Wearing a prison uniform was 'symbolically a sign that you had knuckled under to the system . . . You would become depersonalised, a sort of instrument or a number who could be moved about.'

As long as the H-Blocks were in the news, the prisoners lived in hope that Government concessions were around the corner. By 1980, as the protests entered their fourth year and the media interest began to flag, a pessimistic mood had set in. Despite the efforts of the Relatives' Action Committee in publicising grievances, there was a feeling that more could be done. McGeown remembers Bobby Sands remarking that 'if our people knew what was going on in here they would break the walls down'.

In the summer the talk in the Maze had returned to the subject of a hunger strike. Two wings actually took a vote which went in favour of a strike, which prompted a debate among the IRA staff officers in the prison. By the end of the year a consensus emerged that the time for a hunger-strike had arrived, but the leaders of the blocks and the cages preached caution and the matter was dropped for a while. Cardinal O'Fiaich had opened negotiations with Mason's successor, Humphrey Atkins, who had been appointed Secretary of State after the Conservative victory in the general election in May 1979, to search for some softening of the regime that would allow the prisoners to call off the protest. But it became clear that the matters under discussion came nowhere near what the prisoners sought. The NIO seemed prepared to move on the issue of prison clothing, by offering a hair-splitting compromise in which the inmates would not be expected to wear uniform but civilian-type clothing issued by the authorities.

In the discussions that had gone on throughout the protest the prisoners had formulated five demands. Apart from wearing their own clothes, they wanted the right to refuse prison work, to receive one parcel a week (as they had done in the cages), to associate freely with one another and the return of remission lost as a result of their protest. Judging by Cardinal O'Fiaich's lack of progress, it was evident that the British had no intention of granting these concessions.

Once again there was talk of a hunger strike. In the middle of 1980 the debate inside the blocks was in full swing. The arguments and counter-arguments were written down and circulated around the blocks, often transported by Bobby Sands who had been the H-Block public relations officer since his arrival in the Maze in 1977. He was responsible for feeding the movement outside with news and conveying the feelings of the men in the Maze and also for keeping the republican prisoners inside the blocks in touch with each other.

The debate spread outside the prison, with Danny Morrison and Gerry Brannigan of the H-Block Committee, both regular visitors to the Maze, reporting the attitude of the prisoners to the Army Council and relaying back the leadership's views.

The prisoners [said Pat McGeown] were fighting the battle from a very sheltered outlook . . . At times they felt they had the power to actually shift the British Government and you did need someone from outside who could see all aspects of the struggle, to come in and say, 'Hold it. Don't over emphasise your importance here.'[1]

In October O'Fiaich's initiative broke down completely and the prisoners could no longer be constrained. The decision to go on hunger strike to force the concession of the five demands had been taken several times in principle, as a weapon of last resort. Most of the IRA men in the Maze now felt that the moment had arrived. Plans had already been made as to how the strike should be conducted. In order to spread the geographical impact of the ensuing drama it had been decided that there should be a hunger-striker from each of the Six Counties as well as one from the INLA. The OCs of each block and the IRA staff had drawn up a list of volunteers who had expressed willingness to make the sacrifice. McGeown, the commander of his block, 'went back to the prisoners and said, "Look, these are the implications," and explained it all again. We had some people pulling out at that stage.' Initially the list had contained hundreds. In the end they were left with 'a core of sixty or seventy people throughout the blocks that you knew were reliable'.[1]

The OC of the H-Blocks, Brendan Hughes, and the leaders of the cages decided that a mass fast by all seventy was out of the question. Sticking to the original formula they decided on an initial team of seven. A decision as to whom should follow them if the first protest failed was put off until the question became necessary. 'The attitude was that if seven people die then there's not much point sending another seventy after them and that we would have to take that decision as each person came close to death.'[1]

The organisers of the 1980 strike had considered the history of republican hunger strikes when working out their strategy. As a way of assessing their chances of success this was not a particularly helpful exercise. In the South, Patrick McGrath, a veteran of 1916, was picked up in a police raid in September 1939 and had been released after a wave of public protest after fasting for forty-three days. In 1946, however, Sean Caughey, locked up in Portlaoise, died after thirty-one days, twelve of them on both hunger and thirst strike in an unsuccessful attempt to get political status. More recently, they had the less than inspiring example of MacStiofain. On the other hand, as McGeown and his comrades saw it, McKee's hunger strike had won political recognition in 1972. If he could do it, so could they. It was essential that the men chosen could be relied on to go to the limit. The planners felt under a certain pressure to shoulder the burden themselves. All seven initial strikers held positions either in their blocks or on the overall prison staff. They had all also proved their stamina by doing their time on dirty protest.

A decision to call off the strike would have to be taken by all seven, and then cleared by a committee of the block OCs.

> Looking at it from the outside [said McGeown, who was the OC of H-Block 6 and one of the organisers] it might seem that we were tying people, committing them to the conclusion of a hunger strike. But it was to impress on them . . . that they weren't there as individuals, they were there as representatives of the prisoners and before they went on hunger strike they had to realise that. There was no point in going on hunger strike and then all of a sudden finding that you weren't capable of taking it through to a conclusion. They had to accept that rule at the start and accept those conditions.[1]

It was clearly vital for the men conducting the strike to have worked out in advance what terms they would settle on. Despite the constant harping on the five demands by the republican propaganda machine throughout the hunger strikes the prisoners never believed they would win all of them. The demands in themselves did not really matter. What was important was to extract a concession from the British that the outside world would interpret as the restoration of prisoner-of-war status. Neither Hughes nor Bobby Sands, who took over as the Maze OC when Hughes began his fast, nor the block OCs appear to have decided in advance what would allow them to claim a victory. This confusion was to bring about the premature end of the first hunger strike, and the start of the second.

On the morning of 27 October the seven, lead by Brendan Hughes, refused breakfast. They seemed reasonably cheerful about the ordeal ahead of them. After all, as McGeown pointed out, 'although you always accept the possibility of death, you don't go on hunger strike to die' (a point Cardinal O'Fiaich used to justify his refusal to condemn the hunger-strikers as suicides). There was a general confidence that the British would shift. For the first two or three weeks of the fast the seven stayed as normal in their cells, before being moved to isolation in one wing. Contact between the hunger-strikers and the rest of the prisoners was reduced to encounters at Sunday Mass but once they moved into the hospital even this ceased. For a long time there was nothing for anyone inside the prison to do but to sit back and wait. Outside, the hunger strike was developing into a major political drama with Cardinal O'Fiaich travelling to Rome to hear the views of the Pope, then on to London to intercede with Atkins on the strikers' behalf.

On 4 December Atkins made a statement to the House of Commons declaring there would be no concessions to the hunger-strikers. It was distributed to the prisoners, who scoured it for signals of compromise but found none. Inside the prison hospital, it was a different story. A visitor from the NIO encouraged Hughes to interpret the statement in the light of political necessity, and suggested that concessions were indeed possible. There could be an arrangement for prisoners to wear their own clothes, for example. Bobby Sands was allowed to visit Hughes to hear a report of the discussions. At a later meeting the clothes issue was less clear-cut. This time the offer appeared to be that prisoners would be allowed to wear *civilian* clothes. It appeared to the organisers of the strike that it was necessary to clarify this matter before any progress could be made. According to McGeown, the authorities now gave 'a typically British answer. What they said was, "We'll consider the point on clothes. There's a possibility you will be allowed to wear your own clothes but we won't go into the finer details until we have arrived at some agreement that ends the hunger strike".'[1] Work, association, the receipt of parcels and letters and the issue of lost remission – all these could be negotiated once the protest was over. The only matter they would not consider was a newly-raised demand for segregation from loyalist prisoners.

After each meeting with the NIO Hughes was able to telephone outside advisers, mostly sympathetic priests, for interpretation and advice. Eventually the NIO committed an offer to paper – a thirty-four page document – and gave it to Hughes. The prisoners thought it 'very vague . . . You had one of those documents that said a lot but didn't say anything.'[1] But at least it was something and the hunger strike was approaching a climax. The eyesight of one of the strikers, Sean McKenna from Newry, was failing, a sign that he was close to death.

According to McGeown, 'we had already accepted by then that they were never going to turn round publicly and say, "We give in. You have it all." What they were always going to do was give you a loose interpretation which would then be hammered out in the months ahead . . . It would really become a series of bargaining negotiations.'

The hunger-strikers called Sands into the prison hospital again to ask his opinion. There seemed to be some genuine movement on the question of work. The prisoners had never objected to it as such, just to menial labour. The document offered greater time for education and vocational training. Sands took it back to the cells with him and for the next three or four days the contents were endlessly debated to see if there were grounds to call off the strike. By McGeown's account, 'On 18 December he went back to the prison hospital and said to them that there was the possibility of a solution — that the rest of the prisoners accepted that if they felt that we should move off the hunger strike and attempt to negotiate a way out that was acceptable to us.' At 7.00 pm the strike was called off. The decision was taken collectively by the six remaining men in the hospital wing, McKenna having been moved to the Musgrave military hospital in Belfast when his condition deteriorated.

The following day Sands asked the prison governor, Stanley Hilditch, about getting clothes into the prison but was told there was no authorisation for this. Sands suggested a compromise. While the matter was being clarified prisoners would come off dirty protest and wear pyjamas. It was rejected. Christmas week had started. Sands and the three block OCs spent it considering what to do next.

The first hunger strike had chastened them. In the discussions that followed three of the four, including Sands and McGeown, argued against the immediate launching of another fast. The alternative was to agree to the new prison regime hoping that some concessions could be negotiated once they were inside. In the end the mutinous mood of the men decided the matter. 'The rest of the lads wouldn't accept it if Bobby Sands had given an order to move into the system,' said McGeown. 'You would have had a major conflict amongst our own prisoners.'

Before taking a final decision Sands consulted the movement outside. There was strong resistance to the idea of another hunger strike. The IRA leadership, Sinn Fein, the Relatives' Action Committee and the National H-Block Committee (which had co-ordinated the propaganda efforts for the prison protests) had all breathed easier with the ending of the first fast. They all now argued that they could not afford to tie up their resources for the foreseeable future in reconstructing another failure, and urged negotiation.

Early in the new year it seemed that the authorities were softening. If the prisoners would stop the dirty protest and move into a clean wing they would discuss the clothes issue. Around 20 January the prisoners from two wings moved out of their vile cells in H-Block 3 and H-Block 5. They washed, shaved and had haircuts. For many of them it was the first time they had done so for three years. Messages were dispatched for their clothes to be sent into the prison. When their families arrived at the prison gates with the garments, the authorities would not pass them on. The prisoners responded by smashing the furniture in their cells and immediately resuming the dirty protest. 'From then on,' said McGeown, 'it was a matter of formalising who would go on the next hunger strike.'

The prisoners, in one of the many letters or 'comms' that passed back and forth between the inhabitants of the Maze and the leadership outside the walls throughout the Hunger Strike period, wrote of the decision:

> We have listened carefully to what you have said and we recognize and accept the spirit in which it was wrote, likewise in view of the situation we do not deny you or

criticize your extreme cautiousness. But however distressing it may be, we regret that our decision to hunger strike remains the same . . . (quoted in David Beresford, *Ten Men Dead*, Grafton 1987, p.54)

The new plan was different. The first strikers would begin their fasts at intervals, spreading the drama. The possibility of including a woman was talked of, to maximise international attention. In February more than thirty women in Armagh jail had gone on dirty protest after a series of disputes with the governor, again against the wishes of the IRA leadership. They had already communicated their willingness to join in a hunger strike, as much as a proof of equality as a gesture of solidarity. At first the women favoured a hunger strike *en bloc*. Then they could not decide who their representative should be. The men in the Maze decided to start without them.

Bobby Sands would be the first. The next striker would begin a fortnight later, thereby allowing a reasonable period for negotiations before the next death if Sands died. After that there would be a new hunger striker every week. Sands was the obvious choice to lead the strike. There was a tradition of the prison OC, as he now was, being in the front-line of any protest. There was some opposition to Sands taking part because it would risk the life of a man whose facility with words and political judgement were highly regarded inside the jail.

Sands' reputation had been made inside prison. He came from a respectable working-class family. His father, a former merchant seaman, worked for the Post Office and his mother was famously devout. In 1972 the family were burned out of their home in Rathcoole, North Belfast by loyalists and moved to Twinbrook in West Belfast. There, aged 18, he joined the IRA. He had only been in the organisation a month when a house in which he was staying was raided and arms discovered, and he was sent off to the cages for three years. On his release in April 1976 he returned to Twinbrook, married (the marriage did not survive), had a son, Gerard, and rejoined the IRA. He also helped to set up a Sinn Fein branch and a tenants' association in Twinbrook and began dabbling in republican journalism, contributing articles and poems to *Liberty*, a community paper. He had learnt to play the guitar in the cages and organised concerts at which he played and sang.

In a short time he became leader of the IRA in Twinbrook. The Belfast Brigade lent him the sevices of some more experienced operators to get the unit moving. His command did not last long. In October 1976 he, Joe McDonnell (who was also to die on hunger strike) and two others were stopped in a car by the security forces after bombing a furniture store, and charged with possession of a revolver found in the vehicle. At Castlereagh interrogation centre he was allegedly kicked and beaten for four days. In September the following year he was sentenced to fourteen years and when he arrived at the Maze immediately joined the dirty protest.

Inside the H-Blocks his talents were discovered. He began writing harrowing descriptions of life on the blanket and poems which were published in *Republican News* under the pen-name Marcella, after his sister. He had a good memory and would entertain the prisoners at night by shouting instalments of Leon Uris's epic romanticised novel of the troubles, *Trinity*, the complicated plot of which he had learnt by heart. He had a caustic wit and 'a viper tongue' with the warders. Father Denis Faul, who met him in the Maze, found him 'a strange character. He wasn't charming and he wasn't soft. He was sharp, irritable and tense.' One of the present authors, who met him in 1979, recalls an emaciated, jumpy figure, radiating nervous defiance. He was slightly-built but had played hurling and gaelic football in his pre-IRA days. The prison authorities regarded him as a formidable figure who would undoubtedly go the distance if necessary.

Before the strike he spent several hours discussing its morality with Father Faul. After they had talked about the grief it would cause his family and the disturbances that would inevitably accompany it, 'he finished up saying to me: ''Greater love hath no man than this, that a man lay down his life for his friends.'' I said to Bobby, ''I won't argue with you after that''.'[7] In the run-up to the strike he seemed to

McGeown to be 'withdrawn . . . wrapped up in himself. It's difficult to explain but you got the impression you were talking to someone who was one step removed from life already. But then the next thing he'd be talking about the Free State election and the possibility of resurrecting support for the hunger strike.'

The possibility of putting up hunger-strikers as candidates in the June 1981 general election in the Republic had been discussed as a way of widening attention. Apart from that, McGeown felt, 'We didn't have much of a strategy. We didn't say, "This is how we're going to win it." We were very much in the position of no option. We could either put ourselves at [the prison authorities'] mercy or we could go back on hunger strike.' Before it began Sands argued forcefully with the other strikers that if he died and no concessions resulted then the fast should be abandoned. They replied that his death would only intensify their commitment.

On 1 March the ordeal began. It was five years to the day that special category status had ended, an example of the movement's obsession with anniversaries. The announcement of another H-Block fast caused a little excitement in the media. The news was overshadowed by a speech by Dr Edward Daly, the Catholic Bishop of Derry, condemning the practice of hunger strikes. Interest stayed slack in the coming days. Outside the Maze the H-Block Committee activists and Sinn Fein workers did their best to rally indignation but it was hard work.

On 5 March an event occurred which was to transform the campaign. Frank Maguire, the Independent republican Westminster MP for Fermanagh and South Tyrone, died. Maguire was regarded as eccentric, even by the tolerant standards of North Ireland politics. He was a well-known figure around Fermanagh, the proprietor of Frank's bar, a dark, cool pub on the quiet main street of the rural town of Lisnaskea where time seemed to have halted in the mid-1920s. His chief political function had been to keep a Unionist out of Westminster. Maguire was a stranger to the place himself, and in his six years as an MP had only been seen in Parliament a handful of times.

Maguire's death simultaneously raised the same thought inside and outside the H-Blocks. To McGeown and the rest of the strike planners it seemed that 'this was our chance to make it a major issue . . . Inside the blocks there was a feeling that this was a chance that we shouldn't allow to go to waste.' The suggestion that Bobby Sands should stand was proposed to the IRA leadership who responded with cautious enthusiasm. But under which banner should he run? Standing as a Sinn Fein candidate would raise the question of the movement's attitude towards elections, an issue that had lain dormant since the troubles began.

In the local H-Block Committees, which had been established around the island, the by-election was the subject of much discussion. How best to exploit it was a matter of urgency as the writ for the by-election had been moved with indecent haste by the Unionists, setting the polling date as 9 April. The Tyrone H-Block Committee had quickly come to the conclusion that Sands would be the best candidate. Fermanagh republicans argued for a local man or woman. In an effort to resolve the dispute, local republicans called a meeting at the Swan Lake Hotel in Monaghan. There was nothing new in putting forward a prisoner as a candidate. It was a time-honoured republican tactic, dating from the nineteenth century. As recently as 1955 Fermanagh and South Tyrone and the Mid-Ulster constituency had returned two republican prisoners to Westminster. At the end of the meeting, which was attended by Daithi O'Connaill, Ruairi O'Bradaigh and Gerry Adams, it was decided to endorse Sands as a candidate, though he would run under the cumbersome designation of Anti H-Block/Armagh Political Prisoner, a label designed to spare the voter the problem of voting for the 'armed struggle' and offer instead the chance for a straightforward protest against what was happening in the jails.[6]

The SDLP was torn between logic and emotion over the by-election. As peaceful, constitutional nationalists they had persistently condemned the IRA. It was hardly consistent to step back and allow an IRA man victory. On the other hand, whether they liked it or not, he was a Catholic and belonged to the same tribe as their supporters. To stand against him would split the nationalist vote, reduce the impact of his campaign and conceivably cost him his life, something SDLP voters would not do lightly. The SDLP withdrew from the race. The view of their leader, John Hume, was that they should 'not do the British government's dirty work for them'.[8]

That left Noel Maguire, Frank's middle-aged brother, who was determined to continue the family tradition and asserted his intention to stand right up until the hour before nominations closed. Sinn Fein members were standing by to withdraw Sands' papers if Maguire went ahead. A visit by Adams and O'Connaill and the intercession of the Sands family finally persuaded him against it.[1]

Despite this almost unprecedented display of nationalist unity there was no expectation that Sands would win. There was an undoubted nationalist majority in the constituency − 33,183 against 28,018 combined Unionist votes in the 1979 general election − but there was no guarantee that all nationalists would vote for an IRA man and the Unionists had decided to field a single candidate to maximise their chances. Sinn Fein guessed that Sands would pool around 12,000. Prisoners in the Maze felt he might get 20,000. Despite the fact that the episode turned out to mark the start of a new political strategy in the republican movement, there was no question that Sands' candidacy was anything other than a piece of opportunism, a heaven-sent chance to pour some light upon the dimly-lit events in the H-Blocks. In this it was an immediate success. The election attracted international attention. As polling day approached one of the authors was asked by a waiter in Nairobi: 'How is Mr Bobby Sands?' The flagging and desultory interest of the American television networks was instantly revived. The old questions about Britain's involvement in Northern Ireland were dusted off and raised anew.

Polling day brought frenzy to the placid areas of Fermanagh and Tyrone. The creaky nationalist election machine was running at an unprecedented pitch, busing to the polling stations rural ancients who had not exercised their democratic rights for decades. The following evening a crowd, augmented by the world's media, gathered outside the council offices in Enniskillen as the returning office relished his moment of fame. Sands had polled an extraordinary 30,092 votes, beating Harry West, the Unionist, by 1,446 votes. That night West, a cheerful local farmer, sorrowfully remarked, 'I never thought the decent Catholics of Fermanagh would vote for the gunman.'[9]

Inside the H-Blocks there was euphoria. Now the British would have to move. How could the Prime Minister allow an MP to die? This view was not shared by Sands. From his isolated wing he sent a number of letter to the blocks.

> They said: 'OK, there's a possibility that it will change things but I think you should bear in mind the probability that it won't . . . It's still going to be a major hunger strike, there are probably still going to be people coming after me. In other words − that I'm going to die.'[1]

After the victory the progress of the hunger strike developed into a succession of proposals and initiatives from outside to end the deadlock. Margaret Thatcher's public pronouncements were unpromisingly forthright, refusing repeatedly to view the prisoners as anything other than criminals. On the other hand, the NIO had once again raised the possibility of a concession on clothes. But when Sands and 'Bik' McFarlane, who had taken over from him as the H-Blocks OC, tried to nail them to a proposal, the offer melted away.

There was an intercession from Rome. A papal envoy, Newry-born Monsignor John Magee, visited Sands in prison bearing a present of a silver crucifix from John Paul. Magee had hoped to broker at least the start of a settlement but left disappointed, feeling that the British had offered little co-operation.[10] The Fianna Fail leader Charles Haughey sent his emissary, Sile de Valera, granddaughter of Eamon, to visit Sands, which in turn led to a visit by a delegation from the European Commission on Human Rights. On 28 April

President Reagan said he was 'deeply concerned at the tragic situation'. By now there was practically no hope of a last-minute intervention. The Government and the world settled down to wait for Sands' death.

He was dying by inches. A medical practitioner in the Maze who was present throughout the hunger strikes noted the stages of prisoners' decline. After a few days without food the initial hunger-pangs wore off to be replaced by a feeling of extreme nausea. Their systems reacted violently to the impurities in tap water, but when this was replaced by mineral water they had difficulty keeping it down. After a week their bowel motions ceased. Lack of vitamins affected their eyes. They developed nystagmus, a condition where the sufferer finds it hard to focus and his gaze wanders. The effect on their balance in turn created a form of sea-sickness. For the first six weeks they vomited repeatedly. Then, at about the forty-five-day stage, the doctors noticed a remarkable improvement. The retching stopped. The hunger-strikers were able to hold down fluids. As a result, they seemed more lucid and demonstrated signs of recovery. This phenomenon aroused suspicions. There were stories outside the jail that the prisoners were secretly taking vitamins. The medical staff even took away samples of the tissues that the men used to moisten their cracked lips and tested them for signs of nutriment. They found nothing. They were soon to realise that the rallying preceded the last stage of decline. The reason that they no longer vomited was because the brain cells that trigger the reaction were too damaged by vitamin starvation to work. As the brain damage developed the prisoners began to slip in and out of coma and were rambling and incoherent when conscious. Blindness and unconsciousness usually accompanied the last stage, though the death of Martin Hurson, who died at forty-six days (the shortest hunger-strike), was preceded by agonising convulsions during which he had to be held down on his bed. At the end, the prison medical staff noticed a similarity with cancer victims, 'hollow cheeks, protruding eyes and floppy, inelastic skin'.[11]

The death of Bobby Sands on 5 May on the sixty-fifth day

of his fast brought rioting on the scale of the early seventies to Belfast and Derry. (There was also rioting in Dublin.) Extra troops were drafted in to Ulster. The newspapers had been full of speculation that his death would be marked by a wave of bombings and shootings. In the event the IRA stayed quiet. Weakened by arrests, drained of resources by the H-Blocks campaign, they simply did not have the capacity for a military spectacular.[3]

Despite Sands' request that no one should follow him, the hunger strike continued. The IRA leadership sent a message into the jail after his death telling the prisoners to call it off. This was in effect a military order and the prisoners chose to disobey it. The four who were now fasting, Francis Hughes, Patsy O'Hara (the INLA OC), Raymond McCreesh and Joe McDonnell, felt that it was more important than ever to carry on. Another eighteen prisoners had volunteered. The organisers discussed 'whether to escalate it, move into a higher number or do we run it down, with the four on strike taking the decision to end it. We decided then . . . we would allow it to escalate.'[1]

To allow a breathing-space for possible negotiations there would be a gap before the next hunger-strikers began their fast. They decided on a shift of emphasis. Sands' death had left the British Government unmoved but it had provoked great anxiety in Dublin. McGeown and his comrades felt 'that because the Free State's political situation would be getting out of hand they would be forced to put more pressure on the Brits'. They also believed that the Catholic Church would be pushed 'into a position of saying something stronger than they had . . . that they should come out and say the hunger-strikers are entitled to political status or to the five demands'.[1]

A week after Sands, Francis Hughes died. Nine days later both Patsy O'Hara and Joe McDonnell died. Each death was marked by rioting and demonstrations. The funerals were occasions for huge displays of nationalist solidarity. They were spectacular and moving affairs — 100,000 attended the burial of Bobby Sands. The funeral processions were led by pipe and drum bands and the coffin flanked by a black-clad guard of honour. The clatter of British Army surveillance helicopters only served to intensify the emotional cohesion of the crowd. Just before interment six uniformed men would materialise at the graveside, fire a volley over the coffin and melt into the crowd while women held up umbrellas to shield them from the helicopters overhead as they stripped off their IRA uniforms. Invariably, at the sound of the gunshots, a great cheer went up from the mourners.

These occasions were not mass gestures of support for the prisoners' demands. From the election results that followed, it is clear that many of those who attended Bobby Sands' funeral did not go on to vote for Sinn Fein. Their attendance was prompted by something broader and deeper: an act of mourning for a symbolic member of their class, race and religion, a mark of reproach towards the attitude of the British. Many who attended would have been indifferent to the question of political status. There was a deeper conviction, that the British had behaved callously and cynically throughout the affair. Margaret Thatcher, and the NIO, had presented the hunger strikes as an exercise to revive the IRA's fortunes. After Sands' death Atkins issued a statement saying that he had committed suicide 'under the instructions of those who felt it useful to their cause that he should die'. On a visit to Belfast on 28 May, Mrs Thatcher declared that 'faced with the failure of their discredited cause, the men of violence have chosen in recent months to play what may well be their last card'. The IRA responded by shooting dead a policeman.

The planners in the Maze hoped to gain some political benefit from Catholic emotion and sympathy in the Dail elections of June. Sinn Fein, hampered by an ard fheis resolution of the previous year, had decided not to run in the local government elections in the North in May, a decision they later regretted. In the poll on 11 June the prisoners did well. Paddy Agnew, a blanket man, and Kieran Doherty, a hunger-striker, were both elected to the Dail and the nine H-Block candidates won 40,000 votes.

After the initial excitement the victory produced nothing. Despite the flood of private expressions of anxiety from

371

Dublin to London throughout the hunger strike and the public criticisms of Mrs Thatcher's inflexibility, neither Haughey's Fianna Fail government, nor Garret FitzGerald's Fine Gael/Labour coalition which replaced it after the election, came anywhere near to endorsing the five demands.

At the beginning of July, as the next batch of hunger-strikers approached death, the organisers accepted that pressure from the Church or the South was not going to shift the British. Cardinal O'Fiaich had seen Mrs Thatcher for an ill-tempered meeting on 1 July. At one point she stated that Northern Ireland had been founded to save the Catholics from civil war and wondered why it was that after two world wars, Britain and Germany managed to be friends but Britian and Ireland could not. 'If you want a simple answer,' the cardinal replied, 'it is that you do not occupy the Ruhr.'[10]

On 4 July the IRA issued a remarkably conciliatory statement. The intended message was 'that in our view the issue wasn't that the British should come out and say openly that we were entitled to political status . . .but that rather they should move to negotiate a solution within the prison'. They also stated that they were happy for any concessions granted to them to apply to all prisoners, loyalists included. A new line of negotiation opened up with the NIO through the conduit of the Irish Commission for Justice and Peace, a sub-committee of the Irish Bishops' Conference. Once again there seemed to be the basis of an agreement on the subject of remission and clothes. The death of Joe McDonnell on 8 July intensified the prisoners' desire to keep the protest going, especially as the British seemed to be moving. By now the prisoners' strategy had become hopelessly confused. Having given ground on the matter of political status, the hunger-strikers were correspondingly anxious to extract as many concessions as possible. When a Red Cross delegation came to visit them as part of a general investigation of prison conditions in Northern Ireland, they began pressing the issue of segregation from loyalist prisoners, something that had scarcely featured in their early demands.

Outside the jail the Church and the Catholic community were

becoming increasingly disheartened and angered by the way the episode was being extended. It was obvious that the five demands were unrealistic. The families of the hunger-strikers grew desperate. On 28 July Father Faul, the Dungannon priest who was a regular visitor at the Maze, held a meeting with them in Toomebridge. All but the parents of Kieran Doherty wanted the hunger strike to end. The idea spread that the fast was being extended at the wish of Sinn Fein. Faul contacted Gerry Adams, now the vice president of Sinn Fein (he was released from the Maze in 1977), and asked him to get the hunger-strikers to call off the fast. Adams replied that it was the prisoners who were perpetuating it but that he would go into the jail and tell the hunger-strikers he was morally opposed to what they were doing. Faul got in touch with O'Fiaich who approached the British Government. Permission was granted for Adams, Owen Carron (who later won the Fermanagh and South Tyrone by-election caused by Sands' death on 20 August) and Seamus Ruddy of the IRSP to visit the Maze.[7]

Adams told the strikers that he was against the fast and that he believed that it was becoming politically ineffective. Since the initial outcry over Bobby Sands, support was waning with every death. If the strike went on he believed that the morale inside the H-Blocks would be drained. 'He said he believed that most of the people if not all the people who were round the table would probably be dead before there would be any sort of solution,' said McGeown, who by this time had joined the fast. He finished by saying that 'each one is an individual and if they came off he would back them. There wasn't any big hang-up about it.' Adams' visit had a profound effect. McGeown and his comrades spent 'four or five hours thrashing around the pluses and minuses of it'. Their decision was determined by the condition of Kevin Lynch, an INLA hunger-striker, and Kieran Doherty, who were both deteriorating fast. They asked Dr Ross, one of the H-Block medical staff, whether the men would live if the strike was called off. He replied that they were beyond saving. In the circumstances they thought it cowardly to give up.

On 31 July the collective responsibility the hunger-strikers had accepted for determining whether to save their lives was broken by the intervention of the family of Paddy Quinn. On the forty-seventh day of his strike, when it became clear that his death was imminent, they insisted that he be fed. The prisoners and the IRA outside the prison had no say in the matter. On 8 August Tom McElwee, a 23-year-old IRA member from South Derry, died after sixty-two days. He was followed on 20 August (the day that Owen Carron was elected as MP for Fermanagh-South Tyrone) by Mickey Devine, an INLA man from Derry. Before Devine died he had a long conversation with McGeown. 'He had this attitude of Bobby's — "Look I'm going to die but the people coming after me, that's where we should break it" — and we said, "Well, if you're talking about breaking it then we should break it before you die." '[1] Two weeks after Devine's death the IRSP announced that no more men would be put on hunger strike. This was bowing to the inevitable. There were no INLA men willing to do so left inside the Maze.

Faul was using all his persuasion now to get families to request medical help for their sons when they reached a critical stage. On 4 and 6 September Matt Devlin and Laurence McGeown were removed from the strike after fifty-two and seventy days of fasting. Bernard Fox sought treatment in his own right on 24 September and Liam McCloskey followed him two days later. The hunger strike was falling apart but it was important to the prisoners that it should end in a disciplined way. The organisers wished to taper it off, only ending it completely when they were sure of what concessions had been extracted. On 2 October, following a meeting with Faul, five of the six remaining hunger-strikers' families decided to intervene if they fell into unconsciousness.

The situation had moved out of the hunger-strikers' control. There was no longer much point in postponing the announcement. At 3.00 pm on Saturday 3 October 1981, 217 days after the protest started, the remaining hunger-strikers announced they were abandoning their fast and were immediately given vitamin injections to haul them back to life. Father Faul felt 'a tremendous feeling of relief in Belfast and all over the North of Ireland, a feeling of peace of which this community has so little experience'. Pat McGeown was unable to witness it, having lapsed into a coma and been taken off the protest by his wife. Two days later the new Secretary of State for Northern Ireland, James Prior, announced that from then on prisoners would be entitled to wear their own clothes and that protestors would have half their lost remission restored.

The IRA had paid a heavy price for the improvements they won by the hunger strike. Arguably, everything they gained could have been achieved at any stage in the protest after the death of Sands. The strike dragged on for several reasons, all to do with the fact of their imprisonment. The intense camaraderie of the blocks meant that the death of each hunger-striker intensified the determination of the man who followed him. The years of isolation during the dirty protest, the lack of radio, television, newspapers and visitors from the outside world meant that the men who planned the strike had only the haziest notion of the calibre of their opponents. The logical models they constructed in the endless hours of discussion and analysis were based on misconceptions. According to a senior prisoner, 'they had no understanding of Mrs Thatcher'. They persistently misjudged her strength of will and credited her with a maternalism and concern for propriety that anyone outside the Maze prison would have found extraordinary. After Sands' election the prisoners were convinced that the phenomenon of an MP on hunger strike would force Mrs Thatcher into concession. The British Government's deliberate vagueness in negotiation and the resolution of the prison authorities against any concession ensured that the ordeal was stretched to the limit.

But on the whole, the hunger strike marked a dramatic improvement in the fortunes of the republican movement. It succeeded in dragging the flighty attentions of the world's television networks and press back to Northern Ireland. What they recorded — the endurance of those who died and the mass demonstrations of sympathy — tended to show the IRA in a good light. It was an irony of the episode that it began with the Government attempting to impose on the prisoners the status of criminals and ended with the IRA restoring their credentials among sections of the Catholic community as freedom fighters.

More importantly the hunger strike — or rather the support it gained at the polls — gave the republican movement the confidence it needed to advance into the political arena, and present itself as an alternative nationalist force. The death of Bobby Sands could be taken as marking the end of the Provisional IRA's purely military incarnation. His election as MP for Fermanagh and South Tyrone marked the start of a new, and — for London and Dublin — potentially more dangerous era.

CHAPTER TWENTY

The Armalite and the Ballot-box

The decision to run Sands in the Fermanagh and South Tyrone by-election had been accompanied by deep misgivings on the part of Gerry Adams, Martin McGuinness and Danny Morrison, not because they opposed the idea of contesting elections but because they were concerned that their candidate might not win. His success convinced them that there was a large body of potential supporters who could sustain a whole-hearted political debut. Adams understood that convincing the average volunteer of the worth of mundane political activity would be a long process. But the excitement that Sands' and Carron's victories had generated persuaded many young members that politicking could be as stimulating as military activity, and without most of the attendant risks. By the time of the 1981 ard fheis the strategy of contesting future elections had gained wide acceptance. There had never been any block on fighting elections, and there was a long history of electoral interventions for propaganda purposes. A policy of persistent electioneering, however, was a different matter.

Even before the hunger strikes much of political discussion at the Sinn Fein ard chomhairle (executive committee) had centred on this question, with the forces in favour of full-blooded electioneering being led by Adams. Ironically, the main opponent of the idea was Ruairi O'Bradaigh, one of the most persistent advocates of electoral intervention. O'Bradaigh believed that what was useful as a tactic would corrupt if elevated to a strategy. Inside the ard chomhairle in 1980 and 1981 the tide of opinion was running strongly against him.*

The Northerners were less ideological and more pragmatic. They were relatively unconcerned about the dangers of ideological contamination. Their question was: Will we win? At the 1981 ard fheis their attitude received a triumphant endorsement from the majority of the delegates. The keynote speech was made by Morrison, and during it he demonstrated his superb propagandist's talent by coining the phrase that sums up the strategy the IRA has followed every since. Waving his notes dramatically at the rows of representatives packed under the elegant early Victorian roof of the Dublin Mansion House, he demanded: 'Who here really believes that we can win the war through the ballot-box?' Then he paused and went on, 'But will anyone here object if with a ballot paper in this hand and an Armalite in this hand we take power in Ireland?'

The overwhelming backing for the policy marked the end of the Southerners' influence and the formal arrival of the Northerners in full control of the republican machine. There was a further humiliation for O'Bradaigh when his beloved Eire Nua was voted down by the delegates (but not by the two-thirds majority necessary to erase it from the party's manifesto).

The by-elections had shown that there was a huge potential supply of support for Sinn Fein to build on. The experience of the local council elections of May 1981 had shown Adams that if they did not capitalise on it, other republican and left-wing organisations would. The Irish Independence Party, a short-lived nationalist group founded in 1977, picked up twenty-one seats and the IRSP and the People's Democracy got two seats each.

The first opportunity to discover whether Sinn Fein's support would decline without the sustaining emotional sap provided

* According to Adams, the ard chomhairle had passed a motion in 1980 accepting that Sinn Fein would fight all future elections but at the time this had been regarded as a theoretical position which would not have to be acted on for several years.

by the hunger strikes was provided in October 1982 with the elections for a new Assembly. Despite the total lack of evidence that there was any basis for agreement between the Northern Ireland political parties, Northern Ireland secretary James Prior began work shortly after his arrival in the Province in 1981 on another political initiative. Prior's contribution to the succession of Ulster's discarded political models was powered by the notion of 'rolling devolution'. The new Assembly (seventy-eight members elected by proportional representation) would start off with consultative powers only, but would gradually acquire some executive powers if it demonstrated that there was 'cross community' support for their transfer from Westminster.

Rolling devolution's slender chances were further reduced by the announcement by the SDLP that they would boycott the Assembly and by a lack of enthusiasm for the project in Dublin. In the end, the main result of the enterprise was to give Sinn Fein the opportunity to demonstrate that they were a serious political force. In 1982 they began opening advice centres to deal with complaints about housing, social security payments and all the other accumulated ills of West Belfast and the Creggan and the Bogside. The incongruity of former gunmen earnestly listening to endless complaints about broken guttering and damp provoked understandable mirth and scepticism among their main political opponents, the SDLP. There were sneers about 'social workers with Armalites'. Nor did a substantial number of the ordinary members of the Belfast Brigade find the idea of shifting to this sort of activity very appealing. Before the Assembly elections Adams went to some lengths to bring the men with him. According to one Belfast IRA member,

All brigades were told to do a survey in their area and sound out what the volunteer attitude was. The people they sent along were people who were able to manipulate. The one who turned up to talk to my battalion was a better speaker than anyone else and he had all the answers when the volunteers said, 'But this means we'll have to run down

379

the war.' He said: 'Only until the election is over.' He had all the answers and the people felt inferior to him so they all agreed in the end. At most meetings they all agreed it was a good idea to go into the Assembly [elections] but after they were in to escalate the war again.[1]

The visitors were sometimes IRA men, sometimes from Sinn Fein. On one occasion

the speaker came in and said: 'Look lads, this is the position. After the Bobby Sands election and then Owen Carron we think we can get a mandate from the people here. People are saying we have no mandate but if we can go in and win these elections we can say we have . . . when we go abroad we'll not be going as terrorists. We'll be going as elected representatives of the people of Northern Ireland.'

The election results were a triumph for Adams and his strategy and dismasted the critics of the new direction. Sinn Fein won five of the seventy-eight seats and Adams, McGuinness, Morrison and Carron were elected. They took 10.1 per cent (64,191) of the first preference votes. This was an advance of 2.5 per cent on the aggregate Anti-H-Block vote in the 1981 local elections. Even more satisfying, in view of Adams' desire to present Sinn Fein ultimately as the authentic voice of Northern Catholics, their success had been at the expense of the SDLP, whose total of fourteen seats was five down on the 1973 power-sharing Assembly, three down on the 1975 Convention (it did make a small recovery in first preference votes compared with the local elections).[2]

Success was the best possible foil to the squabbling that the new leadership could expect around the election issue. A few weeks after the elections the Northerners were able to enjoy once more the plaudits of the movement at the Sinn Fein ard fheis. The delegates voted at last to remove Eire Nua in its entirety from the constitution of Sinn Fein. Ruairi O'Bradaigh was to hang on to the presidency for another year before ceding it to Adams. In his resignation speech he cited the rejection of Eire Nua and the commitment to the electoral strategy as the reasons for his departure. 'During my fourteen years as head of Provisional Sinn Fein,' he told the delegates in a speech with a prophetic ring, 'there were no splits or splinters. Long may it remain so, as it will provided we stick to basic principles.'

'Going political' meant a shift in the movement's resources away from the IRA and toward Sinn Fein. Sinn Fein had been a feeble organisation before the hunger strikes. It had a respectable number of members but on the whole they were men and women who felt unable to commit themselves to the IRA, and older republicans whose years meant they were no longer eligible for the active list. After the hunger strikes Sinn Fein became a much more attractive option for republican-minded young people. According to one IRA man, 'for years you couldn't really be a member of the republican movement without being an IRA man. You could be in Sinn Fein but you got no recognition. In the early 1970s Sinn Fein was just a cover-up. The spokespeople were all IRA men acting in a Sinn Fein capacity. Now everybody accepts that Sinn Fein is contributing to the war and they are acceptable members of the movement.'[1] The influx of young people was combined with an increase in the number of ex-prisoners who did not go back to the IRA but joined Sinn Fein instead. 'They'd been educated in jail and they'd learned a lot and they believe that it was the right way to do things. They accept that their value as operators is finished but they still want to contribute to the movement so they go and join Sinn Fein.'[1]

The domination of the Northerners was reflected in the make-up of the ard chomhairle, presided over by Gerry Adams. By 1986 only six of its members were from the South (and despite Sinn Fein's strenuous efforts to present itself as an egalitarian organisation only one, Aine ni Murchu, was female). Its policies were augmented by a standing committee, the coiste seasta, drawn from the ard chomhairle's member-ship, which meets weekly. Below this there is a system of regional committees, the chomhairle limisteir, consisting of delegates from local committees; the chomhairle ceanntairs, which in turn are composed of the smallest unit in the Sinn Fein pyramid; the cumanns or local associations. In 1986 there were 350 in the whole of Ireland with memberships ranging from five in country areas to fifty in Belfast. The growth of republican political activity meant that however notional the division between Sinn Fein and the IRA had been in the past, by 1985 Sinn Fein had developed its own distinct organisation and personalities. But there were still numerous cases of dual membership. The main bridge between the two bodies is provided by Gerry Adams, but in 1986 there were eight members of the ard chomhairle who were in the IRA, and there are many further points at which the two are tied. One man who was a prominent Sinn Fein councillor in 1986, for example, was also on the brigade staff of the IRA in his area.

Although Sinn Fein began to develop a separate existence from the IRA there was no doubt about who was the senior partner in the arrangement. Even in matters of electoral strategy the IRA could have the last say. This was illustrated in the choice of Sinn Fein candidate for an Area D by-election to Belfast City Council. The episode also reveals that Adams' authority in the movement is not as autocratic as has been suggested. On the morning before the Sinn Fein meeting to select a candidate the Belfast Brigade held their own caucus and decided they wanted Alec Maskey, a young hard-liner. Adams was disappointed and suggested his own choice, Sean Keenan, but reluctantly agreed to nominate Maskey that evening. Maskey's other rival was Patrick Wilson. According to one of those present both were told that if they were nominated they should decline:

So Sean Keenan was nominated and he said, 'I'm sorry, I'm too busy and the kid's just started school.' Patrick Wilson was nominated and he said, 'I'm just out of jail and I'm too young yet to take on that role.' Then somebody in the IRA got up and said, 'I nominate Alec Maskey' and somebody said, 'I second it' and all the IRA men clapped Alec in.[1]

382

Adams had previously been thwarted at the Assembly elections when the Brigade staff again insisted on Maskey over his choice, Tom Cahill, who they regarded as too much of a crony.

The publicity the republican movement had received from the hunger strikes and its subsequent electoral achievements had revived the interests of foreign left and revolutionary bodies in the organisation. The PLO in particular had been impressed by the sympathy the IRA had been able to manufacture during the episode. In July 1981 they had invited two senior republicans to the Lebanon, one a leading Sinn Fein organiser and the other William 'Blue Boy' Kelly, a veteran IRA man with the benefit of a clean police record who had long experience as a republican envoy in the US, Europe and the Middle East. On arrival in Beirut they were taken to see a number of middle-ranking PLO officials. According to one of the men the Palestinians 'couldn't understand how the hunger strike was attracting so much attention and they were considering using it as a weapon of propaganda among their own prisoners in Israeli jails'.[1] The pair were taken to training camps in the Chouf mountains and Bekaa valley where the Palestinians declared their willingness to help the IRA with weapons and training. The offer was declined. For one thing, the PLO was fighting a conventional war with conventional weapons and most of those on offer were ludicrously over-powered for Irish conditions. For another, the republicans believed 'there wasn't much point because nothing moves out of the Mediterranean without the Israelis knowing about it'.[1]

Far more significant was the growing friendliness of sections of the left of the British Labour Party towards Sinn Fein. Until 1981 general electoral revulsion in Britain towards the IRA's behaviour ruled out any demonstration of friendliness to the IRA cause. The flood of emotion released by the hunger strikes and the ability of Adams and McGuinness to put themselves forward as 'elected representatives' after the Assembly elections emboldened some figures on the left of the Labour party to begin extending their contacts with Sinn Fein. The first signal that the taboo was about to be comprehensively broken came in July 1981, when Ken Livingstone, leader of the Greater London Council (GLC), entertained at County Hall Mrs Alice McElwee, whose son Thomas was on the forty-fourth day of his fast. Livingstone had made a number of remarks supporting the hunger-strikers' demands and calling for British withdrawal from Ireland but they had unaccountably failed to generate the press outrage his utterances usually provoked. He told one paper that 'the H-Block struggle is part of the struggle to bring about a free, united Ireland. They have my support, and they have the support of the majority of the Labour Party rank and file. I have been consistently in favour of withdrawal from Ireland and to get away from the idea that it is some sort of campaign against terrorism. It is in fact the last colonial war.'[3]

Later that month, as London prepared to celebrate the wedding of Prince Charles to Lady Diana Spencer, a group of IRA supporters began a forty-eight-hour fast on the GLC steps and released hundreds of black balloons over London under the approving eye of Livingstone who declared that he was unable to think of 'a more appalling contrast between this wedding beanfeast and what is happening in Ireland'.[4]

The furore that erupted after these incidents did not prevent two Islington councillors, Steve and Cathy Bundred, from attending an internment anniversary rally in Belfast on 12 August nor Livingstone the following year from backing an invitation circulated around the GLC by Steve Bundred, for Adams and Morrison to visit London for private talks at County Hall. Adams had been all in favour of extending Sinn Fein's links with the British left. Historically, the Labour movement had never shown the slightest sympathy for the IRA. Indeed, some elements of the trade unions were staunchly unionist. But Adams was encouraged by the leftward drift of the party, exemplified by the rise of such figures as Livingstone, and he was eager to forge as many contacts as possible.

The visit was scheduled for 14 December. On 6 December, a few hours after the event had been announced, a bomb went off in the Droppin' Well, a crowded disco-pub in Ballykelly near Derry, where British soldiers from the barracks in the village went to meet local girls. Sixteen people were killed and sixty-six injured. The decision as to whether Livingstone should withdraw the invitation — as the Labour leader Michael Foot was demanding that he do — was taken out of his hands by the action of the Home Secretary, William Whitelaw. On 8 December he issued Adams and Morrison with 'exclusion orders', banning them from mainland Britain under a section of the Prevention of Terrorism Act entitling him to keep out anyone 'who is or has been . . . involved in the commission, preparation or instigation of acts of terrorism'. Sinn Fein was able to claim the debacle as a propaganda victory anyway. How could the Government assert that the Six Counties of Ulster were part of Britain yet ban British citizens from entering another part of its territory?

The general election results confirmed that Sinn Fein's electoral support was not ephemeral. Its share of the poll went up 3.3 per cent to 13.4 per cent (102,601 votes). The SDLP faltered again, falling nearly one per cent to 17.9 (137,012). Gerry Adams was elected MP for West Belfast, but the achievement was diminished by the fact that the nationalist vote was split three ways, with both an SDLP candidate and an Independent (Gerry Fitt) also standing. With his election the Government withdrew its exclusion order, thereby enabling Livingstone to issue another invitation to Adams. On 26 July he arrived at Heathrow Airport where Labour MP Jeremy Corbyn was waiting to greet him. At County Hall he was greeted with all the solemnity and dignity normally given to a head of state. There were numerous television and press interviews, as Adams, looking modish and thoughtful in his aviator spectacles, neat beard and pipe, explained that the visit was part of a long-term attempt to open up a dialogue with the British people and their representatives and to break down the wall of disinformation erected by the media.[5]

Encouraging though these encounters were, the progress of relations between Sinn Fein and the Labour Party was always ultimately regulated by the activities of the IRA. On Saturday 16 December, a little more than four months after Adams had expressed his desire for warmer relations with the British people, an IRA team drove two cars packed with explosives to

Knightsbridge in London and parked them behind Harrods department store. The streets were filled with shoppers buying their Christmas gifts. Half an hour before the bombs were set to explode, one of the IRA men telephoned a warning. It was hopelessly late. The blasts tore through the crowd as they were still struggling to get out of the area, killing eight.

The wave of anger and disgust that the bombing produced made the IRA reluctant to claim responsibility for the attack. Even Adams expressed 'regret' at the action, though he stressed that he was not indulging in 'the politics of condemnation'.[6] For some time it was suggested that the unit had been acting independently and that authorisation would never have been granted. In fact the bombers were on an official mission. They had received specific approval to attack Harrods (though not to cause civilian deaths). It was, the Army Council felt, a symbol of British prestige, and 'an opportunity to let the Brits know we could still strike at their hearts'.[1]

CHAPTER TWENTY-ONE

Armed Propaganda

The growing visibility of Sinn Fein during the early 1980s did not mean that the submerged portion of the republican movement — the IRA itself — was becoming any less important. Gerry Adams was highly sensitive to accusations that the electoral strategy meant a slackening of enthusiasm for violence and at the 1982 ard fheis it had been made clear that all Sinn Fein candidates in elections would be required to be 'unambivalent in their support for the armed struggle.'

By 1985 the IRA was a much smaller part of the organisation than it had been ten years before, but the needs of the movement, as defined by the new philosophy, meant that there was no longer the necessity for a large force. Republican strategy required a certain level of violence — but only enough to distort the private and public life of the North, and to make sure that the military arm was properly exercised. From the peak of about 1,000 activists in the mid-seventies the numbers declined to about 250 by the mid-eighties, a figure which has stayed constant. As Adams and McGuinness became increasingly public figures they stepped back from intimate involvement in the planning of the IRA campaign. McGuinness stood down as chief-of-staff shortly before the Assembly elections, to be replaced first by Ivor Bell, then by a little-known Tyrone man who had been active along the border in the early years of the troubles. Both McGuinness and Adams retained their seats on the Army Council which remained the supreme authority of the republican movement. Its seven members met irregularly at different venues around Ireland to discuss the general progress of the campaign, to propagate or to sanction particular operations and to act as the ultimate court of appeal in matters of internal discipline. It approved or initiated major operations or departures from the normal pattern of approval.

After the end of the hunger strikes the Army Council decided to carry out a symbolic act of punishment against the unionists for their triumphant behaviour during the drama. This decision was passed on to the GHQ staff who then issued an instruction to the brigades of Belfast, Derry, South Armagh and South Tyrone, to suggest some suitable targets. The Belfast Brigade proposed the assassination of Robert Bradford, a former Methodist minister and an Official Unionist MP for South Belfast. Bradford's strident style was more in keeping with the populist loyalism of Democratic Unionists than with his own party, and the Democratic Unionist leader Ian Paisley was a close friend. According to a Belfast IRA man it was 'because Bradford had been making outlandish sectarian remarks'[1] that he was chosen to die.

Before the assassination was carried out, the Army Council considered the consequences of the action. On the whole both the loyalists and the IRA had desisted from killing each other's politicians. For the Provisionals to start now would represent an important development. The council calculated that there was a strong likelihood that the death would spark off reprisal attacks by Protestant crowds or the paramilitaries of the UDA and the UVF against the Catholic areas. 'They were going to cause a backlash,' said a Belfast republican. 'The UDA were on the streets of the Shankill throughout the hunger strike. The IRA was going to exploit that situation.'[2] The leaders of the Belfast units were instructed to prepare for the onslaught. Arms were pulled out of dumps and plans made to set up a medical care network in the event of rioting. On Saturday 14 November 1981 five Provisionals walked into a community centre in Finaghy in south-west Belfast where Bradford was holding a surgery and shot him dead. A caretaker who was in the way also died. The expected backlash never materialised.

Since 1976, when the British Army had been pulled back from the forefront of the conflict, most IRA attacks had been directed against Protestant Irishmen in the uniforms of the UDR and RUC.

Down the years there had been several attempts at political collusion between the IRA and the Protestant paramilitaries. Maire Drumm, a vice-president of Sinn Fein between 1972 and 1976, held a number of meetings with loyalist groups, pressing the old message that the Catholic and Protestant working class had an equally bad lot and pushing advantages of working together.[3] In 1976, while she was recovering from an eye operation in the Mater Hospital in Belfast, three loyalist gunmen, two of them wearing doctors' coats, walked into the ward and shot her dead. The Shankill Road UDA sent a message of sympathy.

Later Drumm's husband Jimmy and Danny Morrison held further meetings with loyalists and by the end of 1976 both sides had nominated representatives to look into the possibility of an independent Ulster loosely federated with the South. The loyalists chose Desmond Boal, a unionist politician and lawyer, and the IRA Sean MacBride, the jurist, diplomat and Nobel Peace Prize winner. The lack of serious intention on either side meant that the talking soon stopped.

Later on, Gerry Adams met John McKeague, another loyalist enthusiast for an independent Ulster, but again the discussion quickly petered out, convincing Adams that 'I was wasting my time. While they [the loyalists] have a chance of preserving their privileges they are going to do so.'[3] Adams came to the conclusion that there was nothing to be gained from the sort of bridge-building exercises attempted by the Officials and that to attempt to heal sectarian wounds would mean 'forgetting the national question. It would mean that we couldn't raise the question of plastic bullets or the RUC or job discrimination. You would have surrendered to the most reactionary elements in loyalism and got nothing in return.'[4]

The few contacts were limited to strictly practical matters, and several pacts were struck with the Protestant paramilitaries which lasted surprisingly well. Following the sectarian carnage of 1975 and 1976 there was an agreement to end assassinations. For several years it succeeded in significantly reducing the number of random killings until it was revoked by the loyalists after the murder of Earl Mountbatten in August 1979. There was also an undertaking by both sides to refrain from car bombing which survived even the rage that followed the La Mon House bombing.

The security forces claim that both sides even co-operated in the killing of Lenny Murphy, a Protestant from West Belfast who had been a member of the Shankill Butchers' sectarian murder gang who were jailed in 1979 for the torture and deaths of nineteen Catholics. On his release from prison in 1983 Murphy resumed his activities, and was involved in the torture and murder of Joe Donegan, a harmless Catholic who was snatched on his way home from the pub. The police believe that since there was a threat of a return to a full-scale campaign of sectarian assassination as long as Murphy was alive, Shankill Road loyalists granted a safe passage to an IRA team to kill him. At the appointed time, Murphy was driving his car in the Shankill Road when he was cut down by automatic rifle fire. His death passed without noticeable regret from his co-religionists.

During the early eighties the operation of Northern Command settled down into a set pattern. Staff meetings were held once a month at different venues around the border which all the brigade commanders attended. Northern command had the authority to order military operations of an accepted type — say an orchestrated wave of police killings — and in some cases to take decisions that would normally be referred upwards, if it was not possible for the Army Council to meet. Initially, Northern Command meetings were large-scale affairs with entire brigade staffs turning up. Later, security considerations dictated that contacts with the brigade areas were as restricted as possible. At discussions concerning operations, for example, anyone not directly concerned — such as the education and recruitment officers — were excluded. Each function was strictly defined and each Northern Command staff intelligence officer encouraged to cultivate his own area of responsibility rather than involve himself in group planning. For this purpose the intelligence officers, security officers and so on held regular meetings with their counterparts on the brigade staffs. Southern Command by now had in theory an exclusively supporting role gathering weapons, maintaining arms and explosives dumps and collecting intelligence.

The decline in membership and activities meant that the IRA on its own was a remarkably cheap organisation to run. In 1983 it cost £2,500 a week to finance the Belfast Brigade, a figure kept low by the meagre wages paid to members. Every full-time IRA member not in work was entitled to £20 a week, but if he took the money he was expected to forgo social security, as the weekly trip to the dole office increased the opportunities for state surveillance. Part-time members and those in work got nothing. Sometimes, when money was tight, wages were not paid at all. All members received the same but special responsibilities brought extra reward. Some brigade staff members in Belfast, for example, were allowed a 'company car', taxed and insured by the IRA, and could claim expenses. Cars were often provided at an advantageous rate by local dealers. According to one IRA man, 'They look at it that, "If I give them this car buck cheap or as near as next to nothing, the next time I need a favour I know they are going to do it and they are not going to come back to me for a year or two . . ." It's a respectable sort of thing, people aren't forced into it as such.'[1]

With the decision to contest elections the potential overall costs of the republican movement rose dramatically. Political activity is an expensive business. The propaganda effort expended during the hunger strikes cost the IRA £1,000,000 and the 1983 general election campaign cost Sinn Fein £30,000. In addition, by 1983 it had to find some £300,000 each year to finance the thirty advice centres. At the same time, the need to court the electorate meant that overt criminal activities like robbing banks and post offices, used to finance the movement in the past, would have to be curtailed.*

By the early 1980s most of the republican movement's income came from legitimate business enterprises or from sophisticated tax frauds in which only the state was the loser and which heightened their economic influence in the ghettoes. To some extent the IRA succeeded in creating a new micro-economy where the money saved by the inhabitants of West Belfast in tax evasion and social security frauds was then circulated in republican-owned bars. The biggest source of finance was the social clubs in Belfast owned by the IRA. By 1986 they had twenty-eight large and, by the standards of West Belfast, luxurious places providing cheap drink and entertainment. The bigger clubs could expect to turn over between £150,000 and £200,000 a year and the IRA would also subtract up to seventy per cent of the taking from the gambling machines. The clubs were scrupulously well run with proper stewards, solicitors and accountants. When the police wished to check the books they were courteously received and offered a drink.[5]

Another major source of money was fraud involving tax exemption certificates in the building trade, which boomed in the 1980s as the old terraces of West Belfast were knocked down and rebuilt. By the end of 1986 about 180 cases of tax evasion involving £55 million had been or were about to come before the courts. According to one policeman, 'In the republican areas the republican organisations actually run the building industry. They decide who's going to work where. None of the builders will take a stand. The unions would love to get in and improve things but they just can't, they're not a strong enough force.'[1] It was possible for the authorities

---

* None the less there continued to be embarrassments. In 1982 the Whiterock post office in the heart of West Belfast was robbed of £7,500 by a gang posing as RUC men investigating giro cheque frauds. Gerry Adams indignantly denied that the IRA was involved but in fact it was the work of a Belfast unit acting against orders.

to see the IRA's involvement in the building trade in an indulgent light. Business was run with brisk efficiency so that the work was done on time and thieving and criminal damage was reduced. The IRA also profited enormously from the construction along the edge of West Belfast of a new road linking the M1 and M2 motorways. Together with some remnants of the Officials they controlled the construction, parcelling the motorway off into 100-yard-fiefdoms.

Another long-standing source of cash was the taxis. The IRA owned several mini-cab firms but also extracted a £15 a week levy from each of the 200 or so members of the Falls Taxi Association, whose black London cabs ferried the population of West Belfast up and down to the city centre at cut-rate fares.

Political considerations meant that straightforward protection rackets were impracticable but business still felt under subtle pressure to contribute to republican funds. One IRA man recalled how a demolition contractor who was about to begin pulling down a bakery in West Belfast had 'got in contact with the local IRA and said, "I'm pulling down the bakery" and they said, "So what?" and he said, "I'll give you £100 a week to leave me alone".'[1]

The multiple layers of the IRA structures conveyed an impression of order and hierarchy but the experience as articulated by one Belfast member at the height of the hunger strike in 1981 reflected the disarray in the ranks of the organisation in North Belfast as the cell structure collapsed out onto the streets at the time and the IRA and the police and army engaged each other in rioting. Christopher Black, the most notorious of the IRA supergrasses, was responsible for terrorist charges being brought against thirty-eight defendants in 1983 after he turned Queen's Evidence in return for a promise of immunity. Although Black's testimony may not have been strong enough to secure convictions in stringent forensic conditions, there is no doubt as to the essential accuracy of his testimony which conveys the flavour of life in at least one section of the IRA in the early eighties.

Black's first encounter with the IRA came after he moved to the 'Bone' during the 1975 ceasefire and was asked to mind a gun. Later he was invited to join the Provisionals and he did so in order to 'be accepted and established in the area. I think I thought it would be a game really, and that there would be excitement.' For three months his duties were as a vigilante on the look-out for 'anti-social behaviour, burglaries . . . thefts.' In December 1975 he went on his first proper IRA operation, an armed robbery at a shop in the centre of Belfast. He was caught and sentenced to ten years in the Maze. Five years later he was out. Three weeks after he was released he received a visitor from the IRA.

> He asked me would I consider coming back into the IRA and I told him I was considering it. A little later another person came to my house. We sat on the stairs and he explained to me that I had the choice of joining an active service unit or going company. He explained what the ASUs done, i.e. going on shooting, taking over houses, perhaps going on the run, leaving your family for days and general terrorist work.

Black decided to 'go company', a matter of keeping order in pubs and clubs and reporting incidents of 'anti-social behaviour'. After a few months, however, he was asked to keep watch while a team fired a few ineffectual shots at some policemen. Black's apparent keenness led to an invitation to join one of the ASUs. In June 1981 he went on his first job. The team met in the home of an elderly sympathiser. The ASU leader told them that they were to take over a house in Ardoyne and shoot at soldiers from it. Before leaving they donned hats and spectacles in a half-hearted attempt at disguise. It was an early job and Black recalled feeling pleased because he would be home in time to see England playing at Wembley on the television.

I knocked the door and a girl about 28 years old answered it. I told her, 'Irish Republican Army, I am taking your house over, don't get excited or panic.' She was alone. I took her upstairs and put her in the front bedroom. I went back downstairs and opened the back door as ordered. I went back upstairs and sat with the girl . . . for about three hours and at about 5.00 pm her husband came to the house. I told her to call him upstairs as if she wanted him . . . The three of us sat to about 7.00 pm. I was looking out of the window and I saw a car stop at the front . . . I saw X and Y get out . . . Y was carrying a plastic bag with something in it . . . I saw him take a Woodmaster rifle out of the bag. I saw Y and X with the rifle get into the attic with a pair of stepladders from the house. I saw Y breaking a slate of the roof facing Twadell Avenue. He told me to go back to the room and keep looking out of the window and I would see another fellow . . . if any of the police or Army were about his coat would be zipped up and that I was to let them know immediately so as they wouldn't shoot. If the zip was open it meant everything was all clear.

This became unnecessary when X remembered that they were within sight of an Army observation post and would be seen running after the shooting. Such frustrations were commonplace. More operations were called off than undertaken. One day when the team were sitting around at their safe house it was decided to try and snipe at the police in the Oldpark Barracks from behind the corrugated iron fence of a building-site. Black was dispatched to warn the watchman to stay out of the way, to note his name, and to instruct him to tell the police that 'it was three fellows with hoods on who done the shooting' when they came to investigate. One of the team was sent to keep guard.

Originally another Provo had been detailed to pull the trigger but his nerve failed and the job fell to Black. A, the leader, came along to supervise.

A turned round and says, 'I wonder if we should hit these fellows getting in and out of these cars, I think they are

395

cops.' I was looking through another wee hole. I could see fellows getting out and into cars but they were dressed with ordinary clothes and not uniform. We took it that their coats were over their uniforms. We decided to wait and see if a better target came along. There were kids playing football in front of the tin where we were going to shoot from and we discussed how we were going to get rid of them. Just then A said, 'There is a cop going into the shop.' I could see he was a uniformed policeman. He had no cap on or tunic. I could see his shirt. A said: 'He has no flak jacket on. Hit him.' A handed me the rifle, told me the safe [safety catch] was off and that it was ready to fire. He told me to take my time. The policeman was just about to go into the shop and I fired about ten shots at him. I knew I didn't hit him because I was not trying. I saw the policeman dive into the shop for cover. As I pulled the rifle out of the tin, A said, 'Did you hit him?' I said, 'I don't know' . . . We ran out of the building site at St Gemma's. A was carrying the rifle. We met B [who] said: 'A couple of kids said there that someone was shot outside the police station.' A said, 'That's sound' and he ordered me to go to my own home and change my clothing.[6]

Jobs were planned on a random and spontaneous basis. The purpose — apart from the basic one of 'stiffing the Brits' — was, in Black's words, to 'keep things on the boil' during the hunger strike. Judging by Black's evidence and that of other former IRA members, the level of violence was almost completely dictated by the enthusiasm of the local commander. Black's boss was dedicated, energetic and impatient with his less zealous subordinates. After one operation fell through,

He . . . said to me did I know a house in the 'Bone' which looks on to the Cliftonville Road. I said 'yes' but I was not sure if the angle was in line with Cliftonville Road. Again the idea was to take the house over and snipe at the Army or police. As I was originally from the 'Bone' I didn't like the idea of me having to take over a house of people

I knew so I called him into the kitchen away from the others. I told him I had promised to take the wife and kids to the pictures and could I go on . . . He wasn't too pleased but he let me go anyway.

Black's story reveals a marked reluctance on the part of many of the ASU operators to be the one to pull the trigger. One day his boss asked him to look out for ways of 'hitting' the Oldpark Road police station which he walked past each morning when delivering his children to school. Black noted that a car drove into the barracks at the same time every morning and passed on the registration number.

He told me that we would hit the policeman. However, I was somewhat afraid of becoming involved in murder and asked for another week to watch the car and its occupant. During the next week I fed [him] incorrect particulars on the movement of the car. I told him that it did not appear when in fact it had.

Another man, B, was ordered to help with the operation.

The first morning B was with me, the car passed us at its normal time . . . B asked me if this was the car and I lied and told him that I was not sure. The next day I did not go and B went alone. He later called . . . at my house at 9.45. I got out of bed and went downstairs. He asked the reason why I hadn't been there and I told him I had got drunk the previous night and had slept in. He told me that he had seen the car, he was a big man and that he was definitely a policeman. I asked him not to tell [the commanding officer] I hadn't been there and he agreed.

After further procrastinations the plan fizzled out when Black was arrested.

The disciplined world conjured up by the 'Green Book' was, on Black's testimony, a long way from real experience. All the activity produced little result. Half the time, as Black's

ASU sniped away from street corners and the attics of commandeered houses, the security forces seem to have been unaware that they were under fire. The operators were more successful organising riots, a relatively simple matter in the emotionally charged atmosphere of the times. One night the ASU were hanging about in a 'call house', when

> we heard that a wee lad had been shot dead . . . this was now an ideal situation to start a riot because the wee fellow was shot and everyone was high. We all went out on to the street and egged people on to start the riot.

It was not until October of 1981 that Black's unit took part in an unequivocally successful operation. One day Black was told to be at a certain address at 10.30 that night. He spent the afternoon in the bookies and the evening in the Shamrock Club. At one point he was asked by one of the team to get hold of a postman's coat. Black remembered an acquaintance in the Post Office and prevailed on him to part with one. By the time Black turned up half an hour late at the rendezvous two of the unit members had still to arrive and he was sent to McLaughlin's Bar over the road to round them up. The plan was that three of the team would spend the night in a safe house. Black and an accomplice were to go to another house and force the man who lived there to lend them his car and to put them both up for the night. As they left, the owner of the house called out, 'All the best lads, watch yourselves.' Black recalled, 'Although I had not been specifically told what was going on I was in no doubt . . . that someone was going to be murdered.' They reconvened at a woman's house where half the team were due to spend the night. In the parlour Black saw a complete postman's outfit: cap complete with badge, grey trousers, black coat and a postman's bag. Unfortunately the coat supplied by Black was too big for its intended wearer, an unemployed labourer, X. He was sent off to find another one and eventually obtained a 'wee, neat grey postman's coat with badges on it' from a man in Ardoyne.

In the early hours of the morning, in the parlour of the safe house, the commanding officer outlined the plan. Their target was a part-time UDR man, Ricky Connolly, who worked at Bellevue Zoo in Belfast. X, disguised as a postman, was to shoot him dead.

As there was no sign of life from the house where Black was supposed to be sleeping and which was expected to provide the car for the operation, they all bedded down where they were for the night. At 6.30 they woke.

We all went down to the living-room where we just talked about the job. Things like, 'Do you think it will come off?' At about seven o'clock we heard a car stop not far away. I looked out of the door and saw that it was sitting outside the door of the house we had been at earlier. I told [the commanding officer]. He told me to go and get the car. I went up to the house and rapped the door. At first he wouldn't open. He refused to open the door. I went down and told [the commanding officer]. [He] said, 'Go back and shout up, "Irish Republican Army!" ' I did this. He said, 'Who is there?' I said, 'Irish Republican Army. Open the door.' He opened the door and said to me, 'You have to be careful now, you never know who is coming to the door.'

Back at the safe house Black was told to write an address on a registered envelope.

I wrote, 'To Mr Ricky Connolly, c/o Belfast Zoo, Antrim, County Down' [sic]. He took this letter from me and handed it to X. I said, 'X, try and bring that back.' [The commanding officer] said, 'It doesn't matter, they will not be able to prove anything.' X and [his accomplice] Y left the house. X had the gun down the waistband of his trousers and hid by the coat . . . 'The two of them left about 8.00 am . . . I saw the car they drove off in. It was a blue colour, I think it had an aerial from the front looped over to the back. It had a lot of badges on the radiator and the wind-screen. About twenty minutes later while me and [the commanding officer] were trying to get the police messages on the radio, X walked in, still in the postman's uniform. [The commanding officer] said, 'Well?' X said, 'He is dead. I hit him twice in the heart and once in the head.'

Black's evidence provides one of the last glimpses of the IRA in the days before the emphasis switched to political activity. As his account makes clear, much energy still went into policing the ghetto, a role the IRA had taken on from the outset. The reluctance of many of the inhabitants of West Belfast to involve themselves with the RUC meant that the Provisionals took responsibility for dealing with a certain amount of conventional crime. Their actions, they frequently pointed out, were usually the result of complaints from the residents of the ghetto, and it was not, they insisted, a task they relished. They divided crime into three categories: petty crime, which could be dealt with merely by a warning (some punishment might follow if the offender persisted); serious crime like armed robbery (except where committed by the Provos themselves) and rape, which were punished by wounding; and crimes against the IRA, such as informing or defrauding the organisation, which were punishable by death.

Before a punishment was carried out there was a rudimentary hearing. There was a theoretical right of appeal but it was rarely exercised. By 1981 the movement's nascent political senses dictated that young joyriders and glue-sniffers were punished by being forced to do 'socially useful work' such as cleaning the homes of old people. The habit of 'knee-capping', however, lingered on. By July of 1986 there had been 1,097 cases. Victims were taken to one of Belfast's many stretches of wasteland, forced to lie down, then shot through the back of the legs with a small calibre pistol. The punishment squad then called an ambulance. The Provos disliked the term 'kneecapping'. They claimed that it was inexact, as the shoot-ings were graded in severity. Some were mere 'stigma' shooting through the fleshy part of the thigh. Firing through the joints was reserved for serious crimes. In exceptional cases offenders were shot through the knees and elbows. If the offender was lucky he was out of the hospital in a week. A combination of bad light, a nervous gunman and a struggling victim made for some horrific injuries.

Eventually Adams decreed that punishment shootings were to be halted completely. According to one IRA man, 'It was bad for the public image. People were asking how we could go out and shoot a wee lad when we couldn't shoot the British.'[1] For a while offenders were beaten with iron bars and hurley sticks instead.

The IRA never gave up the right to shoot its enemies in the community. The organisation had been plagued with informers from the beginning, but the problem became particularly acute with the opening of the Castlereagh interrogation centre in 1977. Many of the informers were IRA men who broke down under questioning and confessed to crimes and then agreed to supply information to the RUC Special Branch in return for immunity. Acting as a 'tout' for the security forces was a bleak, nerve-fraying existence. On his release the informer was given a codename ('Rugby man', 'Jelly'), a telephone number on which to contact his 'handler' and three designated meeting-places. In Belfast these were on Lisburn Road, Shaftesbury Square and around the University, at a safe distance from the usual haunts of the Provisionals who rarely moved out of the security of West Belfast. On arrival, the handler would cruise the streets ensuring that he was not the victim of a set-up, then take his contact off to a city centre pub for a drink. The informer is expected to provide details of personnel, weapons and forthcoming actions. Often the RUC will allow a minor operation to go ahead rather than risk compromising a source. Sometimes, if the informer is taking part, he will be asked to baulk the operation by sabotaging the detonator or the car. At the end of the session the informer is rewarded. The fee is rarely more than £20. It is fear, not money, that cements the relationship.

Despite the persistence of the problem it was not until 1980 that the IRA set up a formal security department to counteract it. Its members were originally drawn from the bomb department who were inactive at the time. The department's first coup was the discovery that Peter Valente, a 33-year-old from the Unity Flats, was a long-standing police informer. Valente, a Provisional volunteer and an H-Block Committee activist, had provided the RUC with a stream of information about IRA personalities and arms dumps over several years. He was discovered when he passed on to his handler the dramatic information that a member of the RUC was selling information to the IRA − including details of informers. Valente was instructed to contact the man by purporting to be acting for the Provisionals, and arrange to meet him to hand over some cash. When they met at a rendezvous in North Belfast, the Special Branch were waiting and the man was forced to resign from the force. The incident sealed Valente's fate. The news of his involvement filtered back to the security department and he was arrested, tried, and executed on 14 November 1981. During his interrogation he provided the names of six other informers who were also shot dead over the next twelve months. They included Maurice Gilvarry, who had worked for the RUC since being taken into Castlereagh in 1977; Paddy Traynor, who began informing after being arrested on the border in 1976; and Vincent Robinson, who was executed in June 1981. Robinson's codename was 'H-Block'. The RUC had done a particularly thorough job in infiltrating the H-Block Committees, and all four were members.

Executions of touts were sometimes accompanied by accusations of torture. The family of Anthony Braniff ('Jelly' to his handler) and a contemporary of Christopher Black in the Ardoyne IRA, claimed that he had been tortured before being shot in September 1981 for giving information about arms dumps. *Republican News* later indignantly denied the charge, announcing that he had made a statement saying he had no complaints about his treatment by his captors before they killed him. The scorch-marks found on his body were attributed to powder burns from the shooting.

In fact the IRA men seemed on the whole to be content with the quality of the organisation's justice. The security department was expected to build up a reasonable dossier of information on a suspect before pulling him in, sidling around the bars of Belfast to pick up intelligence, a practice that soon brought its members the inevitable unpopularity of the policeman. Like policemen, they worked on hunches. According to a former Belfast IRA man in the case of one man,

> They didn't know what it was but they just had a feeling about him. Some people seen him in town, drinking the wine and offering a Brit some of the wine in Barry Street. So they found out that wee snippet and a few other things, like he was arrested with stolen property and wasn't charged, so there was a strong feeling he was up to something. They didn't know what it actually was. So what they did was they set the house up and lured him there by hook or by crook. They could have picked him up, a carload of them and pushed him into the car but they didn't want that because they weren't really sure. So they just said, 'the boys want to talk to you.' So he comes.[1]

The suspect was then blindfolded, bound hand and foot, and his shoes and socks removed before the interrogation began. The technique involved is 'the usual good guy, bad guy. One would be saying: "Look, you done this you bastard," and the other would say "Leave him alone, we don't know, we'll see." ' He eventually confessed that he had been working for the police for several years since he had got out of jail. He signed a confession which was shown to the Belfast Brigade OC who gave his approval for him to be 'nutted'. As the sentence was about to be carried out, however, a security force patrol came on the scene, the executioners fled and he made his escape through a fog which had helpfully descended.[7]

Punishment shootings and executions were carried out with the same detachment as the rest of the IRA's activities. According to a former IRA man, once sentence had been passed, an execution squad would be told, ' "Get ready, stand by. You might be doing a nut job." They'd go and pick him up and take him to such and such a place. They'd have a car and take him away and nut him without getting into any general conversation, like. To them he would just be another baddie.'[1]

For many years it had been IRA practice to subject members

released after interrogation at Castlereagh to an exhaustive debriefing. This was to find out if they had given anything away and to discover what line of questioning the police had taken, an invaluable guide to the state of the RUC's intelligence. The experience with Valente and the others eventually led the IRA to try more subtle methods of dealing with informers. In January 1982 they announced a two-week amnesty for informers. Since that time the policy has been that repentant informers will not be punished and *Republican News* occasionally publishes salutary stories to that effect. The 27 March 1986 issue reported that a 24-year-old from Whiterock, West Belfast who was picked up on motoring charges 'foolishly agreed to act as the eyes and ears of the RUC in his area', but that later 'the strain of living with the continual pressure became intolerable and although very frightened of the RUC, [he] approached Sinn Fein Councillor Sean Keenan and asked for his help'.

Executions continued, however. In September 1985 a young couple, Catherine and Gerard Mahon, were shot to death in Turf Lodge, West Belfast, trying to escape from an IRA execution squad. Mr Mahon, a 28-year-old mechanic, had been recruited by the RUC Special Branch after being arrested for driving offences. With the encouragement of the police, he allowed the IRA to use his house to dump weapons. The dump was fitted with an electronic device which alerted the local Woodburn police station every time it was interfered with, allowing a surveillance team to monitor the movements to and from the house. This led, the IRA claims, to three operations being 'set up'. The horrified reaction of local people to the shooting was regarded by the IRA as having only beneficial results. According to a senior member of the IRA security department, the bodies of executed informers are deliberately left in public places as a warning to others. 'Usually when a body is left on the street two or three people come forward and give themselves up,' he said. 'That's two or three less to do us damage and two or three less to be executed.'[1]

Life in the IRA induced paranoia. Its members had a

tendency to credit the security forces surveillance equipment with extraordinary qualities. According to one member,

> The IRA believe that a house can be bugged through a telephone when the telephone is not being used. The houses in which the IRA meet where there is a telephone they will leave the room or disconnect it. Or they'll go to the kitchen and turn on the tap or the radio to make a crackling noise to disrupt the feedback. They also believe that the Brits leave bugs when they search houses so when they talk of IRA things they will play some sort of music in the background.

The helicopters that constantly hover over the ghettos are thought particularly sinister by some of the volunteers.

> If there is a helicopter in the air they very rarely get an operation off the ground . . . they say that he [the pilot] is probably nicking them with field glasses . . . they also believe that they can pick up sound and hear people talking and that, going along the streets. There are people who believe that the helicopters actually follow them and in one case it did happen, when three girls were caught in Navan Green with incendiary devices. One of the girls came up from the Andytown [*Andersonstown*] Road, and walked straight into a house and five minutes later the Brits and Peelers were in on top of them.[1]

In the mid-eighties the Provisionals were finally able to carry out wide-scale monitoring of the security forces themselves. They first obtained radio equipment capable of breaking into Army and police networks in the early seventies but it was not extensively available until they purchased twenty or thirty sets equipped with an electronic scanner which could sift through the security force frequencies and lock on to a particular signal, tracking the movements of patrols. Their use cut down the need for the large numbers of scouts 'doing dick' at street corners. They also used radios to communicate with each other. During operations they worked in code, using the jargon of mini-cab drivers and gas men to frustrate any security force surveillance of the networks.

The paranoia of the IRA was intensified in 1981 by the advent of a seemingly new type of informer, the 'supergrass'. The term dated from 1974 and had first been used in connection with five English criminals who had taken part in armed robberies and who turned Queen's Evidence against their accomplices in return for reduced sentences. There was nothing in law to prevent the same practice arising in Northern Ireland. What was lacking was a compliant body.

On the night of Friday 21 November 1981 Christopher Black and other members of the ASU, armed, and masked and wearing combat jackets, set up road-blocks around the 'Bone' to check cars entering and leaving the area. It was purely a propaganda exercise, designed to show the Catholics of West Belfast that the IRA was ready to defend them in the event of sectarian violence provoked by the death of Robert Bradford, MP whom they themselves had killed the previous Saturday. Later that evening, still in his combat jacket, Black was stopped by the police, who discovered his hood in an alleyway where he had thrown it on seeing them. He was arrested and taken to Castlereagh. All Sunday and Monday he obeyed the Provisional's golden rule and said nothing. On Monday evening, during his third interview, he asked the two detective sergeants interrogating him: 'Look, if I admit my part, will youse keep me right?' According to the police interview notes:

Black was told to tell us what he knows and it is up to the courts to decide what will happen to him. Black said 'If I help youse, will youse help me?' He was told we can't give any promises. Black said 'I have been about and know a lot and could help youse.'

Senior officers were brought in. Black had three demands before he would talk: a guarantee for his and his family's safety, passage out of the country and immunity from prosecution. The officers, according to their own evidence, offered no promises but said they would put the request to the authorities. Describing the scene in his summing up at the subsequent trial, Mr Justice Kelly said that Black sat for a long time wondering what retribution the IRA would exact.

> He sat nervously drinking tea, smoking cigarettes. He was hesitant and thoughtful. He did not speak for some time. Then he said: 'I suppose I'll have to trust youse then. I want to get out. I'm fed up with this whole thing. I'm sorry I ever got mixed up with the Provos. They are no good.'

Like all supergrasses, bar one, who were to follow him, Black was motivated by entirely selfish considerations and like the vast majority of IRA prisoners he expressed no regret for his actions. The exception among the supergrasses was Kevin McGrady, who after leaving Belfast for Holland in 1976 fell in with a Christian evangelical sect and decided to come back and give himself up.

Until Black, the IRA membership had shown an extraordinarily solid face to the police and the courts. This was partly motivated by self-interest, partly an expression of the camaraderie of a group of men who, however darkly fanciful it might seem to the outside world, regarded themselves as soldiers in a legitimate army and who, on capture, had a soldier's obligations towards his comrades. Black's betrayal, and that of the other supergrasses, was an expression of warweariness. He was 27 years old. Five years of his youth had been spent in the Long Kesh cages. If he had thought that he could get away with it, no doubt he would have maintained his silence. But in the circumstances of his capture, a conviction for membership of the IRA seemed inevitable and the prospect of another lengthy term of imprisonment became unbearable.

Black's decision produced panic in the IRA. No one was sure how much he knew. The senior members of the Belfast IRA prepared to go on the run. After the initial hysteria had subsided, however, the leadership decided on the cooler but more risky tactic of staying put and gambling on being able to discredit both Black and the immunity deal that was being struck. Adams announced publicly that he expected to be arrested at any moment. In the end, the upper reaches of the movement were untouched by any of the supergrasses (with the possible exception of Jim Gibney, whose activities by then were entirely political, who was convicted on the word of the evangelical McGrady).

At first the development seemed disastrous. The existence of the IRA depended on the maintenance, whether by fear or loyalty or both, of silence in the face of the enemy. If this were to crack the whole organisation could be brought crashing down. Black was followed by McGrady, whose evidence resulted in ten being charged. After that there was John Grimley, a drunkard and a braggart whose testimony led to twenty-two republicans being charged. With the decision of a Belfast IRA man, William 'Bo' Skelly, to co-operate, the situation grew more alarming. One of those named by him, Robert Lean, decided to turn supergrass himself. Once a prisoner learnt that he was implicated in another's testimony the temptation to talk was enormous.

As well as avoiding prison, potential supergrasses were offered the prospect of a new life and identity in the country of their choice, private education for their children, a healthy pension for life — 'like supplementary benefit only far more'[8] — and even elocution lessons to neutralise their Belfast accents.

These blandishments were competing with some powerful forces. Most of the supergrasses went through prolonged agonies of indecision before making their choice. The very act of breaking silence to talk to the police was enough to put them under a cloud when they were returned to be debriefed by the security department. If they stayed silent, most of them faced life imprisonment. If they talked, they faced death outside. After the decision had been taken supergrasses had the psychological trauma of being brought face to face with former comrades. One remembers a veteran member of the IRA who was brought in front of him in Castlereagh vomiting as he named him.[7]

After the initial panic the IRA worked out a two-handed approach to winning the supergrasses back. As long as their evidence had not been corroborated it was possible for them to retract it, thereby destroying the basis of the prosecution case. In order to encourage them they broadcast the fact, via their families, that no harm would come to them if they withdrew their charges. In March 1982 they publicly announced an amnesty, promising supergrasses a safe passage to the South. When this was not enough they made implicit or explicit threats against their families. The wife of Robert Brown was kidnapped until he retracted. One by one the supergrasses went back on their stories.

At the same time the supergrass system was coming under pressure from other quarters. It had been a controversial development from the beginning, and considerably stretched the original and discredited concept which had been used in Britain to break up organised robbery gangs. In British supergrass trials, no one had been convicted on the word of one witness without any corroborating evidence, a sharp contrast to the Northern Ireland experience, where fifty-four per cent of those convicted in the ten cases that came to court were found guilty on such evidence.

Concern about the system was voiced by prominent Catholic and Protestant clergymen, trade unionists, Canadian and American legal observers, the British Liberal and Labour parties, Amnesty International and the Irish Government. Disquiet about the quality of the justice was increased by the poor quality of the supergrasses' evidence. John Grimley and Raymond Gilmour appear to have been police agents; John Morgan had been convicted of his brother-in-law's manslaughter before becoming a member of both the INLA and the IRA; Robert Quigley, another IRA man, claimed at the trial of those charged on his evidence that he felt no remorse for the widows or families of the IRA's victims, that he had lied on oath and he had turned Queen's Evidence merely to save his own skin.[9]

One of those implicated in an attempted murder by the supergrass Kevin McGrady turned out to have been in prison at the relevant time, whereupon McGrady substituted the name of his brother. After the McGrady trial in November 1983, presided over by Lord Lowry who described some of the evidence as 'contradictory, bizarre and in some respects, incredible', Northern Ireland judges became less willing to convict on supergrass evidence, and as the number of witnesses grew, the system fell into disuse. Even the Christopher Black case turned out badly from the security forces' point of view when the appeals of eighteen men convicted on his word were upheld in July 1986. Supporters of the system had claimed that supergrass trials could have a devastating effect on paramilitary activity — republican and loyalist — possibly wiping them out altogether. These claims were shown to be wildly exaggerated. Indeed, some legal observers later claimed that the disrespect for the law in Northern Ireland that the system bred could be on a similar scale to that generated by the introduction of internment.[10]

CHAPTER TWENTY-TWO

The Politics of Revenge

After the intoxicating success of the early days of the electoral strategy, Sinn Fein came down to earth as Adams knew it must. The sobering draught was provided by the elections to the European parliament held on 14 June 1984. The contest posed greater difficulties for Sinn Fein than its previous excursions to the polls. For one thing, the election would have to be fought on a broad front, as Northern Ireland was regarded as one constituency electing three members, and the party would be unable to concentrate its efforts in the areas where it knew it was strong. For another, if Adams stood, he would be pitting himself against the formidable figure of the SDLP's John Hume. Adams' defeat would provide republicanism's enemies with a powerful propaganda weapon. Adams prudently decided to forgo the candidacy and Danny Morrison ran instead.

The SDLP fought a vigorous and skilful campaign and, compared to Hume, Morrison cut a frivolous figure with Catholic voters. When the count was announced, Sinn Fein had only managed to attract 91,476 votes, 11,125 fewer than they had polled in the general election the previous year. Adams had always been concerned that the early victories would create a climate of expectation which could lead to disillusionment when the first, inevitable reversal came. He and the rest of the party leadership put the most constructive gloss possible on the result, assuring the movement that it was a necessary dose of reality. Despite this setback the political strategy was by now well entrenched in the movement and political activities were absorbing an increasing amount of its time. To maintain the momentum created by elections, the Sinn Fein leadership had decided in 1984 to allow its members who were elected to local authorities in Northern Ireland to take their seats, just as their counterparts in the South had already done.

The local councils had few powers but they provided a useful forum for political activity. By 1986 there were fifty-six Sinn Fein councillors on local authorities and their presence in the chambers enraged Unionists, especially when they deliberately set out to provoke them by such calculated insults as refusing to stand in silence to honour assassinated UDR men. Membership of the councils also helped Sinn Fein's efforts to establish itself as the most effective guardian of the social welfare of the Catholics. For, as Adams remarked, 'the plebs are fickle', and constant nurturing was necessary to promote the process of 'republicanisation'.[1] By 1984 Sinn Fein was established in the ghettoes of Belfast and Derry as the most efficient means of redress against the agencies of the State, with more advice bureaux than the rest of the Northern Ireland political parties put together. In Belfast they had two advice centres, where Adams led a team of councillors and helpers tirelessly processing complaints against the Housing Executive and the Department of Health and Social Security. Its money and greater energy meant that it easily overshadowed the SDLP. At the same time there were frequent unofficial interventions into domestic strife. Sinn Fein members often arbitrated in cases of wife battering, rape and child abuse, presenting themselves as an alternative to the social services offered by the State.

Outside the ghetto Sinn Fein was regarded with a complicated ambivalence by the Catholic population which was reflected in voting patterns. Despite the anathemas regularly handed out by the church, despite the regular, alienating acts of murderous stupidity, at the end of the day many 'respectable' Catholics were prepared to cast a vote for Sinn Fein if only to keep the Protestant, Unionist out. The single transferable vote, multi-candidate constituency system that operates in Northern Ireland allows voters to vote in order of preference. Citing a candidate as a second choice increases his chances of election as he will receive a proportion of your first choice candidate's surplus votes about the quota necessary to get elected.

A study carried out by S. Elliot and F. J. Smith of Queen's University Belfast (Northern Ireland: The District Council Elections of 1985, The Queen's University of Belfast 1986) revealed that in the 1982 Assembly election the average transfer of votes from the SDLP to Sinn Fein was 22.4 per cent and from Sinn Fein to the SDLP 55.8 per cent.

In the 1985 district council elections, 34 per cent of SDLP voters gave their transfers to Sinn Fein, with 50.5 per cent of Sinn Fein votes passing to the SDLP.

The message of these figures is that despite being in no doubt of Sinn Fein's policies a large majority of constitutional Catholics still felt able to give them their support, if it meant excluding a Unionist from office. This fundamental tribalism among a sizeable proportion of Catholics outside the ghettoes has been a common source of comfort to Adams and Sinn Fein, that as long as Unionism remains so unsympathetic to Catholics, Sinn Fein will retain a viable level of support.

The heavy concentration on such activities was not popular with everyone. Inevitably, complaints that Adams had lost heart in the military aspect of the campaign continued. In 1985 the militarists launched their most serious challenge so far. The main personality behind it was Ivor Bell, the veteran OC of Northern Command and Adams' friend, companion in prison, and co-author of the reconstruction of the IRA in the late 1970s. Bell's grievance was that the organisation's resources were being concentrated on the Sinn Fein political machine and that there was not enough money to pay volunteers or to fund operations. Bell's supporters claimed that Paddy Adams, Gerry's brother, had been imposed on the Belfast IRA in order to stifle military activity in the city. At one point Bell canvassed the idea of a special general army convention at which the direction in which Adams was taking the movement would be challenged. When news of the planned confrontation reached Adams he moved quickly. Those whom

Bell had approached for support were interviewed and made to swear statements. A court martial was called but Bell declined to attend. Although Adams made several attempts to repair the old friendship it was made plain that whatever happened he would not be allowed to play a role in the movement again.[1]

The episode demonstrated the pervasiveness of Adam's control over the movement. Although the argument over the electoral strategy was to break out in public again two years later, and result in a split in the movement, these internal rebellions were the dying kicks of a form of republicanism that was outmoded, outvoted and outgunned. Most IRA members accepted that military activity was largely affected by external factors. For one thing, weapons and ammunition were becoming harder, more expensive and riskier to come by, especially in America. The international intelligence organisations' efforts against the IRA were increasingly cohesive. In February 1982 a joint surveillance operation involving the British, Irish, Canadian and American security services ended in the arrest of one of the main IRA men responsible for arms procurement overseas, Ted Howell, and a companion, Desmond Ellis, who were carrying a shopping list for 200 cases of mixed ammunition and remote control model aircraft capable of transporting twenty-five pounds in weight. These, the intelligence services concluded, were to be converted into flying bombs. Seventeen months later three Irishmen were jailed for plotting to smuggle 'Redeyes', the ground-to-air missiles the IRA longed to obtain in order to knock down Army helicopters, into Ireland.

The most dramatic illustration of the dangers of running guns from America came in the autumn of 1984 when the IRA spent an estimated £1.5 million in the US on a massive shipment of seven tons of rifles, machine-guns and ammunition. The arsenal had been assembled by an American-born former Marine, John Crowley. Before the cargo, stowed in the merchant ship the *Valhalla*, left the East Coast on 23 September 1984, an informer among republican sympathisers in Boston tipped off the American authorities. The FBI informed British intelligence who tipped off Dublin. As the *Valhalla* steamed eastwards it was tracked by an American satellite 300 kilometres above the earth. A hundred and twenty kilometres off the coast of Ireland it recorded the gun-laden cases being transferred to the trawler *Marita Anne*. As she made her way back to her home port of Fenit, County Kerry she was intercepted by two Irish navy vessels and the crew was arrested. The three men on board, who included Martin Ferris, a former member of the Sinn Fein, were sentenced to ten years' imprisonment each.

One result of these disasters was to shift the IRA's procurement efforts to Europe and the conventional arms-dealers, but the IRA's reputation did not prevent them from being cheated on a number of occasions. Amsterdam, with its scores of camouflaging nationalities and its liberal disinclination to probe the credentials of strangers, became a centre of IRA operations. It was also easy to get to. It was a simple matter for an IRA man to sail with a sympathetic merchant crew from Waterford, Sligo or Cork to Le Havre, and board a train to Paris or Amsterdam without encountering a single passport check. Even if operators were stopped, IRA forgers were now masters of their art and could produce decent false documents at eight hours' notice.[2] The route worked equally well in reverse, and arms purchased in Belgium or Holland could be loaded on to a ship in Rotterdam and slipped ashore with the cargo in the Republic with relatively little fuss.

This conduit became dangerous following a raid one freezing morning in January 1986 when, following a tip-off from Scotland Yard, the Dutch security police raided a smart modern apartment in a suburb of Amsterdam and arrested Brendan 'Bik' McFarlane, who had been on the run since escaping from the Maze in October 1983; Gerry Kelly, another Maze escaper; and the ubiquitous 'Blue Boy' Kelly. Inside the flat they found maps of numerous European cities, false Irish and British passports, several thousand pounds' worth of currency in different denominations, guns and keys. There were also some volumes of poetry. The keys turned out to fit a lorry container parked by the docks, which was piled with drums of nitrobenzine explosive.

The increasing technical sophistication of the IRA's enemies from the late seventies onwards meant that the pattern of violence in Northern Ireland changed. With the success of the Army and police in Belfast and Derry the battleground had steadily been moving away from the cities and into the countryside. IRA assassinations increasingly took place in the rural areas where the security forces' surveillance was less concentrated and the IRA could rely on good local intelligence. They attacked them where they were most vulnerable: off duty and unarmed, as they relaxed at home or in a bar, or in the case of the part-time soldier or policeman, as they went about their civilian work. For long periods, almost all the killing was confined to the countryside. In the first six months of 1985, the IRA killed eleven RUC men, eight police reservists, one soldier and two members of the UDR. Only one, the soldier, was killed in Belfast. In the last six months of 1986 they killed 6 RUC men, 1 RUC reservist, 4 soldiers and 6 members of the UDR, none of them in Belfast. Even so, the ability of the IRA to inflict casualties on the security forces declined steadily after the hunger strikes. In 1981 forty-four members of the police, Army and UDR died at the hands of the IRA, in 1982, forty and the following year, thirty-three. In 1984 it fell again to twenty-eight. It rose again to twenty-nine in 1985 but the downward trend reasserted itself in 1986 when it dropped to twenty-four.

The falling casualty rates were partly due to the increasing efficiency and aggression of the security forces in the countryside. Around 1980, after the disaster at the Narrow Water, the RUC had created a new, highly trained squad directed at confronting the IRA on its own terms. The unit's official name was E4A and it was based at Gough Barracks in Armagh. Its thirty members, all volunteers, were trained by the Special Air Service (SAS) at its headquarters in Hereford, England. The main elements in their new approach, as the Deputy Chief Constable of the RUC, Michael McAtamney, was to declare in court later, were 'firepower and aggression'.

A practical demonstration of their tactics was given on 11

November 1982 when three IRA men, Gervais McKerr, Eugene Toman and Sean Burns were shot dead by members of the squad at a police road-block outside Lurgan. The RUC claimed that they had opened up on the vehicle after it 'tried to escape'. No weapons were found in the car. In the same month there was another incident involving E4A. Michael Tighe, a 17-year-old Lurgan boy, and his 19-year-old friend Martin McCauley, went at teatime to check that all was well at the house of a neighbour who had gone away to look after a sick sister. According to McCauley, they were peering through the window of a hayshed near the cottage when they saw 'the tops of some bits of metal'.

> I didn't know what they were. Neither did Tighe. When we got in the window which was half open we saw three old rifles sitting on a bale of hay. Tighe went to investigate. He had just climbed on to a bale of hay in line with the window when two shots made my ears ring.

Tighe fell back, killed instantly. McCauley 'hunkered backwards' towards cover and was hit by some shots fired through the door.

> There was a second burst of gunfire. I was bleeding heavily with blood spouting from my thigh and I had been hit twice in the back. When the shooting stopped they started to break down the door. I tried to get to my feet. Once one of them saw me he hit me with the butt of the rifle then grabbed me and pulled me through the rest of the door. They dragged me about forty-five yards and dumped me on the grass. One got down on his knees and held my shoulders down. The other guy held a rifle to my head. They asked me my name and who was in the shed. They asked about explosives. I said I didn't know what they were talking about.[3]

With this incident E4A's brief anonymity vanished. Catholic politicians claimed that the RUC was operating a 'shoot to kill' policy to wipe out IRA suspects without having to resort to the tiresome processes of the law. Unlike McKerr, Toman and Burns, Tighe and McCauley had no IRA record. The episode was replete with unanswered questions. The guns were of a pre-war vintage and, ballistics experts later asserted in court, had not been fired for decades. What were they doing stacked openly in the shed? The shed, the police admitted, had been fitted with listening devices, but the tapes had run out before the incident could be recorded. A few weeks later, E4A were in action again. Two INLA men, Roddy Carroll and Seamus Grew, were shot dead near a road-block outside a housing estate predominantly inhabited by nationalists in Armagh City.

Disquiet over the shootings was not confined to Catholic politicians. The magistrate presiding over the inquests of Grew and Carroll resigned over the conduct of the police inquiry. After pressure from the Director of Public Prosecutions, Sir Barry Shaw, the RUC Chief Constable, Sir John Hermon, announced an inquiry. The man chosen to conduct it was the Deputy Chief Constable of Manchester police, John Stalker. At the end of May 1986, before Stalker could complete his inquiries, he was suspended from duty, on suspicion of unprofessional conduct in his choice of off-duty companions (he was later cleared and returned to duty) and the inquiry was passed over to Colin Sampson, Chief Constable of West Yorkshire. The fruits of the Stalker-Sampson inquiry were not to emerge until January 1988. The contents of the report remained a secret. In a statement to the House of Commons on 25 January the Attorney General, Sir Patrick Mayhew, said that after studying the evidence dug up by Stalker and Sampson Sir Barry Shaw had concluded that there had been no 'shoot to kill' policy, and no 'incitement to murder'.

There was, however, evidence that RUC officers had conspired to pervert the course of justice during the inquiry. Despite this admission and the widespread belief in Northern Ireland that up to eight policemen would be prosecuted, Sir Barry decided that it would be against the interests of national security for charges to be brought against anyone. Stalker's work had been dogged from the outset by the security forces' desire to shield details of its informer network. Stalker was repeatedly stalled in his efforts to hear the tape planted by MI5 in the barn where Tighe had been killed, and only granted permission when he promised not to compromise the organisations' field agents. In the end it was the belief that any prosecution would reveal too much about the secret workings of the security forces and the intimate relationship between Army Intelligence, MI5 and the RUC Special Branch that ensured that charges were not brought.

The decision provoked a predictable furore in Dublin and among British Labour politicians. Coming in the same week as the Appeal Court rejected the appeal of the six men convicted of the 1974 Birmingham pub bombings, it contributed to a deep depression in relations between London and Dublin

The security forces continued to confront the ASUs head-on whenever they could. On the evening of 21 February 1984, for example, Declan Martin, 18, and Henry Hogan, 21, two IRA men from Dunloy in North Antrim, were killed when they encountered an undercover patrol of the SAS, an episode which also claimed the life of a soldier. Two years later another undercover Army patrol tracked down the most famous member of the IRA border ASUs. Since breaking out of the Maze prison the previous October, Seamus McElwaine had returned to the border country. He spent much of that winter living rough with other members of the unit, roaming the wet wind-scoured country where Fermanagh meets Monaghan, planting and blowing mines and occasionally sniping at military and police patrols. They slept in barns and outhouses, sometimes slipping back over the border to recuperate in the relative safety of their base near Monaghan town. Three hours before dawn on the morning of 26 April 1986, McElwaine and a companion were trekking up a farm track laden with packs and rifles on their way to detonate a mine they had buried on the Roslea-Donagh Road at the passing of the first patrol. As they moved through a gap in a rough stone wall the Army team opened up, hitting McElwaine in the chest and killing him. Later, at the funeral, Martin McGuinness declared over his grave: 'In prison yards all over Britain and Ireland, they remember him. He was a brave, intelligent soldier, a young man who willingly gave up his youth to fight for the freedom of his country . . . he will be remembered in the towns and villages of Fermanagh and Monaghan. His name will live for ever.'

One new element in the conflict in the countryside was the refinement of a weapon which had been previously used with erratic results by the IRA, the mortar bomb. The development of the mortar gave the ASUs the means of striking the police in what they had hitherto regarded as the relative safety of their barracks. Mortars had first appeared in 1974 but they were crude and unreliable devices and it was not until 1979 that they succeeded in killing anyone. The 'engineers' continued experimenting, test-firing prototypes on the lonely strands of Donegal. Eventually, after going through about ten modifications a reasonably efficient missile was constructed. The bombs themselves were welded out of steel pipes, flighted by heating vanes and fired from industrial tubing. The first indication of the power of the new weaponry came in February 1985. Members of the specially created mortar unit parked a lorry a few hundred yards away from the Edward Street Barracks in Newry. Bolted on the back was a crude mortar battery loaded with bombs. The team then withdrew leaving a timing device to provide an electrical charge which sent the bombs arching through the sky to drop with devastating effect inside the barracks wall. The attack killed nine policemen. The border teams were delighted with the new weapon. One spoke of 'the exhilaration of watching the bombs climbing up into the night sky and falling like a stone on the police station'.[4]

After the Newry attack mortars were used regularly, but with less spectacular results. In 1985 there were ten attacks. Poor intelligence before an attack on the Enniskillen police training centre in 1985 meant that thirty cadets who were expected to be lying in their beds asleep were eating breakfast when the bombs landed, a mistake which saved their lives. In November 1986 there was another attack on the Edward Street police station in Newry. A flight of bombs fell short of their targets and rained down on houses in the centre of the city, seriously wounding a 4-year-old Catholic girl and injuring another thirty-eight people. The incident provoked a grudging admission from the IRA that 'this incident left us open to justified criticism'.

One benefit of the use of mortars was that the damage wreaked on the fabric of police barracks meant that extensive rebuilding programmes were soon under way, offering the IRA another opportunity to disrupt and intimidate. Most of the work was put out to local contractors. Shortly after the first Newry attack the IRA announced that any builder involved in the repairs would be shot. This form of 'collaboration' with the British forces had been unaccountably overlooked by the IRA in the past. Once the decision had been taken, the IRA leadership began to regret the fact that they had not done so years before. Such a policy could have stretched the building of Meghaberry, the new high security prison next to the Maze, into the twenty-first century. As it was, there was still great potential for disruption. The first victim was Seamus McAvoy, who supplied Portakabins to the RUC. He was shot dead at his Dublin home in August 1985. An Armagh electrical contractor, who had previously supplied the lighting to the Catholic cathedral, but also to several police stations, was shot dead on a lonely road in County Armagh. Inevitably the supply of builders willing to risk their lives for a contract disappeared. The police were forced to use Army engineers to build and repair police barracks, a development which had the welcome result of returning British soldiers to a more vulnerable position.

The concentration of IRA violence in the countryside in the mid eighties, and the general pressure of IRA's operations in Northern Ireland was a cause of great concern for the IRA leadership. Belfast remained the psychological and political centre of the organisation, yet the IRA were finding it highly dangerous to operate there. One way of maintaining morale was to resume attacks in Britain. The campaign there had suffered a considerable set-back in March 1979 when Brian Keenan, regarded by his friends and enemies alike as possessing the best organisational brain in the IRA, had been arrested in Belfast and returned to stand trial in Britain on the strength of fingerprints found at two of the Balcombe Street gang's bomb factories in London. It was a measure of his importance that plans to rescue him were immediately hatched. The IRA team, which included Gerard Tuite, who had taken part in a British bombing campaign the previous year, two senior IRA men, Bobby Campbell and Bobby Storey, and a middle-aged republican, Dickie Glenholmes, were under police surveillance from the moment they arrived and were eventually picked up and incarcerated in Brixton prison, from which with the aid of a helicopter they had planned to liberate Keenan.

In the wake of the hunger strikes there had been a further upsurge of operations in Britain. In autumn 1981 a team including Paul Kavanagh and Thomas Quigley, both of whose brothers had been shot dead by the security forces, travelled to London. In October they exploded a bomb outside Chelsea Barracks injuring forty soldiers and civilians and killing a woman passer-by and a teenage boy of Irish descent. Later, a bomb disposal expert was killed trying to defuse one of their bombs, and they blew up but failed to kill Sir Steuart Pringle, the Commanding Officer of the Royal Marines, as he got into his car at his home in Dulwich. In November the Wimbledon home of the Attorney General, Sir Michael Havers, was virtually demolished by a bomb.

The police were unaware of the bombers' identities until the end of 1983 when forestry workers felling trees in a Berkshire wood came across some clumsily buried dustbins. The fingerprints on the guns and explosives inside were soon identified as belonging to Kavanagh and Quigley, as well as to two well known IRA activists, Evelyn Glenholmes and Patrick Magee. Quigley was arrested in Belfast in December. Kavanagh, however, was still at large in Britain where the police believe he took part in the Harrods bombing that month. He was eventually arrested when he returned to Belfast to celebrate St Patrick's day in 1983. Both he and Quigley were sent to prison for thirty-five years.

In 1982 bombs went off in Hyde Park and Regents Park killing eight people and injuring fifty-three. These operations were routine, however, compared to what was planned. Sometime after the death of Bobby Sands, the leadership had decided to concentrate their efforts on a spectacular demonstration of the IRA's power to extract revenge.

As a result of the hunger strike Margaret Thatcher had become the most hated figure in the demonology of republicanism. Gerry Adams considered her 'an Irish folk memory. She will be remembered when even some of the names of the hunger strikers are forgotten. All the 6- and 7-year-olds have the memory of Thatcher in their heads.'[1] Before the hunger strikes were over, the leadership had decided to try and kill her. In 1982 the mainland planners began tracing the pattern of her movements, deciding that their best opportunity would come at the annual Conservative Conference, when the political desirability of allowing the foot soldiers and the party's high command to mingle, plus a certain sentimental attachment to the free and easy arrangements of the old days, meant that security checks were abnormally lax.

Two IRA scouts made a preliminary reconnaissance at the Brighton conference of September 1982, moving among the delegates as they mixed with the mighty in the bars of the Grand and Metropole Hotels on the seafront. The next year's conference was at Blackpool. A veteran of the mainland campaign, Patrick Magee, and another man visited the town early in the new year but in the end it was decided to delay until 1984.

Magee was born in Belfast in 1951 but his family had moved to Norwich in East Anglia while he was still young. At the age of 15 he attracted the attention of the police and appeared before a juvenile magistrates court charged with breaking into shops. For this he was given two years' probation but before the term was up he was in court again for stealing from a car. When he was 18 he was convicted a third time, for stealing books from a shop. In 1971 Magee returned to Belfast and moved into Unity Flats, then a perpetual battleground between the IRA and the security forces. In June 1973 he was arrested under an interim custody order, admitting membership of the

IRA, and was not released until November 1975. In 1978, together with Gerard Tuite, he arrived in Britain and planted sixteen bombs in London, Manchester, Liverpool, Coventry and Southampton.

The rumour that an attempt was about to be made on the Prime Minister's life reached the RUC who passed it on to Scotland Yard, but the details were vague. The Prime Minister's security advisers decided that the most likely point of attack was on her twice-weekly drive from Downing Street to the House of Commons for Prime Minister's Question Time and for a while there were systematic checks of cars lining the route and searches of the sewers and service tunnels.

Around lunchtime on 15 September 1984 a taxi picked up Magee, bearded and wearing a leather jacket, at Brighton station and drove him down the hill to the Grand Hotel. There he signed in under the name of Roy Walsh of Braxfield Road, Lewisham, South London and paid £180 for three nights' accommodation and half board. 'Roy Walsh' was a risky piece of bravado − it was the name of a member of the team that had bombed the Old Bailey in 1974. When telephoning the reservation a few days previously he had specified a room with a sea-view at the front of the building. In calculating where to place the bomb Magee and his companions had reckoned on it being a tempestuous conference. The miners' strike was dragging on and the bitterness of the strikers towards the Government was deepening. A march to confront Thatcher at Brighton was planned. Magee calculated that rather than take her customary first-floor suite overlooking the sea, the Prime Minister would opt for a room higher up the building − just in case the miners occupied the hotel. Also, the higher the bomb was placed, the less likelihood there was of its discovery. The planners guessed that as the search teams worked their way through the rooms in the pre-conference sweep their enthusiasm for the job would slacken.

Magee booked himself into a room on the sixth floor, number 629. During his three-day stay he left his room rarely, lunching once in the main restaurant. The staff remember a male companion who was in his room for part of the weekend.

At some point he unscrewed the hardboard bath panel in the bathroom and placed behind it a packet of commercial explosives wrapped in numerous layers of cellophane to mask its distinctive smell. According to the police evidence the explosive weighed between twenty and thirty pounds and was about a foot square. The IRA later insisted that the bomb was much bigger — one hundred pounds — but it is hard to see how such a bulky device could have been successfully hidden in the room. Attached to it was a 'memo park timer' (used in parking meters) and another more sophisticated electronic timing device. The latter was by now a common piece of IRA technology. It was based on the commercial timers found in video recorders and it allowed the bomb to be set to explode months in advance. The first time the Provisionals had used one had been during a visit by the Queen to the University of Coleraine in 1977. The device was buried in the grounds several days before the visit and exploded after she had already departed. Magee had set the timer to detonate the bomb twenty-four days from the date he checked in.

It went off at 2.54 am on Friday 12 October, the last day of the conference. At that moment Mrs Jeanne Shattock was in room 628 apparently running a bath. The blast tore through the wall peppering her with shards of tile, 'driven into her like bullets' the trial later heard, and scorching her flesh. She died instantly. In the room where the bomb was planted were Donald Maclean, a senior figure in the Scottish Conservative Party, and his 54-year-old wife Muriel. Astonishingly, he survived the explosion. Mrs Maclean's leg was shattered and her lungs damaged by the shock wave from the blast and she died a month later.

The explosion broke the back of a massive central chimney stack, sending it crashing down through the twenty-eight rooms below. In room 528 Jennifer Taylor was in bed with her husband.

I remember going to sleep about 2.00 am. We were both terribly tired and I fell asleep very quickly. The next thing I remember is a loud bang. I was lifted upwards and then had the sensation of falling and falling. When I had finished falling I opened my eyes believing I had been dreaming, but I couldn't see anything. My eyes slowly cleared and I found myself sitting on the ground. I saw a wall and a light to my left about four feet away. There was debris all around me — a stainless steel sink, girders, bricks and water, and lots of smoke and dust.

In all, five people died, including the MP for Enfield-Southgate, Sir Anthony Berry, and Roberta Wakeham, the wife of the Government Chief Whip. Thirty others were injured and some permanently disabled. The same day the Provisionals issued a triumphant statement:

> The IRA claim responsibility for the detonation of 100 pounds of gelignite in Brighton, against the British cabinet and the Tory warmongers. Thatcher will now realise that Britain cannot occupy our country, torture our prisoners and shoot our people on their own streets and get away with it.
> Today we were unlucky, but remember, we have only to be lucky once. You will have to be lucky always. Give Ireland peace and there will be no war.

It was signed with the traditional pseudonym 'P. O'Neill' and issued by the Irish Republican Publicity Bureau in Dublin.

The IRA had failed to kill Thatcher or any of the cabinet (they had almost succeeded in the case of the Conservative Party chairman, Norman Tebbit, who was buried for hours under the rubble before being dug out). None the less the leadership regarded the operation as a success. A senior IRA official emphasised this later in comments that illustrate the complicated processes of IRA logic, as well as the fundamental misunderstanding of Thatcher's character:

> It proved the capacity of the IRA to strike where it wanted. Essentially anyone would know that removing Margaret Thatcher as an individual would not necessarily weaken

British policy in Ireland but the fact that you can attack Mrs Thatcher might weaken her resolve to stay in Ireland.

Thatcher has set herself up as a strong leader, therefore the person to weaken is the strongest person and you do that by bringing the war to her front door. Her dying or living is unimportant, but the fact that you can strike at her is important. Without weakening the resolve of that type of person you can never get them to even consider Ireland. The fact that she did not die but now has to look over her shoulder every time she goes out means she can never forget Ireland as a problem. If someone is under that degree of pressure then he or she begins to wonder how valuable Ireland is to that life.[2]

According to the same man, Mrs Thatcher 'will always be a target and if the IRA get the chance to kill her they will'.

Much of the police investigation that followed the blast concentrated on the hotel records. One by one the previous occupants of room 629 were traced and eliminated. No one, however, had heard of Roy Walsh, particularly at Braxfield Road in Lewisham. His hotel registration card was sent to Scotland Yard. There, using a laser and a chemical which reacts to sweat, police experts found prints of a finger and a palm. By the middle of January 1985 the anti-terrorist squad knew that they belonged to Magee but they were reluctant to act immediately. An RUC informer had revealed that another bombing campaign was being prepared and that Magee was once again involved. This knowledge was restricted to a tiny circle of policemen, who spread the fiction that they were still seeking information about the identity of 'Roy Walsh'.

The new offensive that Magee and his companions were working on was a departure from previous bombing operations. The plan, outlined in a document later found on Gerard McDonnell, was for a succession of explosions in London and in a number of holiday resorts. The bombs, planted in hotels or on beaches, would go off every day (except, for some reason, Sundays) around noon for sixteen days. Bombing resorts was their own idea and did not have the specific approval of the

Army Council. The damage done to Adams' attempts to forge links with the British left after the Harrods bomb had persuaded the leadership away from bombings that carried a risk of civilian carnage.[2]

The attacks were to begin in Brighton on 19 July. The following day there would be an explosion at Dover, then Ramsgate, London, Blackpool, London, Eastbourne, and London again. On 28 July there were to be two, one at the Rubens Hotel, near Buckingham Palace, and another at Bournemouth. The remainder were at Torquay, Great Yarmouth, Folkestone, Margate, Southend and Southampton. These bombings, spectacular though they were, were essentially only a diversionary operation. The location and timing of the attacks were designed to throw the British police into confusion, stretching their resources to breaking-point. This would leave the team with an easier task in attacking their main targets: a number of high-ranking politicians and military figures, such as General Sir Frank Kitson, still hated for his counter-insurgency work in Northern Ireland.[2]

The team was led by Gerard McDonnell, a 35-year-old from the Falls Road, known in West Belfast at 'Bloot' because of his bullet-like bald head. He had been arrested in Britain once before, in connection with a bombing in Liverpool in 1977 but had been returned to Belfast for trial in another case, brought after explosives and false documents were found at his home. He was sent to prison for seventeen years, but was one of the thirty-eight prisoners who escaped from the Maze in September 1983. Two women members played a subordinate role, acting as couriers, to front dealings with landlords, and to lend a touch of innocence and normality to the group. Martina Anderson was a former beauty queen who had once entertained the idea of being a model. Instead, she joined the Derry Provisionals and in January 1982 at the age of 20 had been arrested and charged with planting incendiary devices and causing an explosion at a local furniture store; she was bailed, and absconded. Ella O'Dwyer was a rarity, a middle-class university-educated girl from the South with no trace of republicanism in her family. She had been studying at

428

University College, Dublin, traditionally the Catholic university, where she was converted to the IRA cause. In background and temperament she seems to have been very similar to Maria MacGuire, the middle-class Dublin girl whose indiscreet memoirs[5] threw harsh light on to the workings of the IRA leadership. Other peripheral members of the team were Donal Craig, 27, and Sean McShane.

The most interesting figure was Peter Sherry. Sherry's career proved that members of Sinn Fein, even highly visible ones, were not barred from taking part in bombings and shootings. Sherry was a respectable young solicitor's clerk when he first came to the notice of the police in 1974. He was arrested for hijacking a lorry at gunpoint during the funeral of an IRA man killed escaping from the Maze. At the time, he was contrite, admitting to the police that he had 'acted like an idiot'. In 1982 he was arrested on the evidence of supergrass Patrick McGurk and accused of attempting to murder a member of the security forces and armed robbery. The charges were dropped when McGurk withdrew his evidence. In March 1984 Sherry stood as the Sinn Fein candidate against a Unionist in a by-election for a seat on Dungannon council, but managed to attract only forty per cent of the Catholic vote and was soundly beaten. Despite his posture as a conventional politician, his military activities scarcely seem to have slackened. Sherry had a reputation as a marksman and, according to the security forces, was part of an IRA gang that lay in wait for a part-time UDR major one morning in October 1984 as he arrived for work at a creamery in Dungannon. The operation had been betrayed by an informer and the SAS were waiting for them. In the subsequent shoot-out, an innocent passer-by was killed, but Sherry and the rest escaped.

The police kept Sherry and Magee under constant surveillance during the build-up to the offensive. On Saturday 15 June they had watched Magee check into the Rubens Hotel, overlooking the Royal Mews of Buckingham Palace, with an unidentified woman. After he left, the police discovered, hidden beneath a bedside cabinet, a three and a half pound bomb attached to a forty-eight-day timing device and a mercury tilt anti-handling booby-trap which would explode if the device was touched. Despite the positioning of the bomb, the IRA subsequently claimed that the intention was to 'embarrass' the Queen rather than kill her and declared that royalty, for the meantime at least, are not considered to be targets.[6]

Magee stayed in London until 22 June, renting a flat in Hackney Road. Then he boarded a train to Carlisle where he met up at a platform bookstall with Peter Sherry who had arrived on a boat from Larne a little earlier. The meeting was observed by detectives — a man and a woman — posing as an amorous couple on a nearby bench. Magee and Sherry went to Glasgow where they met up with McDonnell and the two women in a ground-floor flat. The police, judging that the bombing offensive was about to begin, decided to move in. The four were sitting down to eat when they burst in.

The membership of the team was an indication of the IRA's difficulties in finding suitable personnel for mainland operations. Sherry, as a Sinn Fein activist, was highly visible; McDonnell was a Maze escaper whose photograph had been blazoned across newspapers and television; and Magee had been the subject of strenuous attempts by the Metropolitan police to extradite him. Of the lesser players, O'Dwyer was a middle-class student of the type the movement had decided to avoid after the Maria MacGuire debacle. One of the minor participants, Donal Craig, was a drunken depressive, who when arrested promptly led the police to another Glasgow safe house stacked with bombs destined for the campaign.

The IRA continued to regard the attempt on Mrs Thatcher's life as a resounding propaganda success, even claiming, on the strength of the relative lack of public outrage at the episode, as measured by the number of insulting telephone calls to the Irish Embassy in London, that it had improved their standing with the British public.[5] Adams and his colleagues believed the attack would frighten the Prime Minister into taking the Irish problem seriously. The attempt on her life certainly caused her to concentrate once again on political formulas. However, the one that was to emerge in the wake of the bombing would give no comfort to the IRA.

CHAPTER TWENTY-THREE

Hillsborough

Since coming to power in 1979 Mrs Thatcher had been involved in several initiatives designed to improve relations between Britain and Ireland. In May and December 1980 she held summit meetings with Charles Haughey of Fianna Fail, who had succeeded Jack Lynch as Prime Minister. Haughey had reiterated the wish of the Irish Government to secure the unity of Ireland but this was to be done 'by agreement and in peace'[1] and any change in the constitutional standing of Northern Ireland would have to be with the consent of the majority in Northern Ireland. Both sides seemed eager to inject more warmth into their relationship. A number of joint studies were inaugurated to examine security and economic co-operation, citizenship rights and possible joint institutional structures.

The hunger strikes in 1981 caused a temporary chill in Anglo-Irish relations but by November of that year they had thawed sufficiently for Garret FitzGerald, whose Fine Gael-Labour coalition had replaced Haughey's government in June, to announce after a summit meeting with Mrs Thatcher the establishment of an Anglo-Irish Intergovernmental Council involving regular meetings between ministers and officials to discuss matters of mutual concern. The following year there was another hiatus in the relationship when the Haughey administration, which returned to power between March and December, gave Britain only limited and grudging support to economic sanctions imposed by the EEC in support of Britain in its war against Argentina in the Falklands.

The Brighton bomb had the effect, as the IRA intended it to, of concentrating the mind of Mrs Thatcher and the media on the Irish problem. It also attracted attention to a significant political event which had been in progress in Ireland for eighteen months but had hitherto drawn only dutiful and sketchy interest from Britain. The New Ireland Forum was set up by Garret FitzGerald in May 1983 but it had been inspired by John Hume, the leader of the SDLP. Hume had begun calling for a 'Council for a New Ireland' to draw up a realistic assessment of how Ireland might be unified during the elections to Prior's inert devolved Assembly in the autumn of 1982. The success of Sinn Fein in that contest gave his proposal an urgency which persuaded FitzGerald to act.

The New Ireland Forum began its discussions in Dublin Castle, the ancient seat of British power in Ireland, on 30 May 1983. It brought together all the constitutional nationalist parties of Ireland — Fine Gael, Labour, Fianna Fail and the SDLP — to articulate their plan for uniting Ireland by consent at the same time as protecting the identity and interests of the Protestant tradition in a new Ireland. The architects of the Forum chose not to invite Sinn Fein because of its refusal to renounce violence to achieve its political aims. On first coming to power FitzGerald, whose parentage embraced the two Irelands (his father fought in the GPO in 1916 and his mother was a presbyterian Unionist), had declared a crusade to reform the constitution, in the process purging it of such elements as the ban on divorce that were potentially repellent to Protestants.

The impetus for the Forum, as the participants frankly proclaimed, was the threat posed to Ireland — North and South — by Sinn Fein, and in particular the prospect that if Sinn Fein succeeded in overtaking the SDLP in the North this would lend a spurious but potentially disastrous legitimacy to republican violence.

In his opening speech, in a passage that showed how power-fully the message of the 'Armalite and the ballot paper' had struck home, FitzGerald declared that by taking part in the Forum the participants were demonstrating a powerful collective rejection of murder, bombing and all the other cruelties that are being inflicted on the population of Northern Ireland in an attempt to secure political change by force. Let the men of violence take note of this unambiguous message from the nationalist people of Ireland: the future of the island will be built by the ballot box and the ballot box alone.[2]

In one sense the Forum was an attempt to eradicate finally the final traces of ambivalence that the Irish State had displayed towards the IRA for much of the period since the trouble began. Sinn Fein and the IRA shared the same heroes and the same fundamental aspiration as the parties of the republic. Indeed, as one historian pointed out, 'the combination of the ballot box and the rifle was the combination which led to the establishment of the twenty-six counties as an independent state'.[3] This historical fact inevitably complicated the reactions of the State to events in the North. At the same time the attitude of the IRA to the Southern state was equally confused. The fact that it was Catholic and Irish did nothing to diminish republicans' contempt for its governments and institutions ('the preserve, by and large, of unprincipled careerists jockeying for the ministerial Mercedes', wrote Gerry Adams)[4] and, if anything, intensified it. At the same time it was an immutable fact that the Twenty-six Counties existed as a hinterland without which the IRA could not operate. It provided it with a launching pad for attacks, a landing point for weapons and explosives, a resting-place when life in the North became too difficult, and a less repressive political climate from which to conduct operations. These considerations imbued a sense of caution in the IRA's approach to Southern sensibilities.

The position of successive Irish administrations since the new troubles began had been to regard the IRA as a subversive and dangerous force at home against which repressive and illiberal measures were justified; at the same time countenancing claims that its crimes were political when it came to the question of IRA men being extradited for offences committed in the North. Section 11 of the Extradition Act of 1965 stated that 'extradition shall not be granted for an offence which is a political offence or an offence connected with a political offence'. In 1971 the Northern Ireland authorities issued thirty-two extradition warrants in connection with subversive activities and a further sixteen in 1972. By October 1982 none had been enforced and early in 1975 the British Lord Chancellor told the House of Lords that not one person had been extradited from the Republic for 'terrorist-type offences'.

The Irish supreme court judges, whatever their private opinions, interpreted the political offence clause with a punctiliousness that infuriated unionists. Some cases aroused special anger. In 1973 Roisin McLaughlin, a 30-year-old Belfast civil servant, was arrested in Cork on a warrant issued in the North alleging that she was one of a group of four girls who had earlier in the year lured four off-duty and unarmed soldiers back to a flat in Belfast with the promise of a party; shortly after they arrived, an IRA man turned up and shot all the soldiers, killing one. The judge discharged McLaughlin with the words: 'There could be no doubt that even murder, and even a dastardly murder such as that described . . . in this case, if carried out by an organisation which, by such methods, sought to overthrow the government of a country by force, was a political offence.'

The prospect of power-sharing in Northern Ireland provided the British Government with a lure to tempt the Irish away from their hard line in this matter. At first, the Cosgrave government had been pressed to abandon the political offence clause, but had resisted. At the Sunningdale conference a Law Enforcement Commission was set up to consider a compromise. After much wrangling the Irish members agreed to support a scheme of extra-territorial jurisdiction in which the courts of each area had the power to try terrorist offenders for offences committed in the other area. This was one of the few acts to survive the collapse of the power-sharing executive and the new arrangement was enshrined in the Criminal Law Jurisdiction Act, introduced to the Dail in November 1974. The measure turned out to make little difference. The legal machinery was rarely cranked into action, and was not used in the Republic until 1980. By 1986 only thirteen prosecutions were undertaken in the South, of which seven were successful. The arrangement satisfied no one. Dublin lawyers complained that the evidence the Northern authorities supplied them with was shoddy and incomplete and accused them of preferring the propaganda advantage of pretending that the South was swarming with terrorist fugitives to undertaking the legal work of bringing offenders to justice.

The lack of progress in devising cross-border legal mechanisms to deal with the IRA contrasted sharply with the vigour shown by the Irish authorities on the home front. When the new troubles began the statute book was already supplied with one formidable measure bequeathed by previous administrations: the Offences Against the State Act, which enabled a person to be convicted of membership of the IRA on the word of a senior police officer. In 1976, following the escape of five IRA men from the basement of the Special Criminal Court in Dublin, Cosgrave's coalition government decided to go further, passing an Emergency Powers Act which gave the police the power to detain suspects for seven days and increased the penalty for membership of the IRA from two to seven years (a move that led to the abandonment of the old practice of refusing to recognise the courts). In another piece of legislation, Dr Conor Cruise O'Brien, the Minister for Posts and Telecommunications, had banned all illegal paramilitary organisations including Provisional Sinn Fein from the airwaves.

These laws were born out of a belief that the IRA was fundamentally to blame for what was happening in Northern Ireland and that if not checked would soon be spreading the same mayhem in the South. In a speech to the Dail in August 1976 Cosgrave declared that 'the principal element in the conflict is undeniably the armed campaign of violence conducted by the IRA against the economy and life of the area'.[5] None the less there were political dangers in emphasising this point. Fine Gael's aggression towards the IRA or conciliation towards the British was invariably exploited by the reflexive nationalists of Fianna Fail, who portrayed such behaviour as supine to British interests and a betrayal of republican principle. The dangers were brought home to Cosgrave in February 1977 when disquiet over the special legislation, exploited by Fianna Fail, contributed to the coalition's defeat in the general election.

This did not deter his successor, Garret FitzGerald, from adopting an unreservedly hostile attitude towards the IRA when he arrived in power. At the same time, partly as a result of new judicial appointments, the attitude of the courts began to harden against the IRA. This became apparent in January 1982 when Dominic McGlinchey, a former IRA man who had joined and eventually become the leader of the INLA and who later boasted of killing thirty people, was arrested on a warrant seeking his extradition to the North. He was wanted for the murder of 67-year-old Mrs Hester McMullan, who had been shot dead when gunmen attacked and wounded her RUC reservist son at Toomebridge, County Antrim in March 1977.

The Irish Chief Justice, Tom O'Higgins, rejected McGlinchey's plea that if returned to the North he would be charged with other offences which were political in nature and in December 1982 gave a judgement which reversed the legal custom of the previous decade. He pronounced that the previous judicial authorities on the subject had been rendered obsolete 'by the fact that modern terrorist violence . . . is often the antithesis of what could reasonably be regarded as political'.[6] The ruling was hailed as a landmark by the incoming Fine Gael administration. The consequence, as the new Attorney General Peter Sutherland pointed out, was that even someone charged with murdering a member of the security forces would no longer be sheltered from extradition by claiming a political motive.

The stiffening of official resolve against the IRA seemed to be matched by a diminution of the sentimental forbearance towards the organisation which the Irish public had displayed so often in the past. The passions aroused by the hunger strikes had died away within a few months of their conclusion, and a spate of incidents served to reinforce the message coming from the courts that the IRA's claims to legitimacy for its actions were ill-founded. In November 1981 an IRA gang kidnapped Ben Dunne, heir to the largest chain of department stores in Ireland, at Killeen, just outside Newry, and held him for six days before releasing him, allegedly after payment of a huge ransom, though this was repeatedly and firmly denied by the Dunne family.

Although the Army Council was fully aware of the effect such adventures had on Irish public opinion a shortage of money, partly imposed by the burdens of running the new political machinery, led them to further kidnappings. The next intended victim was Galen Weston, the dashing, wealthy, polo-playing owner of the international company Adams Foods, which had among its holdings Quinnsworth stores, another shop chain found all over Ireland. A senior IRA source informed the Irish police that the operation was under way and when the kidnap gang arrived at Weston's house just outside Dublin, the Gardai's anti-terrorist unit was lying in wait and captured all the members after a gunbattle. In December 1983 one of Weston's employees, an Englishman called Don Tidey, was kidnapped and held for several weeks before being recaptured in a shootout that left one policeman and an army cadet dead.

The work of the New Ireland Forum then was taking place at a time when public sympathy for the IRA was at a particularly low ebb. When the report was finally unveiled with great fanfare at Dublin Castle, it proved to be something of an anti-climax. The main participants had differing expectations and ambitions for the Forum. Charles Haughey regarded it as a means of constructing a basic constitutional proposal which could then be put to an all-Ireland constitutional conference, convened by the British and Irish governments as a prelude to British withdrawal. In the end the differences between the participants meant that not one but three political models were advanced for consideration. The first, and the one that with a certain amount of prodding Haughey had persuaded the report to endorse as its favoured option, was the traditional aspiration of a 'unitary state', covering the island of Ireland ruled by one government and one parliament elected by all the people of the Thirty-two Counties. The second option was a highly complicated federal or confederal arrangement in which North and South would have their own parliament and executive, presided over by a national government with responsibility for security. The third offering was that Northern Ireland should come under the joint authority of London and Dublin who would have equal responsibility for all aspects of its government. These options were dismissed as 'a bag of dolly mixtures', by Sinn Fein.[7]

The sections of the report condemning terrorism and recognising the validity of the Protestant tradition received expressions of approval from all the British political parties when the report was debated in the House of Commons on 2 July 1984, but the Forum participants would have to wait until 19 November and the summit meeting between Dr FitzGerald and Mrs Thatcher to hear the definitive reaction from the British Prime Minister. That afternoon, at a post-summit press conference, she crushed in a few words the political models that the Forum had so carefully crafted.

> I have made it quite clear [she said when asked her opinion of the three options] . . . that a unified Ireland was one solution that is out. A second solution was confederation of two states. That is out. A third solution was joint authority. That is out. That is a derogation from sovereignty.[8]

Mrs Thatcher's words, or more particularly, the cruel emphasis she gave to each repetition of the word 'out' dismayed and angered many of the Forum participants. In fact there were some aspects of the report that the British Government had taken to heart. One passage had referred to the need for new structures and institutions to overcome the 'alienation' of the nationalist population, a point that had been taken up by the Northern Ireland Secretary James Prior. Two months after the report appeared he spoke of the need for greater recognition of the 'Irish identity' and for a system of communication with Dublin, and by September officials had begun talks to examine ways in which constitutional nationalism could be buttressed.

Brutal though Mrs Thatcher's rejection of a constitutional

role for Dublin had been, she was prepared to concede its right to an advisory voice in the affairs of the North. Douglas Hurd, the new Secretary of State for Northern Ireland, in a new round of meetings with Irish ministers began to see how this might be achieved. The result was unveiled on 15 November when FitzGerald and Thatcher met at Hillsborough Castle outside Belfast. The central element of the new agreement was the establishment of a new Intergovernmental Conference concerned with Northern Ireland and the relationship between the two parts of Ireland. The two also signed a pact declaring the aims of the Anglo-Irish Agreement to be 'promoting peace and stability in Northern Ireland; creating a climate of friendship and co-operation between the people of the two countries; and improving co-operation in combating terrorism.'[9] The most important ingredient in the accord was the right it granted to the Government of the Republic of Ireland through the medium of the Intergovernmental Conference, to 'put forward views and proposals on matters relating to Northern Ireland within the field of activity of the conference'. That meant Dublin now had a legally guaranteed say in political, security and legal matters, including the administration of justice.

The agreement had been forged without a word of consultation with the unionists. They were suspicious from the outset. The DUP MP Peter Robinson said that it was a device 'to trundle Northern Ireland into an all-Ireland republic'. They responded with bitterness and violence. Respectable unionists embarked on a succession of boycotts, withdrawing from meetings with ministers and local councils. There were marches and rallies, many of which ended with the 'loyalists' fighting with police. Policemen's homes were attacked in protest at the banning of a loyalist march in Portadown, and by the end of the first six months of the agreement 300 police houses had been damaged. At an official lunch in Belfast City Hall, a unionist manhandled the new Northern Ireland secretary, Tom King.

Despite the rage it provoked among loyalists, the Anglo-Irish Agreement had few concrete achievements to parade after a year of existence. The Conference had not even managed to bring about the rescinding of the Flags and Emblems Act, let alone achieve the reform on the Diplock Courts and their replacement by a three-judge arrangement sought by the Irish government. Sinn Fein had sneered that the predictable unionist reaction was actually welcome to the Agreement's framers as it exaggerated the concessions that Britain had granted.

Adams' verdict on the agreement was that

> it represents . . . a coming together of the various British strategies on an all Ireland basis, with the Dublin government acting as the new guarantor of partition.
>
> In the final analysis the agreement is about stabilising British interests. It is about what the British and Dublin governments quaintly call 'security'. It addresses itself to a problem for the British outlined in Brigadier Glover's 1978 report [a British military intelligence assessment of future trends in violent republicanism leaked to the IRA and later published in *Republican News*]: British army intelligence could do nothing about the structures and organisation of the IRA in the 26 counties; only 'security' harmonisation with Dublin could remedy this lack.[10]

Adams conceded however that the agreement also concerned

> the political context of what they call the 'security problem'. It is an attempt to isolate and draw popular support away from the republican struggle while putting a diplomatic veneer on British rule, injecting a credibility into establishment 'nationalism' so that British rule and the interests it represents can be stabilised in the long term, and insulating the British from international criticism of their involvement in Irish affairs.

None the less the republican leadership was acutely aware of the potential damage the Agreement could do to their political and military fortunes. The wholehearted security co-operation of the Dublin government was clearly going to pose serious problems, at the very least of logistics and supply to the IRA. More menacing was the potential the Agreement had for undermining political support. It did not matter that IRA violence had created the conditions that made the Agreement possible. For this they could expect no credit and nor could they logically ask for it. The benefits of the Agreement, no matter how intangible they might seem, would inevitably be attributed to John Hume and the SDLP. The proof of this contention was to be swiftly demonstrated. One of the first moves in the unionist campaign against the agreement had been to resign their fifteen Westminster seats in order to create a mass by-election as a medium for opposition to Hillsborough. The polling day was set for 23 January 1986.

This news put Sinn Fein in a difficult and highly unwelcome quandary. The poll offered the architects of the Agreement a chance to demonstrate the success of one of the fundamental aims of Hillsborough: to restore the SDLP to its commanding position among Northern nationalists. Adams' first response to the election was to try to join forces with the SDLP for a joint boycott. When this was, unsurprisingly, rejected, Sinn Fein elected to fight only four constituencies where there were large nationalist populations: Mid-Ulster, Fermanagh and South Tyrone, South Down and Newry and Armagh. On polling day there were heavy reversals on all fronts: in Fermanagh and South Tyrone, the Sinn Fein vote slumped by 5,000 votes against the 1983 general election result; in Mid-Ulster Danny Morrison dropped 2,000 votes; in South Down they lost 1,000; most dramatically of all, in Newry and Armagh Sinn Fein dropped more than 3,000 votes and the seat was won by the SDLP candidate Seamus Mallon, thereby doubling his party's representation at Westminster.

The republican leadership advanced a number of reasons for the setback. The Agreement was new and nationalist voters' hopes were high, heightened further by the violent dislike the accord had aroused in unionists. They even cited the fact that the poll was taking place in mid-winter, supposedly dampening party workers' enthusiasm.[11]

As well as being popular with Northern nationalists, the Anglo-Irish Agreement was equally well received in the Republic. The evidence of the polls was that Charles Haughey's assertion that, far from hastening the dawn of a united Ireland the Hillsborough accord actually conceded the principle of British sovereignty over part of the national territory, was not widely shared. The overwhelming opinion was that Hillsborough was a good thing.

The episode illustrated once again to Adams the feebleness of the republican presence in the Twenty-six Counties and added a new urgency to a policy that he had been pressing for for seven years but which had so far made only slow progress. Once the decision to shift the republican movement on to the twin paths of violence and electoral politics had been taken, it was logical that political activity should not be confined to Northern Ireland but extended to the Republic. As Adams wrote, 'We cannot hope to build a 32 county alternative if we do not build a 32 county struggle.' Military activity, kidnappings notwithstanding, was emphatically not to be a part of republican strategy in the South and the 'armed struggle' was to be waged only in the North.

Sinn Fein's weakness in the republic was the result of a number of factors. For one thing, the basic aspiration of the republican movement was already represented in the manifesto of the country's single largest party, Fianna Fail. For another, the state had been careful to starve the party of publicity and, under section 31 of the Broadcasting Act, disseminating Sinn Fein's views on the airwaves was a criminal offence. Finally, the party lacked the machinery to make its presence felt, and was entirely without the vigorous and healthy political organisation that Sinn Fein had forged in the North. In one area, Adams was discovering that the triumph of the North in the contest for control of the movement had been too complete. Southern republicanism lacked any political personalities equivalent to those in the North and even any readily identifiable leadership.

Adams' plan was to attempt to move Southern republicanism out of its attitude of exclusivity, which had limited its role to

442

little more than a protest movement against both British and Free State perfidy, and into the centre of Irish politics.

He wrote:

> In order to realise our potential we have to develop our organisation very considerably and we have to move into the mainstream of political relevancy. A problem we experience is that many republicans have long had a compartmentalised attitude to their republican activities whereby they pursue republican 'politics' in isolation from their involvement in community groups, trade unions, co-operative or tenant organisations. We are seeking to change that, to break down self isolation and to develop policy and strategy that will encourage our members to work in their trade unions and other organisations as republicans.

Adams also urged members to seek recruits from the ranks of the supporters of the Labour Party, Fianna Fail and the Workers' Party. In the cities, he believed that Sinn Fein's natural constituency lay in the working-class areas. Outside, 'working farmers, small business people and rural working class' were the most fertile areas of potential support. Adams was also encouraged by the potential of the Republic's huge youth vote. With half the population aged under 25, there was an enormous section of the electorate whose outlook was seldom reflected in the manifestos of the major political party.

In one respect Adams' political creed was basically the same as the prescriptions offered by O'Bradaigh. 'National independence' was the prerequisite of a socialist state. 'Socialism' was a 'form of society in which the main means of production, distribution and exchange are socially owned and controlled and in which production is based on human need rather than private profit'.[12] Added to this venerable formula, though, were a number of policies which put Sinn Fein in the vanguard of social change in Ireland and which, Adams believed, made it potentially attractive to young voters. At successive ardfheiseanna delegates had voted in favour of allowing divorce and contraception. A 1985 motion endorsing abortion on demand was reversed the following year however and the movement itself restricted to condemning the 'attitudes and forces' that forced women to terminate their pregnancies. Adams was a believer in positive discrimination and boasted that of Sinn Fein's thirteen national departments, seven were headed by women.[13]

The most obvious way for Sinn Fein to develop in the South was by fighting elections. The party's machine in Northern Ireland had been forged by its participation in the electoral process. There had been fewer opportunities for the movement to develop in the South: there had been only local government elections since the country went to the polls in December 1981. In that contest, even though it came within a few months of the ending of the hunger strikes, Sinn Fein had performed dismally, collecting only five per cent of the vote. In the local elections, none of the Sinn Fein victories would have translated into a seat in the Dail in a general election.

Adams had long ago come to the conclusion that electoral interventions in the South would never be effective unless Sinn Fein abandoned its policy of abstentionism in the Twenty-six Counties. The South, he argued, was different.

> A large part of the nationalist and republican population in the 6 counties regards abstentionism as posing no problems in terms of giving their votes because they do not see participation in the institutions of the state as having anything to offer them. But in the 26 counties, while people may be very scornful of the performance of their politicians and cynical about the institutions of the state they nevertheless expect the people they elect to represent them in these institutions.[14]

In taking this line Adams and his supporters were confronting once again one of the totemic beliefs of republicanism, and resurrecting an issue that history had shown had a tremendous destructive potential, an issue that had contributed to the 1969 split and the birth of the Provisional movement. Until 1983 the rules of Provisional Sinn Fein prevented discussion of the matter at the ard fheis. After this rule was overturned by an ard fheis vote, a debate on the future of abstentionism was held in the 1985 ard fheis. The motion was framed obliquely to avoid a direct collision with the traditionalist upholders of abstentionism. The meeting was asked whether abstentionism 'was a principle or a tactic' as far as the South was concerned. The result was encouraging for Adams. Most of the delegates expressed the view that it was a tactic, but not by the two-thirds margin necessary for this to be translated into official party policy. As the 1986 ard fheis approached Adams was determined to try again. The delegates gathering in the Mansion House were presented with a motion, put by the party ard chomhairle. It read:

> That this ard fheis drops its abstentionist attitude to Leinster House [the seat of the Irish parliament]. Successful Sinn Fein candidates in 26-county elections;
> a. Shall attend Leinster House as directed by the Ard Chomhairle.
> b. Shall not draw their salaries for personal use.

The scene was set for another confrontation between the traditionalist and modernist forces of republicanism.

CHAPTER TWENTY-FOUR

Full Circle

On the morning of 1 November some six hundred delegates filed slowly past the security guards and into the circular auditorium of the Mansion House in Dublin to begin the first full day's proceedings of the ard fheis. There was an atmosphere of amiable purposefulness. The morning papers carried stories that evoked memories of a similar occasion nearly seventeen years before. The champions of abstentionism, lead by Ruairi O'Bradaigh, had made a pilgrimage to the sole surviving member of the Second Dail, Tom Maguire, to ask his judgement on the matter. He replied as he had done when his opinion was sought before, that abstentionism was a basic tenet of republican principle. Further stories predicted that if the vote went against them, O'Bradaigh and his supporters would walk out of the conference just as they had in 1970.

That afternoon Gerry Adams rose to make his presidential address. After a long preamble examining the Anglo-Irish Agreement he finally came to the point:

> I can understand [he said] that some comrades view a change in the abstention policy as a betrayal of republican principle. Some of you may feel that a republican organisation making such a change can no longer call itself 'republican'. If there are delegates here who feel like this, I would remind you that another republican organisation has already done what you fear we are going to do tomorrow . . .

446

Adams then announced that at an extraordinary convention of the IRA three weeks before there had been an overwhelming vote to drop the ban on republicans entering the Dail. Adams went on:

> The decisions of a General Army Convention are not binding on Sinn Fein *ard fheiseanna*, but the logic of those who would consider withdrawing support from Sinn Fein if we change the abstentionist policy must be applied also to your attitude to the army. And the logic which would dictate withdrawal of support from Sinn Fein if decisions go against you means that you have already decided to withdraw solidarity and support from the IRA and the armed struggle.

If a clinching argument was needed, Adams had provided it. The end of his address was marked by several minutes of stamping, clapping and cheering. The backing of the army protected the leadership from the accusation that their desire to end abstentionism was evidence of a loss of commitment to violence. Abstentionism had become an abstract principle, whose upholders were mostly elderly republicans who for several years had played little part in the movement.

When the actual debate was held the following day, it was clear that among the old brigade, the tide of opinion was behind Adams. John Joe McGirl, the 70-year-old County Leitrim republican, made a passionate speech, laced with references to dead colleagues and former prisoners, in which he described abstentionism as 'a millstone and a handicap'. Raising the spectre of the 1969 division he said:

> A year before the split it was clear that the then leadership had abandoned Irish Freedom but today we have an army which has been fighting for sixteen years and will continue to fight until British rule is ended . . .

After enthusiastic applause he concluded by saying:

In no way am I abandoning colleagues who were brought out and executed by the Free State, but I do not think we are going to convince the youth of Ireland that abstentionism is the right road. The answer I always get, no matter how I try to convince them, is 'Why will you not represent us here?'

O'Bradaigh's speech, which centred on the ancient legalistic assertion of the authority of the Second Dail and the illegitimacy of all subsequent parliaments, was received in near silence, broken only by the odd burst of applause from the fringes. Before he began, Adams had come forward to shake his hand, to be told by O'Bradaigh sourly, 'I'll shake hands with any man, any time, not just for the cameras.' It was left to Martin McGuinness to point out the historical significance of the confrontation that was taking place. It was not merely the abstention policy that was under discussion, he said, it was also a question of the style of the leadership of the movement:

> The former leadership of this movement has never been able to come to terms with this leadership's criticisms of the disgraceful attitude adopted by them during the disastrous eighteen-month ceasefire of the seventies. If those of that leadership who remain leave the movement today it will not be just because of the abstentionist vote.

He concluded: 'If you allow yourselves to be led out of this hall today, the only place you will be going is home.'

Of the 628 delegates present, 429 voted to end the ban on abstention and 161 voted to retain it. From now on, Sinn Fein members would enter the Dail if elected. Once the result was announced there was a stirring at the back of the room and O'Bradaigh, closely followed by his old comrade Daithi O'Connaill, marched from the hall accompanied by a small group of supporters. At a hotel just outside Dublin hired in advance, they reconvened under the banner of 'Republican Sinn Fein'. With their departure passed the last traces of the old Southern Provisional leadership.

After the ard fheis a number of operations of a type that

had not been seen in the North for several years were carried out. In Belfast a 600-pound car bomb went off in the Lisburn Road, damaging hundreds of houses. Later a number of hotels were blown up, in the process causing the loss of scores of jobs. The new year opened with a message of fierce belligerence from the Army Council to republican prisoners.

> Morale [it said] is the vital key to our success and the key to high morale is successful operations . . . 1987 will see tangible successes in the war of national liberation. We have the correct strategy and with the full authority which we command we will be pursuing the war . . . In 1987 we will be calling for greater sacrifice . . . in 1987 the British Government and the British media will not be able to ignore the chapters of Irish resistance about to unfold.

Anyone searching in the abstentionism episode for traces of the benign corruption dreamt about in Dublin and London (whereby war weariness and the growth of a political awareness in the republican movement would transform its members from revolutionaries to mere radicals) was to be disappointed. Adams might claim that 'obviously I would prefer a situation where the armed struggle was unnecessary'.[1] Armed struggle, on the other hand, provided the 'vital cutting edge. Without it the issue of Ireland would not be an issue.' Violence is what gives the IRA its importance.

This realisation, combined with the IRA's monochromic view of the world and its implacable and unappeasable nature, means that it is possible to predict with gloomy confidence that the troubles will continue for the foreseeable future. Even if the attitude of leadership were to change, it seems highly likely that a proportion of the rank and file would continue the tradition if only as a monotonous act of revenge.

The history of republicanism since Wolfe Tone has shown that as long as there is a British presence in Ireland it is an ineradicable tradition. The events of the last seventeen years have only planted its spores deeper.

CHAPTER TWENTY-FIVE

Reversals

The IRA's boastful New Year message promising 'tangible successes in the war of national liberation' in 1987 very soon came to seem rash, even hubristic. The year was to turn out to be possibly the worst in the Provisionals' history. On the military front they were battered by ambushes and arms seizures that paralysed activities for long periods. On the electoral front they failed once more to jerk their bandwagon out of the rut into which it had settled in the early 1980s. In the all-important propaganda battle their stained credentials as freedom fighters engaged in a legitimate struggle were further besmirched by a massacre of civilians that united all but the most fanatical republican supporters in a chorus of disgust.

In February Sinn Fein's popular appeal was once again put to the test when elections were called in the Republic of Ireland. This time the contest would have an added dimension. For the first time since the civil war the electorate was being given the opportunity to grant an unequivocal IRA supporter a seat in Leinster House.

The election had been looming for many months and the party organisation had had plenty of warning to prepare for it. Nonetheless Adams prudently declared at an early stage of the campaign that he would not be disappointed if no seats were won. 'We're really concentrating on the next election,' he said. (Quoted in *Daily Telegraph* 10 February 1987.) From the outset the outgoing Taiseach Garret FitzGerald directed a withering attack at the Republicans denouncing Adams and Morrison as 'evil men' responsible for wreaking a 'tragedy on the Lebanese scale' in the North. (*Glasgow Herald* 9 February.)

The Fianna Fail leader Charles Haughey was forced by latent republican sentimentality inside his own party to be more circumspect.

Sinn Fein put up 27 candidates in 24 multi-member constituencies, their first full-blooded venture into the electoral arena of the republic on a nationwide basis. By now the party had perfected a brand of aggressive, publicity-grabbing campaigning, confronting the party leaders as they toured the country in a tactic designed to circumvent the ban on their views being broadcast in Ireland.

Faced with Sinn Fein the electorate seemed curiously uninterested in the issue of violence. The candidates did not encourage the subject, concentrating on indignation at unemployment and tax evasion, denouncing cross-border security co-operation and promising safe jobs for those employed by the State.

The twin of the republican strategy had already put in an unhelpful appearance shortly before the campaign began, however, when two INLA men were shot dead by their erstwhile comrades in Drogheda, a town where Sinn Fein entertained high hopes.

When polling day came on 17 February, republicans did disastrously. Sinn Fein candidates managed to attract only 32,933 votes, or 1.85 per cent of those cast. As Adams had anticipated, the party failed to win a seat. Later on, addressing the Sinn Fein ard fheis, Adams was to ruefully remark that the 'election and its results show clearly, if anyone ever doubted it, the enormity of the task we have undertaken.'

Why had Sinn Fein fared so dismally? Republicans were at first inclined to heap the blame on Section 31 of the Broadcasting Act which according to Adams had 'won for this part of Ireland an international reputation equalled only by South Africa's censorship stance.' The bitterness and regularity with which it was attacked was proof of the measure's effectiveness, and also of the crucial position that publicity and propaganda held in the Republican plan. McGuinness believed in retrospect that they had spread themselves too thin, standing in areas where the republican tradition was weak, and should have concentrated their efforts in their known areas of strength: Dublin and the border country.

But Adams also blamed the movement itself. At the 1987 ard fheis commenting on a dismal year he attributed Sinn Fein's poor showing at the polls to 'the failure in the past to utilise the many opportunities for immersion in the affairs of ordinary people.'

> Most people will not struggle, never mind vote, for abstract things. They will not fight for ideas. They will fight to bring material benefits, to improve the quality of their lives, to guarantee the future for their children. The 'big ideas' which we have concerning liberation, nationalism, independence and socialism must develop out of the 'small ideas' concerned with local grievances, local protests and local aspirations

It was the strictly practical things of life that had dominated the election, notably the rotten state of the Irish economy. In such a context, and with the emotional capital generated by the hunger strike now exhausted, Sinn Fein had subsided into irrelevancy.

As the winter turned into spring most of the movement's energies went into killing, spurred on by a desire to prove to O'Bradaigh and the renegades of Republican Sinn Fein that ending abstentionism had not diminished the IRA's appetite for violence. By the end of April they had killed nine policemen, compared with 12 in the whole of the previous year.

On the morning of Saturday 25 April Lord Justice Maurice Gibson, Northern Ireland's second most senior judge and his wife Cecily were driving along the A1 road that connects Dublin to Belfast. The couple had arrived in Dun Laoghaire that morning on the ferry from Liverpool and were escorted on the 75 mile journey to the border by armed Garda officers.

At 8.35 they arrived at the border, stopped the car and shook hands with their escorts. Then they climbed back in and drove over the border along a mile-long stretch of no-man's land to where their RUC police guard was waiting.

Their car, Mrs Gibson at the wheel, never arrived. As it passed by a car at the side of the road an IRA team detonated by radio signal a 500lb bomb concealed in the vehicle. It blew the car, and the Gibsons, to pieces.

As a senior member the Northern Ireland judiciary Judge Gibson was a natural target for the IRA. His attractiveness as a victim was enhanced by the fact that he had presided over the trial of some RUC men accused of the murder of three IRA members, Toman, McKerr, and Burns, outside Lurgan in 1982, which had been at the heart of the 'shoot to kill' controversy. Judge Gibson acquitted the three officers observing that they had brought the IRA men 'to the final court of justice.' The murders re-ignited a predictable controversy over the tender question of the efficacy of cross border co-operation between the RUC and the Gardai. The matter of security co-ordination had been discussed at almost every meeting of the Anglo-Irish Conference since the agreement was signed. Only the week before the outrage a high level security group had been set up to extend links between the police and military on both parts of the island.

Even so, the RUC and British government remained dissatisfied with the efficiency of their Southern Irish counterparts.

In this case it seemed that if any blame was to be apportioned it probably lay with the RUC. It transpired that they had ceased to collect their VIP charges from the border proper since an explosion at the same spot where the Gibsons died in May 1985 which killed four officers. How a police escort would have prevented the blast, triggered by remote control, was never explained by the RUC's critics.

The IRA's delight at the attack was short lived. It took less than a fortnight for the British security forces to take their revenge. The evening of 8 May was clear and pleasant in the County Armagh hamlet of Loughgall. The pink and white blossom on the apple trees that cluster over the hillsides was in full bloom. Inside the church hall a group of schoolgirls were playing games. At 7.20 a JCB digger made a noisy appearance in Loughgall's main street. One man was at the controls and two more armed with Heckler and Koch sub-machine guns wedged in behind the shovel. Cruising sedately in their wake was a blue Toyota Hiace van of the sort you see all over Ireland ferrying labourers to and from the building sites. Inside were five other IRA men.

They were members of the East Tyrone brigade augmented by Jim Lynagh from Monaghan in the Republic, a veteran of border operations many of which he had carried out with his friend Seamus McElwaine.

The raid was a routine affair, designed as part of the unceasing war against the RUC as well as the wider campaign to dislocate normal life in the North. The plan was to blow up the low, functional police station in the middle of the village and retire. It was not even known whether anyone was inside it as the station was only manned part-time. Death threats would then be issued against any workmen who contracted to repair it. Only the day before members of the gang had thrown a grenade into a courthouse at Dungannon where builders were putting right damage caused by a previous bombing.

As the digger drew level with the police station, a 200 pound bomb balanced in its shovel, the driver swung across the road and swept through the high, supposedly mortar-proof perimeter fence, wedging the JCB against the station wall. The detonator was fired as they dashed back towards the van waiting to speed them away.

The explosion that ensued demolished half the police station and echoed five miles away in Armagh. As the sound rolled off the hillsides another, sharper noise was heard, the stutter of automatic weapons. Firing had broken out on all sides. Lying concealed around the police station were a combined team of Special Air Services soldiers and members of the RUC special support group who had been trained by the SAS. The three IRA men riding the JCB were cut down long before they reached the van. As those inside it struggled to get out, three were riddled with bullets punching through the flimsy walls of the vehicle. The other two died stumbling away in a hopeless attempt to escape. Hundreds of rounds were fired. About a hundred yards from the ambush Anthony Hughes and his brother Oliver were driving innocently through the village when their Citroen was rocked by the impact of bullets. Anthony died instantly after being hit several times in the head. Oliver was hit in the head and chest but survived. They were the victims of SAS marksmen hidden in a wood who took them for part of the team.

The encounter was the biggest loss of life the IRA had suffered since 1921 and it provoked ill-suppressed glee among the security forces and the British government. The ambush had been ruthlessly executed but it was a ruthless conflict and the IRA team had been caught red-handed. Spokesmen presented it as a devastating set back for the IRA. The perverse psyche of republicanism had already turned the disaster into an emotional triumph. At funeral after funeral in dripping graveyards around the border all through the following week, orators exulted in the righteousness of their cuase. Surely if any proof was needed of the justice of the IRA's campaign it had been provided by the brutal efficiency with which the SAS had gone about their task. Speaking over the grave of Paddy Kelly, the 30-year-old leader of the East Tyrone brigade, Martin McGuinness declared that out of the bitterness and anger engendered by the killings '. . . will come a greater strength . . . as the British themselves will see, a greater number of IRA recruits not just in Tyrone but throughout the Six Counties.' (Quoted in *An Phoblacht/Republican News* 14 May 1987.)

The strong, angry fervour, thick in the air at the requiem masses and the gravesides suggested he was right. Jim Lynagh was buried in Monaghan. Thousands of mourners gathered outside the blank, utilitarian Victorian house in Old Cross Square from where he planned his sorties to accompany the coffin to St Macartan's cathedral. Most of them were solid and soberly dressed, middling people with cars and houses and plots of land.

A tremulous soprano sang a religious version of the London-derry Aire at the Mass. The priest avoided all mention of the circumstances of Lynagh's demise in the homily. 'You would think he'd died of pneumonia,' Gerry Adams remarked later in his graveside oration. Lynagh was 31 when he died, a good looking man with a strong sense of humour. He joined the IRA in his teens and began operating with the East Tyrone brigade. He was badly injured in 1973 when a bomb he was carrying went off prematurely. As a result of the incident he was sentenced to ten years in the Maze. On his release he became a Sinn Fein councillor in Monaghan while continuing to shoot and bomb across the border. In 1982 he was sentenced to five years in Portlaoise. On his release he resumed his activities with the East Tyrone brigade. At the time of his death he was privately cited by the army and police as their main terrorist target in the border areas.

The life stories of the other dead men had a monotonously familiar ring. Paddy Kelly was born into a fourth generation republican family, tradition that was reinforced by regular encounters with the police. 'It was the RUC's beatings which made Paddy a volunteer' his father is reported to have observed.

Padraig McKearney was the brother of Sean McKearney who was killed 'on active service' in 1974. He had met Jim Lynagh in prison and after breaking out of the Maze in the mass escape of September 1983 joined up with him on the border where he was 'a key figure on some of the most daring and innovative missions in the last few years,' according to his official obituary.

The youngest were 21-year-old Declan Arthurs and Seamus Donnelly, 19, from the strongly republican area of Galbally. Both joined the IRA after the death on hunger strike of a neighbour, Martin Hurson. As their coffins were lowered into the grave together at Galbally, Martin McGuinness declared: 'We will remember Loughgall. We will remember Loughgall forever. We will see to it that the British government remembers Loughgall as well.'

This defiance did not disguise the fact that the operation had been a disaster for the IRA. How had the security forces' intelligence been so complete? At least one senior IRA man was convinced that the only explanation was that the Provisionals had a highly placed informant inside their ranks. There had been a two-year-old series of arrests, raids on arms dumps in the East Tyrone area including the killing of two IRA men in an ambush as they went to retrieve weapons from a cache near Dungannon that seemed to support the view. The army council as a whole remained unconvinced. Nonetheless it was agreed that henceforth knowledge of operations should be restricted to the smallest possible number of people and that never again would so many people take part in a single operation. Even so, after Loughgall IRA operations in the countryside virtually halted for the rest of the year.

The disaster and the sympathy it evoked might have been expected to bring some benefit to Sinn Fein in the British General Election held the following month. The Sinn Fein campaign opened under the banner 'Freedom, Justice, Peace'. The manifesto retailed the familiar demands. Britain must publicly renounce Northern Ireland as its territory and repeal the Government of Ireland Act, disband and disarm the RUC and the UDR and set a date for British withdrawal prior to an All Ireland Constitutional Conference.

But it made no mention of the IRA, concentrating instead on pledges to improve the material lives of Nationalists in the North.

The reticence on the subject of the 'armed struggle' and the emphasis on practical measures was a recognition of the ground that the SDLP had gained with the nationalist electorate. Since the signing of the Hillsborough accord, the SDLP had repeatedly claimed that the lot of Catholics had improved as a result of the agreement. As was usual with elections in Northern Ireland all other issues once again were to be subordinated to another posing of the national question.

Shortly after the election was called, *Republican News* succinctly summed up the way the contest would be fought.

Unionists will ask for a massive unionist vote against

the Hillsborough Agreement and against Sinn Fein; the SDLP will ask for a massive nationalist vote for the Hillsborough Agreement and against Sinn Fein.

So it was to be. Polling day turned out to be another setback for republicanism. The Sinn Fein vote sank from 13.4 per cent in 1983 to 11.3 per cent. In practically every area of republican strength the vote dipped depressingly. In Foyle Martin McGuinness's support dropped by nearly two thousand. In Mid Ulster, where Danny Morrison had once entertained hopes of a seat, the vote fell by three and a half thousand. The only success was in West Belfast where Gerry Adams beat his SDLP rival Dr Joe Hendron by a comfortable 2,221 votes.

Elsewhere the SDLP triumphed. John Hume, the party leader and an architect of the Anglo-Irish agreement, would be joined in the next parliament by two colleagues: Seamus Mallon from Newry and Armagh and Eddie McGrady from South Down who had ousted after 13 years the dour Unionist stalwart Enoch Powell.

The notion that the agreement would erode support for the IRA had been one of the principal arguments that had persuaded Mrs Thatcher to pursue it. At first sight the results would seem to be a vindication of her policy. Adams and the leadership had long accepted that whatever the tangible benefits of the Hillsborough accord, the SDLP would be richly rewarded for its involvement in it. The fruits of the arrangement were small and provided little practical nourishment. Nonetheless, the arrival of a permanent presence from the South in the councils of the North, in the shape of the foreign minister at the regular Anglo-Irish conferences, had sent a tremendous charge of optimism through the Catholic community.

Through the fog of claim and counter claim the precise shape of the deal may not have been immediately discernible. But the Nationalists felt that it was large and momentous, an impression that was reinforced by the loud squeals of pain and outrage that had been emanating from the Unionists ever since its signing.

With the establishment of a secretariat, jointly manned by

officials from the republic and the North at Maryfield outside Belfast, the agreement provided some practical help to Catholics too. Through it were channelled hundreds of complaints about police harassment, official unfairness in matters of housing and jobs; all the grievances that contributed to nationalist sympathy and ambiguity towards the republican movement.

The attitude of Catholics towards their co-religionists in Sinn Fein and the IRA was to come under painful self-scrutiny following an atrocity on a November Sunday in the charming Fermanagh town of Enniskillen that shook even Adams into a rare public apology for the wanton disregard for life displayed by the perpetrators.

Enniskillen is a Protestant town set in a sea of predominantly Catholic countryside. On the morning of 8 November hundreds of Protestants were gathered in the centre to watch a parade and take part in a service to commemorate the dead of two world wars. Just as the wreath laying ceremony was about to begin at 11 o'clock a bomb exploded inside the St Michael's Reading Rooms, a Catholic social club that lay beside the cenotaph. The bomb was not a big one by Northern Ireland standards, weighing between 30 and 50 pounds, but the effect it had was devastating. It blew out the gable wall cascading rubble onto the crowd waiting outside, killing 11 and injuring 63. All the dead were Protestants. Only two, an off duty and a retired policeman, could remotely be said to fall within the IRA's flexible parameters embracing legitimate targets. One, 20-year-old Marie Wilson, was a nurse at the Royal Victoria Hospital, in the heart of the Catholic Falls Road, where generations of nationalists had been cared for.

The disgust that the killings produced towards the IRA was intensified by the attitude of the victims. Marie Wilson's father, Gordon, made no mention of revenge when he was interviewed about his loss.

> I bear no ill will [he said]. That sort of talk is not going to bring her back to life. She was a great wee lassie. She loved her profession. She was a pet and she's dead. She's in heaven and we'll meet again. Don't ask me please for

459

a purpose. I don't have a purpose. I don't have an answer but I know there has to be a plan. If I did not think that I would commit suicide. It is part of a greater plan and God is good and we shall meet again.

In Dublin thousands of people, politicians, students, businessmen, tramps, filed through the door of the Mansion House, scene of the annual Sinn Fein gathering, to sign books of condolence. The Soviet Union, which had previously regarded the Northern Ireland question as a useful propaganda stick for beating the repressive and 'colonialist' British, was moved to denounce the killings as 'barbaric' through the official news agency, TASS.

It was nearly 30 hours before the IRA admitted that the massacre had been its work. The statement was defensive and arrogant but reeked of guilt. It is the nearest that the Provisionals have come to a statement of remorse.

> The IRA admits responsibility for planting the bomb in Enniskillen yesterday which exploded with such catastrophic consequences. We deeply regret what occurred.

> GHQ has now established that one of our units placed a remote control bomb in St Michael's aimed at catching Crown forces personnel on patrol in connection with the Remembrance Day service but not during it. The bomb blew up without being triggered by our radio signal.

> There has been an ongoing battle for supremacy between the IRA and British Army engineers over the use of remote control bombs. In the past some of our landmines have been triggered by the British Army scanning high frequencies and other devices have been jammed and neutralised.

> On each occasion we overcame the problem and recently believed that we were in advance of British counter measures.

> In the present climate, nothing we can say in explanation will be given the attention which the truth deserves, nor will compensate the feelings of the injured or bereaved.

This last was a considerable understatement. Even among

460

their own supporters the initial reaction was one of shame and disgust. The anonymous leader writer in the *Republican News* the following week prophesied: 'That was a monumental error for which republicans have paid, and will continue to pay, dearly' before concluding that '. . . ultimately Britain is to blame.'

What had happened? Despite elaborate theories at the time that this was a ghoulish attempt by 'hawks' in the movement to wreck the political strategy and drag it back to the old doctrine of physical force the truth is almost certainly simpler.

The attack seems to have been what the IRA communiqué said it was — an attempt to kill members of the security forces taking part in the Remembrance Day activities. It was carried out by a local unit with the approval of the local brigade staff. It was aimed at UDR soldiers who the IRA believed habitually took up position close to the reading room gable wall. As it was never intended as a 'spectacular' but part of the ongoing war against the 'Crown forces' permission did not need to be sought from the army council or GHQ.

Forensic tests at the time of writing have failed to determine how the bomb was exploded prematurely, though the possibility that army scanners may have triggered it has been comprehensively ruled out.

According to a senior IRA man the most dismaying element in the episode from the Provisionals' point of view was the continuing ignorance of their followers.

> Enniskillen was worse than La Mon (see p.336) because we thought our volunteers were more sophisticated and politicised 10 years on not to put a bomb at the Cenotaph where there was such a risk to civilian life. (Interview with authors, Belfast, December 1987.)

Initially, even to the stoical and assured inside the movement, it seemed that the atrocity must hobble Sinn Fein's political progress, especially in the South, for years to come. How could even the most cynical London Labour politician or the wooliest Dutch liberal claim the Provisionals as freedom fighters now? One immediate effect of the episode was to press the Irish government into implementing the Extradition Act which would speed up the passage of wanted IRA suspects from the Republic to the North. The Taoiseach, Charles Haughey, had been threatening to delay the implementation in order to force the British government into judicial reforms in the North − notably increasing the number of judges in a Diplock Court from one to three. Danny Morrison feared that more anti-Republican measures were on the way

> Enniskillen came close to pushing the people of the 26 counties into the arms of those urging internment, proscription of Sinn Fein, the banning of *An Phoblacht (Republican News)* and the ending of the right to silence. We have weathered the storm in the short term but we are unable to quantify the damage in the long term. (Interview with authors, Belfast, December 1987.)

In the view of Gerry Adams: 'I don't think there can be more Enniskillens and I think the IRA, in accepting responsibility for what happened and in its explanation, signalled that they are going to ensure that there are no more Enniskillens.' (Interview with authors, Belfast, January 1988.)

Enniskillen came in the wake of another depressing event for the Provisionals. On 31 October, while the ard fheis was in session, news came through of the seizure of a freighter off the French coast believed to be carrying arms for the IRA. As the story developed, it became clear that the French customs had intercepted an arms delivery of massive proportions. Aboard the Eksund, they discovered 20 Sam-7 ground to air missiles, mortars, recoilless rifles, rocket propelled grenades and their launchers, 1000 Kalashnikov rifles and two tons of plastic explosives. The crew were all Irish. After initial scepticism the police decided that the weapons had been obtained in Libya and despite the scale of the haul − far more than the IRA's campaign required − were for the Provisionals' sole use.

Not only that, it emerged that this was merely part of a series

462

of large scale importations from Libya, at least three in the two years before the discovery of the Eksund. On 23 November Irish policemen combed the countryside searching for signs of the earlier consignments. A 55 foot underground bunker was discovered in County Wicklow but no guns. Several other caches were found but few weapons.

At the start of the New Year the security forces were in a state of nervous anticipation about the missing weapons. The Chief Constable of Northern Ireland held a press conference in which he declared: 'We are satisfied there was a considerable amount of weapons brought into this island. Lethal weapons have arrived here in quantity and they must be found.'

Shortly afterwards the secretary of state for Northern Ireland Tom King announced the setting up of a new Army Brigade headquarters in Armagh City with responsibility for combatting IRA activity along the entire length of border. The security forces are convinced that the IRA has now obtained the ground to air weapons they have sought for so long which will enable them to attack the army helicopters that constantly buzz in the skies along the border. As a precaution the aircraft have been fitted with missile-confusing deflectors. Nonetheless, the shooting down of a helicopter is regarded by both sides as only a matter of time. This was the happy thought that the IRA carried with them into 1988. The previous year had been a disaster, yet they could take satisfaction that even in their darkest moments no-one had seriously suggested that their defeat was imminent. In fact there were some things they could take some satisfaction from. In a perverse way the massacre at Enniskillen had proved their durability.

Despite the revulsion it caused and the calls for the removal of Sinn Fein it was clear that the politics would survive the catastrophe. By early in the New Year, John Hume the leader of the SDLP was engaged in talks with Gerry Adams.

Sinn Fein, the general election results showed, seemed to have settled down on a bedrock of support that was unlikely to subside very much because of events, Hillsborough notwithstanding. As for Enniskillen, the view both inside and outside the movement was that by the time the next election arrived some action by the security forces — another Loughgall perhaps — would have providentially provided Sinn Fein with a propaganda event to counterbalance the memory of Enniskillen.

At the end of the day, despite all the good intentions, politics in Ireland, as Adams discerned, was still a matter of tribalism. Whatever happened the IRA and Sinn Fein had grown too permanent a feature of the political landscape of Ireland to be left out of any serious discussions about its future.

References

2 The Roots of Republicanism

1 Quoted in Robert Kee, *The Bold Fenian Men*, Quartet, London, 1979, p. 31.
2 Eoghan O Loinsigh, 'Bri an Teidil', *Saoirse*, Summer 1986.
3 Quoted in Kee, *op. cit.*, p. 4.
4 *Irish Times*, quoted in Robert Kee, *Ourselves Alone*, Quartet, London, 1982, p. 18.
5 Quoted in Tim Pat Coogan, *The IRA*, Fontana, London, 1980, p. 41.
6 Bowyer Bell, *The Secret Army*, The Academy Press, Dublin, 1979, p. 20.
7 Quoted in Kee, *Ourselves Alone, op. cit.*, p. 88.
8 Quoted in Kevin Kelley, *The Longest War*, Zed Books, London, 1984, p. 64.
9 For full account see Bell, *op. cit.*, p. 290.
10 Quoted in Bell, *op. cit.*, p. 291.

3 Becalmed

1 Jimmy Drumm, interview with authors, July 1985.
2 Martin McGuinness, interviews with authors, 1985-6.
3 Jim Sullivan, interviews with authors, October 1985; February and April 1986.

4 Tomas MacGiolla, interview with authors, December 1985.

5 Quoted in Rosita Sweetman, *On Our Knees*, Pan, London, 1972, p. 141.

6 Sean MacStiofain, *Revolutionary in Ireland*, Gordon Cremonesi, Edinburgh, 1975, p. 92.

7 Ruairi O'Bradaigh, interviews with authors, 1985-6.

8 Tom Barry, *Guerrilla Days in Ireland*, Anvil Books, Dublin, 1981, p. 39.

9 MacStiofain, *op. cit.*, p. 93.

10 *Ibid*, p. 92.

4 Civil Rights

1 Danny Morrison, interviews with authors, 1984-7.

2 Campaign for Social Justice pamphlet, 15 June 1969.

3 Gerry Adams, *Falls Memories*, Brandon Books, Dingle, 1982, p. 136.

4 Raymond Shearer, interview with authors, October 1985.

5 Terence O'Neill, *Autobiography*, Hart Davis, London, 1972.

6 *The Plain Truth*, Campaign for Social Justice document, 1969.

7 *Fortnight*, no. 80.

8 Fred Heatley, interview with authors, October 1985.

9 Private information from RUC member.

10 *Irish Times*, 5 December 1969, quoted in Philip Beresford, unpublished PhD thesis, *The Official IRA and Republican Clubs in Northern Ireland 1968-74 and their Relations with Other Political and Paramilitary Groups*, University of Exeter, 1979, p. 137.

11 MacGiolla, interview with authors, December 1985.

12 Eamonn McCann, *War in an Irish Town*, Pluto Press, London, 1980, p. 35.

13 *Ibid.*, p. 43.

14 Quoted in Beresford, *op. cit.*, p. 102.

15 *Ibid.*, р. 144.

16 *Ibid.*, p. 103.
17 Michael Farrell, *The Orange State*, Pluto Press, London, 1980, p. 250.
18 *Ibid.*, p. 249.
19 Interview with authors.
20 Margot Collins, interview with the authors, December 1984.

5 The Return of the Troubles

1 Joe Cahill, interview with authors, 1985-6.
2 MacStiofain, *op. cit.*, p. 15.
3 *Ibid.*, p. 18.
4 Cathal Goulding, interview with authors, January 1986.
5 Quoted in Beresford, *op. cit.*, p. 144.
6 Quoted in Sweetman, *op. cit.*, p. 190.
7 McMillen lecture, 'The Role of the IRA 1962-67', Dublin, 1972.
8 *Belfast Telegraph*, 9 December 1969, quoted in Beresford, *op. cit.*, p. 153.
9 O'Bradaigh, interviews with authors, 1985-6.
10 MacStiofain, *op. cit.*, p. 113.
11 MacGiolla, interview with authors, January 1986.
12 MacGiolla, interview with authors, December 1985
13 Goulding, interview with authors, April 1986.
14 Eamonn McCann, *op. cit.*, p. 57.
15 All witness accounts of Derry rioting taken from evidence to the *Scarman Inquiry into Violence and Civil Disturbances in Northern Ireland*, HMSO 1972, unless otherwise stated.

6 August 1969

1 *Violence and Civil Disturbances in Northern Ireland in 1969, Report of Tribunal of Inquiry (The Scarman Report)*, Her Majesty's Stationery Office, Belfast, April 1972, volume 1, p. 29.

2 *Ibid.*, p. 27.
3 *Ibid.*, pp. 55, 56.
4 *Ibid.*, p. 59.
5 Interview with authors, January 1986.
6 Paddy Kennedy, interview with authors, September 1984.
7 *Ibid.*
8 *Ibid.*
9 Interview with authors, July 1986.
10 Tom Conaty, interview with authors, 1985.
11 Quoted in Scarman, *op. cit.*, p. 193.
12 *Ibid.*, p. 192.
13 *Ibid.*, p. 221.

7 The Birth of the Provisionals

1 O'Bradaigh, interviews with authors, 1985-6.
2 Joe Cahill, interviews with authors, 1985-6.
3 Private information.
4 Cahill, interview with authors, November 1984.
5 Conaty, interview with authors, October 1985; February and April 1986.
6 Beresford, *op. cit.*, p. 189.
7 Quoted in Sweetman, *op. cit.*, p. 191.
8 Phil McCullough, interview with authors, December 1986.
9 James Kelly, interview with authors, March 1985.
10 Interview with authors.
11 MacStiofain, *op. cit.*, p. 129.
12 *Ibid.*, p. 122.
13 Beresford, *op. cit.*, p. 212.
14 MacStiofain, *op. cit.*, p. 137.
15 *Irish Press*, 5 January 1970.

8 Defenders

1 MacStiofain, *op. cit.*, p. 145.
2 *Ibid.*, p. 143.

3 Private information.
4 Billy Kelly, interview with authors, March 1986.
5 Sullivan, interview with authors.
6 MacStiofain, *op. cit.*, p. 138.
7 Barry, *op. cit.*, p. 13.
8 Beresford, *op. cit.*
9 Beresford, *op. cit.*, p. 275.
10 Kennedy, interview with authors, September 1984.
11 Interview with authors.
12 Sweetman, *op. cit.*, p. 195.
13 Gerry Adams, interview with authors.
14 Beresford, *op. cit.*, p. 243.
15 Cardinal Tomas O'Fiaich, interview with authors, 1976.
16 Sean Donnelly, interview with authors, November 1984.
17 Beresford, *op. cit.*, p. 282.
18 Eamonn McCann, interview with authors, September 1984.
19 Interview with authors, March 1985.
20 Interview with authors.
21 *Sunday Telegraph*, quoted in Beresford, *op. cit..* p. 340.
22 MacStiofain, *op. cit.*, p. 168.
23 Richard Deutsch and Vivien Magowan, Chronology, Vol. 1, p. 96.

9 'This is War'

1 Cahill, interviews with authors, 1985-6.
2 Major-General Sir Frank Kitson, interview with authors, December 1984.
3 Lord Carver, interview with authors, July 1984.
4 Private information.
5 *Republican News*, May 1971.
6 Sir Anthony Farrar-Hockley, letter to authors.
7 Morrison, interview with authors, 1984-7.
8 Deutsch and Magowan, *op. cit.*, Vol 1, p. 90.
9 'McShane', interview with authors, February 1985.
10 Interview with authors.

11 Kennedy, interview, *op. cit.*

12 Tom 'Donnelly', interview with authors, November 1984.

13 McGuinness, interview with authors, 1985-6.

14 Deutsch and Magowan, *op. cit.*, Vol. 1, p. 114.

15 McCann, *op. cit.*, p. 90.

16 Deutsch and Magowan, *op. cit.*, Vol. 1, p. 114.

17 John Taylor, interview with authors, 1985.

18 Beresford, *op. cit.*, p. 370.

19 John McGuffin, *Internment*, Anvil Books, Dublin, 1973, p. 86.

20 Deutsch and Magowan, *op. cit.*, Vol. 1, p. 121.

10 After Internment

1 'McShane', interview with authors, February 1985.

2 Belfast Graves, The National Graves Association, Dublin, 1985, pp. 85-7.

3 Interview with authors.

4 Private information.

5 Armagh journalist, interview with authors.

6 Interview with authors.

7 Desmond Hamill, *Pig in the Middle*, Methuen, London, 1985, p. 85.

8 See Raymond McClean, *The Road to Bloody Sunday*, Ward River Press, Dublin, 1983, p. 127.

9 Quoted in Hamill, *op. cit.*, p. 86.

10 McClean, *op. cit.*, p. 127.

11 *Ibid.*, p. 130.

12 *Ibid.*, p. 133.

13 Quoted in *Daily Telegraph*, 2 February 1972.

11 Fighting and Talking

1 O'Bradaigh, interviews with authors, 1985-6.

2 MacStiofain, *op. cit.*, p. 209.

3 *Ibid.*, p. 210.

4 Tom Caldwell, interview with authors, January 1986.
5 Private information.
6 MacStiofain, *op. cit.*, p. 238.
7 Merlyn Rees, *Northern Ireland: A Personal Perspective*, Methuen, London, 1985, p. 15.
8 Cahill, interviews with authors, 1985-6.
9 MacStiofain, *op. cit.*, p. 241.
10 *Ibid.*, p. 242.
11 *Ibid.*, p. 251.
12 Deutsch and Magowan, *op. cit.*, Vol. 1, p. 178.
13 *Ibid.*, p. 167.
14 Quoted in Kelley, *op. cit.*, p. 177.
15 MacStiofain, *op. cit.*, p. 258.
16 MacStiofain, interview with authors, 1986.
17 McGuinness, interviews with authors, 1985-6.

12 Bloody Friday

1 Martin McGuinness, interview with authors, 1985-6.
2 MacStiofain, *op. cit.*, p. 289.
3 Private information.
4 McCann, *op. cit.*, p. 116.
5 Quoted in David McKittrich, unpublished history of the UDA.
6 Quoted in Martin Dillon and Denis Lehane, *Political Murder in Northern Ireland*, Penguin, London, 1973, p. 61.
7 Quoted in *ibid.*, p. 250.
8 Hamill, *op. cit.*, p. 136.
9 Joe Cahill, interview with authors, 1985-6.
10 *Republican News*, 9 April 1972.

13 Bombing Britain

1 Quoted in Kee, *Bold Fenian Men, op. cit.*, p. 51.
2 Peter McMullen, unpublished interview with David Blundy and John Shirley, 1979.

3 Daithi O'Connaill, interview with *Weekend World* (LWT), 17 November 1974.
4 Chris Mullin.
5 For a full account of the evidence see Nick Davies and Ros Franey, 'The Case of the Guildford Four', *Observer Magazine*, 29 June 1986.
6 Private information.

14 On the Sidelines

1 Brian Faulkner, *Memoirs of a Statesman*, Weidenfeld and Nicolson, London, 1978, p. 144.
2 *Ibid.*, p. 191.
3 O'Bradaigh, interview with authors, November 1986.
4 Faulkner, *op. cit.*, p. 239.
5 Paddy Devlin, *The Fall of the Executive*, published by Paddy Devlin, Belfast, 1975, p. 9.
6 *Ibid.*, p. 32.
7 Seamus Twomey, interview with authors, February 1986.
8 Rev. William Arlow, interview with authors, October 1985.
9 Rees, *op. cit.*, p. 159.

15 Ceasefire

1 Morrison, interview with authors, 1985.
2 McGuinness, interviews with authors, 1985-6.
3 Interview with authors, 1986.
4 Rees, *op. cit.*, p. 224.
5 *Ibid.*, p. 217.
6 Morrison, interviews with authors, 1984-7.
7 Quoted in Beresford, *op. cit.*, p. 879.
8 Interview with authors.
9 David McKittrick, unpublished history of the UDA.
10 Maria MacGuire, *To Take Arms: A Year in the Provisional IRA*, Macmillan, London, 1973.

16 Other People

1 Francis Kelly, police statement, recorded in Kelley, *op. cit.*, p. 133.
2 Quoted in *ibid.*, p. 225.
3 Gerry Adams, interview with authors, February and March 1986.
4 *Belfast Graves, op. cit.*, p. 147.

17 Allies Abroad

1 Quoted in Kee, *op. cit.*, Vol. 11, p. 11.
2 Peter McMullen, quoted in *Boston Globe*, 4 September 1979.
3 McMullen, unpublished interview with David Blundy and John Shirley.
4 Michael Flannery, interview with authors, 17 March 1986.
5 Martin Galvin, interview with authors, 17 March 1986.
6 Court evidence recorded in the *Sunday Times*, 21 November 1982.
7 Court evidence recorded in the *Daily Telegraph*, 31 October 1982.
8 MacGuire, *op. cit*
9 Quoted in Coogan, *op. cit.*, p. 127.
10 *Sunday Telegraph*, 22 December 1974.
11 Michael McKinley, essay, *'The International Dimension of Terrorism in Ireland'*, edited by Yonah Alexander and Alan O'Day, Croom Helm, London, 1984, p. 13.
12 Cahill, interview with authors, November 1984.
13 Interview with authors.

18 Northern Command

1 Interview with authors.
2 Bobby Sands, interview with authors, 1980.
3 Adams, *op. cit.*, p. 134.

4 Brother Bosang, interview with authors, 1986.
5 Adams, *op. cit.*, p. 134.
6 Gerry Adams, *The Politics of Irish Freedom*, Brandon Books, Cork, 1980, p. 10.
7 Collette McArdle Adams, interview with authors, December 1986.
8 McGuinness, interviews with authors, 1985-6.
9 Adams, interview with authors, 1986.
10 *Republican News*, 14 August 1976.
11 Jimmy Drumm, interview with authors, July 1985.
12 Interview with authors.

19 Hunger and Dirt

1 Pat McGeown, interview with authors, 1985.
2 Interview with authors.
3 Private information.
4 Ciaran Nugent, interview with authors, November 1985.
5 Cardinal O'Fiaich, interview with authors, 1986.
6 Adams, interview with authors, May 1986.
7 Father Faul, interview with authors, February 1985.
8 John Hume, interview with authors, December 1986.
9 Harry West, interview with authors, 1981.
10 Cardinal O'Fiaich, interview with authors, February 1985.
11 Prison medical staff, interview with authors, May 1986.

20 The Armalite and the Ballot-box

1 Interview with authors.
2 W. D. Flackes, *A Political Directory of Northern Ireland*, Ariel Books, London, 1984, for all electoral statistics.
3 *London Standard*, 21 July 1983, quoted in John Carvel, *Citizen Ken*, Chatto and Windus, London 1984, p. 88.
4 *Daily Mail*, 29 July 1983.
5 Carvel, *op. cit.*, p. 161.
6 *Irish News*, 18 December 1983.

21 Armed Propaganda

1 Interview with authors, 1985.
2 Interview with authors.
3 Jimmy Drumm, interview with authors, July 1985.
4 Adams, interview with authors, May 1986.
5 Private information from RUC.
6 Evidence of Christopher Black, Regina v. Donnelly and others.
7 Private information.
8 Robert Lean, quoted in Tony Gifford, *Supergrasses: The Use of Accomplice Evidence in Northern Ireland*, The Cobden Trust, 1984.
9 Steven C. Greer, 'Supergrasses and the Legal System', *Law Quarterly Review*, April 1986, p. 241.
10 *Ibid.*, p. 249.

22 The Politics of Revenge

1 Adams, interview with authors, February and May 1986.
2 Private information.
3 Martin McCauley, interview with authors.
4 Interview with authors.
5 MacGuire, *op. cit.*
6 Interview with authors.

23 Hillsborough

1 Quoted in Anthony Kenny, *The Road to Hillsborough: The Shaping of the Anglo-Irish Agreement*, Pergamon, Oxford, 1986, p, 37.
2 *Ibid.*, p. 40.
3 *Ibid.*, p. 41.
4 Gerry Adams, *The Politics of Irish Freedom*, Brandon Press, 1986, p. 38.

5 Quoted in Farrell, *Sheltering the Fugitive*, Mercier Press, Dublin, 1986, p. 73.
6 *Ibid.*, p. 98.
7 Press release issued by Belfast Republican Press Centre, 2 May 1984.
8 Quoted in Kenny, *op. cit.*, p. 82.
9 Quoted in *ibid.*, p. 113.
10 Adams, *The Politics of Irish Freedom, op. cit.*, p. 105.
11 Sinn Fein official, interview with authors, January 1987.
12 Adams, *The Politics of Irish Freedom, op. cit.*, p. 120.
13 *Ibid.*, p. 162.
14 *Ibid.*, p. 158.

24 Full Circle

1 Adams, *The Politics of Irish Freedom, op. cit.*, p. 65.

Index

Index

481

489

REBELS
by Peter de Rosa

'*Rebels* is the saddest story I've read since *The Tale of Two Cities*. I've wept for Ireland a hundred times since reading your book ... well written. Well read. Well done'.
Dr Catherine O'Mahoney-O'Shea
(Grand-niece of Michael Collins)

. . . The British soldiers were bellying along the gutters, then across the bridge, past dead and dying comrades. Some of them, goggle-eyed, spluttering, legs jerking, tongues stiffening, slithered in agony in all directions like hooked fishes on a bank...

Peter de Rosa, bestselling author of *Vicars of Christ,* here dramatically recreates the extraordinary story of how, at Easter 1916, a thousand Irish men and women, armed only with pikes and rifles, challenged the military might of the British Empire and forever changed the course of Anglo-Irish history. The sounds, sights and smells of the moment all come sharply alive in Peter de Rosa's brilliantly evocative narrative. *Rebels* holds the reader in thrall as poignant comedy blends with harrowing scenes of war.

'An extremely readable, exciting and well-documented account'
Tom Glennon, *Irish Times*

'Brings the international reader close to the heart of the watershed in Irish history'
Des Hickey, *Sunday Independent*

'Should be required reading for every member of the British Cabinet and every member of Parliament'
J. Enoch Powell, *Sunday Telegraph*

0 552 13679 4

MOSSAD
by Ronald Payne

No intelligence service is surrounded by more myth and mystery than Mossad. Hailed by the CIA as 'the best in the world', it is held in awe by its friends and feared by its foes. It can boast the most devoted, patriotic agents in the world.

It was Mossad who pulled off the spectacular rescue of Israeli hostages from Entebbe and Mossad agents who pinpointed the target for Israeli bombers to destroy Iraq's nuclear reactor. Since the 1940s, Mossad has been a crucial weapon in Israel's constant struggle to survive.

Mossad is the first full history of this organisation. It is a penetrating, gripping and suspense-filled account. Here are the heroes, the dare-devils, the masters of intelligence, and their incredible stories of kidnappings, Nazi hunts, high-tech espionage, smuggling, nuclear weapons and counter-terrorist operations.

It reads like a thriller . . . but every word is true.

0 552 13311 6

INSIDE THE BRITISH ARMY
by Antony Beevor

'Absorbing, immensely detailed, yet wholly unpompous, written with great style'
Anthony Powell, *Spectator*

No Army in the world is quite like the British Army, with its tribal systems of regimental loyalties and customs. This riveting account of life in today's Army includes virtually everything – Guardsmen on basic training, barrack routine, nights on the town, patrolling the streets in Northern Ireland, parties in the sergeants' mess, the impossibility of normal family life, officer selection, ambition and failure on the way to the top, and the Byzantine world of the Ministry of Defence.

This new edition covers both the end of the Cold War and the Army's success in the Gulf. It describes an Army, over-loyal to the past, now anxiously waiting to know its future and which regiments will disappear. Writing with an insider's understanding and an outsider's freshness of view, ex-Army Officer Antony Beevor has pieced together a vivid, witty and compellingly frank portrait of Army life. Granted unprecedented access at every level, he has produced a candid, entertaining and definitive study of the British Army today.

'Entertaining and informative . . . the civilian reader is likely to be fascinated, flabbergasted, amused and incredulous'
Julian Thompson, *Observer*

'You do not need to be going for a soldier to read this. There is matter here for the historian, the sociologist and the curious, essential reading for civil servants and politicians.
Alan Judd, *Sunday Times*

0 552 13818 5

THE PAST IS MYSELF
by Christabel Bielenberg

'It would be difficult to overpraise this book. Mrs Bielenberg's experience was unique and her honest, intelligence and compassion makes her account of it moving beyond words'
The Economist

Christabel Bieleberg, a niece of Lord Northcliffe, married a German lawyer in 1934. She lived through the war in Germany, as a German citizen, under the horrors of Nazi rule and Allied bombings. *The Past is Myself* is her story of that experience, an unforgettable portrait of an evil time.

'This autobiography is of exceptional distinction and importance. It deserves recognition as a magnificent contribution to international understanding and as a document of how the human spirit can triumph in the midst of evil and persecution'
The Economist

'Marvellously written'
Observer

'Nothing but superlatives will do for this book. It tells its story magnificently and every page of its story is worth telling'
Irish Press

'Intensely moving'
Yorkshire Evening News

0 552 99065 5

NOT WITHOUT MY DAUGHTER
by Betty Mahmoody

'You are here for the rest of your life. Do you understand? You are not leaving Iran. You are here until you die.'

Betty Mahmoody and her husband, Dr Sayyed Bozorg Mahmoody ('Moody'), came to Iran from the USA to meet Moody's family. With them was their four-year-old daughter, Mahtob. Appalled by the squalor of their living conditions, horrified by what she saw of a country where women are merely chattels and Westerners are despised, Betty soon became desperate to return to the States. But Moody, and his often vicious family, had other plans. Mother and daughter became prisoners of an alien culture, hostages of an increasingly tyrannical and violent man.

Betty began to try to arrange an escape. Evading Moody's sinister spy network, she secretly met sympathisers opposed to Khomeini's savage regime. But every scheme that was suggested to her meant leaving Mahtob behind for ever . . .

Eventually, Betty was given the name of a man who would plan their perilous route out of Iran, a journey that few women or children had ever made. Their nightmare attempt to return home began in a bewildering snowstorm . . .

'The horrific situation in which Betty Mahmoody found herself would give any loving mother nightmares. Hers is an amazing story of a woman's courage and total devotion to her child that will have you rooting for them along every inch of their treacherous journey'
Susan Oudot, *Woman's Own*

'Compelling drama ... fascinating, if disturbing ... a moving story of one person's fortitude, courage and faith'
New York Times Book Review

0 552 13356 6

A SELECTION OF RELATED TITLES
AVAILABLE FROM CORGI BOOKS

PRICES SHOWN BELOW WERE CORRECT AT THE TIME OF GOING TO PRESS.
~WEVER TRANSWORLD PUBLISHERS RESERVE THE RIGHT TO SHOW NEW
TAIL PRICES ON COVERS WHICH MAY DIFFER FROM THOSE PREVIOUSLY
VERTISED IN THE TEXT OR ELSEWHERE.

All Corgi/Bantam Books, are available at your bookshop or newsagent, or can be ordered from the following address:

Corgi/Bantam Books,
Cash Sales Department,
P.O. Box 11, Falmouth, Cornwall TR10 9EN

UK and B.F.P.O. customers please send a cheque or postal order (no currency) and allow £1.00 for postage and packing for the first book plus 50p for the second book and 30p for each additional book to a maximum charge of £3.00 (7 books plus).

Overseas customers, including Eire, please allow £2.00 for postage and packing for the first book, £1.00 for the second book, and 50p for each subsequent title ordered.

NAME (Block Letters) ....

ADDRESS ....

....